S0-BIK-159

UNIVERSITÀ DI SIENA
FACOLTÀ DI GIURISPRUDENZA
COLLANA DI STUDI "PIETRO ROSSI"
NUOVA SERIE - VOLUME IV

UNIVERSITÀ DI SIENA - FACOLTÀ DI GIURISPRUDENZA
COLLANA DI STUDI "PIETRO ROSSI" - NUOVA SERIE - VOLUME IV

ITALIAN REFORMATION STUDIES IN HONOR OF LAELIUS SOCINUS

Edited by JOHN A. TEDESCHI

FIRENZE - FELICE LE MONNIER - EDITORE - MCMLXV

№ 0996

302-64 – Stabilimenti Tipografici « E. Ariani » e « L'Arte della Stampa » – Firenze

PREFACE

Lelio Sozzini of Siena died four hundred years ago in Zurich at the age of thirty seven. He left only a handful of letters and a few short theological treatises, the first of which was not published until a century after his death. Yet he holds an important place in the religious history of the sixteenth century.

Fausto Sozzini, Lelio's nephew and junior by fourteen years, who lay the foundations of that religious system first known as Socinianism (and much later in modified form as Unitarianism) in several instances in his writings made evident his indebtedness to his uncle. In a letter to another Italian evangelical in exile, Marcello Squarcialupi, he wrote in 1582:

I recognize no one as my master in any way in these matters of those who live today; I had God alone as my preceptor and sacred scriptures. Nay, even in all that knowledge of divine things, whatever that may be finally in me, it happened that I had none for a teacher besides one man, Laelius, my uncle, or rather certain little writings of his and many notes.

Bibliotheca Fratrum Polonorum, I, 362.

In the preface to one of his major works, the De Jesu Christo Servatore *(1594), Fausto gave credit to certain no longer extant letters addressed by Lelio to Calvin in 1555 for planting in his own mind the first doubts about the validity of the traditional doctrine of the mediatory office of Christ.*

Socinianism, which developed late in the sixteenth century in Poland, far from Italian soil, owed much to the young and questful Lelio. Its distinctive doctrines, including religious toleration, that was known in the next century as the domma *(dogma)* sociniana, *unified and institutionalized the most characteristic elements of the Italian evangelical spirit.*

In the evolving Socinian tradition in the 17th and 18th centuries, Lelio and not Fausto was the coryphaeus *of the sect. He was given an importance which went far beyond his seemingly limited achievements. True, we have Fausto's declarations of indebtedness. But there is another factor still. Lelio assumed psychological significance for the Socinian historians. Fausto was of the second generation. Lelio had been closely associated with the great reformers, Calvin, Bullinger and Melanchthon. He was of their age and with them he had debated and exchanged ideas. He became the figure symbolic of the continuity and connection which Socinianism had with the Classical Reformation. Serving ourselves of an image, Lelio is like the point where the branch of a tree is attached and feeds from the main trunk, but also is projected toward the light in a separate and fruitful direction.*

Lelio made a favorable impression on his contemporaries. The young, cultured, detached and adventurous Sienese patrician who wandered restlessly in a personal search for truth through foreign lands still stands forth as one of the most appealing figures in the gallery of Italian reformers.

Lelio Sozzini is only partially the subject of these collected essays marking the anniversary of his death. It has been our first intention that the scope of our research should include some of the issues and problems related to the Italian reformation of the sixteenth century. Attention has been focused on various aspects of Valdesianism, one of the most important and controversial spiritual currents of the sixteenth century. The Beneficio di Cristo *which has traditionally been considered its doctrinal manifesto is analyzed for the sources and influences which underly it. The hopes of this movement in reforming action from Pope, Emperor and Council, which endure even after the closing of Trent, are suggested to explain why an important segment of reform minded Italian society did not break with Rome.*

The characteristic impatience of the Italian radicals with dogmatic subtleties and their disposition to reduce theological formulations to scriptural simplicity are treated in a study of Camillo Renato and through the questions and doubts on the resurrection, baptism and justification contained in letters addressed by Lelio Sozzini to Calvin in 1549 and 1555.

The cause of religious toleration championed heroically by Italian evangelicals in the sixteenth century is illustrated by two writings, the Carmen *of Camillo Renato and the pseudonymous* Apologia *of Lyncurio (now known to be from the pen of Curione) protesting the execution of Servetus in Geneva in 1553. An important unpublished Inquisitorial trial draws us into the clandestine atmosphere of an evangelical conventicle in Catholic Italy, enabling us, through the detailed testimony, to gain an exact picture of its doctrinal and sacramental usages. The numerous documents in translation we hope are only the prelude to larger and more systematic collections of Italian Reformation writings in modern critical editions.*

The volume closes with material of Socinian interest, including notes for a history of the Sozzini family and a brief study of an unknown essay by Fausto Sozzini revealing that at an early age he possessed a knowledge of logical theory which may contradict the traditional account that his education was unsystematic, and that he had never studied philosophy or dabbled in Logic until late in life.

JOHN TEDESCHI

THE RHAETIAN REPUBLIC (federated with the Swiss)
Grey League [GR]: Ilanz, Thusis
League of the X Jurisdictions [X]: Davos
League of the House of God [GD]: Chur, Poschiavo
Valley of the Inn (Engadin): Zuoz, Süs, Lavin, Fetan
Valley of the Mera: Casaccia, Vicosoprano
Condominium:
County of Chiavenna: Mera continued: Piur, Ch., Mesa
Valtellina [V], following the Adda: Tirano, Teglio, Sondrio, Caspano, Morbegno, Traona
Bormio: Bormio
SWISS CONFEDERATION
BASEL
ZURICH
ST GALL
BERN
LAUSANNE
RHAETIA
LOCARNO
SAVOY
PIEDMONT
FRANCE
SALUZZO
GENOA
REPUBLIC OF GENOA
VENETIAN REPUBLIC
BERGAMO
BRESCIA
BASSANO
VICENZA
PADUA
VENICE
MANTUA
TRENT
COMO
MILAN
PAVIA
PIACENZA
PARMA
MODENA
BOLOGNA
FERRARA
CERVIA
RIMINI
PESARO
URBINO
ANCONA
MACERATA
PERUGIA
ASSISI
VITERBO
ROME
PAPAL STATES
LUCCA
PISA
FLORENCE
DUCHY OF FLORENCE
SIENA
Nuovo Stato
STATO DEI PRESIDI
To Spain 1557
DUCHY OF CARNIOLA
CAPODISTRIA
HAPSBURG HUNGARY
Croatia
OTTOMAN EMPIRE
MODRUS
SEGNA
DURAZZO
CORFU
LEPANTO
NAUPLIA
MALVUSIA
CRETE
CYPRUS
VENICE IN THE EAST
chy of Modena: Borgo, Carpi, Fiorano, Maranello,
onantola, Reggio, Staggia -
chy of Parma: Fiorenzuola, Piacenza
chy of Milan: Como, Casalmaggiora, Cremona, Pavia
KINGDOM OF NAPLES
NAPLES
PAOLA
SAN FILI
COSENZA
Calabria
ITALY IN 1562
MESSINA
PALERMO
TRAPANI
CATANIA
SYRACUSE
CARTHAGE
G H Wms
1962
SPANISH DOMINIONS:
Kingdom of Naples } in personal union since 1504
Kingdom of Sicily
Kingdom of Sardinia
Duchy of Milan, since 1535; Spanish appanage 1556
Stato dei Presidi, since 1557

ROLAND BAINTON

FOUR REVIEWS

Delio Cantimori, *Prospettive di storia ereticale italiana del Cinquecento* (Bari: Laterza, 1960), pp. 125.

If the review of this collection of essays is slight, the reason is that the booklet itself is slight in comparison with the monumental contributions of Cantimori to our understanding of the reformatory movements in Italy in the sixteenth century. But although the bulk is meagre the ideas in these essays are important. In the initial essay Cantimori indicates the manner in which the heretical reform movements of the period should be envisaged. The time has come to go beyond a series of biographies of the martyrs and instead to see the deviations from orthodoxy in the context of the vast efforts at Catholic reform in the sixteenth century. This in turn must be viewed in relation to the entire culture.

Cantimori sees four phases in chronological terms. The first ran from the Fifth Lateran Council (1513-17) to the death of Valdés and the establishment of the Roman Inquisition in 1541-42. This period is called that of "evangelism," when the liberal reform was not yet sharply demarked from the intransigeant. The second is the time of crisis from 1541-60 and the third that of the debacle of liberalism from 1560-80 signalized by the execution of Carnesecchi. In this period in particular one must take account of the exiles and of their influence abroad. The fourth period from 1580-1624 saw the publication of many irenic utopias.

The remaining essays well show how Cantimori is able to turn from the comprehensive to the minute and then to draw from the minute to the comprehensive. He takes, for example, an Italian translation of Calvin's tract "On Fleeing Superstitions."[1] There is a preface by the translator which squarely recognized that the Reformation never succeeded without the support of the civil authorities. In Italy the civil authorities were all hostile. Therefore the "evangelical" had the choice either of exile or of external conformity to the practices of the Church. This conclusion was unpalatable to Calvin because it meant the abandonment of the evangelization of Italy.

---

[1] *Del fuggir le superstitioni che ripugnano a la vera e sincera confessione de la fede...* M.D.L.III.

In connection with the editions of the work of Minus Celsus on religious liberty Cantimori moves into the plans late in the century for the unification of the confessions.

Benedetto Nicolini, *Ideali e passioni nell'Italia religiosa del Cinquecento* (Bologna: Libreria Antiquaria Palmaverde, 1962), pp. 177.

If any man in the sixteenth century wished to conceal anything from posterity he would have done well to burn every trace, for if he left even so much as a scrap of manuscript it would not escape the vigilant scrutiny of Nicolini. But his work reaches far beyond the level of mere documentation. He knows how to relate what he finds to the broader currents of the times. The present volume is the first of a series of collected articles from comparatively inaccessible journals dealing with various aspects of the reformatory movements in Italy in the sixteenth century.

Three of the articles deal with notable women of the Reformation: Isabella Bresegna, Vittoria Colonna and Giulia Gonzaga. Isabella moved from Valdés to Calvin in her views and when her patron Ferrante Gonzaga fell from power in Milan took refuge with Vergerio at Tübingen, only to discover that Vergerio was Lutheran rather than Calvinist. In consequence she withdrew into Italian Switzerland, resisting staunchly the efforts of her husband and sons to reclaim her for Italy and the orthodox faith.

Vittoria Colonna presents a problem as to the interpretation of her religion. Some call her Protestant, some Catholic. Nicolini says they are both mistaken. She was a papist Protestant or a Protestant Catholic. Quite right, yet I would suggest that her case needs to be seen in relation to that of many others who are similarly claimed by both camps. Erasmus, for example, has lately been treated by Nulli [1] as neither Catholic nor Christian. Telle [2] would call him Christian, but not Catholic. Bouyer [3] insists that he was both. Again take Valdés himself. The Protestant missionaries in South America present him as an example of Spanish Protestantism, whereas Domingo de Sta. Teresa [4] seeks to vindicate his complete orthodoxy. The real point is that all these persons and many more in many lands belonged to a particular variety of Catholic reform in the earlier decades of the sixteenth century, a reform latitudinarian in doctrine, disciplined in life, warm in piety, with leanings in varying degrees toward mysticism. Only after Trent

---

[1] Siro Nulli, *Erasmo e il Rinascimento* (Torino, 1955). Ed.

[2] Emile Telle, *Érasme de Rotterdam et le septième sacrement; étude d'évangélisme matrimoniale au XVI siècle et contribution à la biographie intellectuelle d'Érasme* (Genève, 1954). Ed.

[3] Louis Bouyer, *Autour d'Érasme; études sur le christianisme des humanistes catholiques* (Paris, 1955). Ed.

[4] *Juan de Valdes, 1498(?)-1541. Su pensamiento religioso y las corrientes espirituales de su tiempo* (Roma, 1957). Ed.

could this position be denied the name of Catholic. The attempt, however, to bring it into line with Trent involves a distortion. In saying this I am of no mind to dissent from the author's treatment of Vittoria. The point is simply that she is an outstanding example of a widespread phenomenon.

Giulia Gonzaga is described as "faithful to fidelity," faithful to the memory of her husband, to the memory of Valdés and to all the living Valdesians even though a number had gone over to Calvin and were in exile. Though the net tightened around her she showed an amazing intrepidity. A timely death may well have saved her from the stake.

Ochino figures prominently in his controversy with Muzio and at many other points.

In reviewing Omodeo's work on Calvin[1] Nicolini rejoices over the progress in understanding with reference to Calvin on the part of Italians since the treatment by Croce.[2]

Benedetto Nicolini, *Aspetti della vita religiosa, politica e letteraria del Cinquecento* (Bologna: Tamari Editori, 1963), pp. 147.

Nicolini has favored us with a second volume of his collected essays. Before speaking of their content I hope that I may be forgiven for a word of public aknowledgement of the dedication to myself. I venture to call attention to it because the circumstance is singular, arising from no personal contact at any time during a quarter of a century of friendship but stemming rather from a common enthusiasm for a figure dead now these four centuries. Twenty five years have now gone by since I was occupying myself with Ochino. During this interval Nicolini has kept me constantly abreast of his indefatigable researches. How amazed Ochino would have been could he have been told that four hundred years after his passing he would constitute a bond between his beloved *Italia* and the *nuevo mundo* but recently discovered.

The first essay produces new evidence on the contest between Bologna, Milan, Venice and Rome to secure the services of Ochino as Lenten preacher in the very spring before his flight to Geneva. There is no reason to suppose, as Negri conjectured, that the invitation to Rome on the part of Paul III had any sinister motivation. The pope wanted Ochino at Rome for the very same reason that the other cities sought him. The new evidence amplifies what we have already known about the vying of the cities that they might be chastened and uplifted by this disciple of the *Poverello* speaking "with the tongues of men and angels." The reading of these documents gives a fresh appreciation of the anguish which Ochino must have experienced when he severed

[1] Adolfo Omodeo, *Giovanni Calvino e la riforma in Ginevra* (Bari, 1947). Ed.

[2] Benedetto Croce, "Il Marchese di Vico Galeazzo Caracciolo," in *Vite di avventure, di fede e di passione*, 3rd ed. (Bari, 1953), pp. 187-291. Ed.

himself from the adoring throngs who were genuinely thirsty for his words.

The second article shows him in exile at Geneva, in poverty and among strangers to his tongue and his person. However interesting the new details as to his sojourn even greater interest attaches to the suggestion of Nicolini as to why he left Geneva. The usual assumption has been that friction had developed with Calvin but Nicolini points out that each spoke well of the other at this point. The solution proposed is that Ochino at first looked upon Geneva as a strategic point from which to launch propaganda looking to the conversion of Italy. For some time he was feverishly engaged in supplying the Genevan presses with tracts in Italian to be smuggled over the mountains. The result was practically nil and the conclusion appeared incontestable that the conversion of Italy was hopeless. For that reason Ochino resolved to devote himself to the Italian diaspora in Switzerland and Germany.

The third article gives details as to what happened in Italy after the flight. Mignanelli, whose career is outlined, was the papal nuncio at Venice and exceedingly vigilant in ferreting out and suppressing the circulation of Ochino's booklets. He kept also a sharp eye on the half dozen Capuchins in Venice and in particular upon their leader Fra Bonaventura. But nothing was done to the latter because he enjoyed the confidence of Carafa.

Number four calls attention to an alleged confusion between a letter of Bernardino Ochino and one of San Bernardino. The fifth article reproduces from a manuscript in the Vatican library the earliest account by Ochino of his sojourn at Geneva. The sixth reports that the *Laurenziana* at Florence has a collection of letters from Ochino to Paul III, all spurious; and the *Biblioteca Nazionale* at Florence has a copy of a letter also spurious from Ochino to Ascanio Colonna. The last three studies in Nicolini's volume deal with miscellaneous but always interesting bibliographical details.

Oddone Ortolani, *Pietro Carnesecchi* (Florence: Le Monnier, 1963), pp. xv-266.

The records of the trial of Carnesecchi lasting over a year in the 1560s is perhaps the most revealing single document with regard to the character and dissemination of heresy in Italy in the sixteenth century. Carnesecchi himself suspected that he had been brought before the Inquisition primarily to elicit information as to the extent of the movement and to incriminate the living by associating them with the dead. The records have already been published [1] but are so relatively inaccessible that the copious extracts in the appendix to this work are

[1] G. Manzoni, "Estratto del processo di Pietro Carnesecchi," in *Miscellanea di Storia italiana*, X (1870), pp. 187-573. Ed.

very welcome. Drawing from this body of material, amplified by items from extensive sources, the author has reconstructed the entire career of Carnesecchi with meticulous care, persuasive interpretation and dramatic suspense. For all the continuity in papal policy one is made to see very vividly how one pope differed from another and how often the fortunes of Carnesecchi fluctuated as a result of the death of one pope and the election of another.

Carnesecchi, himself a Florentine, throve under the Florentine pope Clement VII who made him a protonotary and richly endowed him with benefices. On the accession of Paul III in 1534 the Florentine lost his office but not his emoluments. During this pontificate he came to be closely associated with the liberal, latitudinarian, moral and mystical variety of Catholic reform. His own fate was the dramatic demonstration of the debacle of this variety in confrontation with the Tridentine.

At Naples Carnesecchi came under the influence of Valdés and at Viterbo of Pole. From these men he imbibed all the tenets and the piety of the "evangelical" reform. But at the same time he acquired from them a deep aversion to rending the seamless robe of the unity of the Church. Like many who later fled to the "heretics" of the north Carnesecchi believed in justification by faith and called into question purgatory and indulgences. Penance should be reduced to voluntary confession and the Eucharist explained in New Testament terms.

He was summoned to Rome, but because of the intercession of friends the case was dropped rather than terminated. For the next five years he withdrew to an abbey in France which had been conferred upon him by Clement VII. His next residences were in Venice and Padua. He was utterly incautious in reading Luther, Melanchthon and Calvin and in consorting with suspects. He carried on a continuous correspondence with Giulia Gonzaga. Pope Paul III died. The "evangelicals" hoped for the election of Pole or Morone, but the choice fell on Carafa, the implacable, as Paul IV. Still worse, Ghislieri was made the chief inquisitor.

Carnesecchi was again summoned to Rome. For some time he declined to come. He even meditated flight to Geneva, but reflected that were he to escape, other suspects would be treated more severely and particularly Cardinal Morone, now himself in prison. But the basic consideration was an unwillingness to cut himself off from the body of the Catholic Church. He waited till the death of Paul IV. When he was succeeded by the Milanese Pius IV Carnesecchi went to Rome and secured a vindication from the Inquisition. Instead then of behaving discreetly he continued his contacts with the dubious and in particular kept up the correspondence with Giulia Gonzaga, confiding to her that he was glad a building of the Inquisition had burned[1]

[1] The building which housed the Roman Inquisition on the Via Ripetta was sacked and burned by a mob after the news of the death of Paul IV (1559). Ed.

and that he sympathized with the remark of Vittoria Colonna that Pole's catarrh was providential since it saved him from attending the session of Trent on justification. When Giulia died in 1566 her correspondence fell into the hands of the Inquisition.

Pius IV died and was succeeded by the Inquisitor Ghislieri as Pius V. Again Carnesecchi was summoned to Rome. Again he contemplated flight and again decided against it. He hoped that Cosimo of Florence would stand behind him, and Morone, but Morone, though released from prison, was still under a cloud. Carnesecchi faced the investigators who plied him a year long with queries about ideas and the personages of the liberal reform movement. He refused absolutely, even under torture, to incriminate the dead or inculpate the living. As for himself he was elusive and ambiguous until confronted with the choice of recantation or the sword. There was no wavering this time. The pope required the entire body of cardinals to attend the public reading of the long indictment and the pronouncement of the sentence of death. Only Morone was excused. The cardinals on a subsequent morning as they came from a conclave saw on the Ponte di Sant'Angelo the charred remains of a one time protonotary of the pope.

Carnesecchi is not a major figure of the Reformation. Italy produced no major figure. He was a man of singular attractiveness, of engaging incaution, of magnificent illusions as to the success of the cause and as to the providential deaths which might save him. Yet when all hopes were shattered he stood unbending and serene.

Domingo Ricart, *Juan de Valdés y el pensamiento religioso europeo en los siglos XVI y XVII* (Lawrence, Kans.: University of Kansas Press, 1959), pp. 139.[1]

Around the middle of the sixteenth century the three most distinguished Spaniards are said to have been Ignatius Loyola, Michael Servetus, and Juan Valdés. The latter was, if anything, more influential than the others in his own day but has since fallen into comparative oblivion. Loyola is remembered because he founded an order and Servetus because he was burned for heresy and his case became the point of departure in the struggle for religious liberty. But Valdés represented that mystical piety which forms no sects and is content with oblivion in the memory of man if only it be possible to enjoy eternity in communion with God.

His career began in Spain in the interlude of liberalism when the spirit of Erasmus was dominant. The revival of intolerance which followed the eruption of Lutheranism led him to withdraw to Naples. There, as has long been known, he enjoyed a considerable vogue as the father of movements which were to separate and solidify as the Catholic and Protestant reformations. We have commonly supposed

[1] This review originally appeared in the *Renaissance News*. Ed.

that his influence in Spain ceased with his departure. But the author shows that his name appeared frequently in heresy trials and disappeared only with the great *auto-da-fé* of 1558. In Italy Valdés profoundly influenced the leaders of the reformatory movements: Giulia Gonzaga, Ochino, Vermigli, Vergerio, Curio, Blandrata, Pole, Carnesecchi: reformers, counterreformers, martyrs, and exiles. It was Curio who, in Basle, brought out an Italian translation of Valdés *One Hundred and Ten Divine Considerations*. In France Claude de Kerquifinen brought out a French translation at Lyons in 1563. In the Netherlands Emden was the center of latitudinarianism and here the Calvinist pastor Gorin printed a Frisian version. He was in consequence dismissed from the ministry. Yet his work found a hearty reception among the followers of Hendrick Niklas, called in England the Familists. But singularly in England there was no translation in the sixteenth century although disciples of Valdés were there in exile. The author wonders why. One may suggest that neither Pole, who aided Mary in the restoration of Catholicism, nor Ochino and Vermigli who battled Rome as Antichrist, could at that time have felt any longer attracted to a mysticism which decried confessionalism. Valdés had to wait for the seventeenth century, when some of those wearied by the contention of the civil wars, such as Nicholas Ferrer and George Herbert, produced the first English translation. Thereafter Valdés passes from notice (save for a brief mention in a letter of John Wesley) until rediscovered by English Quakers, Benjamin Wiffen and Usos de Rio. In our own day Valdés has come to be prized not only as a great mystic but also as an architect of the Spanish language.

The author of this work has delved fruitfully into remote corners and has produced a fascinating picture of the influence of a man and his works.

ODDONE ORTOLANI

THE HOPES OF THE ITALIAN REFORMERS IN ROMAN ACTION

Recent studies of the movement for Reform in sixteenth century Italy attempt to give us an increasingly precise and explicit understanding of the great events of the period, through an analysis of particular aspects which previously had hardly been noted or not sufficiently investigated. Through such an approach, many traditional judgments become more exact or even undergo significant revision. The period as a whole has emerged in a somewhat different light, and appears more complex, more spiritually vital than it did a few decades ago.

In contrast with the great revolutions in Germany, Switzerland, and other European countries, the Italian movement has often been considered a reflection of those great events, a weak, sporadic and even awkward imitation, without real vitality or originality. It was certainly thought to be lacking in daring initiative and in that enthusiasm that results in profound changes, which affect all aspects of life, renew man's conception of it and even transform its ultimate purpose. Today interested scholars are discovering a surprising originality of thought, variety of attitudes, and strength of personal conviction, which, at the same time, give rise to new and more delicate problems.

One particularly intriguing problem arises as soon as one observes the spiritual wealth of the Italian reformation. One asks why so much energy in individuals, and also so much ferment among groups, did not lead to more significant events with deeper repercussions and more impressive developments, but instead exhausted itself in a series of personal adventures which had no significant consequences for the whole. Why, on the contrary, did it ultimately establish more firmly those very aspects of the religious life which it had intended to combat, weaken or even incorporate into a different spirituality? Today the reasons for this course of events cannot be solely attributed to weakness of thought, to skepticism, or to passive inertia. They must be sought elsewhere, and it is becoming generally accepted that the key to the problem lies in the ideas behind human action. It is found in man's attitude towards events, which disposes him to act or not to act, and to sacrifice himself or not, that accelerates or retards his movement until the historical occasion, possible for a certain moment, has vanished.

A feeling of religious uneasiness was common to the whole of Europe at the beginning of the sixteenth century. Attitudes and their intensity may vary, but it was unquestionably a general phenomenon, which it inherited from the tormented final decades of the fifteenth century.

Those who acutely sensed the discrepancy between the official religious discipline and prevailing customs, and their own spiritual longings, searched for the means of making these vague, abstract and personal aspirations into a more extensive guiding principle, which could create an environment more akin to their own desires, in which such desires could be freely realized and which would enable the largest possible number of people to share in the same advantages and personal satisfaction, which they themselves had attained and considered superior. This attempt developed into a dominant passion for many peoples, and certainly was one of the great factors in the history of the sixteenth century.

With respect to this goal, the prevalent theme in Italy was not one of rebellion but of hope in a peaceful reform from above that would restore the order and Christian harmony which the people of Europe sensed they had lost, but that they felt they could and must regain. The familiar image of the road illustrates well: one did not need to construct a new way, but only to rediscover the old one, that, if retraced, would take one back to the point of departure, to the origins and to the perfect and genuine moment of the Christian religion. The ideal itself was not at all revolutionary, but the most violent upheavals were about to take place in its name, and the reformation in all its aspects (including the Catholic counter-reformation) was to be accomplished.

Originally the ideal of loyalty to a distant past did not include the idea of an overthrow of the existing disciplinary system; rather it required the concept of an expectant trust in those who were divinely invested with the power to act on behalf of mankind. The mental inheritance of the Middle Ages clearly indicated that the responsibility for a correct, fervent, and disciplined religious life lay with two authorities, the Emperor and the Pope, each in the fields of action that were variously ascribed to them. The notion that one could act independently and substitute oneself for the two, arose much later and was to be one of the most conspicuous results of the revolution, not its premise. The awareness of this possibility grew out of other Renaissance ferments which were already active in the sphere of the finite and temporal affairs of this world, but which only later invaded the area concerned with eternal and spiritual matters.

In Germany's religious revolution, the crystallization of this consciousness took place unexpectedly, more as a consequence of the dynamics of events and passions than as a condition which was clearly achieved prior to the action. The substitution of a local heresiarch for the traditional universal authority was, in fact, a reaction (perhaps logical but violent and impulsive) to the unskillful and impractical policy of the Papacy. On a deeper level, however, this decisive action came into being as a provisional attitude, which awaited a definite sanction from above, and which worked towards universality as a final goal. For many years, the door remained open for a general accord, which would bring the advantages produced by the reform to all Christians.

The Swiss reformers, who were already clearly aware of the necessity to act alone and not to wait for others, operated with a different dynamic, but not with a dissimilar spirit. Their intention was to create a reform which would not only save those who were capable of enjoying its fruits, but also serve as an example, guide, and orientation to other Christians of good will. There was always the possibility that these others would be not merely simple, isolated followers, favored by an extraordinary grace, but the mass of Christianity, guided by its traditional pastors who were finally reformed.

In the Italians, this readiness to substitute themselves for the traditional authority was lacking. First of all, there was a different historical situation, which placed the potential rebels under much more difficult operating conditions than those in Germany, Switzerland or, other parts of Europe. The Italians were also restrained by the thought that if one wanted to return to the origins, the most direct way was certainly not to break with the institutions which, although corrupt, still remained the direct heirs of the original and perfect situation of primitive Christianity.

With respect to the need for action, or the lack of it, the Italian reformers were basically moved by the fear, which they more or less expressed, that a change occurring outside the traditional structures of Papacy and Empire, signified revolution and not a return to antiquity, innovation and not loyalty to a past that they sought to restore. There was, therefore, a prevailing spirit among Italians of waiting for action from above, of trust that the desired reform would take place through the interest and wisdom either of the Pope, of the Emperor or of both, finally united and in agreement on the need to act in the interest of divine things.

Various psychological factors, typical of Italian nature and mentality (which is inclined to conceive all of man's essential problems on a universal scale) played a role in this attitude. As long as was possible, it was thought that all responsibility rested with Rome, seat of the Papacy and ideal center of the Empire. The individual efforts flourishing distant from this center were considered as evidence, experiences or even manifestations of divine revelation, but they needed some kind of Roman recognition in order to become a useful norm for all of humanity.

A second circumstance that favored this conception of religious reform was provided by the historical situation as it unfolded during the first decades of the century. To visualize the triumph of one's ideas through the establishment of a national church or even simply in a local form (for example, within the limits of a principality) was utopian. It did not require great political sensitivity to realize this; in the face of Northern experience, the Italian reformed rapidly became aware of it, quite apart from their meagre ability to conceive a church limited by national and local boundaries. Thus, the only way to solve the problem was to reform Catholicism, and to ensure that it absorbed the new ideas and propagated them to the whole Christian world.

Finally, one can find a rather subtle third element which influenced the attitude of the reformers and reformed. It is evident in the aristocratic conception of society, typical of the Renaissance world, which lacked the conception of a law that originated from below. The Italians, rather, conceived of authorities that headed society, but which were amenable to modification through certain accepted channels. It was always possible to influence authority, especially in the case of the Papacy, where the head was elected and, therefore, could be chosen from the ranks of those who supported certain trends and currents. However, it was not always just a problem of the Pope's person, in whom the power was centralized. In the Catholic organization, there always existed the possibility of exerting influence by means of councillors, secretaries, and the creation of a powerful public opinion that would sway the ultimate decisions of the supreme authority. All this was apart from the Council, that vast assembly which could consider and absorb positions held by Christians in so many countries, including the Italian minority which, in this way, could find the necessary support for the triumph of their point of view.

Recent studies on the reformation in Italy have tended to emphasize precisely the complexity of religious life in that country, over against the simplifying tendency that would reduce it merely to the history of Popes or Councils. There was a deeply-rooted web of ideas in action which connected religious life with the moral, political, and social world.[1] The hopes and expectations of the Italian supporters for a profound religious reformation were another reflection of this complexity. It is not surprising that a thrust towards action was lacking if one considers the movement that developed from the teaching of Juan de Valdés.

In Valdesianism, there was the possibility of a flexible attitude towards the official church precisely because of the sentiment that the movement sought to arouse in the heart of the Christian, which it considered infinitely more compelling than any external law or dogmatic decision of an official authority. On account of this, Valdesianism has aptly been defined as "neither a church, nor sect, but a force," a force primarily mystical and individualistic, tending, at least in its beginning, towards indifference about any legal act or ecclesiastical decision.[2]

From such an initial position, one observes a development in various directions, according to the individual history of each personality. But, in every case, a real passion and an authentic conviction about the effects of human action, are always missing at the basis of those practical decisions, which could effect tangible changes in collectively orga-

---

[1] Preface of D. Cantimori to G. Alberigo, *I Vescovi italiani al Concilio di Trento* (Florence, 1959).

[2] D. Ricart, *Juan de Valdés y el pensamiento religioso europeo en los siglos XVI y XVII* (El Colegio de Mexico, 1958), pp. 22, 23. See also J. Longhurst, *Erasmus and the Spanish Inquisition: The case of Juan de Valdés* (Albuquerque, 1950).

nized life. In this sense, one can say that Valdesians maintained a conception of history which was bound more to the Middle Ages than to the triumphant Renaissance in which they lived. They were men who expected more from God's providence than from human efforts. The typical medieval presupposition, which attributed developments on earth to God's mysterious will, restrained them from acting, or at least kept them passive and uncertain about it. This attitude is quite obvious in Pietro Carnesecchi, a typical personality of the movement, who, nevertheless, at the end, knew how to crown his faith in reform with the sacrifice of his life.[1]

The hope for a reformation achieved by the church itself, through the work of high prelates or even the Pope was clearly expressed in the Catholic camp from the earliest years of the century, long before the unleashing of the Lutheran storm, [2] and it endured even after this. In 1536, when Pole had overcome an acute crisis of conscience, he was ready to collaborate with the Papacy in the preparation of the Council that Paul III proposed to convoke. His acceptance was inspired by the conviction that the renewal of the Christian life could also be achieved by docilely participating in the life of the Church and attempting to put across one's own point of view through spiritual conduct and example. Even in the eyes of such a man as Carnesecchi, Pole possessed the qualities necessary to lead the Christian community back to the harmony of apostolic times. One could cite examples of the persistence of this hope, although they became increasingly weaker, for many years until the eve of the closing of the Council of Trent. It is enough to reflect on the wave of expectation and, on the other hand, the anxiety aroused by Seripando's nomination as Cardinal in 1560.

In contrast, the hopes in imperial action had a briefer fortune. After Luther's decisive and extreme move, and the definite political form it began to assume, it was logical that Catholic hopes should veer in the direction of Charles V, who alone commanded the high authority and power capable of confronting an event of such dimensions. At the same time, it was also reasonable that those who hoped for an even more radical reform should have looked with confidence to the political authorities who seemed more disposed, either because of real conviction or because of opposition to Empire or Papacy, to undertake a different policy. Thus, they entertained flashes of hope in the support of a prince or of a republic (Renata of France in Ferrara, the Duke of Florence, and Venice).

According to Cantimori,[3] after the coronation at Bologna (1530), Italian reformers no longer hoped for direct action on the part of

---

[1] O. Ortolani, *Pietro Carnesecchi* (Florence, 1963), p. 82.

[2] See Contarini's letter to Guerini dated 13 June, 1514, in H. Jedin, "Contarini und Camaldoli," *Archivio Italiano per la Storia della Pietà*, II (1953), 45-46.

[3] See D. Cantimori, "L'influence du manifeste de Charles Quint contre Clement VII (1526) et de quelques documents similaires de la litterature philoprotestante et anticuriale d'Italie," *Charles Quint et son Temps* (Paris, 1959), pp. 133-141.

Charles V, but for his intervention in favor of a rapid convocation of the council. In the next twenty years, almost all of them were scattered and they no longer constituted a body capable of concerted action. Many had emigrated across the Alps, while others lived fearfully as Nicodemites in their homeland, without any practical possibility of revealing themselves. Their liberation could come from the council and they hoped in it, just as the Catholics also did. The clash of ideas took place over how this council was to be conceived. Catholics understood it as a reunion of bishops faithful to the Papacy and obedient to Papal orders, while Protestants and filo-Protestants conceived it as an assembly open to all opinions, a grand dialogue in which all might be heard and from which would emerge such broad definitions of faith that one could call oneself a Catholic and live freely, even while following the new religious views and certain new forms of cult.

The reality of Trent did not produce an attitude of complete opposition in all the Italian reformed. Indeed, there were many who exerted themselves so that the council might issue decisions inspired by moderation. In fact, among the Council fathers, there were men who, because of their past, and because of a frequently shown attitude of openness and even of toleration towards the new needs, could give rise to serious hopes. Vittoria Colonna, Giulia Gonzaga and Pietro Carnesecchi were not wholly deceived; they had good reason to place their hope in Pole, Morone, Soranzo, Zentani, Sanfelice, all of whom were present at Trent.

A recent study of Italian bishops at that Council[1] tends to modify the older opinion that the Italian episcopate was passive in the face of the more reactionary tendencies of the Roman Curia. The possibility that new air could circulate at Trent and that the influence of Protestant sympathizers might carry some weight was not then to be wholly excluded. However, it must be remembered that the reformed were men of faith, awaiting a heavenly act, who believed the Spirit must be present for the truth to come to light. The Spirit could aid a minority, and illuminate and convince a majority. For Carnesecchi, the Spirit would be the one to reveal truth to the Council; the various parties rather than seeking the triumph of their own points of view, should have prepared themselves to accept divine revelation.[2]

In fact, when the decisions began to issue from Trent that these reformed could not accept (such as the famous decree on justification), their explanation was to deny that the Spirit had presided over the assembly. They said that the Spirit could not be present at a meeting in which all Christians were not represented; he could not illuminate the activities of a mere faction. It is well known how the illness that prevented Pole from attending the sessions at which the doctrine of justification was formulated, was interpreted as an act of God " to

---

[1] Cf. G. Alberigo, *op. cit.*

[2] O. Ortolani, *op. cit.*, pp. 62, 63.

prevent the Cardinal from participating in such a decree."[1] In other words, God was watching over Trent not to illuminate those Fathers, but, by means of a prodigious intervention, to preserve one of his faithful from complicity in definitions considered to be contrary to the truth. The hoped for dialogue between those faithful to the Roman tradition and the few who represented Valdesian aspirations had failed. The attempts to influence by means of visits, recommendations, and letters from men, by now far from Rome but still hopeful that Rome would accept their ideas and allow them to feel they were Catholics, had also failed.[2]

It was thought possible that the decrees of the Council could be revised through the efforts of a truly oecumenical council, representing all the new Christian churches along with the old. Here the Spirit of God would not fail to make his voice heard. In the meantime, having lost his initial illusions, Carnesecchi followed the progress of Trent with the intolerance one reserved to provisional decisions, and thereby also justifying his Nicodemism. Thus the Council of Trent was devalued, but the conciliar ideal was not lost. Vergerio, for instance, scathingly defined Trent as a tribunal where criminals and debtors were the judges, instead of the accused, but in the same breath he continued to speak of another council, to be convoked by the Doge of Venice and by the Germanic nobility, in which this absurd situation would not be repeated.[3]

In general, from this second council one expected broad definitions which would summarize the common elements of the Christian faith without specifying the differences. One awaited also the possibility for criticizing and correcting the abuses of religious authorities. Even as late as the eve of the closing of Trent, 24 March, 1563, Piero Gelido, wrote to Cosimo I from his asylum in Geneva, that he should persuade the Pope to assemble "a legitimate council in the heart of Germany" which the Pope should attend in person "so that the church might be truly reformed."[4]

Lastly, there was no lack of hope for the succession to the throne of Peter. At the death of each Pope, from Paul III to Pius V, the desire for the election of a Pontiff who could alter the course of events and reopen the way to the affirmation of the new ideals renewed itself among the reformed Italians. There was no clearly defined program, nor could there be; it would have been defined according to the person elected. We notice this attitude especially in men who knew that in the Curia the course of events and the climate of opinion were closely bound

---

[1] G. Manzoni, "Estratto del Processo di Pietro Carnesecchi," *Miscellanea di Storia italiana*, X (1870), 549-550.

[2] On the presence of cripto-Lutherans at Trent, cf. H. Jedin, *A History of the Council of Trent*, 2 vols. (Saint Louis, 1957-1960), II, 28. Among these, Luciano degli Ottoni abbot of Pomposa, is defined "a typical exponent of Italian evangelism."

[3] F. C. Church, *The Italian Reformers, 1534-1554* (New York, 1932), pp. 178-179.

[4] C. Cantù, "Spigolature negli archivi toscani," *Rivista Contemporanea*, XXI (1860), 387.

to the seat of authority. They thought that if a man of determined character and broad views should ascend to the chair of Peter, it would not be difficult to give a different tone to the Council.

Later, after the termination of Trent, it was thought that a providential Pope could give a sympathetic emphasis to the practical implementation of the Tridentine decisions, if not to completely undo what was accomplished and to turn Catholicism in a completely new direction. In the long and troubled conclave which followed the death of Paul III, the hopes of the reformed Italians were anything but unfounded. At one point, Pole's election was an accomplished fact and only the Cardinal's well justified scruples, in desiring canonical repetition of his election by homage, changed the course of events.[1]

Similarly, at the death of Paul IV, a few years later, Pietro Carnesecchi, a representative figure, anxiously longed for the election of Cardinal Morone. He thought that Morone's presence as Pope would open a new era of harmony not only among Christians but for all humanity, and Moslems and Jews would not have hesitated to receive Baptism once the internal strife among Christians had ceased.[2] These are hopes of a millenarian type, bordering on the fantastic dreams of a visionary, but they are exemplary for indicating the limits reached by certain Italians in their aspirations for a universal religious peace achieved under the aegis of Rome.

---

[1] O. Ortolani, *op. cit.*, p. 71 ff.
[2] G. Manzoni, *op. cit.*, 382; O. Ortolani, *op. cit.*, pp. 107 ff.

THE *BENEFICIO DI CRISTO*

TRANSLATED, WITH AN INTRODUCTION BY

RUTH PRELOWSKI

INTRODUCTION

The *Beneficio di Cristo* is considered one of the most important works of the Italian Reformation, chiefly because it was so popular and controversial in its own day. It has also become an object of controversy among modern scholars who discuss the nature of the Italian Reformation, and consequently it provides an excellent starting-point for a study of this complex phenomenon.

The first known edition of the *Beneficio* was published anonymously in Venice in 1543, the year after the Roman Inquisition was reorganized.[1] It was a short work,[2] written in Italian in a lucid style, and its theological vocabulary was simple and untechnical; all its features point to the idea that it was designed to reach a very wide audience, and contemporaries considered this was its purpose.[3] In this respect, it was very successful for, according to Vergerio, 40,000 copies were sold in Venice alone during the next six years.[4] The *Beneficio* was also reprinted and circulated at Modena, by the order of Cardinal Morone, who found the book " very spiritual. "[5] Other important ecclesiastics such as Cardinal Tommaso Badia, the Master of the Sacred Palace, Cristoforo Madruzzo, the Cardinal of Trent, and Cardinal Gregorio Cortese (previously the reformer of the Benedictines) highly approved of it.[6] Cardinal Pole and his entourage (including Marcantonio Flaminio and Alvise Priuli) defended the *Beneficio* and had it circulated.[7]

---

[1] The full title of this edition runs: *Trattato utilissimo del beneficio di Giesu Christo crocifisso, verso i Christiani*. Venetiis apud Bernardinum de Bindonis. Anno Do. MDXXXXIII.

[2] The first edition was 72 ff. in small 8º. Contemporaries referred to the book as a " libretto " or " libriccino. "

[3] In his preface to the 1552 Lyons edition, the French translator noted that its author seemed to have written expressly for " simple men, who do not have a great amount of knowledge. " This edition is reprinted in *The Benefit of Christ's Death*, edited by Churchill Babington (London: Bell and Daldy; Cambridge: Deighton Bell and Co., 1855); cf. a similar statement by Vergerio, quoted by Babington, *op. cit.*, Introduction, lxxi, n. 2.

[4] His statement, made in 1549, is quoted by Babington, *op. cit.*, Introduction, xli.

[5] For his reprinting and circulation of the work, cf. Costantino Corvisieri, ed., " Compendio dei processi del Santo Uffizio di Roma (da Paolo III a Paolo IV), " *Archivio della Società Romana di Storia Patria*, III (1880), 268, 272, 459, 467. For Morone's opinion of the *Beneficio*, cf. Cesare Cantù, *Gli eretici d'Italia*, 3 vols. (Turin: Unione Tipografica-Editrice, 1865-67), II, 180.

[6] Morone also reported the reactions of Cortese and Madruzzo. Cantù, *op. cit.*, II, 180. Badia's approval of the book was mentioned in a deposition to the Inquisition; Corvisieri, *loc. cit.*, 469.

[7] The source of this information is a statement by Vergerio, quoted by Babington, *op. cit.*, Introduction, lxiv.

The book had to be defended because it was immediately attacked by Ambrogio Catharino, a Dominican monk, who asserted it was full of "Lutheran errors and deceptions."[1] It was publicly burned in Naples in 1544, and was opposed in Verona (probably by Luigi Lippomani, the coadjutor bishop of the city).[2] Most important of all, it was included in the first Venetian index, published by Giovanni della Casa in 1549.[3] Subsequently, one of the most frequent charges made in heresy trials, was that the defendant had owned or read the *Beneficio*.[4] The Inquisition considered the book so dangerous that it tried to suppress it completely, and was almost successful. In the early nineteenth century, both Ranke and Macaulay thought that no copy had survived, but to everyone's delight John Ayre found and reprinted an English translation. Then Churchill Babington discovered a copy of the original Venetian edition, at St. John's College Library, Cambridge, and had a facsimile of it printed in 1855.[5] Following this, more editions and translations were unearthed in various European libraries; some were reprinted and several new translations were also made.[6]

At the same time as editions of the *Beneficio* were being recovered, a controversy over its authorship was taking place. It was generally thought that Aonio Paleario[7] was the author, because, in a speech made in 1542, he refers to an Italian work he wrote in that same year, "on the great benefits which mankind had derived from his [Christ's] death."[8] Ranke disagreed with this position, basing himself on a Compendium of the Inquisitors, cited in Caracciolo's *Vita di Paolo IV*, which stated that the *Beneficio* had two authors, a Benedictine monk

---

[1] The full title of Catharino's polemic runs: *Compendio d'errori, et inganni Luterani, contenuti in un Libretto, senza nome de l'Autore, intitolato, Trattato utilissimo del benefitio di Christo crucifisso.... Frate Ambrosio Catharino Senese de l'Ordine de Predicatori, A gli amatori de la verità.* In Roma. Ne la Contrada del Pellegrino. MDXLIIII. Together with Girolamo Muzio, Catharino was one of the foremost controversialists of the day. Babington reprints some passages of this work; *op. cit.*, Introduction, lvi-lx.

[2] L. Amabile, *Il santo officio dell'inquisizione a Napoli.* 2 vols. (Città di Castello: S. Lapi tipografo-editore, 1892) I, 195. For its reception in Verona, cf. Corvisieri, *loc. cit.*, 272.

[3] Della Casa's Index was reprinted by Emilio Comba in *I nostri Protestanti*, 2 vols. (Florence: Libreria Claudiana, 1897), II, 692-695. Vergerio's commentary on this Index is an important source of information both for the *Beneficio* and for the period generally.

[4] Frederick Church, *The Italian Reformers 1534-1564*, (New York: Columbia University Press, 1932), pp. 46-47. This was one of the charges brought against Pietro Carnesecchi; cf. G. Manzoni, "Estratto del processo di Pietro Carnesecchi," *Miscellanea di Storia italiana*, X (1870), 553, 567.

[5] Babington describes the search for copies of the *Beneficio* in his Introduction, lxix-lxxiv.

[6] Following the text, there is a bibliography of original and modern editions of the *Beneficio*.

[7] Aonio Paleario was a humanist poet and scholar, and a friend of Bembo and Sadoleto, who was charged with heresy several times, and eventually executed by the Inquisition in 1570.

[8] Babington, Introduction, xxxvi. Babington summarizes the long tradition behind this attribution and presents the case for Paleario; Introduction, xxxii-l. Young also does, with slight differences; cf. M. Young, *The Life and Times of Aonio Paleario* (London: Bell and Daldy, 1860), I, 324-341.

and Flaminio.[1] As more documents of the period were published, it became evident that Ranke's position was stronger. In an article published in 1876, Benrath presented all the available evidence on the question.[2] He noted various weaknesses in the Paleario thesis, and showed that all of the four contemporary sources which speak about the *Beneficio* in any detail mention two authors, neither of which was Paleario.[3] In addition, the title of the book to which Paleario referred in his speech, was found to be *Della pienezza, sufficienza et satisfactione della passione di Christo*.[4] Taking all these things into consideration, Benrath concluded that Paleario could not be the author,[5] and his opinion has been generally accepted. Also, no further evidence has since come to light which would in any way vitiate these conclusions.

The now-accepted authorship is pieced together from the evidence of the four contemporary sources that Benrath mentions. In his 1549 commentary on Della Casa's Index, Vergerio argues that the *Beneficio* did not deserve such a condemnation, and then he mentions that

> There are two persons, who have had a hand in it; one began it, and the other finished and polished it; and both of them are in Italy and well-known and cherished by the foremost members and clergy of Rome.... [6]

When Cardinal Morone was on trial for heresy, he commented as follows on the *Beneficio* in his *Difesa* of 1557:

> I wish to repeat that I was never able to learn who the author of the book was until several years later, since it was said to be Flaminio, and he denied it; afterwards I heard it was a Benedictine monk, I believe either Sicilian or from the Kingdom [of Naples], whose name I did not know. [7]

The fullest statement on the matter was given by Pietro Carnesecchi, a good friend of Flaminio, at his trial in 1567.

---

[1] Leopold von Ranke, *History of the Popes in the sixteenth and seventeenth centuries*, 3 vols., translated by E. Foster (London: George Bell and Sons, 1878), I, 105, n. 1. Caracciolo's biography was written about 1610 and is a defense of Paul IV and of the Inquisition.

[2] Karl Benrath, "Über den Verfasser der Schrift 'Von der Wohltat Christi'," in *Zeitschrift für Kirchengeschichte*, I (1876), 575-596.

[3] *Ibid.*, 584-90.

[4] Cf. Giuseppe De Leva, *Storia documentata di Carlo V, in correlazione all'Italia*. 5 vols. (Venice, vols. 1-3; Padua, vol. 4; Bologna, vol. 5, 1863-1894), III, 369, n. 1. Benrath defended the validity of De Leva's finding: *loc. cit.*, 575-77, 595-96. More recent research shows that the content of Paleario's work differs from the *Beneficio*; cf. Giuseppe Morpurgo, *Un umanista martire, Aonio Paleario e la riforma teorica italiana nel secolo XVI* (Città di Castello, 1912), pp. 285-87.

[5] Benrath, *loc. cit.*, 594.

[6] Vergerio's statement is guoted bay Babington, Introduction, xliii.

[7] Morone's *Difesa* is reprinted by Cantù, *op. cit.*, II, 176-190. For this statement, *Ibid.*, 180-181. Corvisieri, *loc. cit.*, 273.

> The first author of this book was a black monk of St. Benedict called Don Benedetto of Mantua, who said he had composed it while staying in the monastery of his order in Sicily near Mt. Etna; since this Don Benedetto was a friend of M. Marcantonio Flaminio, he gave him the said book, asking him to polish and clarify (illustrare) it with his beautiful style, so that it would be more readable and pleasing, and so Flaminio, while preserving the subject entire, corrected (reformò) it as it seemed proper to him... [1]

The last source that Benrath mentions is the Compendium of the Inquisitors, cited by Ranke. Benrath cautioned that its notes on the *Beneficio* may have been drawn from the records of Carnesecchi's trial, and consequently cannot be considered independent evidence.[2] In addition, Ranke's citation does not carry full weight, because he did not quote from the Compendium directly, but from Caracciolo. The latter's statements on the *Beneficio* differ slightly from those appearing in the Compendium, which was published by Corvisieri in the late nineteenth century. Caracciolo's version runs as follows: "Its author was a monk of S. Severino [a Benedictine house] in Naples, a disciple of Valdés. The reviser of this book was Flaminio..." [3] The Compendium states that "its author was a monk of St. Benedict, a friend of Valdés," and that "its reviser was Flaminio." [4] Corvisieri also quoted a 1564 deposition from another collection, which states that "the book of the *Beneficio di Christo* was composed by a Mantuan monk of S. Severino, a disciple of Marc-Antonio Flaminio..." [5]

Weighing and comparing all these sources, one can gather that the *Beneficio* was written by a Benedictine monk called Don Benedetto, who was originally from Mantua, but in Sicily or Naples at the time. He knew Flaminio and Valdés, and may have been a disciple of either or both of them. The book was then revised by Flaminio, but his contribution was limited mainly to improvement of its style.[6]

Of these two authors, Marcantonio Flaminio was well-known to historians as a humanist poet and scholar, a friend of Valdés and a member of Cardinal Pole's circle at Viterbo, but Don Benedetto was a very obscure figure. However, for about sixty years after Benrath's article, no research was done on him. Then in 1940, independently and within two months of each other, Croce and Caponetto published conflicting articles on two diffeient Don Benedetto's.[7] Croce straigh-

---

[1] Manzoni, *loc. cit.*, 202-203.

[2] Benrath, *loc. cit.*, 593-594. Some of the Compendium's notes on the *Beneficio* are derived from the records of Morone' trial; cf. Corvisieri, *loc. cit.*, 459, 467.

[3] Ranke, *op. cit.*, I, 105, n. 1.

[4] Corvisieri, *loc. cit.*, 272.

[5] *Ibid.*, 469.

[6] Carnesecchi's evidence on this point carries more weight than Vergerio's since he was closer to the event.

[7] Cf. Benedetto Croce, "Il 'Beneficio di Cristo'," *La Critica*, XXXVIII (1940), 115-125, and Salvatore Caponetto, "Il 'Beneficio di Giesù Cristo' e don Benedetto da Mantova," *Gioventù Cristiana*, June 1940, 38-43.

tened out the confusion in a second report; he acknowledged Caponetto's findings and presented the results of some further research he had done.[1] It turned out that the first author of the *Beneficio* had made his vows at Mantua in 1519, and then resided at S. Giorgio Maggiore in Venice until at least 1534, when he was a " decanus " there.[2] At this time, the monastery was headed by Gregorio Cortese, and was a center both for the reform of the order and for humanist studies.[3] From the late 1520's to 1538, Flaminio divided his time between this monastery and Ghiberti's residence at Verona,[4] and he may have met Don Benedetto here rather than in Naples. During the 30's, Pole and other dignitaries such as Contarini and Giberti, visited the monastery, so the monk was probably fairly well-known in ecclesiastical circles.[5]

In 1537 Don Benedetto was transferred to S. Nicola all'Arena, a monastery in Catania (the district in Sicily near Mt. Etna), and he was officially stationed there until his death, which may have been in 1544. [6] Early in 1540 Flaminio came down to live in Naples, on account of his health; Don Benedetto also visited the city, although we do not know when.[7] According to Carnesecchi the monk said he had written the *Beneficio* in Sicily, possibly after a stay in Naples where he came under Valdés' influence.[8] Carnesecchi did not provide any details on when and where the manuscript was given to Flaminio, but he mentioned that he was the first to read and approve the revised version.[9] He was also staying at Naples from early 1540 to May of 1541, and the sentence pronounced against him accuses him of having read the *Beneficio* in Naples.[10] Thus it seems likely that the work was

---

[1] Croce's reply to Caponetto appeared in *L'Appello* (a semi-clandestine review put out by the editors of the suppressed *Gioventù Cristiana*), in no. 3, 1942, 68-69. These three articles are summarized by Giovanni Gonnet in " Il ' Beneficio di Cristo ', " *Bolletino della società di studi valdesi*, n. 79 (1943), 31-33. I was not able to obtain the three original articles, and relied on Gonnet for information about them.

[2] Gonnet, *loc. cit.*, 32.

[3] Church, *op. cit.*, p. 22; Ludwig Pastor, *History of the Popes*, vol. X, edited by R. F. Kerr (London: Kegan Paul, 1910), 416.

[4] Young, *op. cit.*, II, 220-222.

[5] Salvatore Caponetto, " Origini e caratteri della riforma in Sicilia, " *Rinascimento*, VII (1956), 233, n. 3. As Gonnet pointed out (*loc. cit.*, 33), if Don Benedetto were well-known, this would tally with Vergerio's description of the authors of the *Beneficio* (cf. above, 25).

[6] Gonnet, *loc. cit.*, 32.

[7] Ercole Cuccoli, *M. Antonio Flaminio*, (Bologna: Zanichelli, 1897), p. 72. According to Caracciolo and to the 1564 deposition cited by Corvisieri, Don Benedetto was at the monastery of S. Severino (cf. above, 26). Also Basilù, a Venetian lawyer, reported to the Inquisition in 1555 that " Don Benedetto da Mantoa dell'ordine di S^{to} Giorgio " had discussed " justification, its consequences and the sacraments " at Naples; cf. Amabile, *op. cit.*, I, 162-163.

[8] Cf. above, 26. Only Caracciolo specifically states that he was a disciple of Valdés. Internal evidence of the *Beneficio* shows he was well-acquainted with Valdés' thought, whether directly or via Flaminio.

[9] Manzoni, *loc. cit.*, 203.

[10] Oddone Ortolani, *Pietro Carnesecchi* (Florence: Le Monnier, 1963), p. 24. Manzoni, *loc. cit.*, 211, 553.

finished at some time between these two dates.[1] None of the sources indicate why the *Beneficio* was published two years later, or who was responsible for taking it to the press. During 1542 and 1543, Flaminio was traveling with Cardinal Pole, but Carnesecchi was in Venice, and he may have had it printed.[2]

* * * *

It is evident that the circumstances surrounding the composition and the publication of the *Beneficio* are still quite obscure and in need of further study. On the other hand, a great deal has been written about the meaning and significance of the book and its place in the thought of the Italian Reformation. The following paragraphs essay a sketch of the various interpretations put on the *Beneficio* by modern historians.

In the nineteenth century, some Protestant scholars saw the *Beneficio* as the heroic manifesto of Italian Lutheranism, just before it was crushed by the "Romish Inquisition." This interpretation was strengthened by their knowledge that its supposed author, Paleario, later became a "Protestant martyr."[3] In a more moderate tone, Ranke cited the Compendium of the Inquisitors to show that the *Beneficio* taught the Lutheran doctrine of justification. He described how the doctrine was first taken up in Venetian humanist circles by such men as Contarini and Pole, and then spread all over Italy even to "pleasure-loving" Naples, where it was accepted by Valdés' circle. As the Compendium showed, the author of the *Beneficio* was a disciple of Valdés; its reviser was a friend of his and also a member of the Venetian circle.[4]

---

[1] There is also the possiblity that Carnesecchi read only Don Benedetto's manuscript in Naples, and that the revision was not finished until later at Florence or Viterbo. Flaminio resided with Carnesecchi at the latter's house in Florence from May to October, 1541 (Manzoni, *loc. cit.*, 505). Then until November 1542, they were both in Viterbo with Cardinal Pole (Manzoni, *loc. cit.*, 213-214; Ortolani, *op. cit.*, pp. 33, 41).

[2] For Flaminio, cf. Young, *op. cit.*, II, 226. For Carnesecchi, cf. Manzoni, *loc. cit.*, 197. Carnesecchi was accused of taking Valdés' books to Venice for safe-keeping (Manzoni, 558), and it is likely that he gave Flaminio's Italian translation of *Le cento e dieci divine considerazioni* (*Ibid.*, 495. The work was originally in Spanish.) to Vergerio, who then gave it to Curione to publish in Basel; cf. *Le cento e dieci divine considerazioni*, edited by E. Böhmer (Halle in Sassonia, 1860), Curione's preface, 432.

[3] For an extreme statement of this view, cf. Young, *op. cit.*, I, 6-7. Also, *The Benefit of Christ's Death*, edited by J. Ayre (London: The Religious Tract Society, no date), Introduction, xvi-xvii.

[4] Ranke, *op. cit.*, I, 102-105. Valdés was a Spanish nobleman in the service of Charles V, who settled in Naples in 1535 and remained there until his death in August, 1541. During this period he wrote several religious works, including the *Alfabeto cristiano* (a spiritual guide for Giulia Gonzaga), *Le cento e dieci divine considerazioni*, and commentaries on the Psalms and the Pauline epistles. He is thought to have influenced Ochino, Vermigli, Flaminio, Carnesecchi, and other figures.

Towards the end of the century, Pastor, the great Roman Catholic historian, formulated a different conception of the *Beneficio.* He agreed with Ranke that it was inspired by Valdés, but unsympathetically characterized the latter as " a lay theologian, wanting in clearness of thought, " who " inclined to a vague emotional religion, compounded of intellectuality and a false mysticism. " Valdés' writings contained " echoes of Lutheran teaching, " and the *Beneficio* " came very close to the Lutheran thesis of justification by faith. " However, Pastor thought that the Valdesians were unaware of this similarity, and he stressed that their intentions were generally not schismatic.[1] Elsewhere, he remarked that the Italian religious situation in the 1530's and early 1540's was extremely confused, and he thought this was a symptom of the transitional nature of the period.[2] In a 1909 study of Giulia Gonzaga and the Valdesians, Paladino agreed with Pastor that they were interested in a more intimate and intense spiritual life within the orthodox communion. On the other hand, he thought that the Italians were aware of Luther's teaching on justification but they modified it. Citing Carnesecchi's testimony, Paladino said Valdés taught that the Christian should try to acquire inherent justice after he was made just in Christ, and that he should show his faith in his works.[3] He also quoted a passage from the *Beneficio,* which was " the most faithful and genuine expression of Valdés' ideas, " and which was for Italians what Calvin's *Institutes* were for the French and Swiss, to show that it did not have a " complete disdain for works, as Luther had preached. "[4]

Church made some comments on the *Beneficio* in his 1932 work on the Italian Reformers. Like Paladino, he termed the *Beneficio* " a product of the circle of Valdés at Naples, " and the " most influential of the literary products of the Italian reform. "[5] To his mind, the essence of Valdés' teaching consisted in his mystical conception of the individual conscience as man's highest spiritual guide; he rejected external authority but did not define any creed to accompany his teaching.[6] The *Beneficio* was written in his " spirit of mystic devotion, " but it " maintains the doctrine of justification by faith, as one would expect of a disciple of Valdés, who translated the thoughts of his master into familiar phrases. "[7] In other words, Church considered the work

---

[1] Ludwig Pastor, *History of the Popes,* XII, edited by R. F. Kerr (London: Kegan Paul, 2nd edition, 1923), 495-496.

[2] Pastor, *op. cit.,* XI, edited by R. F. Kerr (London: Kegan Paul; St. Louis: B. Herder, 1912), 498-499.

[3] Giuseppe Paladino, *Giulia Gonzaga e il movimento valdesiano* (Naples: F. Sangiovanni & Figlio, 1909), pp. 41-43.

[4] *Ibid.,* p. 39. A recent biography of Valdés follows Paladino in terming the *Beneficio* the " quintessence " of Valdesianism; cf. Domingo Ricart, *Juan de Valdés y el pensamiento religioso europeo en los siglos XVI y XVII* (El Collegio de Mexico, 1958), p. 36.

[5] Church, *op. cit.,* pp. 47, 54.

[6] *Ibid.,* pp. 50-51.

[7] *Ibid.,* p. 47.

an adaptation and popularization of the master's esoteric thought. In a 1940 article on the *Beneficio*, Meozzi followed Paladino's interpretation, asserting that it was typical of the Valdesian school in its delicate balancing of the claims of faith and work; the position that resulted from this "subtle dialectic" could be considered neither completely orthodox nor properly heretical.[1] Meozzi also tended to think that the "protolutheran" elements in the *Beneficio* should be attributed to common Pauline and patristic sources rather than to direct contact with Lutheran literature.[2]

Two years later, in *L'Appello*, a semi-clandestine journal, the *Beneficio* was the subject of an interesting exchange of views.[3] Minaci argued that it represented the attempt of Valdés and his followers to re-evaluate Catholic theology, reviving Pauline and Augustinian elements which had become obscured. They hoped that this would lead to the internal reform of the Church, and consequently to the revival of a sense of Christian unity. Thus the *Beneficio* was the manifesto not of the Italian Reform but of what was almost a pre-Tridentine "counter-reform" against the Lutheran schism, "in the name of Erasmian humanism and Spanish mysticism." Minaci denied that the *Beneficio* reflected any Lutheran influence, and thought it came to be suspected of heresy because it overemphasized Pauline and Augustinian insights.[4] In reply to this thesis, Miegge claimed that the Valdesian movement was basically a "Reformed spirituality," independent in its development but inspired to some degree by the Lutheran doctrine of justification. Taking the *Beneficio* as an example of the thought of the movement, he discussed its position on justification. First, he distinguished between Luther's concept of forensic and imputed justice, and Augustine's conception of justice infused by grace through the agency of the Holy Spirit. Then he cited a "locus" in Melanchthon, where these two conceptions are distinguished and then harmonized as successive stages of the process of justification;[5] the *Beneficio* followed Melanchthon's analysis of this process, combining the doctrine of the gratuitous imputation of Christ's merits with the consequent gift of the Holy Spirit, the source of good works. With regard to the first stage of justification, Miegge pointed out that the *Beneficio* employs

---

[1] Antero Meozzi, "Per la storia del Valdesianesimo in Italia (Il Beneficio di Cristo)", in *La civiltà moderna*, XII (1940), 68-69.

[2] *Ibid.*, p. 75.

[3] Since *L'Appello* was not obtainable, the information on Minaci and Miegge's letters was taken from two later articles that summarize them; cf. Gonnet, *loc. cit.*, 39-40, and S. Caponetto, "Significato del 'Beneficio di Cristo', alla luce di recenti interpretazioni," *Bolletino della società di studi valdesi*, n. 104 (1958), 43-44.

[4] Gonnet, *loc. cit.*, 39; Caponetto, *loc. cit.*, 43. In his new biography of Carnesecchi, Ortolani views the Valdesians and the *Beneficio* very much as Minaci did: cf. Ortolani, *op. cit.*, p. 28.

[5] Neither Gonnet nor Caponetto specify this "locus" that Miegge noted, but he is probably referring to a passage in the 1521 *Loci Communes*, in the section "On Grace." Cf. *The Loci Communes of Philip Melanchthon*, translated by Charles Leander Hill. (Boston: Meador Publishing Co., 1944), pp. 170-171, and pp. 195-198.

the Lutheran metaphor of the marriage of Christ and the sinful soul, which illustrates how Christ's merits are imputed to the Christian through faith. He also noted affinities with Luther's thought in its treatment of doubt about salvation as a wicked temptation of the devil, and its prescription of prayer, frequent communion, and the memory of baptism and predestination, as remedies against doubt.[1]

In an article the following year, Gonnet agreed with Miegge's analysis of the *Beneficio*; he thought it " undeniable " that its treatment of justification accorded with Luther and Melanchthon's thought, but preferred to leave it an open question whether this was due to direct influence or to the parallel development of an " indigenous spiritual current. "[2] Then Gonnet raised an interesting question — did Valdés really inspire the *Beneficio*? He noted it shared Valdés' conception of original sin and man's subsequent depravity, of the pedagogic offices of the law, and of justification by faith, and then pointed out some significant differences. Valdés ultimately maintained an eclectic view of justification, in which salvation depended on grace, but the amount of heavenly glory depended on the quantity of good works following the gift of grace. This division corresponded to the two levels on which God's will operated, the immediate level, on which his grace worked freely and irresistibly, and the mediate level, which followed the natural order and demanded that a person earn salvation by his good works. Valdés also considered " inspiration " superior to the Holy Scripture (like the light of the sun to that of a single candle), and he maintained a moderate view towards the visible Church and its sacramental system. By contrast, the *Beneficio* insisted on justification by faith alone, allowing subsequent good works no merit; it considered Holy Scripture the highest spiritual authority, and constantly supported its arguments with citations from the Bible, particularly from the Pauline epistles, and also from the Church fathers. Its author conveyed the urgent need for Christians to reform themselves spiritually, implying dissatisfaction with the Church. From this analysis, Gonnet reached conclusions which differed interestingly from previous ideas. Like Minaci, he thought that the Italian movement followed the " humanistic-liberal eclecticism " of Valdés, and consequently he disagreed with Miegge that the *Beneficio* was representative of the movement. He rather thought that it reflected the German Reformers' desire for a " theological and organizational clarification " of the religious situation.[3]

---

[1] Gonnet, *loc. cit.*, 40; Caponetto, *loc. cit.*, 43-44.

[2] Gonnet, *loc. cit.*, 33, 40, 43. The phrase, " indigenous spiritual current, " was coined by Casadei in his rebuttal of Church's theory that Spanish influence gave the Italian Reform its " peculiar character. " Cf. Church, *op. cit.*, pp. 2-5; Casadei's review of Church's book in *Religio*, XI (1935), 422-448, and his review of Cione's biography of Valdés in *Religio*, XIV (1938), 110-131. Gonnet applied Casadei's general critique to the thesis of the Valdesian inspiration of the *Beneficio*.

[3] Gonnet, *loc. cit.*, 41-43. According to Caponetto, a recent biographer of Valdés has noted the same differences between Valdés' thought and the *Beneficio* that Gonnet

In his first volume on the Council of Trent, Jedin commented that the *Beneficio* was " typical of Italian evangelism. "[1] He saw " evangelism " as a European phenomenon, an expression of the heightened religious consciousness of the 1530's which was " undoubtedly influenced, directly or at least indirectly, by the German schism. " Theologians and educated laymen, both Protestants and Catholics, discussed the Scripture and the writings of the Church Fathers, particularly Paul and Augustine, in order to rediscover the central meaning of Christianity. Jedin characterized the result as a " riot of individualism, " which was " undefined, fluid and fraught with many possibilities for good and evil. "[2] His reaction to this phenomenon was very similar to Pastor's attitude towards Valdesianism. He was shocked by its " appalling confusion " of thought, and described it as a " characteristic symptom of a period of transition " (before the Council of Trent set up firm standards), in which " old, sound, traditional Catholic material lay thick by the side of what was new, questionable, false. "[3] This general judgement is reflected in his statement that " it is not easy to detect any open heresies in the small book ' On the Benefit of Christ ' — *Del beneficio di Christi* — ... for all that the Roman Inquisition acted in the interests of the Church when it suppressed this work... "[4]

In a 1953 article, Jung developed Jedin's ideas with specific reference to Italian evangelism.[5] She described it as a " spontaneous phenomenon " but also pointed out its antecedents in Italian thought. Following Church, she stressed the importance of Valdés' influence on the movement, and stated that it arose " often under the influence of the German Reformation, sometimes, however, without any direct contact with it. "[6] The *Beneficio* was " the best mirror of the spirit of Evangelism, " and like Meozzi, she thought it embodied the attempt of the movement to retain " justification through faith without omission of good works. " Citing Valdés' *Alfabeto cristiano*, she described his teaching that good works are the inevitable fruit of true faith, although they are not meritorious. She also noted that the *Beneficio* adopted the same theological compromise stated in Cardinal Pole's advice to Vittoria Colonna: " She should believe as if she could be saved only by faith, but on the other hand, she should act as if her salvation would depend upon her good works... "[7] Like Pastor, she characterized the

---

did. Cf. Caponetto, *loc. cit.*, 44, for his description of the comments in Fr. Domingo De Santa Teresa, O.C.D., *Juan des Valdés. Su pensamiento religioso y las corrientes espirituales du su tiempo* (Roma, 1957), chap. XI.

[1] Hubert Jedin, *A History of the Council of Trent*, vol. 1. Translated by Dom Ernest Graf, O.S.B. (St. Louis: B. Herder, 1957), 366.

[2] *Ibid.*, 364-366.

[3] *Ibid.*, 368-369.

[4] *Ibid.*, 366.

[5] Eva-Maria Jung, " On the Nature of Evangelism in 16th. Century Italy, " *Journal of the History of Ideas*, XIV (1953), 511-527. In the first two pages, she gives the derivation of the concept of evangelism.

[6] *Ibid.*, 513-514.

[7] *Ibid.*, 521.

movement as a weak, ambiguous religion, suitable for salons, humanists and cardinals; its indifference towards dogma and the Church tended to reduce Christianity to "nothing but a religious attitude." Thus "the *Beneficio* had to be destroyed: not for what it said, but for what it omitted; not for its heretical teachings, but for its silence, its complete indifference towards the Church."[1]

In the previous year, Vinay came out in support of Miegge's analysis of the *Beneficio.* He stated that the work obviously taught the doctrine of justification in its pure Lutheran form, and that it reflected the influence of early Lutheran works in its treatment of the Lord's Supper and of predestination. Vinay termed it the "most genuinely evangelical" writing of the Italian Reform.[2] To account for the denial of the Lutheran character of the *Beneficio* by scholars such as Paladino and Minaci, he made the interesting suggestion that Italian scholars are generally unable to deal objectively with Luther's influence. They have a deep-seated bias against him, both "Catholic and national" in character, which stems from Luther's dislike of all things Roman, and the corresponding exaggerated reaction against him by the Counter-Reformation.[3]

More recently, Caponetto discussed the *Beneficio* in terms of "evangelism" as defined by Jedin. He considered it typical in its attempt to return to the truth of the Gospel through Paul and Augustine, and in its repetition of Pole's advice to Vittoria Colonna, that Jung had already noted. However, he agreed with Miegge that its theory of justification was of Lutheran origin, and that it differed from Contarini's theory of double justification, which was supported by Seripando and Pole. He accounted for this important difference by reference to Jedin's conception of the fluidity and heterogeneity of the movement.[4] Like Gonnet, he contrasted Valdés' dogmatic indifference with the *Beneficio*'s concern for re-establishing the truth of the Gospel. He also noted that the work oscillated between a joyful exposition of the benefit of Christ, and sharp polemics against the "false Christians," who refused to accept this and held onto justification by faith and works.[5] Caponetto thought that Don Benedetto considered the true Church the community of the elect, because whenever it named the Church, he added in apposition, "every faithful soul." Also he never referred to the Church as a juridical and hierarchical institution, but any allusions to the hierarchy occurred in a polemic context. Caponetto concluded that the monk sensed there was a split between the real and the legal Church, which was persecuting true believers in Christ.[6] Like Meozzi he raised the question whether

[1] E. M. Jung, *op. cit.*, 522-523.

[2] Valdo Vinay, "Lutero e il Luteranesimo nel giudizio della cultura italiana negli ultimi quarant'anni," *Protestantesimo,* VII (1952), 98, 111.

[3] *Ibid.*, 111-112.

[4] Caponetto, *loc. cit.*, 48.

[5] *Ibid.*, 45, 47.

[6] *Ibid.*, 46-47.

the *Beneficio* was orthodox in terms of pre-Tridentine Catholicism, and decided that its response to " the laceration of the Christian republic " was unconsciously heretical. Don Benedetto had crossed over the line when he made the belief in " sola fede " the distinguishing mark between true and false Christians, and when he abandoned the conception of the universal Church in favour of the invisible community of the elect, who were truly guided by the spirit of Christ.[1]

* * * *

Looking back from Caponetto's analysis to the early statements of Protestant scholars, one sees that comments on the *Beneficio* have centered around three main problems: its Valdesian inspiration, its relationship to the thought of the Northern Reformers, and its significance as a representative work of the early Italian Reformers. Each of these problems is complex and has evoked a great diversity of opinions.

For a long time, it was generally assumed that Valdés inspired the *Beneficio*, and that it represented the thought of his circle at Naples.[2] However, Gonnet's detailed comparison of the thought of Valdés and the *Beneficio* has shown that this assumption must be qualified. While granting that the *Beneficio* drew some of its main ideas from Valdés,[3] he pointed out that the orientation of its thought was closer to that of the Northern Reformers. In particular, he supported Miegge's claim that the *Beneficio* held the same position on justification as Melanchthon. Other scholars, such as Paladino, Meozzi and Jung, thought that the *Beneficio* embodied a compromise position that tried to reconcile the Lutheran and Roman Catholic doctrines. If one closely examines the thought of the work, it is evident that Miegge and his supporters have analysed it correctly.

Don Benedetto devotes almost the first half of the *Beneficio* to expounding the Lutheran doctrine of justification by faith alone. He first lays the theological groundwork for the doctrine by describing the depravity of man after original sin. In this context, the Law functions pedagogically in five steps, revealing man's inability to justify himself before God through works, and compelling him to seek Christ,

---

[1] Caponetto, *op. cit.*, 47-49.

[2] Despite this assumption, scholars differed greatly in their characterization of Valdés' thought, and this lack of agreement was reflected in the interpretation of the *Beneficio*. Valdés has always been a controversial figure; his biographers have conducted a long-standing dispute over whether there was any Lutheran influence on his thought. Cf. Gonnet, *loc. cit.*, 36-37.

[3] In addition to the similarities noted by Gonnet, the *Beneficio* takes up or at least mentions many other characteristic themes of Valdés. These will be noted as they occur in the text.

the promised mediator.[1] Then the author develops his main point, namely, that through faith the merits of Christ crucified are imputed to the Christian (the benefit of Christ).[2] Like Melanchthon, he adds that through faith the Christian also receives the gift of the Holy Spirit, which inspires him to a love of God and to good works.[3] Then he states that good works must follow justification as the fruit and testimony of true faith, but that they have no merit attached to them.[4] It is precisely with regard to this point, that Paladino and his followers have misunderstood the intent of the *Beneficio*. They thought that its insistence on the need for good works implied a compromise on the doctrine of justification by faith alone. This view fails to distinguish between the Lutheran abhorrence of good works in connection with justification, and its equally strong insistence on them as an effect and sign of justification. Actually, some passages in the *Beneficio* on the justified Christian's love of good works are very similar to statements made by Luther in *Freedom of a Christian*.[5] Don Benedetto is less clear about the degree of sanctification that the Christian can obtain in this life. He generally stresses man's frailty and the continuing imperfection and deficiency of his works, but in one passage he speaks inconsistently in Valdesian terms about the Christian's attainment of spiritual perfection.[6]

---

[1] This material is covered in the first two-and-a half chapters; see below, pp. 47-53. In *Freedom of a Christian*, Luther states the pedagogic function of the Law; cf. *Martin Luther, Selections from His Writings*, edited by John Dillenberger (Anchor Books, 1961), pp. 57-58. (Citations of the work are to this edition). However, the description of the result of original sin, and the five-fold division of the Law are drawn from Valdés, as Gonnet pointed out. For the exact place where these descriptions occur in Valdés' work, see below, p. 47, note 4, and p. 50, note 8.

[2] See below, pp. 53-68. To make his point clearer, the author employs the analogy of the marriage of Christ and the sinful soul, that Luther used in his *Freedom of a Christian*, and Valdés' parable of the holy king from his *110 Divine Considerations*. (For exact references of these sources, see below, p. 57, note 3, and p. 60, note 3. He also supports his position with citations from the Pauline epistles and from Augustine, Origen, Hilary, Basil, Ambrose and Bernard.

[3] See below, pp. 61, 68, and *The Loci Communes of Philip Melanchthon*, translated by C. L. Hill (Boston: Meador, Publishing Co., 1944), pp. 196-197. (Citations are to this edition.) Luther credits the Holy Spirit with a similar function, but does not specifically say he is imparted to the Christian; cf. *Freedom of a Christian*, pp. 76, 67.

[4] See below, pp. 67-68, 69-70, 71. The author makes two interesting arguments by analogy to show how good works are related to faith. He also distinguishes between the renovating power of true faith, and the mere assent of illusory, historical faith. Cf. Melanchthon, *op. cit.*, pp. 196-197, 206-207. Contrary to the *Beneficio*, Valdés holds that the quantity of the Christian's works subsequent to justification determines the amount of his heavenly glory; cf. Carnesecchi's testimony on this point, in " Estratto del processo di Pietro Carnesecchi, " edited by G. Manzoni, *Miscellanea di Storia italiana*, X (1870), 534-535.

[5] See below, pp. 68, 74 , and Luther, *Freedom of a Christian*, pp. 74-76.

[6] For the two statements on perfection, see below, pp. 75 76. Valdés develops the conception of Christian perfection in his *Alfabeto cristiano*. Cf. *Alfabeto cristiano*, translated by Benjamin Wiffen (London, 1861), pp. 82-83, p. 89, p. 146. This conception reflects his view that the Christian who is justified by faith should also try to acquire inherent justice, and thus increase his heavenly glory.

Don Benedetto also spends a great deal of time discussing problems related to his position on justification. As Miegge pointed out, he analyzes the crucial problem of doubt about one's own justification in the same way as Luther, and he also proposes four Lutheran remedies for it.[1] When he deals with the third of these remedies, the frequent use of holy communion, he describes the sacrament as the sign of Christ's testament, which contains the essence of the mass. In *The Pagan Servitude of the Church,* Luther also describes the Lord's Supper in these terms.[2] Moreover, Don Benedetto paraphrases Calvin's 1539 *Institutes* in his passages on the proper reception of the sacraments, and its spiritual effects on the Christian.[3] Yet it is interesting to note that he ignores Calvin's theory of double predestination, that appeared in the same edition of the *Institutes*. The *Beneficio* treats predestination only as an assurance for the elect of their salvation, and consequently cites the remembrance of it as the final remedy for doubt. Besides dealing with the problem of doubt, Don Benedetto also makes a point of raising and then answering some important objections to his doctrine of justification. He rebuts the medieval argument that certainty of justification can come only from a particular revelation, and his reinterpretation of a Scriptural text in this connection paraphrases Calvin's treatment of the same text.[4] In addition, he answered the significant charge that certainty of justification and predestination gives scandal and leads to immorality.[5]

---

[1] See chapter 6 below, pp. 78-94. Exact references to the similarities between the *Beneficio* and Luther's writings on this subject will be given in the footnotes to these pages.

[2] See below, pp. 79-80, 82. Vinay generally noted their similarity on this subject. Cf. Luther, *Pagan Servitude of the Church*, in *Martin Luther, Selections from His Writings*, edited by Dillenberger (Anchor Books, 1961), pp. 273-282. The long passage describing the assurance that the sacrament gives to the Christian also has a Lutheran ring to it; see below, pp. 81-82.

[3] See below, pp. 80-81, 83-84. All the passages on communion that are paraphrases from the *Institutes* first appeared in the 1536 edition. However, one of them includes a section inserted in the 1539 edition, and the *Beneficio*'s paraphrases of Calvin on other topics generally refer to material that first appeared in the 1539 edition. Thus it is likely that Don Benedetto saw the enlarged 1539 version of the *Institutes*, rather than the first edition of 1536. The influence of Calvin's *Institutes* on the *Beneficio* has not been previously investigated, except in a short study by Tommaso Bozza, entitled *Il Beneficio di Cristo e la Istituzione della religione cristiana di Calvino*, which I have not read. Professor Cantimori recently gave a notice of this study (a pamphlet of 16 pages published privately in Rome, February 3, 1961) which asserts that the *Beneficio* is mainly a clever compilation of passages from the works of Northern Reformers, particularly from Calvin's *Institutes*. (See Delio Cantimori, "Il mestiere dello storico," *Itinerari*, 47-48 (March-April, 1961), pp. 10-15). Professor Bozza intends to present these ideas more extensively when he publishes a new Italian edition of the *Beneficio*, based on a manuscript of the work that he has discovered. Hopefully this new edition will ascertain, among other things, the extent of Flaminio's contribution as reviser.

[4] See below, pp. 87-90. (For the exact citation of the reference to Calvin, see below, p. 89, note 2). In support of his claim that the Christian must believe with certainty, he then cites passages from Hilary, Augustine and Bernard; see below, pp. 91-93.

[5] See below, pp. 68-69, 71, 93-94.

Given such close similarities between the thought of the *Beneficio* and that of the Northern Reformers, one tends to conclude that Don Benedetto was acquainted with their writings. It is true that he does not acknowledge any Northern influence, and we have no proof that he actually read their works, yet indirect evidence favours this possibility. It is known that many of the Northern works did circulate in Italy, both in Latin and in Italian translation.[1] With respect to the *Institutes*, we have Carnesecchi's statement that Flaminio had shown him a little (un poco) of the work in Florence in the middle of 1541.[2] Thus, it is quite conceivable that it could have circulated in Naples the previous year.[3] We also know that Luther's *Freedom of a Christian* and Melanchthon's *Loci Communes* were translated into Italian and circulated bound together, sometime after 1530.[4] Moreover, we know that Don Benedetto's friend, Flaminio, and his associates were familiar with the works of the Northern Reformers.[5] Carnesecchi expresses their common opinion that Luther was a good theologian, who had "interpreted many places in Scripture very well."[6] Although they disliked Luther's prideful schism from the universal Church, and his inspiration of further heresy, this did not prevent them from quite consciously accepting many of his doctrines.[7] As Carnesecchi put it, they drew ideas from him "as if collecting gold from dung, and the rest (as they say) they gave back to the cook."[8] One cannot argue, as Pastor did, that they were unconscious of the similarity between their thought and Luther's.

Catharino and the Inquisition were also well-aware of this similarity; they considered the *Beneficio* Lutheran and consequently heretical, particularly in its treatment of justification. This raises the question whether those who approved of the work really understood its doctrinal position. Looking at Morone's statement of his own reaction, one gets the impression that he had very little theological perception.[9]

---

1 Those works originally in Latin, such as Calvin's *Institutes*, could circulate immediately in Italy among the educated classes.

2 Manzoni, *loc. cit.*, 195. Unfortunately, we do not know whether Flaminio owned the 1536 or the 1539 edition. An Italian translation of the *Institutes* was only made in 1557 by Giulio Pascali.

3 Don Benedetto may have seen Flaminio's copy, or he could have obtained the work in various ways, from another friend or perhaps from a bookseller.

4 Melanchthon's work went under the title: *I Principii De La Theologia Di Ippofilo Da Terra Negra*, the Italian pseudonym being an anagram of his true name. It was possibly translated by Ludovico Castelvetro, and was published at Venice between 1530 and 1550. Bound in with this work was a translation of *Freedom of a Christian*, under the title: *Opera Divina della Christiana Vita*.

5 At his trial, Carnesecchi confessed that he, Flaminio and perhaps Priuli had read heretical books. Cf. Manzoni, *loc. cit.*, 194-195, 197, 203, 504-505, 553-554.

6 Carnesecchi reports this opinion of Luther for himself, Flaminio, Priuli, and Soranzo; cf. Manzoni, *loc. cit.*, 325-327. Paleario speaks similarly of all the Northern writers in his 1542 Oration; cf. Young, *op. cit.*, I, 311-312.

7 Manzoni, *loc. cit.*, 325-327.

8 *Ibid.*, 327.

9 Since this statement was made to the Inquisition during his trial for heresy, there is also the possibility that he was being purposely naive for his own protection.

> It [the *Beneficio*] seemed to me to be very spiritual, and I especially remember the section on communion with affection, and because I had a guiding rule (prima massima) that heretical books were contrary to all the sacraments, it did not seem to me that this little book that spoke so well of the most blessed sacrament, could contain any hidden evil.... [1]

This comment acquires ironic significance, when one remembers that the section on communion reflects both Lutheran and Calvinist thought. On the other hand, Carnesecchi was quite aware of the similarities between Italian and Lutheran thought, and yet he told the Inquisition that the *Beneficio* was " good, Catholic and holy. " [2] Underlying this assertion is his argument that the doctrine of justification by faith was not heretical by pre-Tridentine standards.[3] It represented the attempt to return to the true Scriptural meaning of justification as it was understood by the apostles and the old doctors.[4] Among the latter, he names Augustine, Bernard, Origen and Hilary, the same doctors that Don Benedetto used to support his arguments on justification.[5] In the *Beneficio*, the concept of " faith alone " is also described as St. Paul's " holy doctrine, " and it is expounded with numerous quotations from his epistles.[6] Since the *Beneficio* implicitly follows this ideal of " return to the sources, " one is then confronted with the question — what role did the Northern Reformers play in the formation of its thought? In other words, how much did Luther shape Don Benedetto's view of Paul, and how much did he serve rather to corroborate and then develop the opinions that the latter already held? [7] We have only the meager evidence that in Naples Don Benedetto discussed " justification, its consequences and the sacraments "; [8] the range of the topics suggests that by this time he was under Northern influence.

Having discussed the various influences on the thought of the *Beneficio*, it is appropriate to look at the work as a whole. In his con-

---

[1] Morone's *Difesa*, reprinted by Cantù, *op. cit.*, II, 180.

[2] Manzoni, *loc. cit.*, 502.

[3] *Ibid.*, 334-335. Carnesecchi made a sharp distinction between the doctrine itself, and the deductions (illationi) that could be drawn from it, such as the denial of purgatory and confession, which he considered specifically Lutheran and heretical. (*Ibid.*, 196-197, 335-337.) His testimony as to the exact doctrine of justification by faith that he held is unclear; he speaks both of infused and imputed faith, of faith alone and of double justification (cf. *Ibid.*, 332-333, 533-535).

[4] *Ibid.*, 333-337, 374.

[5] *Ibid.*, 334. Cf. below, pp. 62-64, 91-93.

[6] For his attribution of the doctrine to Paul, see below, pp. 54-55, 90. His citations of Paul occur all through the work, but in particular see below, pp. 49-56, 61-62. He also claims that all the passages in Scripture which seem to contradict Paul's doctrine have been properly " elucidated "; see below, p. 55.

[7] Carnesecchi interestingly describes how this second process took place in his own case; Manzoni, *loc. cit.*, 194-195, 333.

[8] This was reported to the Inquisition by Basilù, a Venetian lawyer, in 1555; cf. Amabile, *op. cit.*, I, 162-163.

clusion, Don Benedetto states that his "principal aim has been to praise and exalt... the stupendous benefit that the Christian has received from Jesus Christ crucified."[1] The author writes from the point of view of a Christian who has experienced the marvelous effects of this benefit, and who wishes to describe them for the edification of his fellow Christians.[2] Thus he traces man's spiritual progress from his original state of depravity, through the central event of his justification and his subsequent imitation of Christ, to his anticipation of eternal life.[3] He emphasizes that the justified Christian shows his gratitude for the great benefit that he has received, by bestowing the benefits of spiritual love on his brethren in Christ.[4] Within this framework, Don Benedetto is also very concerned to achieve his second aim, "to demonstrate that faith of itself justifies," and to show that it is always accompanied by good works.[5] This doctrinal position is the theological expression of his spirituality, and he ultimately justifies it on the ground that it "exalts Jesus Christ and humbles man's pride."[6] Correspondingly, he polemicizes against the doctrine of faith and works because it has the reverse effect, and he describes those who uphold it as "arrogant and half-witted," Christians with "Hebrew minds," or more emphatically "false Christians."[7] The author's concern with the doctrine of "faith alone" is also shown in the last chapter, which he devotes to resolving the problems and objections connected with it.[8]

In following out these two strands of thought, Don Benedetto produced a work which, as Caponetto suggested, resembles an extended meditation rather than a systematic treatise. It has some inconsistencies in its thought, and it is not particularly well-organized. Besides the already-noted inconsistency of his thought regarding sanctification, its author reveals an interesting discrepancy between his ideals and his own practice. While he states that the Christian should avoid all verbal contentions and cheerfully suffer the impositions of false Christians, he himself is actively arguing a theological position and he makes most un-Christian remarks about his opponents.[9] With respect to the organization, several topics in the *Beneficio* are mentioned at one point, and then restated and developed later.[10] The work also reveals a range

---

[1] See below, p. 94.

[2] He usually speaks in the first-person plural, and the "we" represents all Christian men. Also, he directly addresses his readers as "most beloved brethren," and he exhorts them to accept his teachings; see below, pp. 55, 56, 86.

[3] The first five chapters of the *Beneficio* are structured in terms of this main theme.

[4] See below, pp. 74-75.

[5] See below, p. 94. In this final paragraph, Don Benedetto even reiterates his argument by analogy, which illustrates the relationship between faith and works.

[6] See below, pp. 94, 70-71.

[7] See below, pp. 64-65, 67, 94.

[8] This final chapter is about one-third of the work in length. Its contents have already been discussed; see above, p. 36.

[9] For his statements on the ideal of Christian conduct, see below, pp. 75, 76-77.

[10] This is the case with his treatment of predestination; see below, pp. 59-60, 84 ff. It is also true of his theme of the imitation of Christ; see below, pp. 71-72, 74-77.

of tone that corresponds with the various aspects of its thought. In his passages on the effects of faith and on Christian suffering, Don Benedetto writes very lyrically and with great spiritual fervour, in contrast with the flatness of those passages that are merely strings of citations.[1] His exposition of theological points is punctuated by exclamations and reflections appropriate to the subject at hand.[2] Occasionally, the author abruptly shifts the focus of his thought, and this results in an awkwardness of style.[3]

Turning to consider the *Beneficio* in its historical context, one encounters a wealth of conflicting opinions on this aspect of the work. Scholars have generally agreed that the *Beneficio* represents a larger trend in Italian thought, but they variously describe this trend as Italian Lutheranism, Valdesianism, an "indigenous spiritual current," and most recently evangelism. In effect, the diversity of opinion about the *Beneficio* reflects the much broader lack of agreement about the thought of the early Italian Reformers.[4] One can also say that the larger controversy has increased the confusion over the *Beneficio*, because some scholars have tended to make generalizations about the work, which support their thesis on the larger issue but which are not always accurate.[5] There have been no studies that compare the *Beneficio* with the contemporary works of the other Italian Reformers, such as Flaminio, Pole, and Ochino, and thus show whether the *Beneficio* can be considered representative of their thought at this time. However, the available evidence suggests that it is one of the more radical expressions of the period. It shares ideals that are common to Valdés and his Italian associates, particularly the desire to return to the Christianity of the early Church, which was considered a truly spiritual religion. In connection with this, the *Beneficio* claims that its doctrine will. prevent the further commercialization of religion because it does not permit the Christian to "make merchandise" of his works and buy his justification from God.[6]

On the other hand, the *Beneficio* reveals radical leanings in its doctrine of justification and its attitude towards the Church. Caponetto pointed out that its Lutheran stand on justification differs from Contarini's theory of double justification, which was supported by Pole and Seripando and also from the eclectic Valdesian position that Carnesecchi held.[7] Don Benedetto's commitment to a definite position on justification stands in contrast with the non-committal attitude that

---

[1] For the two lyrical passages, see below, pp. 60-61, 76-77. For passages of citations, see below, pp. 59-60, 65.

[2] Among other places, see below, pp. 51, 53, 58, 74, 82, 88.

[3] The most striking example of this occurs on p. 70; also cf., p. 61.

[4] This term roughly connotes those people who were connected with religious circles around Venice in the 1530's or with Valdés' circle in Naples, and covers their thought before it developed into dogmatism of various kinds or a speculative rationalism.

[5] Jedin's and Minaci's remarks are of this kind; see above, pp. 30, 32.

[6] See below, pp. 65-66, 71.

[7] Manzoni, *loc. cit.*, 533-535.

is expressed in Pole's advice to Vittoria Colonna.[1] As Carnesecchi noted, Pole disapproved of curiosity about theological matters, and his advice to Vittoria was intended to stimulate her spiritual efforts, while curbing her curiosity about justification.[2] Caponetto perceptively noted that Don Benedetto's position on justification also influenced his attitude towards the Church. Because he refused to consider his theological opponents as real Christians, he had to abandon the ideal of a unified Christendom that was represented by one Church.[3] Consequently, he moved towards the conception of an invisible Church of the elect, composed of the true Christians who are justified by faith, and infallibly guided by the spirit of Christ.[4] He saw this true Church existing side-by-side with the historical Church, which contained both true and false Christians, and was weakened by schisms.[5] In this respect, Don Benedetto had departed from the conservative attitude towards the Church expressed by contemporaries, such as Carnesecchi and Vittoria Colonna. They continued to equate the historical with the universal Church, and held that it alone possessed divine truth and could lead the Christian to salvation.[6] In contrast to this, Don Benedetto hoped that the *Beneficio* would save other Christians by winning them for the elect.[7]

---

[1] For the quotation of this advice, see above, p. 32. Jung incorrectly says that the *Beneficio* copies Pole's advice, whereas it crucially changes the first part of the advice to an affirmative statement; cf. below, p. 93, and Jung, *loc. cit.*, 521. Caponetto notes that the second part of Pole's advice is repeated in the *Beneficio*, but he does not recognize that while the *Beneficio* assures the Christian of his predestination, Vittoria Colonna is given no similar assurance. Cf. Caponetto, *loc. cit.*, 48.

[2] Manzoni, *loc. cit.*, 503-505.

[3] Don Benedetto distinguishes between the true Christians, who accept justification by faith and are God's elect, and the false Christians, who are reprobates, and whose opinion on justification causes their own damnation; see below, pp. 67, 85, 93-94. He implies that the issue of justification has rent Christianity, and that every Christian must take a stand on it; see below, pp. 70-71.

[4] Caponetto argues this idea from Don Benedetto's two direct references to the Church as " every faithful soul. " This reference can be explained by the context in which it occurs (see below, pp. 57, n. 3, and 58, n. 4), but the conception of the Church of the elect is clearly implied in his treatment of the elect as the closely-united body of Christ, for whose sake Christ was made a redeemer; see among other places pp. 75-76, 83, 94. Don Benedetto also stresses that the elect are guided by the spirit of Christ; see below, pp. 86-87.

[5] Except for one reference to the early Church (below, p. 67), Don Benedetto does not directly mention the Church as an institution, which has led Jung to conclude that he is completely indifferent towards it. Caponetto more accurately thinks that the polemic passages about " false Christians " are intended for the hierarchy; see below, pp. 53-54 in particular. Carnesecchi notes that he derived the same conception of the elect, who were distinct from the historical Church, from Valdés and Flaminio; cf. Manzoni, *loc. cit.*, 334, 534.

[6] After Ochino's flight over the Alps, the common reaction was that he should have submitted himself to the judgement of the inspired Church, instead of placing himself outside the pale of salvation; see Pastor, *History of the Popes*, XI (London: Kegan and Paul, 1912), pp. 493-497, and Manzoni, *loc. cit.*, 505.

[7] Caponetto stressed Don Benedtto's awareness that the elect were in the mynority, and he quoted his single statementehat referred to the persecution of the elect by the " false Christians " (see below, p. 75). However, the author implies that when he explains

To sum up this discussion of the various aspects of the *Beneficio*, one could characterize the work as the product of an Italian Reformer who was gravitating towards the position of the Northern Reform. While Don Benedetto retained the basically spiritual ideals of men like Pole and Valdés, he had become deeply involved in the related theological issues, and committed himself to the Lutheran position on justification. He was well-aware of the strong opposition towards this doctrine manifested by part of the Church, and this led him towards the ideal of an invisible Church, comprising all the true believers in Christ. As Gonnet puts it, his ideas closely approach the " theological and organizational clarification that characterizes the German Reform. "[1]

* * * *

Up to now, only two English translations of the *Beneficio* have been made and neither of them is satisfactory. In the middle of the nineteenth century, Ayre discovered a copy of an old English translation and had it reprinted.[2] It was the fourth edition (1638) of the English translation of 1573, which was made not from the original Italian text but from the French translation of Lyons.[3] By the time of the 1638 edition, the text had undergone several changes, and its accuracy leaves much to be desired.[4] When Babington published the facsimile of the original Venetian edition, he also included another old English translation in the volume. Edward Courtenay had made this version in 1548 directly from the Italian; it was not intended for publication, and Babington had it printed from the original ms.[5] He noted that the ms. had been transcribed by an ignorant hand, and felt obliged to correct the orthography and other errors, besides supplying occasional phrases and punctuation.[6] Both these translations are naturally

---

his views to the " pious Christian, " the latter will accept them, because they are " more true, more holy and more worthy of being preached " than the views of his opponents, ultimately because they are more Christian; see below, pp. 53, 70-71. Don Benedetto also knew that part of the hierarchy were tacitly in sympathy with his ideas.

[1] Gonnet, *loc. cit.*, 43.

[2] *The Benefit of Christ's Death....* edited by J. Ayre (London: Religious Tract Society, no date). For a full citation and description, see the bibliography following the text, § 20.

[3] No one has identified which Lyons edition was used by the English translator. It was probably the edition of 1552, because its preface appears in English translation in the 1573 edition. Also, its alterations of the original text are carried over into the 1573; these include one major change of passage, and alterations and additions of some phrases.

[4] The English translator also added some changes. The most amusing of these is his rendition of St. Bernard's work, " sur le Cantique, " as the " Ballet of Ballets. " There are also differences between the 1573 and the 1638 editions, including a major change in one passage, and omissions and additions of phrases.

[5] For a citation and description of the ms., see the appended bibliography, § 9), and Babington, *op. cit.*, Introduction, lxxx-lxxxi.

[6] Babington, *op. cit.*, Preface, vi-viii.

in the language of their times, and as a result they sometimes employ obsolete words or archaic phrasing. In addition, they are not easily accessible.

It is hoped that this translation will fill the gap and supply the English reader with an accurate and readable version of the *Beneficio*. It is based on Babington's facsimile of the original Venetian edition, with some reference to Paladino's Italian text and to the 1638 English edition.[1] The text does not pose great problems for the translator in terms of meaning; the few places that are ambiguous or unclear have been noted and reproduced as accurately as possible. The main difficulty, rather, has arisen with the sentence structure, which is quite stereotyped and repetitive, and sometimes extremely cumbersome. Following Paladino's lead, the translator has introduced additional punctuation to break up the longer sentences. A few phrases and clauses, which would be very awkward if translated literally, have been slightly simplified or rearranged within the sentence.[2] Also, the translator has taken the liberty of omitting some of the more redundant and unnecessary connectives,[3] and of dividing the chapters into paragraphs. In making these changes, the aim was to preserve faithfully the meaning of the original text, while making it more intelligible to the modern reader.

All the Scriptural references in the margin of the facsimile and in Ayre's edition were checked for accuracy,[4] and others have been added by the translator. When the citation refers to an inexact quote or merely notes a Scriptural allusion, it is preceded by a cf. sign. This occurs frequently, since the author of the *Beneficio* was well-acquainted with the Scripture and employed it very freely. With respect to the patristic references, the translator has checked those given by Ayre,

---

[1] For full citations of Babington's facsimile and the Paladino text, see the bibliography, § 24,43). Paladino modernizes the spelling and punctuation of the Venetian edition, and makes some changes that clarify the text. However, a few of his changes alter the meaning. The Paladino edition, p. 31, line 30, should read "dicono" instead of "diciamo" (cf. Babington, f. 35, verso, last line). Paladino, p. 33, l. 24, should read "dedito" instead of "debito" (cf. Babington, f. 38, line before last.). Pal., p. 54. l. 15, should read "cogitazione" instead of "agitazione" (cf. Bab., f. 66, line 1). Pal., p. 39, line 19, should read "dall" instead of "dell" (cf. Bab., f. 46, line 11), Pal., p. 20, line before last, should read "è vacua" instead of "evacua" (cf. Bab., f. 21, verso, lines 6-7). Pal., p. 48, line 1, should read "e si fa" instead "è si" (cf. Bab., f. 57, line 13).

[2] For instance, cf. Babington, f. 69, lines 15-19, and its translation below, p. 93, lines 35-37; cf. Babington, f. 23, verso, line 18 - f. 24, line 4, with the corresponding passage below, p. 63, lines, 3-7.

[3] For instance, cf. Babington, f. 21, verso, lines 7-8, with the phrase below, p. 61, lines 13-14; cf. Babington, f. 47, verso, line 11, with below, p. 80, line 5. Introductory "and" 's have been generally omitted, and redundant clauses placed in parentheses. Also the parenthetical phrase "dico" has been omitted when it serves no grammatical function.

[4] In the facsimile, the references are given only by chapter, and some of them are inaccurate. Ayre added verses to the citations, also changing the incorrect references of the 1638 edition. This editor collated the two sets of references before checking them.

and then cited them according to the *Patrologia Graeca* and the *Patrologia Latina*.[1] Since the original text does not separate its quotations from the body of the narrative, the translator has introduced quotation marks; they are used to indicate any citation of a sentence or more which is fairly accurate.[2] The similar device of asterisks has also been introduced to mark off the passages in which Don Benedetto paraphrases other authors without acknowledgement. In the original edition, there are marginal comments on the text, but since they usually paraphrase it and add nothing of significance, they have been omitted here. On the other hand, the original table of contents has been included in the translation. Inadequate as it is, it gives an indication of what contemporaries considered important in the *Beneficio*.

Of course, even the most careful translation can never completely succeed in conveying the flavour of the original, and the reader with knowledge of Italian is urged to look at Babington's facsimile or at the Paladino edition. However, the editor hopes that this version of the *Beneficio*, with its introduction and bibliography, will be of use to the English reader and that it will encourage further study of the work.

---

[1] Ayre's citations refer to seventeenth and eighteenth century editions.

[2] Most of the quotes follow those that Ayre inserted in his edition. With respect to quotes, Paladino's edition is not so satisfactory, because he has not looked up the references. Cf. the inaccuracy of a passage from Paul (Rom. viii, 35-36), in his edition, p. 47, line 5. Also, in previously citing Origen, he only puts part of the passage in quotes, whereas it should be entirely enclosed or not at all; see his edition, p. 22, lines 10-35.

A MOST USEFUL TREATISE ON THE BENEFIT OF JESUS CHRIST CRUCIFIED FOR CHRISTIANS

TO THE CHRISTIAN READERS

Since we have acquired one of the most pious and learned works composed in our times, entitled *On the Benefit of Jesus Christ Crucified, for Christians,* it seemed to us that we should print it for your consolation and profit, and without the name of the writer, so that the content rather than the authority of the author will move you.

A TABLE OF SOME OF THE MAIN PASSAGES OF THIS WORK

Chapter I

ON ORIGINAL SIN AND THE MISERY OF MAN

*The Holy Scripture says that God created man in his own image and likeness,[1] making him impassible[2] in regard to his body and just, truthful, pious, merciful and holy in regard to his mind. But when, overcome by greed for knowledge, he ate of the apple forbidden by God, he lost that divine image and likeness, and became like the animals and like the devil who had deceived him. In regard to his mind, he became unjust, lying, cruel, impious and hostile to God, and in regard to his body, he became passible[3] and subject to a thousand inconveniences and infirmities, not only similar but even inferior to brute animals. If our first parents had remained obedient to God, they would have left us their justice and holiness as an inheritance. Instead, because of their disobedience, they willed us their unrighteousness, impiety and hatred towards God, so that it is impossible for us to love God through our own efforts and to conform to his will.**[4] On the contrary, we are hostile to him, regarding him as a judge who justly punishes our sins, and we can never rely on his mercy. In short, our nature has become completely corrupted through the sin of Adam,[5] and although at first it was superior to all creatures, then it became subject to all of them, a servant of the devil, of sin, and of death, and condemned to the miseries of hell. It lost the power of judging things, and began to call the good evil, and evil good, and to consider false things as true, and true false. Reflecting on this, the prophet says

---

[1] Gen. i, 26-27.

[2] A theological term; incapable of suffering.

[3] Capable of suffering.

[4] This description of man before and after original sin paraphrases passages in Considerations I and L of Juan Valdés' *Le cento e dieci divine considerazioni.* The work was translated into English by Nicholas Ferrar in 1638 under the title *110 Divine Considerations* and the translation was recently reprinted (London: John Lane, no date, "Sacred Treasure" series). Citations are to this reprint. Cf. pp. 2, 181-182.

[5] In his 1539 *Institutes,* Calvin laid great emphasis on man's inherited corruption. See the English translation of the 1559 *Institutes,* 2 vols., edited by John T. McNeill (Philadelphia: The Westminster Press, 1960. Library of Christian Classics, XX and XXI). Citations are to this edition. Symbols indicate in which edition of the *Institutes* passages originally appeared and when they were changed; see I, xxvii. For the passage on corruption, cf. I, 246-254.

that every man is a liar,[1] and that there is no one who does good,[2] since the devil, like a strongly armed man, peacefully rules his palace, that is, this world, of which he became the prince and lord. There is no language that could express a thousandth part of our calamity, that we who were created by God's own hands, have lost that divine image and have become like the devil, acquiring his nature and identity, so that we want everything he does and equally reject all that displeases him. Because we have so abandoned ourselves to this evil spirit, each of us is ready to commit even the gravest sin, unless we are restrained by the grace of God.

This loss of justice and the inclination and readiness towards every unrighteousness and impiety is called original sin,[3] and we carry it with us from the womb of our mother, so that we are born children of wrath;[4] it originated in our first parents, and it is the cause and source of all our vices and the iniquities that we commit. If we wish to be freed from these things and to return to that first innocence, regaining the image of God,[5] we must first recognize our misery. For no one ever looks for a doctor unless he knows he is sick, and he does not acknowledge the excellence of the doctor or the debt he owes him, unless he recognizes that his illness is pestilential and deadly. In the same way, no one recognizes Christ, who is the only doctor for our souls, unless he sees that his soul is sick.[6] Also he cannot know Christ's excellence or the obligation that he has towards him, unless he comes to realizeh is grievous sins and his pestilential illness, contracted through the contagion of our first parents.[7]

---

[1] Psalm cxv, 11; cf. Rom. iii, 4. Citations of the Psalms will follow the Vulgate numbering. The author refers to David as the prophet instead of the psalmist, as Ambrose does in his comment on Rom. iv, 5-6, which the author later cites; see below, p. 63.

[2] Psalm xiii, 3.

[3] This definition of original sin is somewhat similar to Melanchthon's description of it as " a native propensity and a certain genial impulse by which we are drawn into sin. " Cf. *The Loci Communes of Philip Melanchthon,* translated by C. H. Hill (Boston: Meador Publishing Co., 1944), pp. 81-82. Citations are to this edition. Cf. also Calvin's definition that first appeared in the 1539 *Institutes*; McNeill ed., I, 250-251.

[4] Eph. ii, 3.

[5] Valdés makes man's recovery of the image of God the point of departure and also the central concern of his thought. Cf. his *110 Divine Considerations*, Considerations I and L, pp. 1-3, 181-185, and his *Alfabeto Christiano* translated by Benjamin Wiffen (London: 1861), pp. 16-20, 89. In his 1539 *Institutes,* Calvin briefly remarks on the same point; cf. McNeill edit., I, 189-190.

[6] Valdés speaks of Christ crucified as the true physician of the soul in his *Alfabeto Christiano*, p. 24; cf. also his *110 Divine Considerations*, Consid. III, pp. 6-11.

[7] In the 1539 *Institutes,* Calvin speaks of the contagion of sin; cf. McNeill edit., I, 248-251.

CHAPTER II

THAT GOD GAVE US THE LAW SO THAT WE WOULD RECOGNIZE OUR SIN, AND DESPAIRING OF OUR ABILITY TO JUSTIFY OURSELVES BY WORKS, WOULD HAVE RECOURSE TO THE MERCY OF GOD AND THE JUSTICE OF FAITH

Accordingly, when our God in his infinite goodness and mercy wanted to send his only-begotten Son to free the miserable children of Adam, he knew that first it was necessary to persuade them of their misery, and so he elected Abraham, in whose seed he promised to bless all nations, and accepted his descendants as his special people.[1] After they had left Egypt and were freed from Pharaoh's bondage, he gave them the Law by means of Moses. The Law prohibits concupiscence and commands us to love God with our whole heart, our whole soul and our whole strength,[2] so that all our hope is placed in God, and we are ready to give up our life for our God, to suffer every bodily torment, to deprive ourselves of our wealth, dignity and honours in order to honour God, choosing to die rather than to do anything, however small, that is not pleasing to our God, and doing all these things with joy and readiness of heart. Next the Law commands us to love our neighbour as ourselves,[3] and by neighbour it means every kind of man, enemies as well as friends;[4] it requires that we be prepared to do unto everyone what we want done unto us, and that we care about others' affairs as we would about our own.[5]

When man looks into this holy Law, as if into a clear mirror,[6] he soon recognizes his own infirmity, and his incapacity to obey God's commandments, and to render the honour and love due to his Creator.[7] Therefore, the first office performed by the Law is to make sin known, as St. Paul states,[8] and he says elsewhere: "I did not recognize sin

---

[1] Cf. Gen. xvii, 4-9: Luke i, 55: Gal. iii, 16.

[2] Deut. vi, 5: cf. Matt. xxii, 37: Mark xii, 30: Luke x, 27.

[3] Lev. xix, 18: Matt. xxii, 39: Mark xii, 31: Luke x, 27.

[4] This may be a reference to the parable of the Good Samaritan, that follows the description of the Law in Luke's Gospel: cf. Luke x, 29-36.

[5] The author's exposition of these two commandments is similar to a passage in Valdés' *Alfabeto Christiano*, in which the latter derives spiritual rules for the Christian from the ten commandments. Cf. pp. 55-66.

[6] Calvin also describes the Law as a mirror in his 1539 *Institutes*. Cf. McNeill edit., I, 355.

[7] In *Freedom of a Christian*, Luther states that the Law should make man recognize his inability to fulfil God's commandments. (Cf. *Freedom of a Christian*, in *Martin Luther, Selections from his Writings*, edited by John Dillenberger Anchor Books, 1961), p. 57. Citations are to this edition.

[8] Cf. Rom. iii, 20.

other than through the Law."[1] The second office performed by the Law is to make sin grow; for since we have separated ourselves from obedience to God and have become slaves to the devil, full of vicious actions and appetites, we cannot bear God to prohibit our concupiscence, and the more it is forbidden the more it grows.[2] St. Paul says that in this way he became a sinner: "Sin was dead, but when the Law came, it rose up again and grew."[3] The third office of the Law is to reveal the wrath and judgement of God, who threatens death and eternal punishment to those who do not fully observe his Law. Thus Holy Scripture says: "Cursed is he who does not constantly observe all the things that are written in the book of the Law,"[4] and St. Paul says that the Law is the minister of death,[5] and that it works wrath.[6] When the Law has uncovered and increased sin, and has demonstrated the wrath and anger of God, who threatens death, it performs its fourth office by terrifying man. Then man falls into despair, for he wants to satisfy the Law but clearly sees that he cannot. His inability makes him fly into a rage against God, and he wishes that he did not exist, because he fears that God will chastise and punish him severely. As St. Paul says: "The wisdom of the flesh is the enemy of God, for it is not subject to the Law of God, nor can it be."[7] The fifth office of the Law, which is its proper end, and the most excellent and necessary one, is that it compels man to go to Christ.[8] In this way, the frightened Hebrews were driven to ask Moses, saying: "Do not let the Lord speak to us, lest we die; you speak to us, and we will obey you and do all things,"[9] and the Lord replied: "They have spoken exceedingly well."[10] They were praised precisely because they asked for a mediator between themselves and God, namely Moses, who represented Jesus Christ, the future advocate and mediator between man and God. Therefore, God said to Moses: "I shall raise them up a prophet from the midst of their brethren like you, and I will put my word in his mouth; he will say all the things that I command him, and I will punish everyone who will not obey my words, which he will speak in my name."[11]

---

[1] Rom. vii, 7.
[2] Cf. Rom. vii, 5, 8.
[3] Cf. Rom. vii, 8-9.
[4] Gal. iii, 10: cf. Deut. xxvii, 26.
[5] Cf. Rom. vii, 13: 2 Cor. iii, 7.
[6] Rom. iv, 15.
[7] Rom. viii, 7.
[8] Cf. Rom. x, 4. This passage on the offices of the Law is similar in thought to Valdés' treatment of the Law in his *Alfabeto Christiano*, pp. 32-34, and also to Calvin's description of the punitive function of the Law in his 1539 *Institutes*; cf. McNeill edit., I, 355-357. Calvin and Valdés likewise cite heavily from Paul's epistle to the Romans. However, the division of the Law's operation into five specific stages is Don Benedetto's own contribution.
[9] Cf. Exodus xx, 19: Deut. v, 25-27; xviii, 16. This citation is a very free paraphrase of the Hebrews' statement, differing from all the Scriptural versions of it.
[10] Cf. Deut. v, 28; xviii, 17.
[11] Deut. xviii, 18-19: cf. Acts iii, 22-23.

Chapter III

THAT THE REMISSION OF SINS, JUSTIFICATION, AND OUR WHOLE SALVATION DEPENDS ON CHRIST

Then our God sent that great prophet he had promised us, namely, his only-begotten Son, so that he might free us from the curse of the Law, reconcile us with our God, make our will capable of doing good works, heal our free will, and restore to us that divine image,[1] which we lost through the fault of our first parents. Since we know that, under heaven, no other name is given to men by which we can save ourselves but the name of Jesus Christ,[2] and since He invites us, crying: "Come to me all you who are harassed and burdened and I will refresh you," [3] let us run into his arms with the footsteps of living faith. What consolation or joy in this life can be compared to what is experienced by the man who feels oppressed by the intolerable weight of his own sins, when he hears such gentle and sweet words from the Son of God, who so graciously promises to refresh him and to free him from that heavy weight? But the essence of the matter consists in a true recognition of our infirmity and misery, for unless one has felt evil, one cannot taste good. And Christ says: "If anyone is thirsty, come to me and drink," [4] as if he wants to say that, unless one realizes he is a sinner and thirsts for justice, he cannot taste how sweet our Jesus Christ is, and how sweet it is to think and speak about him, and to imitate his most holy life.[5]

If we know our infirmity through the office of the Law, then behold John the Baptist points us to the most kind physician, saying: "Behold the lamb of God who takes away the sins of the world." [6] He frees us from the heavy yoke of the Law, abrogates and annihilates its curses and harsh threats,[7] restores our free will, and returns us to our pristine innocence, restoring the image of God in us. As St. Paul says, just as we all died through Adam, so we have all been revived through

---

[1] Cf. Col. iii, 10.
[2] Acts iv, 12.
[3] Matt. xi, 28.
[4] John vii, 37.
[5] The author later discusses the imitation of Christ's life in more detail; see below, pp. 74-77. Valdés also treats this topic in his *110 Divine Considerations*, Consid. LXIV, LXXXIX, pp. 227-229, 328-335.
[6] John i, 29.
[7] Cf. Gal, iii, 13.

Christ;[1] and let us not believe that our sin, which we have inherited from Adam, is more efficacious than Christ's justice, which we have likewise inherited through faith. It seemed man could grieve that, without his causing it, he was born and conceived in sin,[2] in the iniquity of his parents, through whom death ruled over all men; but now there is nothing to lament, for similarly without our causing it, the justice of Christ has come to us, and through him we have been given eternal life and death has been slain.[3]

St. Paul has a beautiful discourse on these things, which I want to record here: "Thus sin, and consequently death, came into the world through one man, and death came to all men because they all sinned. Although sin was in the world, it was not imputed as there was no law, yet death reigned from Adam to Moses even in those who did not sin in the likeness of the transgression of Adam, who is a symbol of the future. However, the gift is not like the sin, for if many have died through the sin of one, many have abounded far more in the grace of God, and in the gift proceeding from it, which comes to us from one man, Jesus Christ. The gift did not come like death from one man's sin, for the condemnation for one crime led to more condemnation, but the gift for many crimes led to justification. Whereas one man's sin caused death to reign through him alone, those who receive the abundance of grace and the gift of justice for life will reign much more through Jesus Christ alone. Just as through one man's sin, evil was propagated unto all men for their condemnation, so through one man's justification, the good was propagated and spread unto all men for the justification of life. Therefore, in the same way that many have become sinners through one man's disobedience, many will also become just through one man's obedience. Although the Law intervened to make sin abound, wherever sin abounds, there grace abounds much more, and, as sin reigned in death, so grace will likewise reign through justice, giving eternal life through Jesus Christ."[4]

Through these words of St. Paul, we can clearly see what was said above, namely, that the Law was given to make sin known; but let us recognize that sin is not as powerful as the justice of Christ, through which we are justified in the presence of God. Just as Christ is more powerful than Adam, his justice is stronger than Adam's sin. If the latter was sufficient to constitute us sinners and children of wrath[5] without any actual fault of our own, the justice of Christ will be far more sufficient to make us just and children of grace,[6] without any of our own good works. For our works cannot be good, unless we ourselves are made good and just through faith before we do them,

---

[1] 1 Cor. xv, 22. In his *110 Divine Considerations*, Valdés meditates on this statement of Paul's; cf. Consid. CVIII, pp. 420-426.

[2] Cf. Psalm L, 5.

[3] Cf. 1 Cor. xv, 54-57: Hosea (Osee), xiii, 14.

[4] Rom. v, 12-21.

[5] Eph. ii, 3.

[6] Cf. Rom. ix, 8: Gal. iv, 26.

as St. Augustine also affirms.[1] From this one sees that those who lack confidence in God's benevolence on account of some grave sins, err greatly. They think that he is not about to remit, cover and pardon any immense sin, when he has already chastised all our sins and iniquities in his only-begotten Son, and consequently granted a general pardon to the whole human race. This pardon is enjoyed by all who believe in the Gospel, that is, in the most happy news which the Apostles published throughout the world,[2] saying: "We pray you, reconcile yourselves with God through Christ, because he who never knew sin has made himself a sinner for us, so that we may become just in him."[3]

Foreseeing this immense goodness of God, Isaiah wrote these most divine words, which depict the passion of Jesus Christ our Lord and its cause so well, that one cannot find it better described in the writings of the Apostles: "Who has believed what we have heard, and to whom has the arm of the Lord been revealed? For he has grown up like a young shoot in his sight, and like a root from the desert soil, and he has neither beauty nor decorum. We have seen him, and his face is not what we hoped for; he is despised and rejected by men, a man full of sorrows, who has felt our infirmities and has endured our sorrows. And we believed that he was wounded and beaten and afflicted by God, but he was wounded for our iniquity and beaten for our wickedness; he was chastised for our peace, and through his beating we have become healed. All of us have wandered like sheep, and each has strayed from the right path, and the Lord has taken all our iniquities upon himself. He has been oppressed and injured, but still he has not opered his mouth; like a lamb he will be led to the slaughter, and like a sheep that stands mute before his shearers, he will not open his mouth."[4]

What great ingratitude, and what an abominable thing it is, if we who profess to be Christians, and who understand that the Son of God has taken all our sins upon himself, and has cancelled them all with his most precious blood by allowing himself to be chastised for us on the cross, still claim that we want to justify ourselves, and to seek the remission of our sins with our own works! As if the merits, the justice, and the blood of Christ are not sufficient to accomplish this, if we do not add our own foul justice, marred by self-love, interest and a thousand vanities, for which we should ask God's pardon rather than a reward! We do not reflect on the threats made by St. Paul to the Galatians, who were deceived by false preachers; they did not believe that justification by faith was sufficient in itself, and claimed that they still intended to justify themselves through the law. St. Paul

---

[1] The author may have places such as these in mind: Augustine, *Enchiridion ad Laurentium*, cap. xxx. (Patrologia Latina, vol. 40, col. 247); *De Fide et Operibus*, cap. xiv, 21. (PL 40, 211); *De Spiritu et Littera*, cap. x, 16. (PL 44, 210).

[2] The same conception of a general pardon proclaimed by the Gospel appears in Valdés, *110 Divine Considerations*. Cf. Considerations XI, XIII and XIV, pp. 35-36, 42-49.

[3] Cf. 2 Cor. v, 20-21.

[4] Cf. Isaiah liii, 1-7. The author omits part of verse 3.

says to them: " Christ will not aid in the least you who justify yourselves by the Law; you have fallen from grace, therefore we wait for the hope of justice with the spirit of faith. "[1]

If seeking for justice and the remission of sins through the observance of the Law, that God gave on Mount Sinai with so much pomp and glory, means losing Christ and his grace, what can be said about those who claim that they want to justify themselves before God, by means of their own laws and observances? Let these people make the comparison, and then decide whether they want God to give to their laws and constitutions, this honour and glory that he is not willing to give his own Law.[2] This honour is only given to his only-begotten Son, who alone has satisfied for all our sins, past, present and future by the sacrifice of his passion, as St. Paul shows in his letter to the Hebrews, and St. John in his first Epistle.[3] Consequently, every time we apply this satisfaction of Christ to our soul through faith, we undoubtedly enjoy the remission of sins, and through his justice, we become good and just in the presence of God. Thus when St. Paul says to the Philippians that, according to the justice of the Law, he had lived irreproachably, he adds: " However, I decided that what was profitable for me was a loss with respect to Christ, rather I think that everything is a loss in comparison with the excellence of knowing my Lord Jesus Christ; for his love I have considered that everything is harmful; I have held that everything is dung in order to gain Christ, and to be found again in him. I do not have my own justice, which consists in the works of the Law, but the justice that consists in the faith of Christ, which is a gift of God, that is, the justice of faith, which allows me to come to a knowledge of him. "[4]

Oh, these are most significant words that every Christian ought to engrave on his heart, and ask God to make him fully appreciate them! Here you see how clearly St. Paul shows that whoever truly knows Christ considers the works of the Law harmful, to the extent that they lead man away from trust in Christ, on whom he should base his whole salvation, and they make him rely on himself. Then extending this judgement (sentenza), St. Paul adds that he holds everything dung in order to gain Christ and to be incorporated into him, pointing out that whoever trusts in works and claims to justify himself with them, does not gain Christ and become incorporated in Him. Since the whole

---

[1] Gal. v, 4-5.

[2] The author's criticism of his opponents at this point is extremely sharp; he charges them with setting up humanly-devised practices, such as indulgences, devotions and pilgrimages, as the criteria of justification, in opposition both to God's will and to his Law. In the *Pagan Servitude of the Church*, Luther makes a similar accusation against the Papacy; (cf. *Servitude of the Church*, in *Martin Luther, Selections from his writings*, edited by John Dillenberger, Anchor Books, 1961.) p. 230, citations are to this edition.

[3] Cf. Heb. vii, 27; ix, 12, 28; x, 12, 14 and 1 John i, 7: ii, 2. The author obviously accepts Paul as the author of the epistle to the Hebrews. Carnesecchi also thought that Valdés accepted this attribution, although the Inquisition was dubious about it. Cf. Manzoni, *loc. cit.*, 495-496.

[4] Phil. iii, 6-10.

mystery of faith consists of this truth, and St. Paul wanted to make his meaning better understood, he adds and impresses upon them that he rejects every exterior justification,[1] every justice founded upon the observance of the Law, and that he embraces the justice given by God through faith. God gives justice to those who believe that in Christ he has chastised all our sins, and that Christ, as St. Paul himself says, " has made himself our wisdom, justice, sanctification and redemption, so that, as it is written, let him who glories, glory in the Lord, and not in his own works. "[2] It is indeed true that one can find some substantiating passages (alcune auttorita) of Holy Scripture, which, if misunderstood, seem to contradict this holy doctrine of St. Paul, and attribute justification and remission of sins to works and to charity. However, some people have already admirably elucidated these passages, and have clearly demonstrated that those who understood them in this sense, did not understand them.[3]

Most beloved brethren, let us not follow the stupid opinion of the foolish Galatians but the truth that St. Paul teaches, and let us give all the glory of our justification to the mercy of God and to the merits of his Son, who with his blood has released us from the dominion of the Law and the tyranny of sin and death,[4] and has led us to the kingdom of God to give us eternal happiness.[5] I say he has freed us from the command of the Law, because he has given us his Spirit, that teaches us every truth, and he has perfectly satisfied the Law.[6] He has given this satisfaction to all his members, that is, to all true Christians, so that they can appear confidently before the tribunal of God, because they are clothed in the justice of his Christ[7] and because he has freed them from the curses of the Law. Thus the Law can no longer accuse or condemn us; it can no longer arouse our affections and appetites or increase our sin, and for this reason St. Paul says that the chirograph,[8] which was unfavorable to us, has been cancelled by Christ and annulled on the wood of the cross.[9] Because our Christ freed us from the dominion of the Law, he has also released us from the tyranny of sin and of death, which can no longer oppress us because they have

---

[1] In interpreting Paul, the author echoes Luther's statement that no external act can produce justification, cf. *Freedom of a Christian*, pp. 53-54.

[2] Cf. 1 Cor. i, 30-31: The last phrase is the author's addition to the Scripture. Cf. 2 Cor. x, 17: Jer. ix, 23-24.

[3] This statement probably refers to the intense controversies of the 1530's over the Pauline epistles, particularly with respect to justification. Don Benedetto leaves no doubt as to which position he supports.

[4] Cf. Rom. vii, 1. Rom. viii, 2.

[5] This statement hints at the author's views on predestination, which are developed later, see below, pp. 84-87.

[6] Cf. 1 Cor. ii, 12-13: Rom. x, 4.

[7] The metaphor of clothing is continually used in the *Beneficio* to show how justice is imputed to man. It is briefly mentioned in Valdés' *110 Divine Considerations*. Cf. Consid. LXXV, p. 269, and in his *Alfabeto Christiano*, p. 20.

[8] A legal term; the simple contract written and signed by the debtor.

[9] Cf. Col, ii, 14.

been overcome by Christ (and consequently by we who are his members) through his resurrection. Thus we can say with St. Paul and with the prophet Hosea: "Death has been conquered and destroyed. Death, where is your sting? Hell, where is your victory? The sting of death is sin, and the power of sin is the law, but let us thank God who has granted us victory through Jesus Christ our Lord."[1] He is that most happy seed, who has crushed the head of the poisonous serpent,[2] namely the devil, so that all who believe in Christ and place their whole trust in his grace, will conquer sin, death, the devil, and hell, with him. He is that blessed seed of Abraham,[3] in whom God promised to bless all nations.

Previously everyone had to fight that horrible serpent on his own and free himself from the curse, but this enterprise was so difficult, that all the forces of the world put together could not accomplish it. Then our God, the father of mercy, was moved to pity by our miseries, and gave us his only-begotten Son who has freed us from the serpent's poison, and who has been made our blessing and justification, provided that we completely renounce all our exterior justifications in accepting him. Most beloved brethren, let us embrace the justice of our Jesus Christ, making it our own by means of faith; let us firmly hold that we are just, not through our works but through the merits of Christ; and let us live, happy and confident that the justice of Christ annihilates all our injustice, and makes us good, just and holy in the sight of God. For when God sees us incorporated into his Son through faith,[4] he will no longer think of us as children of Adam, but as his own children, and he will make us, together with his legitimate Son, heirs of all his riches.

---

[1] Cf. 1 Cor. xv, 54-57: Hosea (Osee) xiii, 14.
[2] Cf. Gen. iii, 15.
[3] Gen. xxii, 18.
[4] Valdés constantly speaks of the Christian as incorporated into Christ through faith in his *110 Divine Considerations*. Cf. among other places, Consid. I, XV, L, XCII, pp. 3, 52, 183, 350.

Chapter IV

ON THE EFFECTS OF LIVING FAITH AND THE UNION OF THE SOUL WITH CHRIST

This holy and living faith is so effective that, whoever believes that Christ has taken his sins upon Himself, becomes like Christ and conquers sin, death, the devil and hell. The reason for this is that * the Church, namely, every faithful soul, is the bride of Christ, and Christ is her spouse. We know the custom of marriage, that from two they become one and the same thing, being two in one flesh, and the property of each becomes common, so that the husband says that his wife's dowry belongs to him, and the wife similarly says that her husband's house and all his riches are hers. And truly, so they are otherwise they would not be one flesh as the Holy Scripture says.[1] In this same way, God has wedded his most beloved Son to the faithful soul, and although she possessed nothing but sin, the Son of God did not scorn to take her as his beloved bride with her dowry of sin. Through the union of this most holy marriage, each possesses what belongs to the other. Thus Christ says: " The dowry of my dear bride the soul (that is, her sins, transgressions of the Law, the wrath of God against her, the boldness of the devil over her, the prison of hell and all her other evils) has come into my power and is my property. It is my right to deal with it as I please, and therefore I want to cast it into the fire of my cross and annihilate it. " When God saw his Son completely soiled with the sins of his bride, he scourged him, slaying him on the wood of the cross; but because he was his most beloved and obedient Son, he raised him from the dead, giving him every power in heaven and earth, stationing him at his right hand.[2] The wife likewise says with the greatest joy: " The realms and empires of my beloved spouse belong to me; I am queen and empress of heaven and earth. My husband's riches, namely, his holiness, innocence, justice, and divinity, with all his virtues and powers, are my property and, therefore, I am holy, innocent, just and divine. I am unstained, shapely and beautiful because my most beloved spouse has no blemish, but is stalwart and handsome; since he is completely mine, all his qualities are consequently mine, and because they are holy and pure, I become holy and pure. " **[3]

---

[1] Cf. Eph. v, 31.
[2] Cf. Eph. i, 20-21: Matt. xxviii, 28.
[3] This passage loosely paraphrases Luther's analogy of the marriage of Christ and

Thus, beginning with his most innocent birth, Christ has used it to sanctify the soiled birth of his wife, who was conceived in sin. The childhood and innocent youth of the bridegroom have justified the childish and juvenile life, and the imperfect actions of his beloved bride, for the love and union between the soul of the true Christian and her spouse Christ is so great that the works of each are common to both.[1] Thus, when one says that Christ fasted, Christ prayed and was heard by his Father, Christ resurrected the dead, freed men from the devil, healed the sick, has died, risen, and ascended into heaven, one can likewise say that the Christian has performed these same works. For the works of Christ are the works of the Christian, for whose sake He has done them all. One can truly say that the Christian was nailed to the cross, was buried, rose again, ascended into heaven, and was made a son of God, a participant in the divine nature.[2] On the other hand, all the works done by the Christian are works of Christ, for He wants them as His own. Because they are imperfect and he is perfect, and he does not want anything imperfect, he makes them perfect through his virtue, so that his wife will always be happy, content, and unafraid. Therefore, although her works are defective, they are still pleasing to God with respect to his Son, on whom he continually looks.[3]

Oh, the immense goodness of God! What a great obligation the Christian has towards him! No human love is so great that it can compare with the love of God, the beloved spouse of the soul of every faithful Christian. St. Paul says that " Christ loved the Church, that is, every beloved soul, his bride, and offered himself to die on the cross for her in order to sanctify her, purifying her with the washing of water through his word, so he could unite her to himself as a glorious Church — one that would have no stain, or wrinkle or any such thing, but would be holy and irreproachable, that is, holy and innocent like himself, and the true and legitimate daughter of God. "[4] As Christ says, " God so loved the world that he gave his only-begotten Son, so that whoever believes in him may not perish but may have life eternal. God did not send his Son into the world so that he might judge it, but so that the world might be saved through him, and whoever believes in him is not judged. "[5]

---

the soul in *Freedom of a Christian*, cf. pp. 60-61. The Scriptural source for this analogy, Eph. v, 21-33, speaks in terms of Christ and the Church, and Don Benedetto probably placed " the Church " in apposition with " every faithful soul " in order to harmonize Luther's version with the Scriptural text.

[1] Here the author enlarges on Luther's analogy, showing the completeness of the " exchange of goods " between Christ and the soul.

[2] In the *Alfabeto Christiano*, Valdés stresses that the Christian should experience for himself every event of Christ's life. Cf. pp. 112-113.

[3] In his treatment of the analogy, Luther was concerned to show that the Christian could be confident of the remission of his sins and his righteousness in Christ, because Christ was both God and man.

[4] Cf. Eph. v., 25-27. Luther quoted this passage with reference to the believing soul; cf. *Freedom of a Christian*, p. 61. Don Benedetto adds interpretive comments to the Scriptural text so that his version incorporates Luther's use of the text.

[5] John iii, 16-18.

Someone could say to me: " In what way is the union of this divine marriage made? How is this connexion of the espoused soul with her bridegroom Christ made? How can I be sure that my soul will be united with Christ and made his bride? How can I confidently glory in his riches, as the bride above did? It is easy for me to believe that others may receive this honour and glory, but I cannot persuade myself that I may be one of those, to whom God gives so many graces; I know my own misery and imperfection." Most beloved brother, I reply that your certainty consists in the true, living faith, with which God purifies hearts, as St. Peter says.[1] This faith consists in giving credit to the Gospel, namely to the happy news that has been published by God throughout the world, namely that God has used up the rigour of his justice against Christ, and has chastised all our sins in him. Whoever accepts and believes this good news really has the true faith and enjoys the remission of his sins; he is reconciled with God, and from a child of wrath becomes a child of grace, regaining the image of God. He enters into God's kingdom and is made a temple of God,[2] who marries the soul to his only-begotten Son by means of this faith, which is a work and a gift of God, as St. Paul often says.[3]

God gives faith to those whom he calls to himself in order to justify and glorify them, and to give them life eternal.[4] Christ testifies to this saying: " This is the will of him who sent me, that everyone who sees the Son and believes in him may have life eternal, and I will raise him up on the Last Day." [5] Likewise he says: " As Moses raised up the serpent in the desert, in the same way, the Son of Man must be raised up, so that no one who believes in him may perish, but may have life eternal." [6] He said to Martha: " He who believes in me will live, even if he dies; everyone who lives and believes in me will not die forever." [7] To the crowd of Jews he said: " I came into the world as a light, so that everyone who believes in me may not remain in darkness." [8] In his Epistle, St. John says: " And in this God's love for was manifest, for God is love, and he sent his only-begotten Son into the world, so that we might live through him. The love consists in this, not that we loved God but that he loved us and he sent his Son as an atonement for our sins." [9] Moreover, he sent him to destroy our enemies, and for this purpose he made him share in our flesh and blood, as St. Paul says, " so that through his death he would destroy

[1] Cf. Acts xv, 9. The author has briefly dealt with an important problem connected with Luther's doctrine of imputed justice, doubt about the certainty of one's own justification. Like Luther, he thinks that the solution lies in an increase of faith. This problem is discussed later in more detail, see below, pp. 78-85.

[2] Cf. John iii, 5: 1 Cor. iii, 16.

[3] Among other places, cf. Rom. v, 15-17: 2 Cor. ix, 15: Eph. ii, 8.

[4] Cf. Rom. viii, 30.

[5] John vi, 39.

[6] John iii, 14-15.

[7] John xi, 25-26.

[8] John xii, 46.

[9] Cf. 1 John iv, 8-10.

the one who commanded death, namely the devil, and free all those who were enslaved throughout their life by the fear of death." [1] Since we have the testimony of Holy Scripture for those promises discussed above (and for many other promises, scattered in various places in it), we cannot doubt that it is so. Scripture speaks generally, so no one should fear that what it says does not apply to him.

Since the whole mystery of faith [2] consists in this, let us take an example to make it better understood. * A good and holy king has it proclaimed in an edict that all rebels may safely return to his kingdom, because, through the merits of one of their kinsmen, he has pardoned them all. Certainly none of the rebels should doubt that they have really obtained pardon for their rebellion, but they ought to confidently return to their homes to live under the shadow of that holy king. If one of them did not return, he would pay the penalty for it, for he would die in exile and in disgrace with his king because of his unbelief. This holy king is the Lord of heaven and earth, who, through the obedience and merit of our kinsman Christ, has pardoned us all our revolts, and as we said above, has had an edict proclaimed throughout the whole world, that we all may safely return to his kingdom. Accordingly, whoever believes in this edict will return to the kingdom of God, from which we were expelled through the guilt of our first parents, and will be happily governed by the Spirit of God. Whoever does not believe this proclamation will not enjoy this general pardon, but because of his unbelief will remain in exile under the tyranny of the devil, and will live and die in extreme misery, that is in disgrace with the King of heaven and earth.** [3] This is rightfully so, for we can offer no greater insult to God than to make him a liar and deceiver, and we do this by not believing in his promises.[4]

Oh, this sin of unbelief is so grave! In as much as it has the power, it deprives God of his glory and his perfection, not to mention the harm of one's own damnation and the continual torment of the mind, that the miserable conscience experiences in this life.[5] On the other hand, God is glorified by the man who approaches him with a true heart in the certainty of faith and who believes in his promises without the least suspicion, firmly holding he will obtain all that God has promised. This man lives in continual peace and joy, always praising and thanking God, who has elected him to the glory of eternal life; he has a most reliable pledge for his most beloved spouse, namely the Son

---

[1] Heb. ii, 14-15.

[2] Cf. 1 Tim. iii, 9: Eph. iii, 4-5.

[3] This parable of the holy king is a shortened version of the one in Valdés' *110 Divine Considerations*, Consid. XIII, pp. 39-45. Cf. Consid. XXXVIII, pp. 133-135 for a variant of the parable.

[4] Luther considers a lack of faith the highest insult to God; cf. *Freedom of a Christian*, pp. 59-60, and *Bondage of the Will* (also included in *Martin Luther, Selections from his Writings*, edited by John Dillenberger, Anchor Books, 1961). Citations are to this edition. Cf. pp. 184-185. Valdés has the same opinion; cf. *Alfabeto Christiano*, pp. 84-85.

[5] Valdés mentions these effects of unbelief in his *110 Divine Considerations*, Consid. IV, p. 13.

of God, whose blood has intoxicated his heart. This most holy faith creates a living hope and a constant trust in God's mercy towards us, which lives and operates in our hearts, and through which we completely repose in God, leaving our welfare to him.[1] As we are sure of God's benevolence, we do not fear either the devil, or his ministers, or death.

This extremely firm and spirited trust in God's mercy expands and stimulates our heart, directing it towards God with the sweetest affections, and filling it with most ardent love. For this reason, St. Paul urges us to go trustfully before the throne of grace,[2] and he exhorts us not to throw away our trust, which has a great reward in store.[3] This holy trust, which never lacks divine love, is generated in the heart by the Holy Spirit, who is imparted to us by faith.[4] Consequently, by this living efficacy we are stimulated to do good, and we acquire so much ability and inclination for this, that we are most ready to do and to endure all intolerable things for the love and glory of our most kind father, God. Through Christ he has enriched us with such abundant grace and favour, and he has made us from enemies into most dear children. As soon as God gives this true faith to man, the force of love impels him to do good works, and like the best of trees, to yield the sweetest fruits to God and to his neighbor.[5] In the same way, it is impossible to set a block of wood on fire without producing light.

Without this holy faith, it is impossible for anyone to please God,[6] and by means of it, all the saints of the Old and New Testament were saved.[7] St. Paul testifies to this concerning Abraham, of whom the Scripture says: " Abraham believed in God and it was imputed to him for justice. "[8] And so he says a little before: " Therefore, we believe that man is justified through faith without the works of the Law. "[9] Elsewherehe says: " So then, in the present time the remnant is saved according to the election of grace, and if it is saved by grace, it cannot be saved by works, for then grace would not be free. "[10] St. Paul says to the Galatians that " it is evident that no

---

[1] Valdés stresses that the Christian should completely conform himself to the will of God; cf. *Alfabeto Christiano*, pp. 56-59, and *110 Divine Considerations*, Consid. XXXV, pp. 115-120.

[2] Cf. Heb. iv, 16.

[3] Heb. x, 35.

[4] Melanchthon characterizes hope and love as the fruits of the Holy Spirit, who is infused into the heart of the justified Christian; cf. *The Loci Communes of Philip Melanchthon*, edited by C. H. Hill, p. 171.

[5] Luther, Melanchthon and Valdés all describe love and good works as the necessary fruit and testimony of true faith; cf. Luther's *Freedom of a Christian*, pp. 74-76, Melanchthon's *Loci Communes*, pp. 204-207, and Valdés' *Alfabeto Christiano*, p. 74.

[6] Heb. xi, 6.

[7] This is a reference to the argument of Hebrews, ch. 11, where it is claimed that Old Testament figures possessed faith.

[8] Rom. iv, 3: Gen. xv, 6.

[9] Rom. iii, 28.

[10] Rom. xi, 5-6.

one justifies himself before God through the Law, because the just man lives by faith, and the Law does not consist in faith; but whoever observes what the Law commands, will live by that observance."[1] And he previously says that man cannot justify himself through the works of the Law, but only through faith in Jesus Christ.[2] A little further on, he says that if man can justify himself through the Law, then Christ died in vain.[3] Comparing the justice of the Law to the justice of the Gospel, he says to the Romans that the former consists in acts and the latter in belief, "because if you confess the Lord Jesus Christ with your mouth and believe in your heart that God has raised him from the dead, you will be saved. For one believes in justice with the heart, and one confesses to salvation with the mouth."[4] Here then you see how clearly St. Paul demonstrates that faith, makes man just without any aid from works.

Not only St. Paul but also the holy doctors who came after him, have confirmed and approved this holy truth of justification through faith. The chief among them is St. Augustine; in the book *Of Faith and Works*, in *Of the Spirit and Of the Letter*, in his *Eighty-Three Questions*, in his Letter to Pope Boniface, in the *Treatise on Psalm 31*, and in many other places, he defends this teaching (sentenza), showing that we are justified through faith without the aid of good works, for the reason that the latter are not the cause but the effect of justification.[5] He also shows that when the words of St. James are soundly understood, they are not contrary to this teaching.[6]

In the fourth book of *On the Epistle to the Romans*, Origen also defends this teaching, affirming that St. Paul "means that faith alone suffices for justification, so that man becomes just through belief alone, even when he has done no works. In this way, the thief was justified without the works of the Law, since the Lord did not look for what he had done in the past, and He did not wait for him to do anything after he believed; but, after he had justified him through his confession alone, he accepted him as a companion for his entrance into Paradise. In the Gospel of St. Luke, that notorious woman at the feet of Jesus Christ also heard him say to her: 'Your sins are remitted,'[7] and a little later, 'Your faith has saved you, go in peace.'"[8] Origen then adds: "In many places in the Gospel, one sees how the Lord spoke

---

[1] Gal. iii, 11-12: cf. Habk. ii, 4: Lev. xviii, 5.
[2] Gal. ii, 16.
[3] Gal. ii, 21.
[4] Rom. x, 9-10.
[5] Cf. Augustine, *De Fide et Operibus*, cap. xvi, 27 (PL 40, 215). *De Spiritu et Littera*, cap. vii, 11 (PL 44, 206). *De diversis Quaestionibus octoginta tribus*. Quaest. lxxvi (PL 40, 87-89). Epistolae Classis III, *Epistola ad Paulinum* (Bonifacium), clxxxvi, 8 ff. (PL 33, 218-220). *Enarrationes in Psalmos*, Psalmus xxxi, Enar. II ff. (PL 36, 258, etc.).
[6] The citation given above for *De diversis Quaestionibus octoginta tribus* is concerned with this point.
[7] Luke vii, 47.
[8] Luke vii, 50.

in such a way as to show that faith is the cause of the believer's salvation. Therefore, man is justified through faith, for which the works of the Law are no help. On the contrary, where there is no faith which justifies the believer, however much man may do the works that the Law commands, they cannot justify him, because they are not built on the foundation of faith; although they may seem good, they lack the faith, which is the mark of those who are justified by God. And who can glory in his own justice, when he hears God say through the prophet: 'Every justice of ours is like the cloth of a menstrous woman.'?[1] Accordingly, it is only lawful to glory in the faith of the cross of Christ."[2]

In his homily, *On Humility*, St. Basil expressly intends the Christian to consider himself just only through faith in Christ, and these are his words: "The Apostle says: 'Let him who glories, glory in the Lord,' saying that 'God made Christ for our wisdom, justice, sanctification and redemption, so that, as it is written, let him who glories, glory in the Lord.'[3] Man achieves the perfect and entire glorification of God, when he does not elevate himself through his own justice, but recognizes that he lacks true justice and that he is justified by faith alone in Christ. And St. Paul glories in despising his own justice and in seeking through faith, the justice of Christ, that comes from God."[4] In the ninth canon of *On St. Matthew*, St. Hilary says: "The scribes were disturbed that sin was remitted by a man, for they considered Jesus Christ only as a man, and that he had remitted what the Law could not remit, because faith alone justifies."[5]

St. Ambrose expounds those words of St. Paul: "Whoever believes in Him who justifies the sinner, has his faith imputed to him for justice, according to the purpose of God's grace, and David also declares the blessedness of the man to whom God imputes justice without works."[6] He comments on them thus: "St. Paul says that whoever believes in Christ, that is, the Gentile, has his faith reputed to him for justice, as Abraham did. How then did the Jews think that, through the works of the Law, they justified themselves in accordance with the justification of Abraham, since Abraham was not justified through the works of the Law, but only through faith? Therefore the Law is not necessary, as the sinner is justified before God through faith alone, according to the purpose of God's grace. Thus Paul says that God has determined that with the cessation of the Law, the unjust man should only ask for faith in the grace of God for his salvation, as David also said. To confirm what he has said, the apostle gives the example of the prophet: 'The blessedness of the man to whom God imputes justice without

---

[1] Isaiah lxiv, 6.

[2] Cf. Origen, *Commentarium in Epistolam ad Romanos*, Lib. III, 9 (Patrologia Graeca 14, 952-954). The author mistakenly says the citation is from Book IV of this work.

[3] 1 Cor i, 30-31: cf. Jer. ix, 23-24.

[4] Basil, *Homilia de Humilitate*, xx, 3 (PG 31, 530).

[5] Hilary, *Commentarius in Evangelium Matthei*, cap. viii, 6 (PL 9, 961).

[6] Rom. iv, 5-6: cf. Psalm xxxi, 1-2.

works.' David means that those are blessed whom God has determined to justify in his sight by faith alone, without any toil or observance, and so he preaches the blessedness of the time in which Christ was born. As the Lord himself says: 'Many just men and prophets desire to see the things that you see and to hear the things that you hear, and they have not heard them.'"[1]

When he expounds the first chapter of the *First Letter to the Corinthians*, the same Ambrose says most explicitly that whoever believes in Christ is justified without works and without any merit, and that he receives the remission of his sins through faith alone.[2] He makes this same point in a letter to Irenaeus as follows: "No one may glory in his works, because no one is justified by his works; he who is just has justice as a gift, because he is justified through Christ. Thus it is faith that frees through the blood of Christ, so blessed is he whose sin is remitted and who is given pardon."[3] In the seventyseventh sermon, *On the Song of Songs*, St. Bernard also confirms this, stating that our merits do not have any part in justification, but that one should completely attribute it to grace, which makes us just *gratis*, and in this way frees us from the bondage of sin. He adds that Christ marries the soul and unifies it with himself through faith, without the intervention of any merit from our works.[4]

However, in order not to be too lengthy, I will end these allegations, after I have given a most beautiful teaching (sentenza) of St. Ambrose. In the book entitled *Of Jacob and of the Holy Life*, this saintly man says that since Jacob was not the firstborn in his own right, he hid himself under his brother's attire, adorned himself with the latter's garments, which gave out a sweet scent, and thus disguised as another person, presented himself to his father to receive the blessing for his own profit.[5] In the same way, it is necessary that we clothe ourselves with the justice of Christ through faith, and hide ourselves under the precious purity of our first-born brother, if we want to be accepted as just in the presence of God.[6] This is certainly true, for if we appear before God without being clothed in the justice of Christ, we will undoubtedly be judged as completely unjust and worthy of every punishment; but if, on the other hand, God sees us adorned with the justice of Christ, he will undoubtedly accept us as just and holy and worthy of eternal life. Those who pretend to achieve justification by observing God's commandments (which are comprised in loving God with one's whole heart, one's whole soul and one's whole strength, and

---

[1] Cf. Luke x, 24: Matt. xiii, 7; cf. *Commentaria in Epistolas B. Pauli* (dubiously ascribed to Ambrose). *Ad Romanos*, cap. iv, versus 5-6 (PL 17, 86-87).

[2] Cf. Ambrose, *Commentaria in Epistolas B. Pauli*; *Ad Corinthianos primo*, cap. i, 4 (PL 17, 194-195).

[3] Cf. Ambrose, Epistolae Classis II. *Epistola ad Irenaeum*, lxxiii, 11 (PL 16, 1038).

[4] Cf. Bernard, *Sermones in Cantica Canticorum*, Sermo lxvii (PL 183 [2], 1107-1108). The author mistakenly cites the seventy-seventh sermon, but that is on a different topic.

[5] Cf. Gen. xxvii.

[6] Cf. Ambrose, *De Jacob et Vita Beata*, Lib. II, cap. ii, 9 (PL 4, 648).

one's neighbour as one's self)[1] are certainly very bold. Who could be so arrogant and half-witted, that he dares to let himself believe he has entirely observed these two precepts, and that he does not see that, since the Law of God requires a perfect spiritual love (dilezione) from man,[2] it condemns every imperfection? Then let each man consider his own actions, which seem partly good to him, and he will find that they should rather be called transgressions of the holy Law, since they are impure and imperfect actions.

Here those words of David ring out: "Do not enter into judgement with your servant, for no one living will be justified in your sight."[3] Solomon says: "Who can say, 'My heart is clean.'?"[4] And Job exclaims: "What kind of a thing is man, that should he be immaculate, and that he who is born of woman appears just? Behold, not one of his saints is immutable, and the heavens are not pure in his sight. How much more abominable and useless is man, who drinks iniquity like water."[5] St. John says: "If we say we are without sin, we deceive ourselves."[6] And the Lord taught us that every time we pray we should say: "Dismiss our debts from us."[7] From this one can see the foolishness of those who make merchandise of their works, presuming that they can use them to save not only themselves but also their neighbour. As if the Lord has not said: "When you have done all the things that were commanded you, say: 'We are useless servants; we have done what we were obligated to do.'"[8] Here you see that even if we had perfectly observed the Law of God, we would still have to consider and to call ourselves useless servants. Now, since all men are extremely distant from this perfect observance, will anyone dare to glory in himself for having accumulated so much more merit than the just measure, that he has some left to give to others?[9]

But, returning to our subject, let the arrogant sinner, who has done some works praiseworthy in the eyes of the world, and then pretends to justify himself in God's eyes, consider that all works which come from impure and unclean hearts are also unclean and impure, and consequently cannot be either pleasing to God or efficacious for justification.[10] We must first purify our hearts, if we want our works to be pleasing to God, and the purification consists of faith, as the

---

[1] Cf. Matt. xxii, 37, 39: Mark xii, 30-31: Luke x, 27.

[2] In *Freedom of a Christian*, Luther states that the Law, particularly the first commandment, must be perfectly fulfilled for a man to justify himself before God; cf. pp. 57, 62.

[3] Psalm cxlii, 2.

[4] Prov. xx, 9.

[5] Job xv, 14-16.

[6] 1 John i, 8.

[7] Matt. vi, 12. Cf. Luke xi, 4.

[8] Luke xvii, 10.

[9] This may refer to the offering of masses for the dead and the granting of indulgences for the souls in purgatory.

[10] Melanchthon makes precisely this point about works previous to justification; cf. *Loci Communes*, p. 196. Cf. also Luther, *Freedom of a Christian*, p. 69.

Holy Spirit affirms through the mouth of St. Paul.[1] Thus one must not say that the unjust and sinful man becomes just, good and pleasing to God through his own works, but one must say that faith purifies our hearts from all sins, makes us good, just and pleasing to God, and consequently ensures that our works, although defective and imperfect, are pleasing to His Majesty. Because we have become children of God through faith, he regards our works like a merciful father and not like a severe judge, and he has compassion on our fragility; he looks on us as members of his first-born Son, whose justice and perfection take the place of our uncleanliness and imperfection, which are not imputed to us and do not come to God's judgement because they are hidden under Christ's purity and innocence. [2]

Thus it happens that, although our works proceeding from true faith are impure and imperfect of themselves, they will nevertheless be praised and approved by Christ in the general judgement, in as much as they are the fruit and testimony of our faith, through which we are saved. For if we have loved Christ's brothers, we will clearly show that we have also been faithful followers and brothers of Christ, and through faith we will be put in full possession of the eternal kingdom, prepared by our God for us from the creation of the world.[3] It is not through our merits certainly but through his mercy, that he has elected and called us to the grace of the Gospel, and has justified us in order to glorify us in eternity with his only-begotten son Jesus Christ, our Lord. He is sanctification and justice for us, but certainly not for those who will not confess that his mercy is sufficient in itself to make man just and pleasing to God,[4] who, through his paternal benevolence, offers and gives us Christ with his justice, without any merits of our own works.

And what can man do in order to merit such a great gift and treasure as Christ? This treasure is given only through the grace, favour and mercy of God, and it is faith alone that receives such a gift, and allows us to enjoy the remission of sins. Therefore, when St. Paul and the doctors say that faith alone justifies without works, they mean that it alone enables us to enjoy the general pardon and to receive Christ, who lives in the heart through faith, as St. Paul says. [5] Christ has overcome the terrors of our consciences, and satisfied divine justice for our sins; he has extinguished the wrath of God against us and the fire of hell, into which our natural and acquired depravity [6] hurled us,

---

[1] Cf. Acts xv, 9. The author mistakenly cites St. Paul instead of St. Peter.

[2] Melanchthon states that the works following justification are impure and therefore not righteous, but they are not imputed because of faith, cf. *Loci Communes*, p. 197.

[3] Cf. Matt. xxv, 34.

[4] Corresponding to their rejection of good works as a cause of justification, Luther and Melanchthon stress the need for complete trust in the mercy of God and in his promises. Cf. Luther, *Freedom of a Christian*, p. 59; *Loci Communes*, 192-198.

[5] Cf. Eph. iii, 17.

[6] Valdés distinguishes between these two kinds of human depravity in his *110 Divine Considerations*, Consid. VI, pp. 20-21.

and he has destroyed the devils with all their power and tyranny. These things cannot be accomplished or done by all the works of all of mankind put together. This glory and power is reserved for the Son of God alone, the blessed Christ, who has power above all others in heaven, on earth, and in hell.[1] He gives himself with all his merits to those, who despair of themselves, and place their whole hope of salvation in him and in his merits.

Therefore, when one hears it said that faith alone justifies without works, he should not be deceived and think like the false Christians who drag everything down to the level of carnal life. For them, true faith consists in believing the story of Jesus Christ in the way that one believes those of Caesar and Alexander. This kind of belief is a historical faith, founded on the mere report of men and writings, and impressed lightly on the mind through established custom. It is like the faith of the Turks, who believe in the fables of the Koran for these same reasons. Faith such as this is a human fantasy; it does not renew man's heart at all or warm it with divine love, and no good works or a new life follow from it.[2] Accordingly, they falsely say that faith alone does not justify but that we need works, contrary to the Holy Scripture and to the blessed doctors of the holy Church. I reply to them that this historical and most vain faith, with the works added to it, not only does not justify but also hurls people into the depth of hell, like those who had no oil in their lamps,[3] that is, no living faith in their hearts.

Justifying faith is a work of God in us, through which our old man is crucified[4] and we are all transformed in Christ, so that we become a new creature and very dear children of God. It is this divine faith which inserts us in the death and resurrection of Christ, and consequently mortifies our flesh with its affections and concupiscences. For since we realise that, through the efficacy of faith, we have died with Christ, we loosen our ties with ourselves and with the world,[5] and we understand that those who die with Christ should mortify their earthly members, that is, the vicious affections of the mind and appetites of the flesh.[6] Since we also know that we have been resurrected with Christ, we endeavour to lead a holy and spiritual life, like the life we

---

[1] Cf. Matt. xxviii, 18.

[2] This distinction between a mere historical faith and the true faith that regenerates man is shared by Valdés and the Northern Reformers; cf. Valdés' *Alfabeto Christiano*, p. 74, and his *110 Divine Considerations*, Consid. XXXV and XXXVII, pp. 117, 127-128. Cf. Luther's *Freedom of a Christian*, p. 65; Melanchthon's *Loci Communes*, pp. 172-176; and Calvin's *Institutes*, McNeill edit., I, 543.

[3] Cf. Matt. xxv, 3.

[4] Cf. Rom. vi, 6.

[5] The phrase in the original runs: " ci risolviamo con noi medesimi, et col mondo. " Valdés makes this process of resolution the subject of Consid. XVII in his *110 Divine Considerations*, cf. pp. 54-57.

[6] Cf. Col. iii, 5, 8. In his *110 Divine Considerations*, Valdés constantly discusses the need for the mortification of appetites and affections. Cf. among others, Consid. XXVII, XXXI, XLIV, LVI-LVII, XCII, pp. 94-97, 102-107, 150-152, 203-214, 345-350.

will lead in heaven after the last resurrection. This most holy faith enables us to enjoy the general pardon announced by the Gospel, it introduces us to the kingdom of God, pacifies our conscience and maintains us in a perpetual, spiritual and holy joy. This same faith unites us with God, and makes him live in our hearts and clothe our soul with himself. Consequently, his Spirit is stirred towards the same things that Christ was while he conversed with men, namely, to humility, meekness, obedience to God, charity and all the other perfections, through which we regain the image of God.[1] Thus Christ rightfully attributes blessedness to this inspired faith, and the former cannot exist without good works and holiness.

How can it be true that the Christian is not holy, if Christ becomes his sanctification through faith? Thus we are just and holy through faith, and for this reason, St. Paul almost always calls saints, those whom we call Christians.[2] If they do not have the spirit of Christ, they do not belong to Him, and consequently they are not Christians. If they have Christ's spirit, which rules and governs them, we ought not to fear that they may become lazy about doing good works, even though they know they are justified by faith alone. For the spirit of Christ is the spirit of charity, and charity cannot be idle or cease from good works. Indeed, if we want to say the truth, man can never do good works unless he first knows that he is justified through faith. Before this, he does the works more for his own justification than for the love and glory of God, and so he soils them with self-love and self-interest; whereas, the man who knows he is justified through the merits and justice of Christ (which he makes his own through faith) works solely for the love of God and of Christ, and not for any self-love or self-justification.[3] Consequently, the true Christian (that is, one who holds himself just through the justice of Christ) does not ask whether good works are prescribed or not, but stirred and impelled by the force of divine love, he offers himself eagerly to all holy and Christian works and never ceases to act well.[4]

Whoever does not experience through his own faith these marvelous effects, which, as we have said, inspired faith causes in the Christian, may know that he still does not have Christian faith. Let him urgently ask God to give it to him, saying: "Lord, help my unbelief."[5] Also when he hears it said that only faith justifies, let him not be deceived and say: "Why should I tire myself out in good works when faith is

---

[1] This sentence suggests the Valdesian idea that the Christian slowly attains spiritual perfection and thus regains the image of God, as a result of his incorporation into Christ through faith. Cf. his *110 Divine Considerations*, Consid. I and L, pp. 3, 183, and his *Christian Alphabet*, pp. 82-83, 89, 149.

[3] Among other places, cf. Rom. i, 7: xv, 25: Eph. i, 1: 1 Cor. xiv, 33: Col. i, 2.

[3] Valdés draws this contrast in his *110 Divine Considerations*, Consid. IX, p. 31. Cf. Luther, *Freedom of a Christian*, p. 68.

[4] In *Freedom of a Christian*, Luther similarly describes the Christian's attitude towards good works, pp. 74-76. Cf. Valdés, *Alfabeto Christiano*, pp. 52-53.

[5] Mark ix, 23.

sufficient to send me to paradise?" I reply to him that faith alone does send one to paradise, but let him notice that devils also believe and they tremble, as St. James says.[1] Oh, would you go with them to paradise? From this false conclusion, brother, you can see how much you err; you think you have faith that justifies, and you do not; you say: "I am rich and prosperous and I do not need anything," and you do not know that you are miserable, wretched, poor, blind and naked. I advise you to buy from God some gold made red-hot with fire, namely true faith inflamed with good works, so that you may become rich and clothe yourself in white garments, that is, in the innocence of Christ, and that the shame of your nakedness, namely the ugliness of your sins, may not be apparent.[2]

Justifying faith then is like a flame of fire, which cannot help but shine forth. It is true that the flame alone burns the wood without the aid of light, and yet the flame cannot exist without light. In the same way, it is true that faith alone burns and extinguishes sins without the aid of works, and yet faith cannot exist without good works.[3] If we see a flame of fire with no light, we know it is painted and unreal, and similarly, if we do not see the light of good works in someone, it is a sign that he does not have the true, inspired faith that God gives to his elect to justify and glorify them. I believe with certainty that this is what St. James meant when he said: "Show me your faith in your works, and I will show you my faith in my works."[4] He meant that, whoever cares about the ambition and pleasures of the world does not believe, although he may say he does, for he does not show the effects of faith in himself.

We can also compare this most holy justifying faith to the divinity that was in Jesus Christ. Since He was true man but without sin, he did amazing things, healing the sick, making the blind see, walking on the waters, and raising the dead, but these miraculous works did not make Christ become God. He was God, and the legitimate and only-begotten Son of God, before he did any of these things, and it was not necessary for him to work such miracles in order to become God, but he worked them because he was God. Thus these miracles did not make Christ become God, but they showed that he was true God. In the same way, true living faith is a divinity in the soul of the Christian, who works marvels and is never tired of good works, but these works do not make him a Christian (that is, just, good, holy and most pleasing to God). It was not necessary for him to do such works in order to become a Christian, but he does them all because he is a Christian through faith (in the same way that the man Christ

---

[1] James ii, 19. Luther also replies to this objection in *Freedom of a Christian*; cf. pp. 67 ff.

[2] Cf. Rev. iii, 17-18. The author has added interpretative comments to the text.

[3] In his *Alfabeto Christiano*, Valdés gives a variant of this analogy, that speaks of warmth instead of light. Cf. p. 74.

[4] James ii, 18.

was God through his divinity). Thus these works do not make the Christian good and just, but they show that he is good and just. In the same way that Christ's divinity was the cause of his miracles, faith operating through spiritual love (dilezione) is the cause of the Christian's good works. It was said that Christ had done this or that miracle, and such miracles not only glorified God but also were of the greatest honour to Christ as man. Because he was obedient even unto death, God rewarded him in his resurrection by giving him every power in heaven and earth, which he did not have before as man; he had merited this through the union of the divine Word with Christ's humanity. Faith works in the Christian in the same way, for through the union of faith with the soul, what belongs to one is attributed to the other. For this reason, Holy Scripture sometimes promises the Christian eternal life on account of his good works, since they are a fruit and testimony of living faith, and they proceed from it like light from a flame of fire, as we have already said above.

This most holy faith embraces Christ and unites him with the soul, and all three, that is, faith, Christ and the soul, become one and the same thing.[1] In this way, the soul merits whatever Christ has merited, and therefore St. Augustine says that God crowns his gifts in us.[2] In St. John's Gospel, Christ himself testifies to his union with the soul through faith. When he prays to the Father for his apostles, and for those who would believe in him through their words, he says: "I do not pray only for them, but also for those who will believe in me through their word, so that all may be one, just as you, my Father, are in me and I in you, and so that they may also be one in us, and the world may believe that you sent me. I have given them the glory that you gave me, in order that they may be one, just as we are one."[3] Accordingly, since we believe the word of the Apostles, who preached that Christ died for our sins and was resurrected for our justification, we become one with Christ, and as he is one with God, so we are also one with God through Christ. Oh, the stupendous glory of the Christian, who through faith is allowed to possess those ineffable things that the angels long to see!

From this discussion, one can clearly see the difference between us, and those who defend justification by faith and works. We agree in that we also uphold works, affirming that justifying faith cannot be without good works, and they say[4] that those who are justified by faith do works which can truly be called good. We differ in that we say faith justifies without the aid of works, and the reason is ready,

---

[1] This mystical statement differs from Don Benedetto's conception of the Christian's incorporation into Christ and his clothing himself with Christ's merits.

[2] Cf. among other places, Augustine, Epistolae Classis III, *Epistola ad Sixtum*, cap. v, 19 (PL 33, 880); *Enarrationes in Psalmos*, In Psalmum cii, Enar. 7 (PL 37, 1321-1322).

[3] John xvii, 20-22.

[4] In the Turin edition of 1860 and Paladino's edition (see bibliography, § 38, 43), "dicono" they say – has been unnecessarily changed to "diciamo" – we say.

that through faith we clothe ourselves in Christ[1] and make his justice and sanctity our own. Since it is true that we are given Christ's justice through faith,[2] we cannot be so ungrateful, blind and impious, as to believe that this is not sufficient to make us pleasing and just before God without our works. We say with the apostle: "If the blood of oxen and goats and the sprinkled ashes of a cow sanctified the unclean with respect to purifying the flesh, how much more will the blood of Christ, who has offered his immaculate self to God through the eternal Spirit, purge our conscience from dead works in order to serve the living God?"[3] Now let the pious Christian decide which of these two opinions is more true, more holy and more worthy of being preached: ours, that explains the benefit of Christ and humbles human arrogance, which wants to exalt its own works against the glory of Christ; or the other, that obscures the glory and the benefit of Christ by saying that faith of itself does not justify, and that exalts human pride, which cannot bear to be justified *gratis* through Jesus Christ our Lord.

Oh, they will say to me: "Yet it is a great incentive to good works to say that through them man makes himself just before God." I reply that we also confess that good works are pleasing to God, and that he will reward them in paradise through his mere liberality, but we say, as St. Augustine also does, that truly good works are done only by those who are justified through faith, for if the tree is not good, it cannot bear good fruit.[4] In addition, those who are justified through faith realize that they are just through the justice of God executed in Christ, and so they do not make trade of their good works with God, and claim that with them they can buy justification from him. Instead, they are inflamed with the love of God and want to glorify Christ, who has justified them and given them all his merits and riches; they make every effort to do God's will and fight vigorously against self-love, the world and the devil. When they fall through the weakness of the flesh, they rise again even more desirous of doing good and so much more enamoured of their God;[5] for they know he will not impute their sins to them, since they are incorporated into Christ, who has satisfied for all his members on the wood of the cross and always intercedes for them before the eternal Father. Because of his love for his only-begotten Son, God always looks on them with a most mild countenance, and rules and defends them as his most beloved children. At the end, he will give them the inheritance of the world, and will make them conform to the glorious image of Christ.[6]

---

[1] Cf. Gal. iii, 26-27.
[2] Cf. Rom. iv, 25.
[3] Heb. ix, 13-14.
[4] Cf. Matt. xii, 33, and Augustine, *De verbis Evangelii Matthei*, cap. xii, 33. Sermo lxii, 1 (PL 38, 467). Cf. also Matt. vii, 16-20; Luther, *Freedom of a Christian*, pp. 69-70; and Valdés *Alfabeto Christiano*, p. 53.
[5] Valdés often speaks of the Christian as enamoured of God. Cf. his *110 Divine Considerations*, Consid. XXIII, pp. 74-79, and *Christian Alphabet*, p. 50.
[6] Cf. Rom. viii, 29.

It is these loving encouragements that stir true Christians to do good works. When they reflect that through faith they have become children of God and participants in the divine nature, they are urged by the Holy Spirit, dwelling in them, to live as becomes the children of such a great Lord, and they are ashamed of not maintaining the decorum of their heavenly nobility.[1] Therefore, they make every effort to imitate their first-born brother, Jesus Christ; they live in the greatest humility and meekness and seek the glory of God in all things; they lay down their lives for their brothers and do good to their enemies; and they glory in ignominy and in the cross of our Lord Jesus Christ.[2] They say with Zachary: "We are freed from the hands of our enemies, so that without fear we may serve God in holiness and justice in his sight all the days of our life."[3] With St. Paul they say: "The grace of the Lord has appeared, so that we might destroy all impiety and wordly desires, and live with sobriety, holiness and piety in this world, while awaiting the blessed hope and the glorious appearance of the great God and Saviour."[4]

Inspired faith works these and other similar thoughts, desires and affections in the minds of the justified. Whoever does not feel these divine affections and operations in one's heart, either in whole or in part, but is given over to the flesh and the world, may know for certain that he still does not have justifying faith. He is not a member of Christ, because he does not have His spirit, and consequently he does not belong to Christ; and whoever does not belong to Christ is not a Christian.[5] From now on then, let human prudence cease attacking the justice of the most holy faith,[6] and let us give all the glory of our justification to the merits of Christ, with whom we clothe ourselves through faith.[7]

---

[1] Valdés discusses Christian decorum in Consid. XC and XCIV of his *110 Divine Considerations*, pp. 335-339, 360. The theme reflects his background as a courtier.

[2] Cf. Gal. vi, 14.

[3] Luke i, 74-75.

[4] Cf. Titus ii, 11-13.

[5] Cf. Rom. viii, 9.

[6] Valdés contrasts the laws of human prudence with man's acceptance of God's justice, in his *110 Divine Considerations*, Consid. III, pp. 6-11.

[7] Cf. Gal. iii, 26-27.

Chapter V

HOW THE CHRISTIAN CLOTHES HIMSELF WITH CHRIST

From what was said above, one can understand fairly clearly how the Christian clothes himself with Christ; still we intend to speak somewhat more about it, for we know that the discussion of Christ and of his gifts to the pious Christian can never seem lengthy or irksome, even if it were repeated a thousand times. I say that the Christian knows that through faith Christ, with all his justice, holiness and innocence, belongs to him. Just as someone clothes himself in a very beautiful and precious robe, when he wishes to present himself before a lord, so the Christian adorns and covers himself with the innocence of Christ and all his perfections. Then he presents himself before God, the Lord of the universe, relying on the merits of Christ, just as if he had merited and attained them all himself. Faith certainly enables us to possess Christ and all that belongs to him, in the same way that each of us owns his own clothes. Therefore, clothing oneself with Christ is nothing other than firmly holding that Christ is ours (as he truly is, if we believe him), and believing that this heavenly garment makes us pleasing and acceptable to God. For it is most certain that, like an excellent Father, he has given us his Son, and he wants all his justice and all that he is, can and has done, to be under our jurisdiction. As a result, it is lawful for us to glory in ourselves, as if we had performed and acquired these things by our own powers. Whoever believes this will find without fail, that what he believes is most true, as we have shown above. Thus the Christian should have a firm belief and conviction that all the goods, graces and riches of Christ are his own; since God has given us Christ, how could it be that he would not give us everything with him?[1] If this is true (as indeed it is) the Christian can truthfully say: "I am a son of God, Christ is my brother, I am lord of heaven and earth, of hell, of death and of the Law; for the Law cannot accuse or curse me, because the justice of my Christ has been made my own."

It is this faith alone that enables man to be called a Christian and one who is clothed in Christ, as we have said, and it can properly be called the great mystery,[2] which contains the marvelous and incredible

---

[1] Cf. Rom. viii, 32.
[2] Cf. 1 Tim. iii, 9.

things of the great God. They cannot penetrate into man's heart unless God softens it with his grace, as he has promised to do through the mouth of Ezechiel, saying: "I will give you a new heart, and I will place a new spirit in your midst; I will take away the heart of stone from your body, and I will give you a heart of flesh." [1] Therefore, whoever does not believe in this way, namely, that he possesses Christ and all his goods, can never be called a true Christian. He will never have a happy and peaceful conscience, or a good mind that is willing to act well (servente al bene operare); he will easily fall away from good works, or rather he will never be able to do truly good things. This faith alone and the trust that we have in the merits of Christ, makes men true Christians, strong, joyous, smiling, enamoured of God, ready to do good works, possessors of the kingdom of God and his dearly-beloved sons, in whom the Holy Spirit truly dwells.

What mind is so abject, vile and cold, that the thought of the inestimable grandeur of God's gift to us, the gift of his most beloved Son with all his perfections, does not enflame it with a most ardent desire to be like Christ in good works? For he was also given to us by the Father as an example, that we should always follow, moulding our life so that it may be an image of the life of Christ.[2] As St. Peter says: "Christ has suffered for us, leaving us an example so that we might follow in his footsteps." [3] From this consideration arises the other way of clothing oneself with Christ, which we can call patterning (exemplare); for the Christian should regulate his whole life by the example of Christ, and conform to Him [4] in all his thoughts, words and deeds, leaving his bad life in the past, and clothing himself with the new life, namely, with that of Christ.[5] Thus St. Paul says: "Let us cast off the works of darkness and put on the weapons of light, not in feasting and drunkeness, not in fornication and lasciviousness, or in contentions; but clothe yourself with the Lord Jesus Christ, and pay no heed to the flesh with its concupiscences." [6] The true Christian, who is enamoured of Christ, then says to himself: "Since Christ, who had no need of me, has regained me with his own blood, and become poor in order to enrich me, I likewise want to give my goods and my life for the love and welfare of my neighbour. Just as I have clothed myself with Christ because of his love for me, so I want my neighbour in Christ to clothe himself with myself and my goods, because of the love that I bear him for the love of Christ." [7]

---

[1] Ezechiel xxxvi, 26.

[2] Valdés discusses the imitation of Christ in his *110 Divine Considerations*, Consid. LXIV and LXXXIX, pp. 227-229, 328-335. In the *Alfabeto Christiano*, Valdés recommended *De Imitatione Christi* as simple spiritual reading for Giulia Gonzaga; cf. p. 164.

[3] 1 Peter ii, 21.

[4] Valdés speaks of conforming oneself to God in his *110 Divine Considerations*, Consid. XXXV, pp. 115-120.

[5] Cf. Eph. iv, 22-24.

[6] Rom. xiii, 12-14.

[7] This description of the true Christian's sentiments is similar to a passage in Luther's *Freedom of a Christian*; cf. pp. 74-75, 79-80.

If someone does not behave in this way, he is still not a true Christian, for one must not say: "I love Christ," unless one loves Christ's members and brethren. If we do not love our neighbour, for the love of whom Christ has shed his own blood, we cannot truthfully say that we love Christ. Although he was equal to God, he was obedient to the Father even unto death on the cross,[1] and he has loved and redeemed us, giving himself to us with all his works and possessions. We who are rich and abundant in Christ's goods should be obedient to God in this same way; we should offer and give our works, all our possessions, and ourselves to our neighbours and brothers in Christ, serving them in all their needs and being almost another Christ to them.[2] Since Christ was humble, meek and removed from contentions,[3] we ought to make every effort towards humility and meekness and flee all fights and contentions, those that consist of words and disputes, just as much as those consisting of deeds.[4] Just as Christ endured all the persecutions and disorders of the world for the glory of God, we should cheerfully undergo the ignominies and persecutions which false Christians impose on all those who want to live piously in Christ.[5] Christ laid down his life for his enemies and prayed for them on the cross,[6] and we should always pray for our enemies and willingly lay down our life for their salvation.

This is how we follow the footsteps of Christ, as St. Peter says; for when we recognize that Christ and all his riches belongs to us (that is, when we clothe ourselves with Christ and become pure and free from all stains),[7] there is nothing else left for us to do but to glorify God by imitating Christ, and to do the same things for our brothers that Christ has done for us. Above all, we know from his own words, that he accepts everything we do for his and our brothers as a benefit for himself. Since we are the true Christian members of Christ,[8] we can certainly do neither good nor evil to true Christians without doing the same to Christ, to the extent that he rejoices and suffers in his members. Just as Christ is our garment through faith, so we ought to be a garment for our brothers through spiritual affection (dilezione). We should also take the same care of their bodies that we do of our own, for they are the true members of our body, of which Jesus Christ is the head. It is this divine love and charity, born in the unfeigned

---

[1] Cf. Phil. ii, 6, 8.

[2] This sentence is similar to a passage in Luther's *Freedom of a Christian*, p. 76.

[3] Cf. Matt. xii, 19: Isaiah xlii, 2.

[4] Cf. 2 Tim. ii, 23.

[5] Cf. 2 Tim. iii, 12. Don Benedetto specifies the persecutors of the Scriptural text as false Christians, indicating his consciousness of the split within Christianity itself. He repeats this idea below, p. 76, last line.

[6] Cf. Luke xxiv, 34.

[7] This parenthetical clause is somewhat ambiguous, suggesting that the Christian becomes pure and spotless in himself as well as in Christ.

[8] Cf. Rom. xii, 5.

faith that God inspires in his elect, of which St. Paul says that it works through charity.[1]

Because the life of Christ, in whose imitation we should clothe ourselves, was a perpetual cross, full of tribulation, ignominies and persecutions,[2] we must continually carry the cross if we wish to conform to his life. As Christ said: " If anyone wants to follow me, let him despise himself and take up his cross daily and follow me. "[3] The main reason for this cross is that, by means of this exercise, our God intends to mortify our mental affections and our physical appetites, so that we may realize in ourselves that perfection, in which we have been embraced by Christ, through our incorporation in him.[4] God wants our faith, refined like gold in the furnace of tribulations, to shien forth in his praise,[5] and in addition, he wants us to illustrate his power through our infirmity. The world to its vexation sees his power in us, when our weakness becomes strong through trials and persecutions, and the more it is attacked and tormented, the stronger and firmer it becomes.[6] Thus St. Paul says: " We have this treasure in earthen vessels, so that the magnificence of power belongs to God and not to us; we endure trials in all things, but we do not suffocate; we are poor but not destitute; we undergo persecution but are not abandoned; we are reviled but do not perish; and we always carry about the mortification of our Lord Jesus in our flesh, so that his life is also revealed in our body. "[7]

Seeing that Christ and his dear disciples glorified God by their tribulations, then let us also joyfully embrace them,[8] saying with St. Paul: " God forbid that I should glory in anything but the cross of our Lord Jesus Christ ".[9] Let us behave so that the world in spite of itself may know and see the stupendous effects, which God produces in those who sincerely embrace the grace of the Gospel. Let the men of the world see how calmly true Christians bear the loss of their goods, the death of their children, ignominies, bodily infirmities, and persecutions by false Christians. Let them see how only true Christians adore God in spirit and in truth, accepting all that happens from his hands, regarding all that he does as good, just and holy; praising God for

---

[1] Gal. v, 6.

[2] Valdés describes the nature of the cross similarly in his *110 Divine Considerations*, Consid. LXIV, p. 228.

[3] Luke ix, 23.

[4] This sentence clearly states Valdés' conception of the spiritual perfection, which is the goal of the justified Christian, and which reflects his theory of double justification. Cf. *Alfabeto Christiano*, pp. 82-83, 89 and *110 Divine Considerations*, Consid. XL, pp. 137-142. It contrasts with his other statements on man's frailty and his imperfect works; see above, pp. 65-66, below, p. 86.

[5] Cf. 1 Peter i, 7.

[6] Cf. 2 Cor. xii, 9-10.

[7] 2 Cor iv, 7-10.

[8] Valdés discusses the necessity and the glory of Christian suffering in his 110 *Divine Considerations*, Consid. XVII and XCIII, pp. 56-57, 350-355.

[9] Gal. vi, 14.

all things, favorable and adverse; thanking him like an excellent and most gracious father; and recognizing that their suffering, which is mainly on account of the Gospel and the imitation of Christ, is a great gift of God. Above all, they know that " tribulation works patience, patience proof, proof hope, and hope is not confounded." [1] * I say that patience works proof, because God has promised to aid those who rely on him in their tribulations; this is proved to us when we stand strong and firm, sustained by God's hand,[2] for we could not do this with our own powers. Through patience, therefore, we find by experience that the Lord offers us the aid that he promised in times of need. This, in turn, confirms our hope, for it would be too great a lack of gratitude not to expect in the future that aid and favour, which we have found so certain and constant through experience.** [3] But why so many words? It should be enough for us to know that through tribulations true Christians clothe themselves with the image of Christ crucified. If we bear this willingly, then we clothe ourselves with the image of Christ glorified.[4] Just as the passion of Christ abounds, our consolation will also abound through Christ,[5] and if we endure, we shall reign together.[6]

---

[1] Rom. v, 3-5: cf. James i, 4-5.

[2] Cf. 2 Cor. i, 4: Psalm ix, 9-10.

[3] This exposition of the text from Romans paraphrases a passage in Calvin's 1539 edition of the *Institutes*. Cf. McNeill edit., I, 704. Valdés also devotes Consid. XV, pp. 49-52, of his *110 Divine Considerations* to the theme of God's aid in tribulations.

[4] Cf. Rom. viii, 17.

[5] Cor. i, 5.

[6] 2 Tim. ii, 12.

Chapter VI

SOME REMEDIES FOR LACK OF CONFIDENCE

Since the devil and human prudence always try to deprive us of this most holy faith (through which we believe that all our sins have been chastized in Christ, and that we are reconciled with God through his most precious blood) it is necessary that the Christian always have his weapons ready to defend himself against this most wicked temptation, which tries to deprive the soul of its life.[1] I think that the most powerful of these weapons are prayers, the frequent use of holy communion, and the memory of baptism and predestination.[2]

In our prayers, let us say with the father of the lunatic: "Lord, help our unbelief,"[3] and with the apostles: "Lord, increase our faith."[4] If we are ruled by an unceasing desire to grow in faith, hope and charity, let us pray continually, as St. Paul commands,[5] for prayer is nothing other than a fervent desire founded on God.[6] With the memory of baptism, we become more certain that we are reconciled with God,[7] for St. Peter says that Noah's ark was the symbol of baptism. Just as Noah believed in the promises of God and thus saved himself from the deluge in the ark, we save ourselves from God's wrath through

---

[1] Luther treats doubt as a wicked temptation of the devil; cf. his *Commentary on St. Paul's Epistle to the Galatians* (included in *Martin Luther, Selections from his Writings*, edited by John Dillenberger, Anchor Books, 1961). Citations are to this edition, pp. 107-108. Valdés thinks that human prudence creates doubt in the Christian's mind, by raising various objections to belief in the Gospel; cf. his *110 Divine Considerations*, XCIX and CIII, pp. 378-382, 394-399.

[2] Luther treats these four practices as remedies for doubt in various places in his writings. Exact references will be given as each remedy is discussed in the text. In his *110 Divine Considerations*, Valdés suggests some other remedies for doubt; cf. Consid. CIII, pp. 394-399.

[3] Mark ix, 24.

[4] Luke xvii, 5.

[5] Cf. 1 Thess. v, 17: Luke xviii, 1.

[6] Valdés cites these two prayers from Scripture, and says the Christian should ask God for more faith in the same way; cf. his *110 Divine Considerations*, Consid. LXIX, pp. 242-245, and *Alfabeto Christiano*, pp. 75-76. Luther also urges the Christian to pray for faith; cf. *Sermons on the Catechism* (included in *Martin Luther, Selections from his Writings*, edited by Dillenberger, Anchor Books, 1961). Citations are to this edition, pp. 216-217.

[7] Luther makes this point in his *Pagan Servitude of the Church*, pp. 294-295. In his *110 Divine Considerations*, Valdés discusses baptism, but in a different context; cf. Consid. CIV, pp. 399-402.

faith, which is founded on the word of Christ,[1] who says: "Whoever believes and is baptized, will be saved."[2] This is very reasonable, because in baptism we clothe ourselves with Christ, as St. Paul states,[3] and consequently are made participants in his justice and in all his goods. The sins we commit in our weakness are covered by this most precious garment, and they are not imputed to us by God. As St. Paul says, we feel that blessedness of the psalm which says: "Blessed are those whose iniquity is remitted and whose sins are covered! Blessed is the man to whom the Lord does not impute sin."[4] However, the Christian guards against taking these words as a license to sin, for this doctrine does not apply to those who honour themselves with the name of Christian, and confess Christ with their words, but deny him with their deeds.[5] It concerns the true Christians who, although they fight vigorously against the flesh, the world, and the devil, still fall every day and are forced to say continually: "Remit our debts from us."[6] We speak to them in order to console and sustain them, so that they may not fall into desperation, as if the blood of Christ did not cleanse us from every sin, and he were not the advocate and atonement for his members.

Therefore, when we are tempted to doubt the remission of sins, and our conscience begins to disturb us, adorned with faith, let us immediately have recourse to the precious blood of Jesus Christ, shed for us on the altar of the cross, and distributed to the faithful at the Last Supper, under the veil of the most holy sacrament.[7] It was instituted by Christ so that we would celebrate the memory of his death, and by means of this visible sacrament would make our afflicted consciences certain of our reconciliation with God.[8] Blessed Christ made a testament when he said: "This is my body, which is given for you,[9] and this is my blood of the New Testament, which is shed for many unto the remission of sins."[10] As St. Paul says, "we know that the testament is made by man, yet if it is authenticated, no one undervalues it or adds anything to it";[11] and no testament is valid before

---

[1] Cf. 1 Peter iii, 20-21.
[2] Mark xvi, 16.
[3] Cf. Gal. iii, 27.
[4] Psalm xxxi, 1-2. Cf. Rom. iv, 6-8.
[5] Cf. Rom. x, 9-10.
[6] Matt. vi, 12: cf. Luke ix, 4.
[7] In the *Sermons on the Catechism*, Luther urges the Christian to use this sacrament as a remedy for his spiritual weakness; cf. pp. 237-239. Don Benedetto treats the sacrament in terms of the spiritual nourishment that it provides for the Christian, and the latter's duty to receive it worthily; he does not discuss the controversial question of the mode of Christ's presence in the sacrament.
[8] This description of the Eucharist is similar to Calvin's definition of a sacrament and his analysis of the Lord's Supper; cf. McNeill edit., II, 1277, 1360-1364. Cf. also Luther's *Pagan Servitude of the Church*. pp. 271-272, 280-282.
[9] Luke xxii, 19: cf. Matt. xxvi, 26: Mark xiv, 22.
[10] Matt. xxvi, 28: cf. Luke xxii, 20: Mark xiv, 24.
[11] Gal. iii, 15.

one's death, but afterwards it is extremely valid. Accordingly, Christ has confirmed his testament (in which he promises the remission of sins, the grace and benevolence of the Father and himself, mercy, and eternal life), by his most precious blood and by his own death, so that it would be valid. St. Paul says that, through this act, Christ " becomes the mediator of the New Testament, so that when his death intervenes for the redemption of those transgressions committed under the first Testament, those who are called may receive the promise of the eternal inheritance. For where there is a testament, it is necessary that the death of the testator interpose itself, because the testament of a dead man is confirmed, while it is worth nothing during the testator's life. "[1] Therefore, through Christ's death, we are confident and extremely certain of the validity of his testament, in which all our iniquities are remitted and we are made inheritors of eternal life. As a sign and a pledge of this, he has left us this most divine sacrament in the place of a seal.[2] It not only gives our souls an assured confidence in our eternal salvation, but it also makes us secure in the immortality of our body, because from now on it is enlivened by that immortal flesh, and in a certain way, it comes to share in its immortality.[3]

* Whoever shares in this divine flesh through faith will not perish in eternity,[4] but if one participates in it without faith, it turns into a deadly poison for him. When corporeal food finds the stomach occupied by vicious humours, it also becomes contaminated and harmful. In the same way, when this spiritual food finds a soul vicious with malice and unfaithfulness, it hurls it into greater ruin, not through its own fault, but because to the unclean and the unfaithful nothing is clean, even if it is sanctified by the blessing of the Lord. As St. Paul says: " He who eats of this bread and drinks of this chalice unworthily, will be guilty of the body and blood of the Lord, "[5] and " he eats and drinks his own damnation because he does not recognize the Lord's body. "[6] Whoever usurps the Lord's meal without faith and charity, does not recognize the Lord's body. Because he does not believe that this body is his life and the cleansing of all his sins, he makes Christ a liar, he tramples on the Son of God, and considers the blood of the testament (through which he has been sanctified) as a profane thing; he injures the Spirit of grace, and he will be most severely punished by God for this unfaithfulness and wicked hypocrisy. He has not placed his trust in his justification in the passion of Christ, and yet since he receives this most holy sacrament, he professes not to place his trust in anything else. Thus he accuses himself, testifies

---

[1] Heb. ix, 15-17.

[2] Luther discusses the Lord's Supper as the sign of His testament in his *Pagan Servitude of the Church*; cf. pp. 273 ff.

[3] Cf. Irenaeus, *Adversus Haereses*, Lib. IV, xviii, 5 (PG 7, 1027-1029) and *Ibid.*, Lib. V, ii, 2-3 (PG 7, 1124-1128).

[4] Cf. John vi, 54.

[5] 1 Cor. xi, 27.

[6] 1 Cor. xi, 29.

to his own iniquity, and condemns himself to eternal death, by denying the eternal life that God promised him in this most holy sacrament.** [1]

At times the Christian feels that his enemies wish to overpower him, namely, when he doubts whether he has attained the remission of his sins through Christ and whether he can endure the devil with his temptations. He feels that the accusation of his doubtful conscience will prevail over him, so that he begins to fear that hell will swallow him up and that death has conquered and killed him forever, because of God's wrath. When the Christian feels these anxieties, let him go to this most holy sacrament with a good mind and with trust and receive it devotedly, in his heart saying in reply to his enemies: "I confess that I merit a thousand hells and eternal death for my sins, but this most divine sacrament that I receive now, makes me secure and certain of the remission of all my iniquities and of reconciliation with God. If I reflect on my actions, there is no doubt that I know I am sinful and condemned, and my conscience would never be quiet, if I believed that my sins were pardoned through the works that I do. But, if I reflect on the promises and the covenant of God, who promises me remission of sins through the blood of Christ, I am as certain of having obtained this and of having his grace, as I am confident and certain that he, who has promised and made the covenant, cannot lie or deceive.[2] Through this firm faith I become just, and it is this justice of Christ which saves me and makes my conscience tranquil. Has he not given his most innocent body into the hands of sinners for my sins? Has he not shed his blood in order to cleanse all my iniquities? Thus, my soul, why are you sad? Trust in the Lord, who bears you so much love that he has allowed his only-begotten Son to die in order to free you from eternal death.[3] Christ took on our poverty, in order to give us his riches; he took on our infirmity, to confirm us with his strength; he became mortal, to make us immortal; he descended to the earth so that we could ascend to heaven; and he became the Son of Man together with us in order to make us sons of God with him.[4] Thus who can accuse us? It is God who justifies us; then who can condemn us? Christ has died for us, rather he has arisen and sits at the right hand of God, interceding for us.[5] Oh my soul, then leave off these wailings and sighs; my soul, bless the Lord; let all that is within me bless his holy name; my soul, bless the Lord and never forget all his gifts. He is the atonement for all your sins, he heals all your infir-

---

[1] This paragraph paraphrases a passage on the Lord's Supper from Calvin's *Institutes*. Most of the passage first appeared in the 1536 edition, but the analogy of spiritual and ordinary food was inserted in 1539. Cf. McNeill edit., II, 14, 17-18.

[2] This passage has a Lutheran ring to it. In *Bondage of the Will*, Luther confesses these same sentiments with respect to justification; cf. p. 199.

[3] Cf. 1 John iv, 10.

[4] This statement of the exchange between Christ and man is similar to a passage that first appeared in the 1536 edition of Calvin's *Institutes*; cf. McNeill edit., II, 1362. Cf. also Luther's *Freedom of a Christian*, pp. 60-61.

[5] Rom. viii, 33-34.

mities, he rescues your life from death, he crowns you with mercy and compassion. The Lord is most merciful and mild; he is slow to wrath, and great in mercy. He does not contend in eternity, and he does not maintain hate eternally. He has not acted according to our sins, nor has he punished us according to our iniquities; for, in accordance with the height of heaven above the earth, he has exercised mercy on those who fear him; and in proportion to the distance of the orient from the occident, he has made our sins distant from us. As the father has mercy on his son, the Lord has had mercy on us and given us his only-begotten Son." [1]

It is with this faith and gratitude, with these and similar thoughts, that we should receive the sacrament of the body and blood of Jesus Christ our Lord. In this way, fear is driven from the soul, charity is augmented, faith confirmed, conscience reassured, and the tongue never seems tired of praising God, and rendering him infinite thanks for such a great benefit. This is the virtue, the efficacy and the unique trust of our soul; the conscience built on this rock does not fear any storm, not even the gates of hell, the wrath of God, the Law, sin, death, or demons, or anything else. [2] Because the whole essence of the mass consists of this most divine sacrament,[3] when the Christian finds himself there, he should always hold the eyes of his mind fixed on the passion of our most gracious Lord.[4] He should contemplate, on one hand, Christ on the cross, burdened with all our sins, and on the other, God who chastises him, beating his most-beloved Son instead of us. Oh, happy is he who closes his eyes to all other sights, and wants to see and understand only Jesus Christ crucified, in whom all the graces and treasures of wisdom and knowledge are stored! Happy is he who always feeds his mind with such divine food and makes his soul drunk with the love of God by means of such a sweet and saving liqueur!

But before I end this discussion, I would first like to point out to the Christian that St. Augustine is in the habit of calling this most divine sacrament the bond of love and the mystery of unity.[5] He says: "Whoever receives the mystery of unity and does not preserve the bond of peace, does not receive the mystery for himself but a witness

---

[1] This exhortation to the soul is a very free paraphrase of Psalm cii, verses 1-13.

[2] It is not clear from the text to what the first word of this sentence refers. Since its gender is feminine in Italian, it cannot refer to the benefit or to the sacrament, but may refer to faith. Caponetto assumes the latter possibility, and considers the second half of the sentence a reference to Luther's reinterpretation of Matt. xvi, 18. Luther claimed that the rock on which the Church was built was not the Papal power, but faith in Christ's Word; cf. *The Papacy at Rome* (in *Works of Martin Luther*, vol. 1 [Philadelphia: The Muhlenberg Press, 1943], pp. 380-381).

[3] Luther asserts that the essence of the mass consists of the words of Christ, which institute the sacrament of the Lord's Supper. Cf. *The Pagan Servitude of the Church*, pp. 271-272, 275.

[4] Valdés encourages this practice in the *Alfabeto Christiano*, pp. 49-50.

[5] Cf. Augustine, *In Joannis Evangelium, Tractatus cxxiv*, cap. vi, Tract. xxvi, 13 (PL 35, 1613).

against himself."[1] Accordingly, we should know that * the Lord ordained this sacrament, not only to make us sure of the remission of our sins, but also to inflame us with peace, union and fraternal charity, for in this sacrament, the Lord lets us participate in his body, in such a way that he becomes one with us, and we with him. Therefore, since he has but one body, of which he makes us all participants, through this participation all of us must also become one body, whose unity is represented by the bread of the sacrament. Just as it is made of many grains, blended and mixed so that one cannot be distinguished from the other, in the same way, we should be joined and united with so much harmony of spirit, that the slightest division cannot intrude among us. St. Paul shows us this when he says: "Is not the chalice of benediction that we bless the communion of the blood of Christ? And is not the bread that we break the communion of the body of Christ? Many of us are one bread and one body, because we all participate in one bread."[2] Therefore, when we receive the most holy communion, we ought to consider that we are all incorporated into Christ, all members of one same body, that is of Christ,[3] in such a way that we cannot offend, defame or despise any of the brethren, without equally offending, defaming or despising Jesus Christ in him. We cannot disagree with the brethren, without equally disagreeing with Christ, and we cannot love Christ, if we do not love him in the brethren. We ought to care as much for the brethren, who are members of our body, as we do for our own body. In the same way that no part of our body feels any pain, without it spreading to all the other parts, we should not let our brother feel any pain, without also being moved to compassion.** [4]

With thoughts like these, we should prepare for such a great sacrament, exciting in our minds an ardent love for our neighbour.[5] * What greater stimulus can incite us to mutual love, than to see that Christ, by giving himself to us, not only invites us to give ourselves to one another, but in as much as he makes himself common to us all, he also makes all of us one in him? **[5] Thus we should desire and take care that all of us may be one soul, one heart and one tongue, harmonious and unified in thoughts, in words and in deeds. * Let every Christian know that each time we receive this most holy sacrament, we are obligated to all the offices of charity, in such a way that we do not offend the brothers in anything, and we do not leave anything

---

[1] Augustine, Sermones de Tempore, Classis II. *Sermo cclxxii, In die Pentecostes postremus.* Ad infantes, de Sacramento (PL 38, 1246).

[2] 1 Cor. x, 16-17.

[3] Cf. Rom. xii, 5.

[3] This is a free paraphrase of a passage that first appeared in the 1536 edition of Calvin's *Institutes.* Cf. McNeill edit., II, 1414-1416.

[4] The remainder of this paragraph is a patchwork of material on the Lord's Supper that first appeared in Calvin's 1536 *Institutes.*

[5] Cf. McNeill edit., II, 1415-1416.

undone which would aid and profit them in their necessity.** [1] * If some who are divided and alienated from their brethren should come to this heavenly meal of the Lord, they may know for certain that they eat unworthily; they are guilty of the body and blood of the Lord, and eat and drink their own damnation. For it does not fall to them divide and lacerate the body of Christ, since they are divided by hatred from their brethren, that is, from the members of Christ, and they have no part in Christ. Yet, by receiving most holy communion, they profess to believe that all their salvation consists in the participation and union with Christ. ** [2] Therefore, let us go and receive this heavenly bread, * to celebrate the memory of the Lord's passion, and by this remembrance, to sustain and fortify our faith and the certainty of the remission of our sins; to excite our minds and tongues to praise and preach the infinite goodness of our God; and lastly, to nourish mutual charity and to declare it to one another through the most intimate union, that we all have in the body of Jesus Christ our Lord. ** [3]

Besides prayer, the memory of baptism and frequent use of most holy communion, the best remedy against diffidence and fear (which is not compatible with Christian charity), is the memory of our predestination and our election to eternal life. [4] This is founded on the word of God, which is the sword of the Holy Spirit,[5] and with which we can kill our enemies: "Rejoice" says the Lord "that your names are written in Heaven." [6] There is no greater joy or consolation in this present life for the Christian who is afflicted and tempted, or who has fallen into some sin, than the memory of his predestination, and the certainty of being one of those whose names are written in the book of life,[7] and who have been elected by God to conform to the image of Christ. [8] Oh, it is an ineffable consolation for a man to have this faith and to reflect continually in his heart on this most sweet predestination! Through it he knows that, even though he may fall, his Father God, who has predestined him to eternal life, will always sustain his hand.[9] Thus he always says in his heart: "If God has elected and predestined me to the glory of his children, who will be able to hinder me?" "If God is for us," says St. Paul, "who can be against us?"[10] On the contrary, in order to accomplish predestination in us, God sent us his most beloved Son, who is the most secure

---

[1] Mc Neill edit., II, 1422.
[2] *Ibid.*, II, 1417-1418.
[3] *Ibid.*, II, 1422.
[4] Valdés says that the Christian should have faith in his election to eternal life; cf. his *110 Divine Considerations*, Consid. XVI, pp. 52-54. Luther considers the certainty of predestination an essential part of the Christian faith; cf. *Bondage of the Will*, pp. 184-85.
[5] Cf. Eph. vi, 17.
[6] Luke x, 20.
[7] Cf. Phil. iv, 3.
[8] Cf. Rom. viii, 29.
[9] Cf. Psalm xxxvi, 24.
[10] Rom. viii, 31.

pledge that we who have accepted the grace of the Gospel, are among the children of God elected to eternal life.

This most holy predestination maintains the true Christian in a state of continual, spiritual joy. It increases his effort towards good works, inflames him with love of God, and makes him hostile to the world and to sin. Who could be so fierce and ironlike that he would not burn full of divine love, if he knew that God in his mercy has made him his child from eternity? Who could be so vile and cowardly that he would not consider all the delights, honours and riches of the world a most vile corruption, if he knew that God has made him a citizen of heaven? The latter truly adore God in spirit and truth; they accept all things, favourable and adverse, from the hand of God their Father; and they always praise, and thank him as a pious, just, and holy father in all his works. Enamoured with their God and armed with the knowledge of their predestination, they fear neither death, sin, the devil, or hell. They do not know what the wrath of God is, for in God they see nothing but love and paternal charity towards them. If they have tribulations, they accept them as favours from their God, and cry out with St. Paul: "Who will separate us from the charity of God? Tribulations, or anguish, or persecution, or fame, or nakedness, or danger, or the knife? As it is written, we die for you every day; we are held like sheep for the slaughter; but in all these things, we conquer through Him who loved us."[1] Therefore, it is not without reason that St. John says true Christians know they must be saved and glorified, and that through this trust they become holy, just as Christ is holy.[2] When St. Paul exhorts his disciples to the pious and holy life, he usually reminds them of their election and predestination,[3] since it is the most efficacious way to stimulate the love of God and the effort towards good works in the minds of true Christians. For the same reason, blessed Christ spoke in public of this most holy predestination,[4] as he knew that a knowledge of it was very important for the edification of the elect.

But perhaps you will say to me: "I know that those whose names are written in heaven have reason to live in perpetual joy and to glorify God with their words and works, but I do not know if I am included in that number. Therefore I live in perpetual fear, especially since I know that I am very weak and frail with regard to sin. I cannot sufficiently defend myself from its violence, so I am overcome by it everyday. In addition to this, seeing that I am often afflicted and vexed with many tribulations, I can almost behold the wrath of God scourging me." Most beloved brother, I say in reply to these doubts of yours, that you should believe with certainty that these are temptations of the devil, who tries in every way to rob you of faith and of

---

[1] Rom. viii, 35-37: Psalm xliii, 22.
[2] Cf. 1 John iii, 4-6.
[3] Cf. Eph. i, 4-6.
[4] Cf. Luke x, 20.

the trust, which is born of faith and which assures us of God's good will towards us. The devil endeavours to deprive the Christian soul of this precious garment, for he knows that no one is truly faithful unless he believes in the words of God, who promises the remission of our sins and his peace to everyone who accepts the grace of the Gospel. I say that whoever is not definitely persuaded by these promises that God is a favourably inclined and indulgent father, and whoever does not wait for the inheritance of the heavenly kingdom with firm faith, is not truly faithful and makes himself completely unworthy of God's grace.[1] Thus St. Paul says that we are the house of God, provided that we firmly maintain the trust and glory of our hope until the end.[2] Elsewhere he exhorts us not to throw away our trust, which has a great reward in store.[3]

Most beloved brether, let us make every effort to do the will of God like good children, and let us be on guard against sins as much as we are able. Even if we sin through our fragility, let us not believe therefore that we are vessels of wrath, or that we are abandoned by the Holy Spirit, because we have an advocate before the Father, the just Jesus Christ, who is the atonement for our sins.[4] Brethren, let us recall that judgement of St. Augustine, who says that no holy and just man is without sin, and yet he does not stop being just and holy, provided he regards holiness with affection.[5] Therefore, if we are afflicted and troubled, let us not believe that God has sent us our troubles because we are his enemies, but rather because he is our most merciful Father. "The Lord," says Solomon, "chastises whomever he loves, and scourges every child that he receives."[6]

Since we have accepted the grace of the Gospel, through which God receives man as his child, we must not doubt of God's grace and benevolence; and knowing that the words of God and the imitation of the life of Christ delight us,[7] we must firmly believe that we are children of God and a temple of the Holy Spirit,[8] because these things cannot be done by the work of human prudence. They are the gifts of the Holy Spirit, who dwells in us through faith, and * is like a seal that authenticates and stamps those divine promises in our hearts, whose certainty he has previously impressed upon our minds, and who was given to us by God instead of a pledge in order to establish and confirm them. The Apostle says: "After you have believed, you will

---

[1] Luther stresses that the essence of Christianity is a firm faith in God's promises: cf. *Freedom of a Christian*, pp. 59-60.

[2] Heb. iii, 6.

[3] Heb. x, 35.

[4] 1 John ii, 1-2.

[5] Augustine, *De ecclesiasticus dogmatibus*, cap. liii (PL 42, 1222). The book is attributed to Gennadius.

[6] Prov. iii, 12.

[7] Valdés states that this delight is one of the marks of true piety in his *110 Divine Considerations*, Consid. XLVII, p. 161.

[8] Gal. iii, 26: 1 Cor. iii, 16.

be sealed in the promised Holy Spirit, who is the pledge of our inheritance." [1] See how he shows that the hearts of the faithful are stamped by the Holy Spirit as by a seal, in such a way that he calls the Holy Spirit, the Spirit of promise, because he authenticates the promises of the Gospel.** [2] This, as we have often said, is the good news that promises the remission of sins and eternal life to those who believe that all their sins have been chastised in Christ. According to St. Paul, all of us who believe in Jesus Christ are children of God, [3] and because we are his children, God has sent the spirit of his Son into our hearts, who cries: "Abba, father." [4] St. Paul says to the Romans: "Those who are judged by the Spirit of God are children of God. For you have not received the spirit of bondage once again in fear, but have received the spirit of adoption, through which we cry "Abba, father," the Spirit himself renders witness together with our spirit, that we are children of God, and if we are children, we are also heirs." [5]

One should note that, in these two places, St. Paul speaks most clearly, not of any special revelation, but of the witness that the Holy Spirit commonly renders to all those who accept the grace of the Gospel. If, then, the Holy Spirit makes us certain that we are children and heirs of God, why should we doubt of our predestination? In the same epistle, St. Paul says: "Those whom God has predestined, he has also called; and those he has called, he has justified; and those he has justified, he has also glorified. Then what shall we say to these things? If God is for us, who will be against us?" [6] If I clearly recognize that God has called me, giving me faith and its effects, that is, peace of conscience, mortification of the flesh and vivification of the spirit,[7] either wholly or partly, why should I doubt that I am predestined? Then let us say with St. Paul that all true Christians (that is, all those who believe in the Gospel), do not receive the spirit of this world but the Spirit who comes from God, through whose inspiration they do the things that God has granted them.[8] Is it any wonder then, if we know that God from eternity has given them eternal life? [9]

However, some people say that no one should be so arrogant as to glory in having the Spirit of Christ. They say these things as though the Christian gloried in having gained it through his own merits and

---

[1] Eph. i, 13-14.

[2] This description of the role of the Holy Spirit paraphrases a passage in the 1539 edition of Calvin's *Institutes*. Cf. McNeill edit., I, 584.

[3] Gal. iii, 26.

[4] Gal. iv, 6.

[5] Rom. viii, 14-17.

[6] Rom. viii, 30-31.

[7] For Luther's description of the effects of faith, cf. *Freedom of a Christian*, p. 58. In his *110 Divine Considerations*, Valdés describes mortification of the flesh and vivification of the spirit as the effect of faith; cf. Consid., XIX, XXXIX, pp. 61-65, 135-137.

[8] Cf. 1 Cor. ii, 12.

[9] In this paragraph, Don Benedetto summarizes his argument for the Christian's certainty of his justification and predestination, before he turns to deal with various objections to his position.

not through the mere mercy of God, and as though it were arrogance to confess to being a Christian. They speak as though one can be a Christian without having the Spirit of Christ,[1] or as though we can say, without plain hypocrisy, that Christ is the Lord, or call God our Father, if the Spirit does not move our heart and tongue to utter such a sweet word.[2] Yet those who consider us arrogant because we say that God has given us the Holy Spirit with faith, not only do not prohibit us from saying " Our Father " every day,[3] but they command us to do so. But let them tell me, how can one separate faith from the Holy Spirit, since faith is the Holy Spirit's own work? If it is arrogance to believe that the Spirit of Christ is in us, why does St. Paul command the Corinthians to examine whether they have faith, affirming that they are reprobates if they do not know that Christ is in them?[4] Certainly it is great blindness to make Christians, who dare to glory in the presence of the Holy Spirit guilty of arrogance, for Christianity could not stand firmly without this glorification.[5] But Christ, who cannot lie, says that his Spirit is unknown to the world, and that it is known only by those with whom he dwells.[6] Then let these people become true Christians, cast away their Hebrew minds,[7] and truly embrace the grace of the Gospel; they will realize that Christians have the Holy Spirit, and know that they have it.

But perhaps someone will say that the Christian cannot know he is in God's grace without a particular revelation, and consequently he cannot know he is predestined.[8] He could chiefly allege those words of Solomon; "Man does not know whether he is worthy of hate or love,"[9] and those of St. Paul to the Corinthians: "I am not aware of anything, nevertheless, in this I am not justified."[10] I think that I have clearly shown above, by means of the words of Holy Scripture, that this opinion is false. It only remains to indicate briefly that these two passages (auttorità), on which the opinion is chiefly based, should not be understood in this sense.

With respect to the statement of Solomon, * although it is not faithfully translated in the usual version, no one is so stupid that if

---

[1] Cf. Rom. viii, 9.

[2] Cf. 1 Cor. xii, 3.

[3] Cf. Matt. vi, 9: Luke xi, 2.

[4] 2 Cor. xiii, 5.

[5] In *Bondage of the Will,* Luther argues that the Christian's knowledge of the immutability of God's will is the mainstay of his faith. Cf. pp. 184-185.

[6] John xiv, 17. This paragraph is similar to a passage in Calvin's 1539 *Institutes*. Cf. McNeill edit., I, 586-587.

[7] Cf. Gal. v, 1-5. Valdés describes Christians who place their faith in the works of the Law, as having a " Hebrew piety. " Cf. his *110 Divine Considerations,* Consid. XCIV, pp. 356-360. Unlike the author, however, Valdés never goes so far as to term Christians with Hebrew minds " false Christians. "

[8] Calvin also argues against this view, which was held by medieval theologians, in a passage first appearing in the 1539 *Institutes*. Cf. McNeill edit., I, 585.

[9] Eccles. ix, 1.

[10] 1 Cor. iv, 4.

he reads all of Solomon's discourse, he cannot clearly see that he wants to say: If anyone wishes to judge whether God loves or hates him by the occurrences of this present life, he strives in vain, because the same things happen to the just and the impious, the sacrificer and the abstainer, the good man and the sinner. From this one gathers that God does not always show his love to those to whom he grants external prosperity, and he does not always show his hatred to those whom he afflicts. Does it seem to you, most dear brother, that one should conclude that man cannot be certain of the grace of God, because this certainty cannot be understood in terms of the various happenings of transitory and temporal affairs? A little before, the same Solomon says that one cannot distinguish the difference between the soul of a man and that of a beast, because one sees the man and the beast die in the same way.[1] On account of this external accident, shall we conclude that our belief in the immortality of the soul is founded only on conjecture? But it is excessive to weary oneself over such a clear matter.** [2]

With respect to the words of St. Paul, I say that, in speaking of the administration of the Gospel, he says he does not know that he has made any mistakes, but, in spite of this, he is not at all certain that he has completely fulfilled his duty, and that in this respect he has obtained the praise of justice from God, like the person who has done all that is just and proper for a faithful steward. In the same way, when a just and discreet majordomo speaks about his office, he would not dare to justify himself and maintain that he has completely fulfilled his duty and the will of his Lord, but he would leave the entire decision to the Lord. No one who reads and reflects well on the preceding and following words will doubt that this is the sense of St. Paul's teaching. I know well that some who expound St. Paul's words say that, even though he did not recognize any sin in himself, nevertheless he did not know that he was just before God, because, as David maintains, no one can know his own sins perfectly.[3] However, they do not notice that St. Paul does not base justice on works but on faith,[4] and that he rejects all his own justice, embracing only the justice that God gives through Christ.[5] They also do not consider that he was most certain he would be justified, if he preserved his Christian faith pure and entire, and he knew that the crown of this justice was prepared for him in heaven.[6] He was certain that no creature, whether of heaven, earth or hell, was strong enough to separate him from the love of God,[7] and

---

[1] Cf. Eccles. iii, 19.

[2] This paragraph paraphrases Calvin's interpretation of the same text. Cf. McNeill edit., I, 585-586. Cf. also Melanchthon's discussion of this text, in *Loci Communes*, p. 211.

[3] Cf. Psalm xviii, 13.

[4] Cf. Rom. iii, 28: v, 1.

[5] Phil. iii, 9.

[6] 2 Tim. iv, 8.

[7] Cf. Rom. viii, 38-39.

he wanted to die, because he knew that he had to be with Christ.[1] All these things would have been false, if he had not been certain that he was just through faith and not through works. Therefore, most beloved brethren, let us cease making St. Paul say what he never thought, rather what he always most bitterly opposed, for he reprimanded those who measured justification by works and not by faith in Christ our Lord.

Other than these two passages (auttorità) of Solomon and St. Paul, they could cite some other places in Holy Scripture that exhort man to fear, which seems to be contrary to the certainty of predestination. If I wanted to explain all these places in detail, it would be too lengthy, but, in general, I say that criminal fear is proper to the Old Testament and filial love is proper to the New. St. Paul testifies to this when he says to the Romans: "You have not received the spirit of bondage again in fear, but the spirit of adoption through which we cry "Abba, father."[2] He also says to Timothy that God has not given us the spirit of fear, but the spirit of power and love.[3] According to the promises made through the mouths of his prophets, God has given us Christ and freed us from the hand of our enemies, so that we can serve him without fear in holiness and justice in his presence all the days of our life.[4] From this and many other similar places in Holy Scripture, one clearly gathers that criminal and servile fear is not proper for the Christian. This is also confirmed for us, in that this fear is contrary to spiritual joy, which is proper for the Christian, as St. Paul clearly demonstrates to the Romans, when he says that the kingdom of God is justice and peace and joy in the Holy Spirit,[5] namely, that whoever enters into the kingdom of evangelical grace is justified by faith, and consequently enjoys the peace of conscience that produces a perfect spiritual and holy joy. Thus St. Paul often exhorts Christians to always live joyfully[6] and St. Peter says that those who believe in Christ rejoice in an indescribable and glorified joy, even though they are afflicted by various temptations.[7]

Therefore, when Holy Scripture threatens and frightens Christians, they should understand that it is speaking to the licentious Christians, who do not observe the decorum of God's children. These people should be treated like slaves and held in fear until they taste how sweet the Lord is, and faith produces its effects in them, and they have enough filial love to maintain them in the decorum of Christian piety and in the imitation of Christ.[8] When the same Scripture exhorts true

---

[1] Cf. Phil. i, 23.
[2] Rom. viii, 15.
[3] 2 Tim. i, 7.
[4] Luke i, 70, 74-75.
[5] Rom. xiv, 17.
[6] Phil. iv, 4.
[7] Cf. 1 Peter i, 6, 8.
[8] Here the author reiterates these Valdesian themes, that he expounded earlier, see above, pp. 72, 74-77.

Christians to fear, it does not mean that they must fear the judgement and the wrath of God, as though he were about to condemn them. As we have already said, they know that God has called and elected them (and this through his mere mercy and not through their own merits), because of the testimony that the Holy Spirit renders to their spirit. Thus, they do not doubt in the least that through his mercy he will maintain them in the happiness, to which he has called them. Scripture does not exhort them to servile but to filial fear, namely, that like good sons they should take care not to offend Christian piety, to commit any act against the decorum of the children of God, and to sadden the Holy Spirit, who dwells in us.[1] It also exhorts us that, since we recognize the depravity of our nature, we should always be attentive and vigilant and never rely upon ourselves; for in our flesh and mind dwell appetites and affections that, as enemies of the spirit, always lay traps for us and strive to make us proud, ambitious, avaricious and sensual.[2] It is this fear to which Scripture exhorts true Christians, who have already tasted how sweet the Lord is, and who make every effort to imitate Christ; and as they cast off the old man, they start to shed this holy fear. However, good Christians should never completely shed this filial fear, which is most compatible with Christian charity, whereas servile fear cannot exist with it.

Through what has been said, one can clearly understand that the pious Christian does not have to doubt concerning the remission of his sins or the grace of God. Nevertheless, in order to satisfy the reader more, I would like to add some passages (alcune auttorità) from the holy doctors, who confirm this truth. In the fifth canon of *On St. Matthew*, St. Hilary says that God wants us to hope without any wavering of an uncertain will, for otherwise, if faith itself is doubtful, one does not obtain justification through it.[3] Here you see that, according to Hilary, man does not obtain the remission of his sins from God, unless he believes without any doubt that he will obtain it. This is rightfully so, for the man who doubts is like a wave on the sea, which is beaten and agitated by the winds, and consequently he should not expect to receive anything from God.[4]

Let us listen to St. Augustine, who teaches us in his *Manual* how to drive out the foolish thought that would deprive us of that pious and holy certainty: "Let foolish cogitation," he says, "mutter as much as it wants, saying: 'And who are you? and how great is that glory? with what merits do you hope that you should obtain it?' I confidently reply: 'I know him in whom I believe; I know that through his great charity he has made me his son; I know that he is truthful in his pro-

---

[1] Cf. Eph. iv, 30.

[2] Luther stresses the dichotomy of flesh and spirit and the dying to the old man in his *Freedom of a Christian*, pp. 53-54. Valdés does the same in his *110 Divine Considerations*, Consid. XIX and XXVI, pp. 61-65 and 89-94, and in the *Alfabeto Christiano*, p. 109.

[3] Cf. Hilary, *Commentarium in Evangelium Matthei*, cap. v, 6 (PL 9, 944-945).

[4] Cf. James i, 6-8.

mises, able to give what he promises and to do what he wishes. If I think of the death of the Lord, the multitude of my sins cannot make me afraid. All my hope is in his death; it is my merit, my refuge, my salvation, my life and my resurrection. The mercy of the Lord is my merit, and as long as the Lord is not lacking in mercy, I am not poor in merit. If the mercies of the Lord are many, so are my merits; and the more powerful he is to save, the more secure I am.' "[1] When the same Augustine speaks elsewhere with God, he says that he would have despaired on account of his great sins and his infinite negligences, if the Word had not been incarnated. Then he adds these words: "All my hope, all the certainty of my trust is placed in his precious blood, which has been shed for us and for our salvation. In him I breathe. Confiding myself in him, I desire to come unto you, Father, not possessing my own justice but that of your Son, Jesus Christ."[2] In these two places, St. Augustine clearly shows that the Christian ought not to hesitate but to be certain of his justification, basing this not on his own works, but on the precious blood of Christ, which cleanses us from all our sins and reconciles us with God.

In the first sermon of *The Annunciation of the Lord*, St. Bernard says most explicitly that it is not enough to believe that you cannot have the remission of sins, unless God grants it; that you cannot have any good desires or actions, unless he bestows them on you; and that you cannot merit eternal life with your own works, unless it is also given to you as a gift. In addition to these things, which must be considered rather as an uncertain beginning and foundation of faith, St. Bernard says that you must also believe that your own sins are remitted by him.[3] Here then you see how this holy man confesses that it is not enough to believe in general about the remission of sins, but you must believe in particular that your iniquities are remitted by Christ. The reason for this is ready, namely that, since God has promised you justification through Christ's merits, if you do not believe that you are justified through them, you make God a liar, and consequently you make yourself most unworthy of his grace and liberality.

You will say to me: "I really believe in the remission of sins and I know that God is truthful, but I doubt that I am worthy of such a great gift." I reply to you that the remission of sins would not be a gift and a grace but a payment, if God granted it to you because of the worth of your works. But, I repeat that God accepts you as just and does not impute your sin to you, through the merits of Christ, which are given to you and become yours through faith. Therefore, following St. Bernard's saintly advice, do not believe only in general of the remission of sins, but apply this belief to your own case, and believe without doubt that through Christ all your iniquities are par-

---

[1] Augustine, *Manuale*, cap. xxiii (PL 40, 961).
[2] *Ibid.*, cap. xiii (PL 40, 957).
[3] Bernard, *Sermones de sanctis, In Festo Annuntiationis Beatae Mariae Virginis.* Sermo I, 1, 3 (PL 183, 383-384).

doned. In this way, you will glorify God by confessing he is merciful and truthful, and you will become just and holy in God's sight, because the justice and sanctity of Jesus Christ is imparted to you through this faith and confession.

Turning now to the discussion of predestination, I say that from what has been said above, one understands clearly that the certainty of predestination does not harm true Christians, but profits them highly. It does not seem to me that it can harm reprobates and false Christians, because, although men so constituted would strain to make themselves believe that they are among the number of the predestined, they could never persuade their consciences, which would always cry out. Yet it seems indeed that the doctrine of predestination may harm them, because they are in the habit of saying: "If I am one of the reprobates, what do good works profit me? If I am one of the predestined, I will be saved without tiring myself out in good works." I briefly reply to you that with diabolical arguments like those, they increase the wrath of God against themselves, for he has revealed the knowledge of predestination to Christians, in order to make them fervent and not apathetic in the love of God, alert and not slow in good works.[1] Thus, on one hand, the true Christian believes with certainty that he is predestined to eternal life and must be saved, not through his own merits certainly, but through the election of God, who has predestined us, not through our own works but in order to show his mercy. On the other hand, he pays attention to good works and to the imitation of Christ, as if his salvation depended on his own industry and diligence.[2] But whoever refrains from doing good because of the doctrine of predestination, saying: "If I am predestined, I will be saved without the effort of good works," clearly demonstrates that he is not acting out of the love of God, but out of self-love. Perhaps his works were good and holy in the sight of men, but in the sight of God, who looks at his intention, they were wicked and abominable. From this one can gather that the doctrine of predestination profits rather than harms false Christians, because it reveals their hypocrisy, which cannot be healed while it stays concealed under the cloak of exterior works.

But I wish that those who say: "I do not want to act well, because if I am predestined, I will be saved without my efforts," would tell me why, when they are sick, they do not say: "I do not want either doctor or medicines, because what God has determined for me cannot fail". Why do they eat? Why do they drink? Why do they till the earth, plant vines and do all that is advisable to sustain the body with so much diligence? Why do they not say: "All these efforts and labours

---

[1] Calvin similarly discusses the different effects that certainty of predestination has on the elect and on the reprobates in his 1539 *Institutes*; cf. McNeill edit., II, 960-961.

[2] Cf. Pole's advice to Vittoria Colonna, as reported by Carnesecchi: "She should endeavour to believe as if she had to save herself by faith alone, and, on the other hand, attend to works as though her salvation consisted in her works...." (Manzoni, *loc. cit.*, 269).

of ours are superfluous, for is it possible that what God has foreseen and decided about our life and death will not take place?" Therefore, if the providence of God does not make them negligent and lazy in bodily things, why should it make them cowardly and slothful in things pertaining to Christian perfection, which is incomparably more noble than the body? However, we see that the scandal of the reprobates deterred neither Jesus Christ nor St. Paul from preaching the truth afforded for the edification of the elect, for the love of whom Christ was made man and died on the cross. Thus the scandal of false Christians should not hinder us from preaching predestination to true Christians, since we have seen that it contains so much edification.[1]

We have arrived at the end of our discussion, in which our principal aim has been to praise and exalt, in accordance with our limited ability, the stupendous benefit that the Christian has received from Jesus Christ crucified, and to demonstrate that faith of itself justifies, meaning that God receives as just, all those who truly believe that Jesus Christ has satisfied for their sins. However, just as the light is not separable from the flame which burns of itself alone, so good works cannot be separated from faith, which justifies of itself alone. This most holy doctrine, that exalts Jesus Christ and humbles man's pride, was and always will be opposed by Christians who have Hebrew minds. But blessed is he who imitates St. Paul, renounces all his own justification and wants no other justice than that of Christ. Clothed in the garment of this justice, he can appear most confidently in the sight of God, and he will receive from him the blessing and the inheritance of heaven and earth, together with his only-begotten Son Jesus Christ our Lord, to whom be glory for ever and ever. Amen.

---

[1] In his 1539 *Institutes*, Calvin strongly insists on the need to preach predestination in spite of the possibility of scandal; cf. McNeill edit., II, 924-925. Carnesecchi thought that the "ancient doctors" had been cautious about preaching predestination in order not to give scandal to the people (cf. Manzoni, *loc. cit.*, 335).

BIBLIOGRAPHY

I. Original editions of the *Beneficio*.

1. *Trattato utilissimo del beneficio di Giesu Christo crocifisso, verso i Christiani.* Venetiis apud Bernardinum de Bindonis. Anno Do. MDXXXXIII.

   In small 8°, ff. [1], 72, [2]. On the verso of the title-page is a short note " Alli lettori Christiani. " This is the first known edition. Babington discovered a copy and printed a facsimile of it in 1855 (see below, § 24).
   Copy: St. John's College Library, Cambridge.

2. *Trattato utilissimo del beneficio di Giesu Christo crocifisso, verso i Christiani.* Venetiis apud Philippum Stagninum. Anno Do. MDXLVI.

   According to Reumont, the title-page of this edition reads as it is given above, and the work is in small 6° of 70 folios. A copy was discovered in the Royal Library at Stuttgart in 1856 (see A. Reumont, *Bibliografia dei lavori pubblicati in Germania sulla storia d'Italia,* Berlin, 1863, p. 99). E. Böhmer also reported that a copy was at the Imperial Library in Vienna (see *Rivista Cristiana,* X [1882], p. 76).

3. *Trattato utilissimo del beneficio di Giesu Cristo crocifisso, verso i Christiani.* In Venetia.

   E. Böhmer reported an edition with the above title, no date or publisher, in small 8°, ff. [1], 78, [2]; a woodcut of a cross on the title-page, and on the verso, a note " Alli lettori. " It was in the Imperial Library at Vienna (see *Rivista Cristiana,* X [1882], p. 76). B. Wiffen also reported a Venetian edition without date or publisher, possibly a 1546 edition by Paulo Gherardo, at the University Library, Cambridge (see Wiffen's list of editions of the *Beneficio* in M. Young, *The Life and Times of Aonio Paleario,* London, 1860, vol I, Appendix p. 567).

4. *Trattato utilissimo del beneficio di Giesu Christo crocifisso, verso i Christiani.* In Tubinga MDLXV.

   Babington reported this edition with the above title, and on the verso, a note to the reader similar to that of the 1543 Venetian edition, except that at the end is added: " Adesso nuovamente restampata & corretta per Antonio Dalmatino & Stephano Istriano. " In 8°, a copy at the University of Laibach (see Babington, *The Benefit of Christ's Death,* London 1855, Introduction, lxxiv-lxxv). Wiffen also reported that copies of a 1563 Tübingen edition in Italian were at the University of Laibach and the Royal Library in Stuttgart (see M. Young, *op. cit.,* vol. I, Appendix, p. 567).

5. *Trattato utilissimo del benefitio di Giesu Christo, con li misterii del rosario, con l'indulgenza in fine di Papa Adriano alle corone de' grani benedetti.*

   Babington reported that this curious title appeared in the 1590 Index of Sixtus V (see *Die Indices Librorum Prohibitorum des sechzehnten Jahrhunderts*, gesammelt und herausgegeben von F. H. Reusch [Tübingen, 1886], p. 518).

6. According to the Compendium of the Inquisitors (see Young, *op. cit.*, vol. I, pp. 333-334), there were several Modenese editions, published by Antonio Gadaldino. However, none is extant, and we have no further information about them.

7. *Du Benefice de Jesus Christ crucifié envers les Chrétiens, traduit de vulgaire Italien en François.*
   A Lyon, par Jehan de Tournes, 1545.

   According to Babington, this title appears in the *Censura* of 1551 of the Theological Faculty of Paris, in the "Catalogus librorum Gallicorum ab incertis auctoribus" (see Babington's Introduction, lxxv). No copies of this edition are extant.

8. *Du benefice de Jesus Christ crucifié, envers les Chrestiens. Traduict de vulgaire Italien, en langage Françoys. Plus, Une traduction de la huytiesme Homelie de sainct Jean Chrysostome, De la femme Cananée: mise de Latin en Françoys. Venez à moy vous tous qui travaillez & estes chargez, & ie vous soulageray.* 1552.

   Babington printed a facsimile of the title-page of this edition. He reports that "it consists of 64 leaves in 12mo, which are numbered, the printer's signatures extending from A to H in eights," and that it was done at Lyons, probably by Johan de Tournes. There is a preface of the translator "A t'ous les Chrestiens qui sont dessoubz le ciel." (See Babington's Introduction, lxxv-lxxvi, and his reprint of this edition).

9. *The treatice most proffitable of the benefitte that true christianes receyve by the dethe of Jesus Christe.* 1548.

   Babington describes in detail this translation made directly from the Italian by Edward Courtenay, Earl of Devonshire, and dedicated to "the right vertuous Lady and gratious princes, Anne Duches of Somerset." Two of the pages contain additions in the hand of Edward VI. (See his Introduction, lxxx-lxxxv and his printing of this translation).

   Copy: in ms. at the Library of the University of Cambridge.

10. *The Benefite that Christians receive by Jesus Christ Crucifyed. Translated out of French into English, by A. G.*
    1573. Imprinted at London for Lucas Harison and George Bishop.

    In small 8º, unpaginated. It contains a note to the English reader in italics, followed by the preface of the French translator. On the last leaf, the colophon: "Imprinted at London by Thomas East for Lucas Harison & George Bishop." The English translator is probably Arthur Golding, who translated many religious works and classics into English for various noble patrons. Babington reprints a facsimile of the title-page (see his Introduction, lxxvii-lxxix).

    Copies: Houghton Library, Harvard University. STC 6699.
    British Museum. 4226 a.a. 33.

11. *The Benefite that Christians receive....*
H. Bynneman for L. Harison and G. Bishop. London.

In 8°, probably printed in 1575. The British Museum Catalogue does not give the full title. Babington also cites an undated English edition (see his Introduction, lxxviii).

Copy: British Museum 4226 a.a. 34.

12. *The benefit that Christians receive by Jesus Christ crucified. Translated out of French into English by A. G.* 1577.
Imprinted nigh unto the three Cranes in the Vintree for Lucas Harrison and G. Byshop.

Babington cites this edition from an eighteenth-century source, which adds that the edition contains both the French and English prefaces (see his Introduction, lxxviii). No copies are extant.

13. *The benefit that Christians receive by Jesus Christ crucified* etc.
1580. T. Dawson for George Bishop and T. Wodcocke. 'Quarto.'
Babington cites this title from another source (see his Introduction, lxxix). The British Museum Catalogue does not give the title but cites the edition as 8°.

Copy: British Museum c. 37, a. 50.

14. *The Benefite of Christs Death, or the glorious Riches of Gods free Grace, which every true beleever receives by Jesus Christ, and him crucified. First compiled and printed in the Italian tongue: And afterwards translated and printed in the French tongue: And out of French into English, by A. G. 1 Cor. 2. 2. For I determined not to know anything among you, save Jesus Christ and him crucified. Phil 3. 8. Yea doubtlesse I count all things but losse, for the excellent knowledge sake of Christ Jesus. The Third Edition.*
London, Printed by I. L. for Andrew Hebb dwelling at the signe of the Bell in Pauls Church-yard. 1633.

According to Babington, this edition is in 12° of 106 pages, and it has the preface of the English translator. Babington prints a facsimile of the title-page (see his Introduction, lxxix).

Copies: Cambridge University Library.
Worcester College, Oxford.

15. *The Benefit of Christs death.... The Fourth Edition.*
London, Printed by E. G. for Andrew Hebb, dwelling at the signe of the Bell in Saint Pauls Churchyard, 1638.

In small 8°, pp. [4], 106. The title is exactly the same as the 1633 edition, and it has the note of the English translator. Babington prints a facsimile of its title-page.

Copies: Biblioteca Nazionale, Firenze, (Guicciardini) 2-4²-54.
British Museum 4225. df. 53.

16. *Tratado utilissimo del beneficio de Jesu Christo.*

Babington cites this Spanish version from several Indexes of prohibited books (see his Introduction, lxxvii). No copies are extant (see Reusch, *op. cit.*, "Index des spanischen generalinquisitors Quiroga von 1583," p. 440).

17. *Beneficium Christi.*
Tübingen [Urach], Primus Truber & Hans Ungnat von Sonneck, 1563.

A copy of this edition, offered for sale in 1963, was described as follows by the dealer: in Croatian, printed in Glagolithic type; 86, [2] ff., small woodcut of crucifixion on title surrounded by a woodcut border, 8°. (See Lathrop C. Harper, Catalogue N. 19, N.Y., N.Y.). According to Badalic, this edition is a translation from the original 1543 Venetian edition, and a note in the work adds that it was revised by Antonio Dalmatino and Stephano Istriano. (See J. Badalic, *Jugoslavia usque ad annum MDC*, (Bibliographica Aureliana II) Baden-Baden, 1960, n. 98, p. 71). Wiffen reported that there was also a copy of a 1563 Croatian edition in Cyrillic script at the University of Laibach (see Young, *op. cit.*, vol. I, Appendix, p. 567).

Copies: Öffentliche Bibliothek der Universität Bäsel.
Staats und Universitätsbibliothek, Hamburg.
Universitätsbibliothek, Jena.
Univerzitetna knjiznica, Ljubljana (Laibach).
Bibliothèque Nationale, Strasbourg.
Landesbibliothek, Stuttgart.
Universitätsbibliothek, Tübingen.

18. *Beneficium Christi.*
Tübingen, 1565.

According to Badalic, this Croatian edition is in 8°, in Roman characters, 68 ff. (See J. Badalic, *op. cit.*, n. 116, p. 87). Babington notes that the preface is similar to that of the 1543 Venetian edition, except for the added note that it was revised and translated by Antonio Dalmatino and Stephano Istriano (see Babington's Introduction, lxxxvi-lxxxvii).

Copy: Univerzitetna knjižnica, Ljubljana (Laibach).

19. German version of 1614.

Reumont and Wiffen mention a German translation of 1614 printed at "New-Hanaw," that was found in the Royal Library of Berlin (see Reumont, *op. cit.*, p. 99 and Young's Appendix).

II. Modern editions of the *Beneficio*.

20. *The Benefit of Christ's Death; or, the Glorious Riches of God's Free Grace, which every true believer receives by Jesus Christ, and him crucified.* Originally written in Italian by Aonio Paleario and now reprinted from an ancient English translation; with an Introduction by the Rev. John Ayre. London. The Religious Tract Society.

This edition is a reprint of the fourth English edition of 1638 (see § 16), with corrected Scriptural references, and patristic citations added. It was the first modern printing of the *Beneficio* in any form; the British Museum Catalogue gives the date of publication as 1847. According to Sampson Low's Catalogue, a new edition appeared in 1851 (see *The English Catalogue of Books published from January, 1835 to January, 1863*, compiled by Sampson Low, London, 1864, p. 580)

Copies: British Museum 4419. d. 32.
Andover-Harvard Theological Library.
Biblioteca Nazionale, Firenze, (Guicciardini), 2-4²-53; 20-2-48.

21. *Benefizio della morte di Cristo di Aonio Paleario.*
Pisa: Tipografia Nistri, 1849.

According to Chiminelli, this edition was a translation of Ayre back into Italian, done by "ex-priest A" (see P. Chiminelli, *Bibliografia della Storia della Riforma Religiosa in Italia,* Rome, 1921, p. 153).

Copies: British Museum. 4255. b. 60.
Biblioteca Nazionale, Firenze (Guicciardini), 2-5-31.
Facoltà Valdese, Rome, 463-11-int. 2; XVI-60-5.

22. *Benefizio della morte di Cristo di Aonio Paleario.*
Florence: 1849.

According to Chiminelli, this was a translation from Ayre back into Italian, which differed from the Pisan edition; it was made by Stanislao Bianciardi (see Chiminelli, *op. cit.*, p. 153).

Copies: Library of Congress, Washington.
Biblioteca Nazionale, Firenze (Guicciardini), 2-5-32.

23. *Benefizio della morte di Cristo di Aonio Paleario.* Sull'edizione di Firenze.
W. Tarn, 56 Paternoster Row, London.

This edition was based on the Florentine edition of 1849 (see above, § 22), but its introduction was copied from the slightly-earlier Pisan edition (see above, § 21). According to the British Museum Catalogue, the date of publication was probably 1855. There is a variant of this edition in the Guicciardini collection; its frontiepiece lacks the acknowledgement to the Florentine edition, and gives the publisher as W. Jones, but with the same address. This also cited in Wiffen's list (see Young, *op. cit.*, p. 567).

Copies: British Museum. 3900. bb. 9 (3).
Biblioteca Nazionale, Firenze (henceforth noted as B. N. F.), (Guicciardini), 2-5-33.

24. *The Benefit of Christ's Death: probably written by Aonio Paleario....* With an Introduction, by Churchill Babington.
London: Bell and Daldy. Cambridge: Deighton, Bell & Co., 1855.

This is the most important modern edition of the *Beneficio.* In it Babington prints a facsimile of the original Venetian edition of 1543 (see § 1); he also reprints the Lyons translation of 1552 (see § 8) and the ms. translation into English of 1548 (see § 9). It includes a valuable introduction, bibliography, and notes.

Copies: British Museum. 3901. c. 31.
Andover-Harvard Theological Library.
Facoltà Valdese, Rome. W-XVI-60-22.

25. *Von der Wohltat Christi.* Das hochberühmte Römische Zeugniss aus dem Zeitalter der Reformation für die Rechtfertigung durch den Glauben. Nach vermeintlicher gänzlicher Vernichtung neulichst zu Cambridge wieder aufgefunden, unter Anfügung des italienischen Originaltextes ins Teutsche übertragen und bevorwortet von einem evangelischen Doctor der Theologie.
Leipzig: Dörffling und Franke. 1855.

Tischendorf made the translation from the proofs of the facsimile sent to him by Babington. Two more editions followed within a year. Wiffen mistakenly says they are all in Italian. The titles for this edition and the five listed directly below were taken from Christian Gottlob

Kayser, *Index Locupletissimus Librorum.... Voilstandiges Bucher-Lexicon, 1853-1858, A-Z, Dreizehnter Theil.* Bearbeitet und herausgegeben von Gustav Wilhelm, Wuttig, Leipzig, 1860, p. 171.

26. *Von der Wohltat Christi.* Das hochberühmte Römische Zeugniss aus dem Zeitalter der Reformation für die Rechtfertigung aus dem Glauben von A. P. Nach vermeintlicher gänzlicher Vernichtung wiederaufgefunden, von einem evang. Doktor der Theologie der deutschen Kirche übergehen, und ausgestattet mit einer ausführlichen historischen Einleitung. Vierte revidirte Ausgabe.
Leipzig: 1856.

A fifth and sixth revised edition with the same title appeared respectively in 1856 and 1857.

Copies: British Museum. 3901. c. 46 (2), (fifth revised edition).
B.N.F. M. 3330.-.10. (fifth revised edition).
Bibliothèque Nationale, Paris, D^2 16509 (sixth revised edition).

27. *Das wieder gefundene Büchlein: Von der Wohlthat Christi.* Aus dem Italienischen übersetzt von Erich Stiller.
Hamburg: Kittler, 1856.

This edition and the three listed below were new German translations made from Babington's facsimile of the original Venetian edition (see above, § 24).

28. *Das wieder gefundene Büchlein: Von der Wohlthat Christi.* Aus dem Italienischen übersetzt und mit einer historischen Einleitung versehen von Erich Stiller. Zweite Auflage. Erste Stereotyp Auflage.
Hamburg: 1856.

29. *Das Büchlein von der Wohlthat des Kreuzes Christ.* Aus dem Italienischen. Nach der in Venedig 1543 erschienenen und in London wieder abgedruckten Ausgabe. Von P. G. Kind.

Chur: Grubenman, 1856.

30. *Die hochnützliche Schrift von der Wohlthat Jesus Christi des Gekreuzigten gegen die Christen.* Im Jahre 1543 zu Venedig herausgegeben. Treu aus dem Italienischen übertragene. Stereotyp Auflage.
Stuttgart: I. F. Steinkopf, 1856.

31. *A Paleario Over de Weldaad van Christus.* Mit inteidung untr den Auteur.
Amsterdam: 1856.

Wiffen cites this title, which is supposed to be the first Dutch edition (see Young, *op. cit.*, p. 567).

32. *Le bienfait de Jésus-Christ crucifié envers les Chrétiens.* Ouvrage célèbre du XVIe siècle recemment retrouvé a Cambridge. Traduit de l'Italien et précédé d'une Introduction historique par L. Bonnet, pasteur.
Lausanne: Georges Bridel Éditeur, Paris: Grassart Libraire Éditeur, 1856.

Wiffen also mentions a French translation of 1856 published at Vevay, but I have been unable to verify it.

Copy: B. N. F. (Guicciardini), 2-5-30.

33. *Trattato del benefizio della morte di Cristo.*
Nice: Coisson e Comp., 1857.

Cited from the *Catalogo Generale della Libreria Italiana dall'anno 1847 a tutto il 1899,* compilato dal Prof. Attilio Pagliaini, Milan, 1901, vol. A-D, p. 742. (The entry is under Della Paglia, Paleario's original name).

Copy: Facoltà Valdese, Rome. W-XVI-60-6, 2.

34. *Bienfaits decoulant de la mort de Christ.*
Toulouse: Société des livres religieux, 1857.

Three reprintings of this edition appeared in 1859 and 1860.

Copy: Bibliothèque Nationale, Paris. D^2 5970.
(The reprintings, D^2 5971-5973).

35. *The Benefit of Christ's Death; or, the Glorious Riches of God's Free Grace, which every true believer receives by Jesus Christ, and him crucified.* Originally written in Italian, and attributed to Aonio Paleario; now reprinted from an ancient English translation: with an Introduction by the Rev. John Ayre.
London: The Religious Tract Society.

According to the Library of Congress Catalogue, this edition, with its slightly changed title (cf. § 20), appeared in 1859. However, its title indicates that it is a reprint of the 1638 English editon, rather than the original 1573 edition, as the Catalogue states.

Copy: Library of Congress.

36. See §. 20 for title.
Boston: Gould and Lincoln, 1860.
New York: Sheldon and Company, 1860.

Copies: Library of Congress.
Harvard College Library.

37. *Beneficium Christi.* Benefit of Christ's Death; or, the Glorious Riches of God's Free Grace, which every true believer receives by Jesus Christ, and him crucified. Originally written in Italian and attributed to Aonio Paleario; now reprinted from an ancient English translation. With a historical sketch of the book and its writer.
Philadelphia, Presbyterian publication committee.
New York, A. D. F. Randolph.

According to the Library of Congress Catalogue, this edition appeared in 1860, and its title indicates that it is a reprint of the 1638 English edition, rather than of the original 1573 translation, as the Catalogue indicates.

Copy: Library of Congress.

38. *Trattato utilissimo del beneficio di Giesu Christo crocifisso, verso i Christiani* [Edited by Piero Guicciardini].
London: The Religious Tract Society, Turin: Un. Tip. Edit., 1860.

According to Gonnet, this edition is an exact reprint of the Italian text given in Babington's facsimile (see *Bolletino della Socierà di Studi*

Valdesi, 1943, no. 79, p. 30), but the editor has modernized the authography somewhat, as is indicated on the title-page.

Copy: B. N. F. (Guicciardini), 2-5-33.

39. *Bienfait decoulant de la mort de Christ.*
Paris: Librairie française et étrangère, 1864.

Copy: Bibliothèque Nationale, Paris, D[2] 5974.

40. *Court résumé du célèbre traité sur le bienfait de la mort de Jésus-Christ.... par Aonio Paleario*, publié en Italien en 1543.
Saint-Ètienne: Cellier, 1871.

Copy: Bibliothèque Nationale, Paris. D. 60854.

41. *Compendio del celebre trattato del Beneficio di Gesu Christo crocifisso verso i Christiani, di Aonio Paleario*, pubblicata per la prima volta nel 1842.

Milano: Tipi della Società Cooperativa, 1871.

Copy: B. N. F. 3289.4

42. *Trattato utilissimo del Beneficio di Cristo....*
Rome-Florence, 1887.

Copy: Facoltà Valdese, Rome. W-463-13-int. 3; XVI-60-6.

43. *Trattato utilissimo del beneficio di Giesu Christo crocifisso, verso i Christiani*, edited by Giuseppe Paladino, in *Opuscoli e lettere di Riformatori Italiani*, I, 1-60.
(Scrittori d'Italia, no. 58) Bari: Laterza e Figli, 1913

This edition is a slightly modernized version of the 1543 Venetian edition, taken from the Babington facsimile.

Copy: Harvard College Library, etc.

44. *Dal trattato utilissimo del beneficio...*, edited by E. Paschetto.
Turin: Il Seminatore, 1941.

Copy: Facoltà Valdese, Rome. W-463-13-int. 2.

45. *Beneficio di Cristo.* Introduzione e note di Mariano Moreschini.
Rome: La Casa Editrice Religio, 1942.

According to Gonnet, this text was made from the 1860 Guicciardini edition, but it has been quite modernized (see *Bolletino della Società di Studi Valdesi*, 1943, no. 79, p. 30). In this edition the author was given as Benedetto Luchino, due to the attribution made by Benedetto Croce in a 1940 article (see *La Critica*, XXXVIII (1940), pp. 115-125).

Copy: Facoltà Valdese, Rome. W-XVI-60-8.

46. *Del Beneficio de Cristo crucificado*, por un reformador italiano anonimo.

(Obras Clas. de la Ref. IV) Buenos Aires: Editorial "La Aurora".

GEORGE HUNTSTON WILLIAMS

CAMILLO RENATO (*c.* 1500- ? 1575)

INTRODUCTION

In the history of religious philosophy three views of immortality have been distinguished.[1] The first view has been called individual immortality *by* the *grace* of God; the second, associated with Averroes (d. 1198), universal but impersonal immortality by nature; and the third, a modification of the last and associated anciently with Plato and in altered formulation with Avicenna (d. 1037), individual immortality *by nature*. In the opening of the Reformation Era the common Christian view of individual immortality by grace (the first view above) had here and there, under the influence of Renaissance Platonism, given way to a belief in a natural immortality of man (the third view above). It was, in any event, on the premise of either individual immortality by grace or by nature that the papal Church militant exercised sway over the vast realm of the suffering Church of purgatory. The V Lateran Council ending in 1517 had confirmed this position; and normative Protestantism, for the most part, perpetuated the traditional Catholic view of immortality, although it eliminated purgatory and otherwise modified the doctrine of the afterlife in the perspective of its strong emphasis upon election, reprobation, and saving faith.

Over against the main Christian positions in the Reformation Era regarding the soul was that of the psychopannychists, soul sleepers, or mortalists. These eschatologically radical Christians, accepting the natural mortality of man and a more or less prolonged interval of psychic death or quiescence, placed their evangelical hope in a re-creative miracle of God at the resurrection and the second advent of Christ.

During the sixteenth century there were three groups among the exponents of the Radical Reformation who, abandoning the traditional

---

[1] Harry A. Wolfson, " Spinoza and the Religion of the Past, " *Religious Philosophy: A Group of Essays* (Cambridge, 1961), pp. 263 f. See also the whole essay " Immortality and Resurrection in the Philosophy of the Church Fathers, " *ibid.*, pp. 69-103. Part I of the present study was originally written in honor of Professor Wolfson, " Camillus Renatus.... and Individual Immortality by the Grace of Psychic Resurrection, " Jubilee Volumes, edited by Saul Lieberman (Jerusalem, 1963).

At the outset I wish to express my deep appreciation to the editor of this Volume, John Tedeschi, for his immense help in the preparation of this biography of Camillo Renato at several stages of its composition at home and abroad and for the great thoroughness, resourcefulness, and selfless kindliness with which he has gone about the editing of the whole of our Volume in honor of the four hundredth anniversary of the death of Laelius Socinus.

Christian view of the general and immediately realized immortality of the individual sentient soul, devised various forms of psychopannychism.[1] Psychopannychism has come to be the generic term for a complex of sectarian views about the death or sleep of the soul after the death of the body, pending the resurrection of all the dead *or* of the elect alone. The three religious groups espousing psychopannychism in the Reformation Era were the Spiritual Libertines, the Anabaptists, and the Socinians.

All three groups seem to have been directly or indirectly influenced by the speculations emanating from two schools of interpreters of Aristotle in the northern Italian universities of Padua, Bologna, and Ferrara: the Averroists and the Alexandrines. Common to these two schools was the acceptance of the natural *mortality* of the soul. In dependence upon Aristotle, both Averroists and Alexandrines, along with the three major schools of late medieval scholasticism (the Scotists, the Thomists, and the Nominalists) had, of course, in dealing with the soul, to come to terms with Aristotle's distinctions among the faculties of the human soul, namely: the nutritive, the sensitive, and the rational-intellective soul. Within the intellect Aristotle had made a further distinction between the passive or potential intellect and the active intellect (*intellectus agens*).

Aristotle's wording permitted some pagan, Moslem, and Christian interpreters through the centuries to consider the *Intellectus Agens* as a universal and eternal power, *independent* of human bodies, operating on individual perishable, passive intellects. Such was the view, for example, of the Averroists. With the aid of Neoplatonist elements, late medieval Italian Averroists propounded a monopsychism whereby it was possible to salvage an impersonal or universal immortality through the reabsorption of the individual soul, the *anima rationalis*, a transient manifestation of the universal, back into the *anima intellectiva* or *anima mundi* or the primal *Intellectus Agens*. By the end of the fifteenth century, one notable Averroist, Agostino Nifo, in his *De intellectu* of 1492 had gone so far in his conflation of the two intellects, active and passive, that he was able, as an Averroist, to approach the Thomist interpretation of Aristotle and to avow the immortality of the personal, intellectual or rational soul.

The Italian Alexandrines, in contrast to the Averroists, had not gone through a comparable Platonizing and Christianizing process. Followers of Alexander of Aphrodisias, commentator of Aristotle of c. 200 A.D., the Italian Alexandrines constituted a vigorous, new school of naturalistic interpreters of Aristotle, called forth by Girolamo Donato's translation in 1495 of *Liber* I of Alexander's *De Anima.*

---

[1] I have traced the various expressions of psychopannychism, including thnetopsychism and quoted the pertinent decree of the V Lateran Council in *Radical Reformation* (Philadelphia, 1962), pp. 20-24, 104-106, 580-592, and *passim.* Le Roy Edwin Froom, ranking Seventh Day Adventist Church historian, projects a comprehensive history of the doctrine of the provisional sleep of the soul, " Conditional Immortality. "

With this publication began, in fact, the great struggle between the spiritualizing Averroist Aristotelians and the naturalizing Alexandrine Aristotelians, which was to dominate the philosophical debate in the northern Italian universities in the sixteenth century and constitute the background of psychopannychism as a distinctively Italian stress on the radical fringe of the Reformation movement.

From the purely philosophical and often medically trained Averroists and from the often humanistically trained Alexandrines the sectarian psychopannychists differed, of course, markedly. For while the psychopannychists accepted from these two kinds of interpreters of Aristotle as practically and philosophically evident the fact that the personal soul (*anima rationalis*) is extinguished with the death of the body, they would not resort to the purely *nominal* affirmation of immortality as a datum of faith based on revelation and authoritative ecclesiastical tradition, nor would they accept as binding the scriptural arguments advanced rather perfunctorily in the condemnation of the Averroist positions by the V Lateran Council.[1] Instead, the radical reformers of psychopannychist persuasion, yielding to the philosophical-medical argumentation in the northern Italian universities, had recourse to a neglected, minor theme running through the New Testament and the Church Fathers which placed the eschatological hope entirely in the general resurrection as a final re-creative action of God. It is apparent that they related this impending mighty act of God to the ongoing operation of his Holy Spirit as *Creator Spiritus* in the resuscitation of the spirits and the bodies of the elect. In any event, they rejoiced in such a scriptural assurance as I Thessalonians 4: 13-18 that the saintly dead would awake to the sound of the trumpet of God; and in the meantime they vigorously attacked all medieval institutions which rested upon the claim of the Church to control allegedly *sentient* souls in purgatory and to manipulate the supererogatory merits of the saints in paradise.

It is plausible that these Italian, sectarianizing Protestants, in their aknowledgment of the philosophically demonstrable mortality of the rational soul and in their confidence in the regenerative and re-creative work of the Holy Spirit effectuating at the eschaton the restoration of the soul of the spiritually redeeemed after a period of sleep or decomposition with the body, were drawing upon a conflation of minor traditions, one going back to the Church Fathers and another deriving perhaps from Moslem speculation.

The Church Fathers had been aware of the possibility that the Spirit in some scriptural passages might be identified with the *Anima Mundi* of Stoic and Neoplatonist speculation, for example, Wisdom 1:7: "Because the Spirit of the Lord filleth the world." [2] In the development

[1] On the conciliar condemnation of Averroism, see S. Offelli, "Il pensiero del Concilio Lateranense sulla demostrabilità razionale dell'immortalità dell'anima," *Studia Patavina*, I (1954), 7-40.

[2] For a discussion of this possibility, rejected by Augustine, see Harry A. Wolfson, *The Philosophy of the Church Fathers* (Cambridge, Mass., 1956), p. 250.

of Christian Humanism during the Renaissance one could have gone further and identified this Holy Spirit with the *Intellectus Agens*, the more so for the reason that in Moslem tradition since the time of the Sufi Alfarabi (d. 950) the holy Spirit or the friendly Spirit, said in the Koran to have brought down the Koran with truth, [1] was expressly identified with the *Intellectus Agens* or external intellect of Aristotle: "And the Active Intellect is that of which it is appropriate to believe that it is the faithful Spirit and the Holy Spirit." [2]

Radical Italian Protestants, against the background of the Averroist-Alexandrine debates, and drawing further on diverse traditions of medieval religious philosophy, could as Evangelical Rationalists and Spiritualists, ground their psychopannychism, their distinctive eschatological hope, both in New Testament revelation and in philosophical reason, that is, in the regenerative Holy Spirit operative from without upon the spirit within.

Liberated from Catholic ecclesiasticism in the general Protestant upheaval of the century, the sectarian psychopannychists, indigenous to Italy, freely avowing the death of the soul with the body, proclaimed the saving gospel that, by a miracle no less prodigious than creation *ex nihilo*, God would at the end re-create the bodies of the dead or form new bodies and, re-animating them, bring them before him for bliss or punishment according to their merit. Psychopannychism, linked with the doctrine of election, was the Italian counterpart of solafideism in Luther's Germany and of predestination in Calvin's Switzerland as the basic thrust in what proved to be an abortive reformation in the northern Italian city-states and principalities.

In the course of the seventeenth century the psychopannychist hope largely subsided among the Libertines who accommodated themselves completely to the world as a cultured, political faction in advanced circles in Italy, France, and Holland. The same somber hope among the Anabaptists of a much humbler walk of life was gradually mitigated by sentiments flowing in from their Catholic or Protestant environment which tended to revive the expectation of a natural immortality. Alone among the original groups of psychopannychists, the Socinians persisted throughout the seventeenth century and beyond in their radical faith in the eventual re-creation of the ensouled bodies of the saintly dead.

Among the influential figures in the rise of Socinianism was Camillo Renato. He was, according to an orthodox but tolerantly pro-Socinian writer,[3] the *praeceptor*, *dux*, and *informator* of the young Sie-

[1] Sura 26: 193; Sura 16: 104. The Spirit is also identified with the angel Gabriel.

[2] Generously pointed out and translated for me by Professor Harry A. Wolfson in the Hebrew translation of Alfarabi, *Sefer ha-Hathalot* in Z. Filipowski's edition (Leipzig, 1849), p. 2, lines 10-11.

For a discussion of the relationship between the Holy Spirit and the highest in the human intellect, see Philip Merlan, *Monopsychism, Mysticism, Metaconsciousness: Problems of the Soul in the Neoaristotelian and Neoplatonic Tradition* (The Hague, 1963), esp. pp. 97, 145 f.

[3] Such is the Socinian tradition concerning the relationship. See Friedrich Bock, *Historia Antitrinitariorum*, II (Königsberg/Leipzig, 1784), 581.

nese Laelius Socinus who became much concerned about the *quies* of the soul and the final resurrection.[1] Dying in 1562, Laelius left his library and his own writings to his nephew Faustus Socinus, the refounder of the Reformed-Anabaptist Minor Church of Poland and the fountainhead of the Socinian movement. According to an early anti-Socinian writer, " the whole system of religion " associated with the names of Laelius and Faustus Socinus goes back ultimately to Camillo Renato,[2] the seminal but erratic psychopannychist, anabaptist, antitrinitarian.

The proto-Socinian Camillo Renato (*alias* Lisia Phileno *alias* Paolo Ricci) was not " the gentle mystic " idealized in the Socinian tradition. He was, rather, a man of brilliance, daring, duplicity, passion, excess, turmoil, and inconstancy. He is to be classed with others on the margins of the Reformation: Michael Servetus, David Joris, and Bernardino Ochino, all four of whom were chameleon-like figures, readily changing their names. All four sought for a season to camouflage themselves, first in inquisitorial-Catholic society and then in established-Protestant lands. In an age of thousands of martyr pyres, they, like the mythical salamander, flourished close to the flames. A trait common to these four men was their espousal of toleration, never without at least a trace of histrionic self-indulgence.

These four men of the Left Wing of the Reformation are difficult to place, however refined our typology. In fact, the major interest attaching to Camillo Renato, who moved like a storm up the Italian peninsula from Palermo in Sicily to Chur in Switzerland, is that he was genetically and morphologically an important nodal point connecting three branches of the Radical Reformation: Spiritualism, Evangelical Rationalism, and Anabaptism. However, Camillo is of interest not only as a representative figure but also in his own right, especially now that we can with certainty annex to his biography several episodes in which he featured under the names of Lisia Phileno and Paolo Ricci, five times apprehended by the Inquisition. [3]

---

[1] Besides his Confession and his correspondence with John Calvin on the subject, see also his " De resurrectione " as edited by Lech Szczucki, " Z Eschatologii Braci Polsckich, " *Archiwum historii filozofii,* I (1957), 5-41. " De resurrectione " was later translated into Dutch as *Van de opstandinge deeser Lichaamer* and into German as *Von der aufferstehung der Leiber.*

[2] Pietro Domenico Rosi da Porta, *Historia Reformationis Ecclesiarum Raeticarum* (Chur, 1771-1774), I: 2, 86.

[3] The identification of Lisia Phileno and Camillo Renato was first suggested by F. C. Church, *The Italian Reformers, 1534-1564* (New York, 1932), p. 39, n. The identification was virtually proved by Alfredo Casadei, " Lisia Fileno e Camillo Renato, " *Religio,* XV (1939), 356-440 (the fifth and last, undistributed fascicule). The identification was accepted by Delio Cantimori, *Eretici italiani del Cinquecento* (Florence, 1939; German edition, Basel, 1949), with a few amplifications. The present writer has come into epistolary contact with Professor Antonio Rotondò, who is engaged in a study of heresy in Modena and Bologna, from 1540 to 1570, in which Camillo Renato features as an important figure. Professor Rotondò has very kindly shared advance notices of his research, which is now in part published as " Per la storia dell'eresia a Bologna nel secolo XVI, " *Rinascimento,* XIII (December, 1962), 107-154 with 6 plates. As my own work, completed about the same time, has been delayed in publication, it has seemed

The life and thought of Camillo Renato fall into two main phases: i) Paolo Ricci - Lisia Phileno: unfrocked Franciscan humanist of Venice, Bologna, Modena, and Ferrara (*c.* 1500-1542) and ii) Camillo Renato: radical Rhaetian reformer of the Grisons and the Valtellina (1542- ? 1575).

most wise to incorporate some of the salient findings of Professor Rotondò, which will be cited as " Bologna. " The main sources for the career and thought of Ricci-Phileno-Renato are 1) the Bolognese *Carmina* of Ricci-Phileno (see below, p. 118 n. 1); 2) the XLIII Articles presumably prepared by Ricci-Phileno for the Bolognese legate (see below, p. 111 n. 2); 3) the " Apologia " prepared in connection with the trial in Ferrara (see below, p. 139 n. 2); 4) the Abjuration (see below, at p. 121 n. 3); 5) the correspondence of and about Renato preserved in St. Gall (see below, p. 130 n. 7); 6) an anonymous tract in Italian on baptism and the Lord's Supper believed to be by Renato (see below, p. 153 n. 5); 7) the *Credo* or *Professio* in rhyme presented by Renato in the Grisons (see below, p. 162 n. 3); and 8) the *Carmen* composed by Renato in Rhaetia on the anniversary of the burning of Michael Servetus (see below, p. 176). Professor Rotondò's study is based primarily on source 3, of which he projects a critical edition; he also draws upon sources 1, 2, 5, 6, 7 and 8. My own study is based upon sources 3, 4, 5, 6, 7 and 8 and on source 2 only where Rotondò himself, in his notes, quotes 12 of its 43 articles. (The MS is described by Rotondò on p. 111, n. 1. Article 1 is given on p. 121, n. 4; article 13, on p. 117 f., n. 4; articles 15, 16 on p. 115, n. 2; articles 36, 37, 38, 40 on p. 124, n. 3).

Part I

PAOLO RICCI OR LISIA PHILENO: RADICAL FRANCISCAN HUMANIST (*c.* 1500-1542) [1]

The life of Camillo Renato before his capture near Modena in 1540 can be only a sketch with traits drawn from a half dozen personal references in the documentation of the year of his arrest and trial and inferences drawn from the full name as given in the final trial: Lysias Philaenus Paulus Riccius Siculus. [2]

1) THE CAREER OF PAOLO RICCI IN SICILY, NAPLES, AND VENICE (*c. 1500-1538*)

Camillo Renato, henceforth in this Part to be called Phileno, was born presumably as Paolo Ricci between 1500 and 1510 [3] in what had until 1503 been the Aragonese Kingdom of the Two Sicilies, hence

---

[1] I here reproduce in amplified form the early career of Ricci-Phileno-Renato as printed in the Jubilee Volumes in Honor of Harry A. Wolfson, ed. by Saul Lieberman (Jerusalem, 1963).

[2] The " Apologia, " prepared by Phileno while in prison in Ferrara and the Record of the trial at Ferrara constitute a major source for the present study. " Apologia Lisyae Philaeni Pauli Riccij Siculi Ferrariae nomine haereseos detenti, feliciter Hercule II imperante, Duce IV, 1540. " This is MS No. B 1928 in the Biblioteca Comunale dell'Archiginnasio of Bologna. See Albano Sorbelli *et al.*, *Inventari dei Manoscritti delle Biblioteche Italiane*, LXXX (Florence, 1954). The " Apologia " records utterances of Phileno during his trial at Ferrara in December 1540. It will be critically edited and interpreted by Antonio Rotondò in a comprehensive account of the sectarian history of Modena. Professor Rotondò will also publish the complete text of the *Trattato sul Battesimo e sulla Eucaristia*, recently printed in part and identified by Delio Cantimori as a later work of Phileno-Renato. Cf. *Per la Storia degli Eretici Italiani* (Rome, 1937), pp. 47-54.

I am most grateful to Professor and Mrs. Rotondò, the latter an expert palaeographer, for the transliteration of folio 26: " Quod sanctorum nondum in Paradisum animae. " For the rest I am depending upon a microfilm of the text and the immense help of Dr. David Pingree, Research Associate of the Oriental Institute, University of Chicago, and of Professor Josephine Von Henneberg of Boston College.

[3] The date is inferred from Tommasino de' Bianchi detto de' Lancellotti, *Cronaca Modenese*, VI (Parma, 1868), *Monumenti di Storia Patria delle Provincie Modenesi*, VII, 410; Casadei, " Fileno, " p. 369. But the governor, p. 112, n. 3, refers to him in 1540 as " giovane di età. " As for the name Fileno, it might have been *originally* a toponymic. We know of a Dominican house in Calabria elevated to the rank of priory " in locum Fileni " in 1558. See Andreas Frühwert, *Acta capitulorum generalium ordinis Praedicatorum*, V (Rome, 1901), 16; cf. 100 where it is spelled " Filenae. "

the recurrent toponymic Siculus (Siciliano). It is less likely that he was born in the Spanish Kingdom of Sicily (commonly called the Kingdom of Naples) than on the island (called the Vice-royalty = *vicereame*). One could conjecture on the basis of the name of Lysias, which he later assumed, that he had some connection with Syracuse; for the Attic orator Lysias who died c. 380 B. C. was the son of an Athenian metic born in Syracuse.[1] It is also possible that he was born in Messina.[2] But our only specific reference to origins in the documentation points to Palermo [3] and the neighboring province of Trapani as the place of his origin. A Franciscan tertiary [4] of high birth and of the same surname who died in Palermo in 1599 might have been a relation. Presumably our Paolo Ricci Phileno came of a family of means and culture, for he was later to move with ease in the habitations of patricians and nobles. He is described as " a big man and well formed. " [5]

[1] Lysias' father earned his living by making shields.

[2] It should not go unnoticed that the family name Ricci also appears in the records of Messina in our period. Of tantalizing interest is an inquisitional report, dated Palermo 26 June 1569, listing among those reconciled to the Catholic Church in that year a Caterinella Rizo with the notation " que su suego y marido la abian enseñedo la setta luterana. " Her husband was Joan Antonio, a shopkeeper of Messina, possibly an apothecary (*boticario*). Among the heretical views confessed by her were that there is no purgatory and that saints are unable to make intercession. One is tempted to see in her father-in-law a possible relation of our Paolo Ricci who taught the same views. Carlo Garufi, " Contributo alla Storia dell'Inquisizione di Sicilia nei secoli XVI e XVII, " *Archivio Storico Siciliano*, XXVIII (1913-1914), 317.

It is of further interest, in view of Paolo Ricci's strong opposition to the doctrine of purgatory and of his later appeal to the Greek view on this matter, that there were many Greeks in Messina who " ensegnavano non esservi purgatorio " and that among those presumably influenced by their teaching and consequently apprehended by the inquisitors were several members of the third order of St. Francis of Paola. Vito la Mantia, " Origine e vicende dell'Inquisizione in Sicilia, " *Rivista Storica Italiana*, III (1886), 530.

[3] The reference to Palermo is found in the letter of the governor of Modena to the duke of Ferrara, 16 October 1540; Casadei, " Fileno, " pp. 364 f.

[4] Geronimo Riccio (Riccius) of Trapani (1514-1599) who went to Rome in 1544 to be elected procurator general of the order of the Discalced Franciscan Tertiaries. See Giuseppe Mira, *Bibliografia Siciliana*, II (Palermo, 1881), 285 and especially Giuseppe M. di Ferro, *Biografia degli Uomini Illustri Trapanesi*, IV (Trapani, 1850), 138-140. It is not certain whether this " gracious " and " celebrated orator " who wrote the statutes of his order in Italian belongs to the family of the somewhat later Geronimo Riccio, baron of S. Anna. This noble family is known to have had connections with Naples. There are several members of this family, renowned in both branches of law, in literature, and theology, who originated in the town or the province of Trapani and ended their careers in Palermo. The Ricci (Riccio) family originating in the province of Trapani would have been keenly conscious, because of the local monuments and traditions, that their ancestors were once within the maritime empire of Carthage and as such had valiantly fought the Romans. The later assumed name of our very literate Siciliano might have been intended to evoke the memory of both the Grecian (Syracuse) and the Carthaginian (Trapani) beginnings of civilization in Sicily: Lysias, of Syracuse; and Philaenus, of Carthaginian Trapani and Palermo at the other extreme of the storied island. On the heroic Carthaginian brothers Philaeni, see below at p. 116, n. 4.

[5] The description of Phileno as " homo grande, e ben formato " is that of Lancellotti, *Cronaca*, p. 410; cf. that of Alessandro Tassoni, " Cronaca di Modena, " *Monumenti di Storia Patria delle Provincie Modenesi: Serie Delle Cronache*, XV (Modena, 1888), 331; Casadei, " Fileno, " p. 373.

It may have been while he was quite young that Phileno joined the Franciscans. In the first third of the sixteenth century this could have meant theoretically one of five main branches of the Franciscan family, namely, the Observants, the Conventuals, the Third Order of St. Francis, the Hermits of San Francesco of Paola in Calabria (d. 1507), and the Capuchins. Phileno surely had none of the distinctive characteristics of a Capuchin. An eighteenth-century literary historian assumes that he was a Conventual, without adducing reasons.[1] This account is based, in turn, upon a contemporary description[2] which says somewhat curiously that Phileno was " della religion de S. Francesco de Napole." It is just possible that *Napole* is the transcribing editor's misreading of *Paola*; and that we have here a reference to the rapidly rising new order of Calabrian Minimi or Hermits of San Francesco of Paola. This order was particularly given to a strenuous " life of Lent " *throughout the year* and to the defense and alleviation of the poor and downtrodden. There was also a third order of the Minimi. Some of Phileno's traits, like his concern for the poor, his later chronic ill health which could have been caused by excessive fasting in his youth, his eschatology, his reforming zeal, and the fact that he is never in the later hearings and trial identified with any of the older branches of the Franciscan family (who might conceivably have sought to protect him) could be explained by his having as a youth joined the Minimi who, though they spread rapidly from Calabria and Sicily to France,[3] were not at the time of his arrest in Bologna strong in Emilia. It is equally plausible that Phileno could have been a Discalced Tertiary of St. Francis, wearing the distinctive habit with scapular and cord.

At some point in his monastic career Phileno was ordained a priest.[4]

---

[1] Girolamo Tiraboschi, *Biblioteca Modenese*, I (Modena, 1781), 12.

[2] Lancellotti, *Cronaca*, p. 410; Tassoni, " Cronaca, " p. 331; Casadei, " Fileno, " p. 373; letter of vicar to bishop of Modena, 26 October 1540; printed in C. Cantù, *Gli Eretici d'Italia* (Turin, 1866), II, 175, also Casadei, " Fileno, " p. 371, n. 1.

[3] It is just possible that *Palermo* in another source is also a misreading of a manuscript *Paola* and that Phileno-Ricci came from the same family in Calabria which produced at the beginning of the next century a bishop for the joined and diminutive Calabrian sees of Cerenzia and Cariati. One Mauritius Ricci became bishop of these two sees in 1619. Pius Bonifacius Gams, *Series Episcoporum* (Regensburg, 1873), p. 869. Girolamo Marafioti, *Croniche et Antichità di Calabria* (Padua, 1601), folios 112 v; 268 v. Cerenzia, a mere village on the Sila, is not distant from the casale San Fili between Cosenza and Paola. The Castello Melicucco is not far off. On the Sila near Cerenzia is located the mother house of Joachimism, San Giovanni in Fiore. In this same region, in a castle between San Fili and Paola, St. Francis of Paola — devoted to the poor and to extreme austerity " of the life of Lent " throughout the year — founded the order of the Hermits of St. Francis of Assisi called the Minimi, with its mother house above Paola and with thirty-two convents established by his death in 1507. For the castle, near San Fili, see Marafioti, *op. cit.*, folio 168 v. In this same region two thousand Waldensians were put to death on the Sila 10 June 1530. Gertrude Slaughter, *Calabria the First Italy* (Madison, Wisconsin, 1939), p. 270.

[4] That he was ordained is inferred from a later statement that he celebrated the Mass in Modena. Lancellotti, *Cronaca*, p. 410; Casadei, " Fileno, " p. 369. That he was *clericus*, though in secular habit, was argued by Ludovicus Boninus in " Consilia " f. 22 v.

A powerful preacher, he became a master in theology.[1] Presumably it was at the University of Naples that he studied.[2] Here he may have established contact with other learned members of his clan, for several Riccis are attested among the *lectores* at the *Studium* of Naples in this period.[3] Perhaps it was at this point in his career as friar, preacher, and *scholaris*, that Phileno became intensely concerned with the reformation of Christendom and the renewal of the Church.

Phileno left Naples for Padua,[4] and perhaps matriculated at its university.[5] He then went on to Venice where, during the nunciature (1526-28) of Altobello Averoldi (bishop of Pola), he was accused of heresy by several people of ill will, detained, and investigated but not condemned.[6]

As it happens another Paolo Ricci appears at about this time in the Venetian records. This was the converted Jew who served as physician and astrological advisor of Maximilian I and Ferdinand I. It was during the nunciature of Averoldi's successor, Girolamo Aleander, that a certain work of this Austro-Italian Ricci, perhaps his *Apologeticus* on the Cabbala, was sequestered and burned.[7] But we have no record,

---

[1] Lancellotti, *Cronaca*, p. 410; Casadei, " Fileno, " p. 369.

[2] Lancellotti, *Cronaca*, p. 410. Paolo Longo, without documentation, says that Ricci was a professor of theology in Naples. " Études sur la Réforme à Modène au XVI siècle, " *Le Chrétien évangélique*, XXI (1878), 125. Longo goes on to call Ricci the first Protestant martyr of the Modenese Reformation. Also without any documentation, several other modern writers have averred by surmise that Phileno became at this time associated with the circle of Juan de Valdés. But Valdés was not in Naples until 1529 and we know that Ricci was already in Venice by this date (see below at n. 6). It is, however, possible that Ricci-Phileno later established contact with that circle by correspondence and that he even revisited Naples himself. Cf. Carlo Garufi, *op. cit.*, XL (1916), note iii, 313, citing Luigi Amabile, *Il Santo Officio dell'Inquisizione in Napoli* (Città di Castello, 1892), I, 129 f. and 133; and Arturo Pascal, " La Colonia Messinese di Ginevra, " *Bolletino della Società di Storia Valdese*, No. 62 (1934), 121; No. 63 (1935), 37.

[3] Giangiuseppe Origlia, *Istoria dello Studio di Napoli* (Naples, 1753), I, 246; II, 39.

[4] This is inferred from his answer to the inquisitorial question whether he had been held for a hearing in Padua. " Apologia, " folio 53 v, " Respondit [Phileno] numquam Patavii hoc nomine accusatum aut inquisitum fuisse *ante* detentionem Venetam. "

[5] Rotondò proposes eventually to explore the Paduan career of Phileno. He suspects that Phileno was already at work there on his eschatological views. He notes that thus far Girolamo Galateo (c. 1490-1541), who studied at Padua, is one of the very few reformers whose extant writings permit us to document clearly the link between psychopannychism and the Aristotelian discussion of the soul at the University of Padua. " Bologna, " p. 136. Galateo's *Apologia* before the Venetian Senate in 1538 was published in Bologna, February 2, 1541. For the section in it on the sleep of saints and his reference to Aristotle, see the edition and article of Renato Freschi, " Girolamo Galateo e la sua Apologia, " *Studi e Materiali di Storia delle Religioni*, XI (1935), 96 f.

[6] " Apologia, " folio 9 r: " Venetiis de hac questione non fui accusatus ullo pacto neque inquisitus ut in actis petere potestis. " Cf. folio 53 v; Rotondò, " Bologna, " p. 109, n. 1. It is scarcely possible that the hearing would have taken place under Averoldi's earlier nunciature in Venice (1517-1523). For these dates, see F. Gaeta, " Origine e sviluppo della rappresentanza stabile pontificia in Venezia, " *Annuario dell'Istituto Storico per l'età moderna e contemporanea*, IX-X (1957-1958), 40.

[7] Aleander refers to his condemnation of one work by Ferdinand's Ricci in a letter to Pietro Carnesecchi, Franco Gaeta, ed., *Nunziature di Venezia*, I (Rome, 1958), item 58, 7 February 1534, p. 165. Pier Paolo Vergerio, later an associate of Phileno-Renato, deli-

apart from a reference in the later trial in Ferrara, of our Ricci-Phileno's hearing in Venice.

For what was at least a decade, 1528-1538, we lose track of Phileno. It is possible that he stayed on in Venice and came to know Pietro Paolo Vergerio who delivered the funeral oration for Averoldi in 1531, who became papal nuncio himself in Germany in 1533, and who in 1536 began a career as reforming bishop successively of Modrus and Capodistria. Vergerio is mentioned at this point because after his exile, he was to become briefly associated in Rhaetia with Phileno (under the name, Camillo Renato) and to propound there a plan for the political unification of the reformation movement. It is plausible to assume that it was in relatively tolerant Venice, full of Greeks, Armenians, Jews, and the ambassadors and merchants from Lutheran cities and principalities to the north, that Phileno formulated his own grand design: " In pacificanda Germania cum Ecclesia Romana. "[1] It is remotely possible that an oration printed as though delivered at the diet of Speyer in 1529 (and from internal evidence composed in 1528), commonly ascribed to Ferdinand's physician, was actually composed by our Paolo Ricci Phileno as his contribution to the unification of Christendom against the Turk.[2] But this is very unlikely, since the oration appeals primarily to Germanic and ancient Roman patriotism in calling for concerted war on Mohammedanism. Our Ricci-Phileno, from his known views, was not interested in the defense of Christendom by war but rather in the reunification of Christendom

---

vered an oration on the death of Averoldi in 1531. Cf. Franco Gaeta, " Un inedito Vergeriano, " *Rivista di Storia della Chiesa in Italia*, XIII (1959), 397. Gaeta here calls attention to a *miscellanea* manuscript in the Biblioteca Nazionale Marciana, which, besides Vergerio's oration on the death of Nuncio Averoldi, contains a list of heretical writings of the north, from John Hus to Theobald Billicanus, and including Paolo Ricci. After this name, Gaeta mentions the specific works condemned: " Apologetica plures charte e Apologetica intera. " It is possible that we have here a reference to the Austrian Ricci's *Apologeticus.... adversus obtrectatorem Cabbalae sermo*. The condemnation of one of the Austrian Ricci's works only adds interest to the fact that Ferdinand was so basically confident in the worth of his Jewish convert that he on two occasions proposed him to Clement VII as bishop for the see of Trent, first in 1531 and then in 1534. See *Enciclopedia Italiana*, XXIX (1936), 247. For the fact that this Ricci was a physician for Maximillian I as well as Ferdinand I and that he was perhaps responsible for the expulsion of Jews by the former from certain Austrian domains, see Emanuel Baumgarten, *Die Juden in Steiermark* (Vienna, 1903), pp. 28 f. For the numerous writings of the Austrian Ricci, see the catalogues of the British Museum and of the Bibliothèque Nationale, and Christian Gottlieb Jöcher, *Gelehrten-Lexikon*, Ergänzungsband VI (Bremen, 1819), coll. 2095 f.

[1] " Apologia, " folio 35.

[2] The oration, *Ad principes, magistratus, populosque Germaniae in Spirensi conventu habito*, is printed by Marquard Freher, *Germanicarum rerum scriptores*, III (Hanover, 1611), 379-386. Here it is dated as of 1544. For earlier editions, all of which except the first are ascribed to Paolo Ricci, see the catalogues of the British Museum and the Bibliothèque Nationale. For a summary of the contents and for the fact that the address was not actually delivered at Speyer, although in German Ferdinand himself expressed some of the same ideas, see Johannes Kühn, *Deutsche Reichstagsakten*, jüngere Reihe, VII: 1 (Stuttgart, 1935), long note on pp. 552 f.

through direct appeal to the Pope and later through a more radical reformation.

It was Phileno's intention to go to Rome and there, at some early but unidentified moment in his career, confer with "the most reverend and learned cardinals"; for he was initially confident that by restoring the Mass "to its dignity and integrity" rather than by suspending it (as in Reformed lands) "the whole of Christendom (*rem Christianam*) and the mutual concord of the whole Church" might be served. He was certain that the more enlightened prelates in Rome, including the Pope himself, would like to see the way to clearing the Church of its superstitions, both those not hitherto recognized as such and those long tolerated.[1] One of Phileno's basic convictions concerning the renewal of the Church was that the priest and his parishioner should alike be able to give a full and refined account of the articles of faith, including the *beneficium Christi*, the will of God, the Fatherhood of God, and the dignity and institution of the Christian life.[2]

Although Phileno remained intensely concerned with reform, it is certain that "for quite a while" before he was to go on trial (in 1540) he had laid aside the habit of his order and had gone about "per longum tempus" in secular garb. It is probable that it was in Venice that our Siciliano changed his habit from that of a Franciscan to that of gentleman scholar, and his name from Paolo Ricci to Lisia Phileno.[3] Eloquent preacher, proud to the point of vanity, our Siciliano probably thought of himself as Lysias (Lisia) reborn to proclaim the reform in classical cadences. Although his assumed name, Phileno, may have been originally a toponymic (spelled Fileno, more specific than Siciliano in reference to an obscure place in the south unknown to the Bolognese and surely unknown to us), his classical spelling of it as Philaenus is a clear allusion to the two Carthaginian brothers of that name who allowed themselves to be buried alive to mark the extreme boundary of Punic Carthage over against Cyrenaica.[4] That Phileno thought of

---

[1] "Apologia," folio 37 v; Rotondò, "Bologna," pp. 109, 123. On Phileno's only views on the limited power of the Pope, who should not take precedence over God and Scripture but rather interpret them, see *ibid.*, pp. 131 f.

[2] "Apologia," folio 36 r. On what was understood by the *beneficio di Cristo*, see elsewhere in this Volume the translation of the most popular evangelical Italian work of this title (*c.* 1540) edited by Miss Ruth Prelowski.

[3] "Consilia," ff. 22 r, v. For comparison, another friar, Giulio della Rovere of the Austin Hermits, who had likewise studied in Padua and who entered Bologna in the same year as Phileno, quit his frock and went about Bologna under the name of Camillo, even though the would resume it and preach the Lenten sermons in Venice three years later. Emilio Comba, "Giulio da Milano," *La Rivista Cristiana*, XV (1887), 269-277; 304-333; 345-356; esp. p. 276, n. 3 (based on two depositions of May 1539).

[4] The story is told by Sallust, *Bellum Jugurthinum*, 79; repeated by Pomponius Mela, *Chorographia*, i, 31-38; Valerus Maximus, *Memorabilia*, vi, 4; and Pliny, *Naturalis Historia*, v, 4. For the possible significance of the choice of a Carthaginian name, see the reference above to the Tertiary Franciscan Geronimo Riccio (1514-1599) of "Carthaginian" Trapani and Palermo, p. 112, n. 4. Alas, for any theory of a fraternal relationship between these two is the assertion that Geronimo was the first born of the illustrious

himself as an academician and as a rhetorician is clear from our documentation. That he would have allowed himself and any brother in faith to be buried alive to mark and hold the easternmost boundary of a reformed Christendom seems less in character![1]

2) RICCI-PHILENO IN BOLOGNA (*1538-1540*)

Lysias Philaenus or Paulus Riccius, presumably *en route* to Rome, stopped off in Bologna in 1538[2] (at least a decade after his brush with the papal nuncio in Venice), perhaps to try out among the patricians, and the *scholares* of the *Studium* of Bologna, his ideas on the sloughing off of superstition and on the inculcation of religious, moral, and civic reform. "You should," he proclaims, "establish a new life for the Temple of the Holy Spirit and worthy of God. There is no need of going about according to the flesh but rather according to the spirit, showing charity towards all the poor, humanity among all men, gentleness in correcting the sins of others, compassion, and fraternity, observing the laws of society (*civitatis*)."[3] Phileno, who seems at some point to have married, had very specific suggestions to make on relations with one's wife, on keeping peace in the home, on bringing up little girls, on reading at home from the New Testament and otherwise learning what it means to be a Christian.[4]

Unlike a Franciscan under conventual discipline, Phileno appears to have spent a good deal of his time in the homes of Bolognese patricians and nobles, like the Lambertini, Danesi, Biancani, Manzoli, Bolognetti, and Bocchi. He appears to have been accepted in their homes as a moral reformer and as a preceptor of several of their children.[5] Count Cornelio Lambertini, whom Phileno names as one of his hosts, later appears in the Bolognese chronicle as a senator. The *cavaliere* Achille Bocchi, was the center of a literary circle which was soon to be formalized as the famous Accademia Bocchiana. From the library of Giacomo Biancani of Bologna are preserved fifteen manuscript

Aloisio and Agnese. We have postulated for Paolo Ricci (Riccio) Phileno a birth c. 1500, at the latest 1510.

[1] The Paolo Ricci who composed an ideal oration for the diet of Speyer, urging a joint Catholic-Protestant war against the encroachments from the East, could more plausibly have called himself Lysias Philaenus, but the *Ad principes* (cf. p. 115, n. 2) is connected with the name Riccius not Philaenus.

[2] The date of 1538 is inferred from Phileno's testimony in the "Apologia," folio 43 r, where he says in 1540 that he had studied in Bologna "biennio fere." Abbot Tiraboschi, working with manuscript materials in the Ducal Archive of Modena, says that Phileno had, on his arrival in Modena, 'deposto l'abito religioso,' *op. cit.*, p. 12.

[3] "Apologia," folio 12 v. Rotondò gives the text, "Bologna," p. 110. It is the great merit of this careful scholar, among other things, to have expatiated on the religious ideas of Phileno, especially during his two years in Bologna.

[4] "Apologia," folio 21 r; Rotondò, "Bologna," p. 110.

[5] "Apologia," folio 44 r. For Count Cornelio Lambertini, either the same as the one referred to by Phileno or perhaps his son, see Salvatore Muzzi, *Annali della Città di Bologna* (Bologna, 1844), VI, 589, 622.

Latin poems (*carmina*) composed by Phileno mostly on domestic personalities and occasions.[1] Phileno thus devoted himself in Bologna to pedagogical activities and to his own literary, philosophical, and theological studies.

He apparently made many friends among fellow *scholares* and discussed with them and his patrons the issues of the hour. He reports somewhat immodestly that he was greatly admired for his ability, erudition, his zeal in humane letters, and his good habits.[2] He was clearly at home *in scholis* as well as in the piazzas and the churches. With his command of patristic and scholastic theology as evidenced by his "Apologia" of 1540, it would appear that Phileno continued in Bologna to engage in formal studies, although there is no record of his matriculation at the *Studium*.

The *Studium* of Bologna had for some time been divided into the University of the Legists, for which the city had long been famous, and the *Universitas Artistarum*, which embraced all the other disciplines besides law, including medicine (cf. the German *Arzt*). Lectures in theology, however, were not given regularly under the auspices of the *Artisti*; and, when announced, they were most commonly by a learned friar lecturing in his own convent.[3]

The Averroists Alessandro Achillini and Tiberio Bacilieri,[4] both doctors of medicine, had taught philosophy at the opening of the century; and the more radical Alexandrist, Pietro Pomponazzi had come to Bologna from Padua in 1512, publishing his *De immortalitate animae* in 1516, teaching that the immortality of the *anima intellectiva*, though a datum of the faith, cannot be demonstrated by reason. It

---

[1] The fifteen *carmina* begin as follows: Ad Annam Parthineam Pontanarum, Dominam, In Fantutii de Fantutiis obitum, Ad Cassandram Troianam, Ad Hilarium Taurum, De Flora, Ad Angelum Danesium, Ad Octavium, Ad Ludovicum, De quodam puero sordidulo, In D. N. Jesu Christi nat., Ad Hemmium de sole, nubibus, tonitru, fulmine, pluvia. These are to be found in *Codice latino* 83 (52, Busta II, No. 1) of the Biblioteca Universitaria di Bologna, ff. 438-450. The titles are listed by Lodovico Frati, "Indice dei codici latini.... di Bologna," *Studi Italiani di Filologia Classica*, XVI (1908), 137 f. One will wish to compare them closely with the only known *carmen* of the same humanist friar under the name of Camillo Renato, in defense of Michael Servetus, 1554. The text of this *Carmen* is printed in Calvin, *Opera Omnia*, XV (*Corpus Reformatorum*, XLVIII), No. 2017, coll. 239-245. As for Giacomo Biancani in whose library the fifteen *carmina* were preserved, he was a near contemporary of Phileno. One must examine the manuscript "Notizie storiche geneologiche della famiglia Biancani di Bologna", by Baldassare Biancani, MS B 2526 of the Archiginnasio; Sorbelli, *op. cit.*, LXXXII, 90. Rotondò, who has studied the *carmina*, identifies further the families, personalities and occasions of the poems. "Bologna," pp. 109-111; 126-129.

[2] "Apologia," folio 43 r.

[3] Paul Oskar Kristeller, "The University of Bologna and the Renaissance," *Studi e Memorie per la storia dell'Università di Bologna*, n. s. I (Bologna, 1956), 320 f. For lectures in theology in a convent instead of the usual precincts of the *Artisti*, cf. Umberto Dallari, *I Rotuli dei Lettori, Legisti e Artisti dello Studio Bolognese*, II (Bologna, 1889), 5.

[4] Carlo Calcaterra, *Alma Mater Studiorum: L'Università di Bologna nella Storia della Cultura e della Civiltà* (Bologna, 1948), pp. 162 f; Bruno Nardi, *Saggi sull'Aristotelismo padovano dal secolo XIV al XVI* (Florence, 1960), ch. viii, ix.

was to this that the already cited spiritualizing Averroist Nifo replied with his *Tractatus de immortalitate* in 1518. In 1520 Pomponazzi came out with his *De fato, de libero arbitrio et praedestinatione*.

At the time of Phileno's sojourn in Bologna, there were three professors of philosophy and medicine who lectured *de anima*. One of them was Antonio Francesco dalla Fava (Faba, Fabius), another Antonio dal Fiume (Flumenius).[1] Both of them had begun their teaching careers within a year or two after the death of Pomponazzi in 1525. It is quite probable that Phileno heard these men lecturing on the mortality of the individual soul. And it is almost certain that he knew the third and last master of Bolognese Averroism, Ludovico Boccadiferro (Buccaferreus), who belonged to the circle of Phileno's protector, Achille Bocchi. Boccadiferro attempted to harmonize Plato, Aristotle, and Averroes in his *Lectiones super tres libros de anima* (Venice, 1556), and in "Quaestio de immortalitate animae."[2]

We know that Phileno, himself, was pressed, as he says, by certain among the students (*ex scholaribus*), on the immortality of the souls of the saints, and that he was amazed to find that there were indeed many passages in scripture and among the Fathers[3] indicating that the souls of not even the saints had yet been admitted to paradise. He specified the books of Irenaeus, Lactantius, Ambrose, and Augustine.[4] He also became much interested in the Council of Basel-Ferrara-Florence and specifically referred to the Greek views about purgatory in the debates of June-July 1438.[5] Phileno was apparently to become quite impressed by the Orthodox arguments for interpreting the New Testament texts eschatologically as referring solely to a future rather than to a provisional, present blessedness or purgation immediately after death. The Greeks were explicit that there was no present purgation by fire. Phileno reports that he at first tried to controvert the testimony of these passages by others of a more traditional content and that he consulted with "other students and friends" over a number of years (*superioribus annis*) and particularly with the otherwise uni-

---

[1] Dallari, *Rotuli*, II, 91; Serafino Mazzetti, *Repertorio di tutti i professori.... di Bologna* (Bologna, 1847), items 1174 and 978; Calcaterra, *op. cit.*, p. 175.

[2] Nardi, *op. cit.*, p. 412; Rotondò, "Bologna," pp. 126 and 132-134. The latter also offers in plate 4 a print from Bocchi's *Symbolicae quaestiones* (Bologna, 1574), showing God, the triune, blowing the Spirit into the world (described by Rotondò, "Bologna,", pp. 132 f.). Cf. Genesis I: 2b.

[3] Cf. Oscar Cullmann, *Immortality of the Soul or Resurrection of the Dead in the New Testament* (New York, 1958) and Georges Florovsky, "The Resurrection of Life," *Harvard Divinity School Bulletin*, 1951, pp. 5-26.

[4] "Apologia," folio 26 r.

[5] Mansi, *Sacrorum Conciliorum.... Collectio, XXXI*, coll. 485 ff. Phileno says that the book of the Acts which he consulted in prison had been "recentissime impresso," "Apologia," folio 8. Phileno will have been particularly interested in the views of Metropolitan Mark Eugenicus of Ephesus. On the possible direct influence on Phileno of Greeks in Sicily teaching their anti-purgatorial view, see above, p. 112, n. 2. The most recent account of the discussion on purgatory is by Joseph Gill, *The Council of Florence* (Cambridge, 1959), pp. 117-125.

dentified preacher (*concionatorem*)[1] of San Petronio in Bologna at the beginning of the year 1540. Phileno claims later, in his " Apologia, " that his fellow students, " who were always eager to discuss all new and wayward doctrines, " involved him so much in speculative discussion that he, as a mature scholar, was implicated as the very fountainhead of student ferment. But there can be little doubt that, despite his later protestations before a tribunal, he himself had come to espouse and even elaborate those views, accepting as probable that " the souls of the elect have not yet entered [paradise or] heaven, " that " they rest (*quiescere*) with Christ until resurrected at the day of judgment, " and that there is no present hell or purgatory.[2] Phileno must have adopted other radical views also which were theologically and socially unsettling.

Yet everything seemed to be going well for Phileno until the Lent of 1540. It was then that there came to San Giacomo, the church and convent of the Austin Friars, a famous preacher of the order from Naples with, from Phileno's lofty point of view, an unwarranted reputation for scriptural learning. Phileno scornfully describes his grave demeanor, his inept pronunciation, and his misconstruing of scriptures. One is relieved, in the interest of safeguarding Phileno's own reputation, to ascertain that he could not have been referring to Girolamo Seripando of Naples, general of the Hermits of St. Augustine and later the papal legate at the Council of Trent.[3] Seripando had, to be sure, been resident in Bologna for six years, and in 1540 he would visit and preach in the city between April 11 and April 30.[4] But Phileno's difficulties with an unnamed Austin Friar from Naples began on Ash Wednesday, 11 February 1540,[5] when the preacher spent two wearisome hours on the trivialia of fasting, " as if every father in Bologna were not fully acquainted with the law of the Church on the subject. " Phileno, " with much civility as was becoming, " made bold to apprise the preacher of his opinion that more edifying and needful topics could be dealt with in the ensuing Lenten sermons. At this the Neapolitan Augustinian was enraged, declared that Phileno was " a prophet of Martin Luther sent into Italy, " and that he was an excommunicated apostate.

---

1 " Apologia, " folio 26 r. Rotondò can go no further than identify the preacher in S. Petronio as " a conventual Franciscan appointed by his General. " " Bologna, " p. 135, n. 2. The Lenten preacher of S. Petronio is not to be confused with the Lenten preacher of S. Giacomo, the also unidentified Austin friar, who got Phileno into trouble. See below at n. 4.

2 " Apologia, " folios 5 v and 26 r.

3 Hubert Jedin, *Girolamo Seripando: Sein Leben und Denken im Geisteskampf des 16. Jahrhunderts*, 2 vols. (Würzburg, 1937).

4 *Ibid.*, II, 412. See below.

5 In " Apologia, " folio 43 r. Phileno specifies " primo die quatragesime. " Easter in that year fell on March 28. Hence we have a specific date for the onset of Phileno's troubles. That Seripando could not have made an earlier visit to Bologna that year is inferred from his itinerary ascertained by reference to his sermons calendared by Jedin, *op. cit.*, II, 407-426. He was in Perugia on January 18 and then went to the Adriatic, moving up the coast from Fermo, February 14; Ancona, February 26, Pesaro, March 6 and 8; Rimini, March 9 - April 2.

It is true that Phileno would later acknowledge that he had read of Luther at least *De abroganda missa privata* (1521).[1] The Lenten preacher in San Giacomo proceeded to inform the local Dominicans of the renegade in their midst.

Bologna was the seat of the Dominican provincial chapter of Lower Lombardy. The Dominicans mobilized to apprehend Phileno wherever he might show up " in the church, in the assembly, in the schools, in the square, and throughout the city. " Given the original provocation, we must henceforth be prepared to find evidence of Phileno's having eaten meat and dairy products during Lent and almost hypochondriacal itemizations of his ailments (that would justify his use of forbidden proteins) all bulking very large in the extant documentation. We shall try to keep our report of this kind of material to a minimum.

Phileno had powerful protectors among the highborn citizens. Moreover, he was confident that his ideas of reform were much closer to those of the reforming Roman Pontiff (Paul III) than the Austin Friar's. Phileno's strategy was, therefore, to appeal from the Dominican inquisitor and from the bishop of Bologna (Alessandro Campeggio) to the papal legate in Bologna, the newly appointed Bonifazio Ferrero, cardinal bishop of Ivrea.[2] It is quite possible that it was at this moment that Phileno " briefly " set forth his convinctions in XLIII Articles[3] to present to Ferrero. In the meantime, the whole of the town became aroused by the charges, the preachers of San Petronio and of the Dominican Church joining with the preacher of the Austin Friars in San Giacomo, to denounce Phileno as a heretic, an apostate, an excommunicate, and a seditious person to be avoided for the religious and social turmoil he was causing both men and women in their homes as also in their parishes. Before Phileno could manage to state his case before the legate, the latter fell ill.[4]

If the anonymous XLIII Articles really do come from the hand of Phileno (or from his reform-minded circle in Bologna), we would have to characterize him at this juncture as a still quite moderate reformer. Although the XLIII Articles refer several times to the churches oppressed " under the yoke of the Pope, " and scandalized " by very corrupt priests, " still they argue against formal separation, noting that Paul and James were loyal to the old rites and institutions of the Temple, even though corrupted or perverted by wicked priests, scribes and Pharisees; and they justified temporizing by quoting Titus

---

[1] " Apologia, " folio 53 r.

[2] " Apologia, " folios 17 v. 45 r. For the appointment of the new legate, see Pompeo Vizani, *Dieci libri delle historie della sua patria* (Bologna, 1608), supplementary book XI, pp. 16 f.

[3] That the XLIII Articles are identical with the " haec omnia, " " in articulos, " " brevius tamen, " presented according to Phileno in his " Apologia " (folio 17 v.) to the Cardinal legate in Bologna, is the very plausible working hypothesis of Rotondò, " Bologna, " p. 111, n. 1. The Articles are found in a Ms. Miscellany of the Archiginnasio of Bologna: B 1859, " Consilia et Vota in materia S. Officij, " ff. 202 r-205 v.

[4] " Apologia, " folio 45 v.

1:15: "To the pure all things are pure."[1] The Articles point out further that Paul did not even call the righteous to withdraw from the notoriously corrupt church of the Corinthians and that Augustine regarded as pernicious the counsel to separate because of corruption in the church.[2] In view of the relative conservatism of the reform being proposed in Bologna and especially in view of the later Rhaetian career of Phileno, it is of special interest that the Articles expressly state that, so long as scriptures are read in the church and the sacraments administered in the words of the Lord, no one should hold "that those who have been baptized by the servants of the Pope should be rebaptized into a more pure church."[3] The fact that the document recoils expressly from anabaptism is nevertheless an indication that the circle from which it came must have engendered more radical postulates than it realized. On the matter of psychopannychism, the Articles are silent except for including the invocation of the saints among the tolerable superstitions.[4] A notable feature of the Articles is the author's recognition that being a citizen, a *paterfamilias*, or a magistrate constitutes a true or rightful vocation (*iustam vocationem*).[5]

3) RICCI-PHILENO IN MODENA AND ENVIRONS (*1540*)

Before the papal legate in Bologna was incapacitated by illness, Phileno had apparently never considered fleeing; but he now decided to depart from Bologna with a view to visiting his *patria*, then Rome itself, and finally to leave Italy altogether, not without visiting "the ancient cities of Modena, Mirandola, and Mantua."[6] Because of an abscess in his right armpit, from which he was suffering at the time, he thought he would perish. In the company of several friends he got away to Nonantola; and to prove his innocence he boldly asked admittance at the local *Dominican* convent, two of whose members he names.[7] He hoped through the intercession of these two learned and reasonable men to vindicate his honor and his orthodoxy. With these friars, whom he presumably had known earlier, at least by reputation, he stayed for five or six days, talking with them at table about all the problems astir in Bologna. They agreed with all that he put forward; but the bishop of Nonantola, a member of the same order, remarked to his brother that Phileno was obviously "maximus Lutheranus."

---

[1] Article XXXIII. Phileno here anticipates his later Spiritual Libertinism, closely akin to Nicodemism.

[2] Articles XXXIV and XL.

[3] Article XXXV.

[4] Article III.

[5] Article VIII.

[6] "Apologia," folio 45 v.

[7] Angelus Valentinus and Bartholomeus Giselinus Mirandulanus, lector of the Dominican convent in Modena. "Apologia," folio 45 v.

As his abscess grew worse, Phileno went on to Modena, staying in bed for almost a month. Scarcely cured, he went back toward Nonantola, to the villa or palace of Thomaso Carandino at Staggia (at that time in the territory of Nonantola; today a *frazione* of the commune of San Prospero). Henceforth Staggia will bulk large in the account of Phileno in his own "Apologia" and in the Histories of the two Modenese chroniclers, the contemporary Lancellotti and the later Tassoni. It is here the place to note that the lady of the villa was the extraordinarily independent and unconventional Anna Carandina, natural daughter of Count Sigismondo Rangoni. The Rangoni family will protect Phileno as long as possible and may prove to have been a factor in compassing his final escape from Italy after his impending trial and incarceration in Ferrara. But this is to anticipate.

The other hearth for the half fugitive Phileno was the Academy in Modena. Here he was received as Messer Lisia Phileno, Siciliano, accomplished in Latin literature and in scriptural learning. It is possible that within the circle of the academicians he assumed still another name, that by which he was solely known after his flight to Rhaetia-Camillo.[1] The Academy of Modena was, at this time, under the direction of the physician Giovanni Grillenzoni, a former student of Pietro Pomponazzi. Other members were the Cretan Francesco Porto, teacher of Greek in Modena from 1536 to 1546 and later, reader at the University of Ferrara and teacher of the daughters of Duchess Renata; the equally learned Lodovico Castelvetro;[2] and Carlo Segonio, the famous historian of Roman and Bolognese antiquities. It is of interest that Castelvetro and Porto ended up as Calvinists in Switzerland. Count Ercole Rangoni had, in a very brief time apparently, come to consider Phileno as a friend, deeply impressed as he was by the unfrocked friar's "*virtù,* imposing doctrine, singular judgment, highest competence in all branches of literature, especially the Bible."[3] The count noted also the accomplished friar's "incomparable magnanimity and love, the holiness of all his ways, exemplary to those close to him and far from any personal ambition and quest for glory."[4] Alas, this evaluation of Phileno as modest is at variance with what Phileno himself freely says with palpable pride in his "Apologia" about his sense of mission and about his achievements as a preacher, conversationalist, and writer, "everywhere esteemed and praised."

It was during his very brief and interrupted visits in Modena that Phileno gave clearest expression to his views about poverty and the duties of the monks and friars to help the poor and to safeguard them

---

[1] There is a bit of evidence that in Modena he took a new name, Camillo Renato. The manuscript evidence for this will be presented by Rotondò in his forthcoming book. As *scholaris* in Bologna he used both Phileno and Ricci.

[2] Letter of Papino (p. 128, n. 4); Casadei, "Fileno," p. 368. Information on Porto is from Francesco Lemmi, *La Riforma in Italia* (Milan, 1939), p. 76.

[3] Tassoni, "Cronaca," p. 331; Casadei, "Fileno," p. 359.

[4] Letter of Count Ercole to Duke Ercole, 18 October 1540, Archivio di Stato di Modena: Particolari; Casadei, "Fileno," pp. 365-367.

from exploitation. His utterances were called forth by the famine[1] caused by extended drought which oppressed the region at this time. That some of Phileno's teaching bore on the Franciscan theme of apostolic poverty and in the socially radical context of a local famine is suggested also by the fact that the *letterati* of the Academy had, even before his arrival, made the demand that the religious in their convents should be expected to give even more for the poor and the needy than Christians living in the world.[2] There was so much commotion stirred up from the pulpits of the churches, including the cathedral, among the various orders, particularly between the Austin Friars and the Observant Franciscans, that the governor of Modena, Battistino Strozzi, had to report to Count Ercole in a long letter of 18 April 1540.[3]

Social and religious reform will surely have been in the air as a consequence of the meeting of the provincial chapter of the Austin Friars after the Lenten season. The principal preacher was a powerful orator, by many thought to be favorable to Lutheranism, perhaps Seripando himself, known to have been present in Bologna April 11 to April 30.[4] Despite Phileno's unfortunate encounter with another Austin Friar earlier in the year in Bologna, one cannot doubt but that he sought out this more congenial representative of the order and that he surely entered into the general discussion following in the wake of his visit. Phileno himself is reported to have preached, possibly from the pulpit of the Conventual Franciscan Church, and to have challenged the religious orders, the Franciscans included, by demanding that they give up their corporate wealth for the benefit of the poor, the better to follow the evangelical counsels which they professed. He is reported to have celebrated the Mass, perhaps in some parish church under the patronage of the Rangoni.[5] The latter phrase could, of course, mean also that Phileno merely conducted the eucharistic service along the simplified lines permitted in the chapel of Duchess Renata in Ferrara, with communion in both kinds. In his sermons Phileno will have approached Luther's doctrine at several points, for example on the preeminence of faith and election.

Taking leave from the conventual churches and from the company of the Court and the Academy, Phileno also sought out, as occasion

---

[1] Lancellotti, *Cronaca*, pp. x, 402 *passim*.

[2] Lancellotti, *Cronaca*, p. 205; Casadei, " Fileno, " p. 362. The date of this entry is 17 September 1539, a year before Camillo's arrival in Modena.

[3] The letter of Strozzi, said to be in the " Ducale Archivio segreto, " is adduced by Tiraboschi, *Biblioteca Modenese*, I, 13. The chronicle of the conflict among the friars is given by Lancellotti, *Cronaca*, pp. 317-336.

[4] The chapter meeting of some two hundred friars began after Easter, March 28. *Ibid.*, pp. xii, 308. On April 18 a preacher of the Austin Friars, Fra Latantio, preached a " most beautiful sermon " in S. Augustino and made known from the vicar of the Dominican inquisitor that his listeners should denounce whoever had or whatever shop sold a little book entitled *El Summario della Sacra Scrittura*. *Ibid.*, p. 321.

[5] Lancellotti, *Cronaca*, p. 410; Casadei, " Fileno, " p. 369.

afforded, the religiously more radical groups[1] which, in rather large numbers before his arrival in Modena, had already been meeting in conventicles and private chapels, as perhaps also at Staggia. In these circles, some of which had friendly contacts with the Swiss and South German divines, Phileno began to read and comment on the epistles of Paul and guided the study of scripture in general. The hostile chronicler Tassoni says that in 1540 the wise and the stupid, men and women, professed to decide the sense of scripture: "Not only men of every condition, learned and ignorant and devoid of a knowledge of letters, but also women, whenever occasion was given — in public places, in squares, shops, and churches, — disputed about faith and the law of Christ, and all out of the Holy Scriptures, promiscuously quoting Paul, Matthew, John, the Apocalypse, and all the doctors whom they never saw."[2]

About the end of August Phileno went out from Modena some twenty kilometers to stay in the palace in Staggia.[3] His hostess, Anna Carandina (1502-1552),[4] and his host, Thomaso Carandino, were possibly induced by Phileno to introduce, as patrons of the local church, a new liturgy (*officium novum*), perhaps modeled on that of Duchess Renata in Ferrara.[5] Phileno is said, however, to have gone only once to attend this service. It was noted by the local rustics, alas, during Phileno's sojourn at the villa in Staggia for a month and a half that his host and hostess did not usually go to Mass and that he himself was often seen walking with others around the grounds of the palace or nearby at the hour of Mass or shortly thereafter.[6] At his trial Phileno would later deny this hotly and recall that, despite the severe trouble which his thirty-eight year old hostess was having with her feet, she, her husband, their children, and the entire household and retinue walked regularly to Sunday Mass; and he would call down upon the false witness the condign punishment of the law.

However truthful his later testimony may be, it is also clear from the same testimony that Phileno was disgusted by the ignorance and

---

[1] Rotondò names two figures in the heterodox movement in Modena, both of them friends of Phileno, Giovanni Bertari Poliziano and Girolamo Teggia. He promises a long study of them on the basis of their trials beginning in March 1541. "Bologna," p. 135, n. 4.

[2] Tassoni, "Cronaca," as given by Cantù, *Eretici*, II, 158. The material is also presented in Girolamo Tiraboschi, *Storia della letteratura italiana*, VII: 1 (Milan, 1824), 135 f.

[3] A sojourn of a month and a half at the palace is based upon the testimony of a Modenese witness at the trial. "Apologia," folio 31 v.

[4] She lived a rather unconventional life, remarried after the death of her husband, was called before the judicatory in Ferrara for mistreating a servant, and because of family altercation was twice interred. Lancellotti, *Cronaca Modenese*, Monumenti, XII, pp. 289 f.

[5] The *officium novum* is mentioned by a witness at the trial. "Apologia," folio 31 v. The local church was S. Maria della Staggia. Cf. G. Tiraboschi, *Dizionario Topografico degli Stati Estensi* (Bologna, 1963), II, 363.

[6] "Apologia," folios 31 v. and 38 r.

the disorderly lives of the two local priests of Staggia.[1] One of them was by common rumor a counterfeiter (*monetarius*), the other so inept at Latin that he made no sense of the liturgy, stringing the words together, and subverting the sense. Moreover, both were utterly superstitious, preying on the credulities of parishioners still more simple than themselves. Shabby priests, they gave themselves over to gluttony, games of chance, and various frivolities, thereby incurring the frequent rebuke of Phileno and his noble companions.

It is clear that Phileno would have been loath to attend Mass celebrated by such priests. He had also compelling physical reasons for abstaining. Besides his recently cured abscess, he was apparently suffering from numerous ailments of the head, liver, stomach, limbs, and notably of his eyes which were so afflicted with discharges that the left one seemed threatened with blindness.[2] All his ailments required medical attention and the therapy of hot and cold baths and medical applications. On some days, he later records, he was scarcely able to rise from his bed in the morning. Then, to compound his difficulties, he seriously hurt his foot on a rock when he was returning from Mirandola and for almost a fortnight he had to keep to his abode.

The best that can be made of the conflicting evidence is that the spirited lord and lady of Staggia undoubtedly attended the local church from time to time in the company of their learned guest but that the center of their religious speculation at Staggia was the palace salon; and our radical Franciscan undoubtedly celebrated the Eucharist in the palace chapel in a quasi-Protestant manner, restored, as Phileno would have explained, to its original " dignity and integrity. "

The rancor of the local priests, the enmity of other denizens of the region, and the persistence of the aggrieved Austin Friars and Dominicans of Bologna finally combined to bring about the capture of Phileno in plain day in the open road. It was " il messo della Croce " or a *missus* of the local sodality of cross-wearing informers, the *societas Crucesignatorum*, usually summoned by a bell,[3] who pointed out Phileno to the detachment of knights in search of him. Phileno says the capture took place on October 14 with many Modenese in the crowd.[4]

The Modenese chronicler, in contrast, says that the arrest took place suddenly on Sunday 17 October 1540 when Phileno and several of his followers were presumably gathered for worship in the villa of Madonna Anna Carandina.[5] The chronicler says further that the knights were retainers of Duke Ercole II, who had ordered the arrest from his seat in Ferrara. It is also reported that but for his foolhardiness (*leggerezza*), Phileno, duly warned, could easily have saved himself.

---

[1] " Apologia, " folio 38 v.

[2] " Apologia, " folio 38 r. It is a further evidence of the identity of Phileno and Camillo Renato that Camillo is known to have died blind. See below at p. 182, n. 4.

[3] Paul Hinschius, *System des katholischen Kirchenrechts*, V: 1 (Berlin, 1893), 461.

[4] " Apologia, " folio 43 r.

[5] Lancellotti, *Cronaca*, p. 410.

Trusting "too much in himself," he wished "to tempt God."[1] The foolhardiness consisted in Phileno's openly moving back and forth between Staggia and Modena, carried in a two-wheeled cart (*cisium*) because of his several ailments, even after he knew himself to be under local suspicion.[2]

Count Ercole Rangoni of Modena almost at once wrote to his superior Duke Ercole in Ferrara, the spouse of reform-minded Duchess Renata (Renée), declaring his confidence in the probity of the "poor innocent" friar, in words quoted more fully above, charging the Dominicans with jealousy and machination in having the attractive Franciscan preacher and humanist arrested. He implored the duke to see to it that the trial, should it come to that, be conducted fairly and if possible by non-partisan judges.[3] Rangoni apparently took steps to arrange the amelioration of the place of Phileno's detention and was presumably seconded by the governor of Modena, Battistino Strozzi, who apprised the duke in Ferrara of the arrest and of the condition of "the highly cultured" occupant of the castle prison.[4]

The vicar of the bishop of Modena had an entirely different opinion of the prisoner from that of the incredulous count of Modena. In a letter of 16 October to his bishop, Giovanni Morone (soon to be named cardinal), at the time papal nuncio in Germany,[5] the vicar described among "the sowers of heresy in the diocese" our radical Franciscan who, "according to his manner, calls himself by various names."[6] The vicar called the friar a "ribaldo" who had, moreover, proceeded to excite social unrest among the peasants and artisans imprisoned with

---

[1] The order for the arrest was dated 10 October. Letter of the governor of Modena (p. 112, n. 3). Lancellotti gives both the date, 17 October, and the name of Anna Caran dina, *Cronaca*, pp. 403, 405, 410. It is of interest that at the trial of Pietro Antonio Cervia, beginning 1563 in Modena, a certain Claudio Carandino is cited as heretical. See elsewhere in this volume John Tedeschi, p. 250. The *frazione* of Staggia continued to harbor persons like Phileno. We have a letter of his fellow academician, Castelvetro, from his villa in Staggia, 8 October 1545. Giuseppe Cavazzuti, *Lodovico Castelvetro* (Modena, 1903), p. 72; cf. p. 197, n. 1. The fact that Phileno courted arrest is inferred from the letter of Cipriano Quadrio to Giulio Milanese, 13 February 1541. See also below at p. 141, n. 1; Casadei, "Fileno," pp. 326, 377.

Rotondò dates the incriminating letter of Cipriano to Giulio in 1541, assuming that, since it was written from Bologna, it referred to Phileno's difficulties there. "Bologna," p. 111 and n. 2. Comba, who excerpts the letter along with others used against Giulio at his trial in Venice after Lent in 1541, gives only the day and month but places Cipriano's letter between one dated 19 March 1541 and another dated 20 November 1540. "Giulio," pp. 325 f. I think that ours should be dated 13 February *1541* and that it refers to Phileno's foolhardiness *at Staggia*, about which Cipriano could have readily learned in Bologna. Cipriano remained in Bologna, studying law until July 1542. "Bologna," p. 111, n. 2. The fact that Giulio remarks that Phileno was *incarcerato* would seem to suggest Staggia and Modena rather than Bologna.

[2] "Apologia," folio 46 v.

[3] Letter of Count Ercole to Duke Ercole, p. 123, n. 4 above.

[4] Letter of governor of Modena, p. 112, n. 3 above.

[5] Morone was named bishop of Modena in 1529, but had not been able to take possession of his see because of the interference of Cardinal Ippolito d'Este. Letter of vicar to bishop, p. 113, n. 2 above.

[6] The vicar gives only the two names already introduced: Fileno and Paolo.

him. Surely the biased vicar was going on rumor only when he included homicides along with heresy among the charges now brought against the friar; for violence does not feature in any of the more circumstantial reports of the hearings and the final trial. At best, we can only conjecture that there is here a distorted echo of the armed attempt on the open roads to prevent the passage of the Dominican inquisitors intent on entering Modena on an errand possibly related to the apprehension or prosecution of suspects associated with Phileno.[1] Morone himself in a letter from Worms to Cardinal Farnese, 27 December 1540, was closer to the truth when he observed in simple dismay that there was more heresy in his Modena than in Bohemia and in Germany and proceeded to specify the teachings that were being openly proclaimed in his diocese, against purgatory, against the Mass, against ecclesiastical power, and against the invocation of the saints, all with the tacit support of the supposed defenders of the city.[2] From Morone's letter and from that of his vicar, as from other sources already cited, it is clear that Phileno did not lack for intercessors who repudiated the charges of sedition, immorality, and heresy, saying that he was being calumniated merely "for being exceedingly learned in scriptures and in Platonic (*sic*) doctrine."[3] The Rangoni and other noble supporters felt so strongly about Phileno that through their direct or indirect armed intervention the Dominican inquisitor of Bologna was prevented from transferring the records of the first deliberations in Bologna to reinforce the findings in Modena.[4]

4) THE TRIAL, RECANTATION, AND IMPRISONMENT IN FERRARA (*late 1540-c. 1542*)

Despite the efforts of Modenese supporters, including the count and the academicians,[5] the hearing of Phileno as a "Lutheran heretic" began in the castle prison in Modena 26 October[6] under the direction of Dominican inquisitors from both Bologna and Ferrara. By 28 October 1540 sufficiently incriminating evidence had been assembled to justify a transfer of the trial to the ducal capital, Ferrara.[7] The evidence brought forward in the Modenese hearings was not of such a character as to undermine the devotion of all the heretical friar's fol-

[1] Letter of Papino, n. 4 below.

[2] Ludwig Cardauns, ed. *Nuntiaturberichte aus Deutschland* (1533-1559), VI (Berlin, 1910), No. 270. Morone repeats himself on the situation in Modena in a letter of 21 May 1542 to Cardinal Contarini, specifying also widespread doubt in the city about the presence of departed saints with Christ. A. M. Quirini, *Collectio Epistolarum Reginaldi Poli*, III (Brescia, 1748), cclxx (cited by Rotondò, "Bologna," p. 135, n. 4).

[3] Letter of vicar to bishop, p. 113, n. 2 above.

[4] The letter of the inquisitor Papino to the duke of Ferrara, 28 October 1540; Casadei, "Fileno," p. 368.

[5] "The Academy wished to help him." Lancellotti, *Cronaca*, p. 405.

[6] Lancellotti, *Cronaca*, p. 405; Casadei, "Fileno," p. 367.

[7] Letter of Papino, n. 4 above.

lowers. The excited populace was perhaps divided in its passions. By armed guard Phileno was taken, bound, out of town by night; and the populace was diverted by an officially inspired rumoı that he would be conducted through the gate leading to Bologna to be burned instead of to Ferrara for another hearing.[1]

In the meantime Gasparo Cardinal Contarini had become interested in Phileno, or rather, in the theological points at issue in the hearings. A letter of 16 November 1540 from Duke Ercole to his ambassador Bonifacio Ruggieri (former *podestà* of Modena)[2] indicates that the most powerful Italian ecclesiastic in favor of irenic efforts to conciliate German Protestants had already made discreet inquiries about the heretical Sicilian.[3] In view of his own very difficult position among his confrères in the Italian hierarchy, Cardinal Contarini will have been perturbed lest the Augustinian (Lutheranizing) doctrine of election and justification be compromised in high Catholic circles by the vagaries of an irresponsible friar. Since the cardinal himself was at variance also with the popular Catholic conception of free will and merit, he was doubtless anxious that the interrelated doctrines of salvation by faith and predestination not be imperiled by the taint of moral improbity on the part of the eloquent Modenese preacher of ecclesiastical reform, divine election, and psychopannychism. The cardinal's inquiries had apparently turned up not only the usual charge of Phileno's being " a very seditious person " but also the extraordinary rumor that Phileno's " ribaldry " was nothing less than bigamy or rather that the friar had " had four [women]. "[4] Since no moral charges will be brought against Phileno in the records closest to the hearings and the final trial at Ferrara, we may assume that this rumor, like the other, even worse, contained in the correspondence with Cardinal Morone, can be ascribed to frenzied inferences and deliberate distortions on the part of the opponents of the popular humanist. It is not to be excluded, however, that in the fellowship of the popular conventicles meeting in the homes of the radicals of several social classes in and around Modena and earlier in Bologna the conduct of the friar was open to criticism.[5] It may be sufficient, however, to safeguard Phileno's honor to state that even after the trial, Duke Ercole continued to speak of Phileno as a man " of quality "

---

[1] Lancellotti, *Cronaca*, pp. 410, 419 f.; Tassoni, " Cronaca, " p. 331; Casadei, " Fileno, " pp. 369, 372 f.

[2] The *cavaliere* Ruggieri was *podestà* in 1538. Luigi Napoleone Cittadella, *Notizie relative a Ferrara per la maggior parte inedite* (Ferrara, 1864), p. 369.

[3] Archivio di Stato di Modena: Dispaccio da Roma, filza 28; Casadei, " Fileno, " p. 371.

[4] *Ibid.*, filza 27; Casadei, " Fileno, " p. 376. In the text the word is *bigomio*. The letter containing it comes after the completion of the trial; but the rumor, reported to the duke by Ruggieri as something mentioned by Contarini, must have been picked up previously.

[5] One is tempted to observe that the last main section in Renato's *Carmen* on Servetus in 1554, lines 341 f., dealing with a father and the suitors and swains of his pretty daughter and which so ill befits the rest of the poem on Servetus' death, may be a telltale autobiographical reminiscence.

and crossed out of his letter the charge against Phileno as " tristo et ribaldo, " replacing it simply with the charge of his being a heretic.[1]

We turn now to the details of this trial of Lisia Phileno *alias* Paolo Ricci in Ferrara. There are two principal sources besides Alessandro Tassoni's " Cronaca di Modena. " The " Apologia " in forty-eight folios was prepared in several copies[2] by Phileno in the prison of the Dominican convent of the no longer extant Santa Maria degli Angeli,[3] where Girolamo Savonarola had once taken his vows. Attached to the " Apologia " are nine folios containing the " Conclusiones " and the names of the *consultores* at the trial, signed by the notary Boethius de Sylvestris. A related document is the " Consilia in causam Phileni sententiati ad carceros perpetuos, "[4] signed by Johannes Ludovicus Boninus, presumably one of the *jurisperiti* or *consultores*. At least, one is tempted to identify this Ludovicus of the independent " Consilia " with the first *consultor* and advocate for Phileno, who is styled in the " Conclusiones " attached to the " Apologia, " " Dominus Ludovicus de Silvestris, civis Ferrariensis. "[5]

The final trial in Ferrara took place in a chamber above the prison of Degli Angeli in four sessions beginning 12 December 1540. The trial proceeded in the presence of two judges: the one, the suffragan bishop as the representative of Giovanni Cardinal Salviati, archbishop of Ferrara; the other, Fra Stefano Foscharara, Dominican inquisitor from Bologna.[6] The presence of the cardinal's vicar, Bishop Ottaviano, would appear to represent Duke Ercole's accommodation to Count Ercole's request that " the poor innocent " be given as impartial a trial as possible. Six consultors heard the testimony of a score of witnesses including at least one woman of Modena.

Before we listen to the verdict of the consultors and hear the sentence of the lord inquisitor and overhear the Abjuration of the heretic, it is appropriate to bring together the main points espoused by Phileno in Bologna, Modena, and Staggia in order to have before us a balanced delineation of the kind of radical reform he was preaching in various circles. They were, in fact, brought out as some IX Accusations at the trial in Ferrara.[7] These and the evidence of other sources make

---

[1] Letter of Duke Ercole to Bonifazio Ruggieri, 28 December 1540; B. Fontana, *Renata di Francia* (Rome, 1893), II, 137; Casadei, " Fileno, " p. 375.

[2] " Apologia, " folio 1 A.

[3] A picture of church and convent, built in 1440, may be seen in Dante Balboni, " Briciole Savonaroliane, " *Studi Savonaroliani*, Atti e Memorie della Deputazione Provinciale Ferrarese di Storia Patria, n. s., III, Part III (Ferrara, 1932-1933), opp. p. 66.

[4] The " Consilia " are found in the same MS codex as the XLIII Articles (above, p. 121, n. 3), namely, Bologna: Biblioteca dell'Archiginnasio, B 1859, ff. 20-23.

[5] Ottaviano da Castello, Vescovo di S. Leone.

[6] Tassoni, " Cronaca, " pp. 331 f.; Cantù, *Eretici*, II, 157-159; Casadei, " Fileno, " pp. 373-375.

[7] The items in the Retractations or Abjuration have been numbered for convenience and inverted as roughly nine presumed Accusations. The Abjuration is printed in Tassoni, " Cronaca, " pp. 331 f.; Casadei, " Fileno, " pp. 373-375. Also important are the XLIII Articles (see above at p. 121, n. 3), of which twelve appear, mostly complete, *passim* in the notes of Rotondò's " Bologna. " Of course, the most important source is the

it possible to group Phileno's convictions under seven main headings, namely: 1) that, although one may draw upon the testimony of the Fathers and the Schoolmen, the sole authority is Scripture, particularly the New Testament; 2) that " superstition " is worse than " heresy "; 3) that salvation depends utterly upon the divine election with no meritorious use of one's free will; 4) that the souls of the righteous and the wicked expire at the death of the body and have no abiding place until the general resurrection and the last judgment (psychopannychism); hence 5) that all the liturgical and penitential practices (superstitions) based on the alleged existence of a purgatory filled with sinners and of a paradise filled with saints constitute a religious deception that has given rise to intolerable social exploitation of simple believers by the professionally religious; 6) that evangelical Christians should, instead, gather for worship and mutual support and mutual correction, confident that the Holy Spirit, promised by Christ, will be among them as they seek to interpret the scriptures (originally inspired by the same Spirit) and as they seek also to do the will of Christ as prompted by his Spirit in their midst; and 7) that the purification or reformation of the Christian community can be properly undertaken by conscientious lords as well as by prelates.

(1) As for the first of Phileno's postulates, our Italian reformer stood with the classical Protestant reformers to the north in insisting on the preeminence of the Bible. He approached the northern sectarian or radical reformers in giving marked precedence to the New Testament and especially to the epistles of Paul. Phileno's emphasis *sola scriptura* was in theory and practice actually quite divergent from that of the classical Protestant reformers, in view of his reliance on communal exegesis and hermeneutics (point 6 below). Moreover, he distinguished not so much between law and grace, as between faith and love. In this connection he distinguished between the first table of the Ten Commandments and the second. The former, Phileno maintained, deals with the postulates of faith; the second, with the implications of faith, namely, love.[1]

(2) Phileno defined " superstition " as directed against the first table of the Law. But going beyond his distinction between error in faith (as belief, the first table) and failure in love (the commandment of the second table), Phileno contended in a most unusual way and on unexpected grounds that " a person who is superstitious (*superstitiosus*) and therefore unfaithful (*infidelis*) is much worse than a heretic (*haereticus*).[2]

" Apologia "; but, as it was prepared in prison in anticipation of the trial, one can only infer the true convictions of its author.

[1] " Apologia, " folios 28 v., 30 v. for his stress on the New Testament; folio 37 v. for his discussion of the two tables. Rotondò has underscored the significance of Phileno's distinction, " Bologna, " pp. 114 f.

[2] " Apologia, " folio 37 r. Rotondò has been very successful in disengaging from the MSS Phileno's theory of the benign heretic and in analysing Phileno's concept of superstition, " Bologna, " pp. 114 f.

A heretic was for him one who did not believe divine truth to be contained in the Holy Scriptures, as, for example, the Jew (in part) and the Turk.[1] So long as anyone regards himself as a Christian, invokes the name of Christ, and seeks the guidance of the Holy Spirit promised by Christ, he should, even though he errs and declares others in error, be regarded as within the faith and within the community of the would-be faithful![2] Ecclesiastical authorities should not do violence to the commandments of the second table (love, *caritas*) in defending the commandments of the first (beliefs, *fides*).

And what were, for Phileno, some specific instances of superstition worse than heresy? "Superstition" appears to have been comprehensive enough to include the papacy whenever tyrannical,[3] canon law, monastic and other vows, and ceremonies to the degree that they impair, obstruct, pervert, or abrogate the faith of Christ and the exercise of love among Christians who would follow the example of Christ.[4] Among the ceremonies he would consider the most superstitious and abominable to be the Mass whenever and wherever it was considered a repetition of Christ's sacrifice rather than, along with the Gospels and Epistles read before communion, a grateful recollection of the original and unique sacrifice.[5] He located the superstition of the ceremony *circa missam*, not *in missa*, and suggested, like Paul, that one should not share bread with those who misconceive the true meaning of the eucharistic fellowship.[6]

(3) As for the third postulate, the doctrine of election, Phileno stood with the Protestant reformers to the north and could therefore be plausibly accused of being a Calvinist or a Lutheran. But, of course, Phileno argued entirely on the basis of Pauline and Augustinian texts. As we have already noted, Cardinal Contarini (himself concerned to preserve or recover the fullness of the Augustinian doctrine which belonged to the common heritage) had found occasion to observe that on this first point Phileno was improperly accused of heresy. And, precisely on this point Phileno, citing several patristic and scholastic authorities, contended against his detractors and misinterpreters that he acknowledged the freedom of the will but he claimed also that because of original sin this will, without being "liberated by the power of the Holy Spirit,"[7] could never perform anything but evil. He adduced in his favor the whole tradition of the Fathers and the Schoolmen, specifying Cyprian, Augustine against Pelagius, Ambrose, the epistles of five bishops to Pope Innocent I, the Council of Mileve against

---

1 "Apologia," folios 34 v. and 2 r.

2 "Apologia," folio 15; XLIII Articles, item 1; quoted by Rotondò, "Bologna," p. 114, n. 4.

3 XLIII Articles, No. 36; Rotondò, "Bologna," p. 124, n. 3.

4 "Apologia," folio 47 v. "Superstition is by far a worse vice and crime than illicit intercourse. "Apologia," folio 37 v.

5 "Apologia," folios 32 v. and 34 r.

6 XLIII Articles, No. 1; quoted by Rotondò, "Bologna," p. 116, n. 4.

7 "Apologia," folio 25 r.; cf. folio 5 A.

Pelagius and Coelestius in 416, the II Council of Orange (under Caesarius of Arles) in 529 against the Semipelagians, Popes Gregory I, and Leo I, and Thomas Aquinas. At the end he was obliged to repudiate the view " that man does not have a free will except to do evil " and to avow instead " that man has a free will both to do good and to do evil, although, to be sure, he cannot perform works worthy of eternal life without the special grace of the Holy Spirit. "

With what Phileno would have preferred to call simply the Pauline (rather than either the Lutheran or the Augustinian) view of predestination and of the bondage of the will and with his fourth main doctrine concerning the provisional death of the soul Phileno had forged a highly sharpened two-edged sword which he could wield with frightening skill in cutting away the vestiges of the ecclesiastical merit system surviving, as he would later say, in even the Reformed churches. We turn to examine the second edge of Phileno's trenchant theology.

(4) The view that the soul at the death of the body falls into a dreamlike sleep and the starker conception of the complete extinction of the soul, in either case, with the hope of resuscitation with the body at the resurrection and for the final judgment are to be found, as was noted by way of our introduction, in the New Testament. It is not likely, however, that Phileno drew his eschatology directly from the scriptures but rather from the theories of the *Studium* of Padua and Bologna where philosophical and medical speculation had worked with the Averroistic idea of the death of the sentient *anima* with the body and the absorption of the individuated *anima intellectiva* into the universal intellect (*intellectus universalis*) and the even more drastically Aristotelian (Alexandrine) idea about the mortality of the soul expounded by Pomponazzi. That Phileno's espousal of the provisional death or sleep of the soul could be interpreted by the inquisitorial court of Ferrara as one with the most extreme heresies, exceeding in gravity even Calvinism, is suggested by the title of a work of the moderate crypto-Protestant Celio Secondo Curione writing in Lucca in the year after Phileno's trial, *De immortalitate animorum*, which was specifically directed against " Anabaptists, " " Epicureans, " and " Sadducees. "[1]

To use as nearly as possible his own words, Phileno presumably held prior to his trial " that the souls of the saints and the others justified have not yet entered heaven and will not enter in fact until after the last judgment " and therefore that they do not yet " enjoy the delights of paradise " nor " the vision of the highest God. "[2] By the same token, the souls of sinful believers are not suffering in purgatory. And this leads to the next major feature of Phileno's radical reformation.

---

[1] It was to be printed in the second edition of Curione's *Araneus seu de Providentia Dei* (Basel, 1544), pp. 89-93. Cf. Markus Kutter, *Celio Secondo Curione* (Basel, 1955), p. 44. On the background, also with special reference to Renato-Phileno, see Delio Cantimori, " Anabattismo e Neoplatonismo nel XVI secolo in Italia, " *Rendiconti della R. Accademia Nazionale dei Lincei*, cl. di. sc. mor., May-June, 1936, pp. 521-561.

[2] These phrases are from the Abjuration, and they appear also in the " Apologia. "

(5) The whole complex of ecclesiastical practices which presupposed the survival of the sentient soul in the interim before the general resurrection completely gives way in Phileno's theology under the pressure of his stress on predestination and eschatology. The saints are not yet in heaven to intercede on behalf of the living. Or at least — so he preferred to argue in the presence of the tribunal — the Old Testament and the New and even the early canons of the Church are aware of the great danger of idolatry and therefore do not require prayers to the saints as a matter of faith. Since like all souls, the soul of the Virgin Mary is at peace until the general resurrection, prayer even to her is of no avail, only the *Pater noster* as taught by Jesus being efficacious.[1] Since, then, all prayers and ecclesiastical practices based upon the assumption of a natural immortality of the sentient soul susceptible of pain or pleasure are without scriptural warrant, not only are all Masses for the dead invalid but also all prayers of intercession, in fact the whole penitential system of confession and fasts, especially during Lent. Moreover, the Mass should be celebrated in its primitive simplicity just as it was instituted by Jesus and recorded by the evangelists and Paul. Chapels, convents, and monasteries which exist partly by reason of the endowments for the saying of Masses for the dead should be disbanded and vows should be dissolved. As for this last point, which was existential for him (as a friar who had once taken vows) and for the devout poor, Phileno declared expressly that "one should not make a vow to God or to the saints and that, even having done so, one should not fulfill it," once liberated by the true gospel.[2]

(6) Phileno converted the whole psychology and practice of monastic vows and vows to the saints into a new evangelical basis for another kind of commitment among reborn Christians. Going beyond the aristocratic interiorization of faith in the circles of Valdesian piety, Phileno stressed the corporate dimension of faith and the egalitarian participation of all in the deliberations of the evangelical fellowship. All have gifts, he argued, appealing to I Corinthians chs. 12 and 14, women as well as men, the poor as well as the noble, the learned and the unlearned, who should all study together and await the counsel of the Holy Spirit. Knowing that all men are fallible, Phileno was confident that fittly joined and guided and illuminated by the Holy Spirit, they were in the best position to learn God's word and will, for the Holy Spirit is the sole interpreter of Holy Scripture in the midst of the faithful. All should, therefore, have them and especially the New Testament in their hands, studying, meditating, conferring, testing the spirits, and mutually seeking the truth, night and day. Who would not say that thus guided they would surely know the truth and not fall into any error? For human opinions can be discussed in common as to whether they conform to the divine and then be received, to the

---

[1] "Apologia," folios 13r., 26 v.

[2] Abjuration and "Apologia," folios 40 v., 41 v., and 8 a.

glory of God the Father and Jesus Christ and for the love of one's neighbor.[1] In his theory of the evangelical community, Phileno went so far, apparently, as to advocate that " it is for Christians to have one heart and one mind and all things in common — but for the glory of Christ. "[2]

(7) Within the socially mixed, evangelically fervent circles to which Phileno had brought his message in Venice (presumably), Bologna, Modena, and Staggia, the initiative of evangelically motivated landowners and princes (like Thomaso Carandino and Duchess Renata of Ferrara) in bringing about a renewal of the Catholic Church in Italian towns and principalities was affirmed, no doubt, on the model of the German princes and patricians but in Phileno by express reference to the reforming kings of the Old Testament, for " in Italy we are under princes no less wise, no less Christian. "[3]

Such were the seven main points in Phileno's conception of the reformation of Christendom as he sat pondering his convictions and improvising responses to the inquisitors in Degli Angeli.

Given the radical character of Phileno's teachings, it is a wonder that the inquisitors in the proceedings, begun at Bologna, continued at Modena, and terminated at Ferrara just before Christmas 1540, took so long to declare Phileno a heretic![4] The fact is that the brilliant rhetorician and well-versed theologian had been so resourceful in parrying the charges of the witnesses by citing such ancient authorities as Cyprian and Chrysostom and such later writers as Scotus and Erasmus (who, not incidentally, was in Bologna in 1506)[5] that the advocate among the six consultors, Lodovico de Silvestris, could contend that Phileno was not " formally heretical, " that he had effectively advanced scriptural, patristic, and scholastic reasons for his doubts, and that he had, all told, offered enough explanation of the spirit in which he was probing for answers " to alleviate his case " and to justify the tribunal in sparing him the ordinary penalties for stubborn heretics. Until persuaded by the majority, Lodovico proposed that the tribunal find some " extraordinary " remedy suitable to the case.

The five remaining consultors found Phileno indeed guilty of heresy; but at least one, Fra Girolamo dei Landi, O. P., lector on metaphysics at the University of Ferrara, urged that the normal punishment be mitigated lest Phileno " fall into despair. " The three consultors who voted for the normal punishment of a clever but obdurate heretic were Fra Giovanni Verato, Carmelite professor of theology at the University of Ferrara, Dom Giacomo Emiliano of Ferrara, doctor of law, and

---

[1] " Apologia, " folios 28 v.-29 r., 32 v., 47 v.; Rotondò, " Bologna, " pp. 118-122.

[2] XLIII Articles, No. 1; Rotondò, " Bologna, " p. 121, n. 4.

[3] " Apologia, " folios 30 v.-31 r.; XLI Articles, No. 38; quoted by Rotondò, " Bologna, " p. 124, n. 3.

[4] The opinions of the six consultors are found with the " Apologia. "

[5] A. Renaudet, *Érasme et l'Italie* (Geneva, 1954), pp. 74-76. Cf. Phileno's references to the reading of Erasmus in Bologna, " Apologia, " folio 30 r.

Fra Andrea da Imola, O. P., lector and priest in the convent of Santa Maria degli Angeli in Ferrara. The most severe in his judgment among the consultors was Dom Lanfranco di Lugo, doctor and professor in Ferrara, who was certain that Phileno, because of his pertinacity in responses, his excuses, evasions, and frivolities, was at heart impenitent, and that he should therefore be given over to the secular arm for the ultimate punishment. It would appear that Lanfranco, though the most pitiless, was also the most discerning of the consultors!

The final sentence was that Phileno should make a public Abjuration (the nine implied accusations of which we have been citing above) and that he should be verbally degraded from his ecclesiastical rank and consigned to perpetual imprisonment. That he was only *verbally* degraded confirms our impression that for some time, perhaps since his stay in Venice, Phileno had not been wearing the habit of a friar.

According to the sentence, Phileno publicly recanted all his heresies. The accounts all agree that after the recantation there was "a solemn procession," at the end of which Phileno's sentence as a convicted "Lutheran" was read and he was mitred.[1] After his confession of the Catholic faith,[2] Phileno went on to promise that he would not in the future adhere to any of the aforementioned heresies; that he would not seek to win any others to them; that he would not harbor any heretical books; that, if in future he should know of any one infected with any of these heresies or to be in possession of such books, he would inform on them before the two ecclesiastics who had conducted his trial; that he would neither flee nor leave without the approval, permission, and consent of the local authorities; that he would not complain about his punishment; and, finally, that if he should ever contravene his solemn promises, he would willingly submit to all the penalties due the relapsed according to the canon law. The provisions here enumerated strangely suggest that there was in fact an effort (inspired perhaps by Duchess Renata) to rehabilitate the much-admired preacher in return for his formal recantation. These provisions point to a kind of house arrest or gentleman's detention on good behavior rather than life imprisonment. Yet the very document which contains the Abjuration and these conditions states elsewhere that he was sentenced to imprisonment[3] for life. A third source, Duke Ercole[4], in the letter to his ambassador in Rome with information for Contarini, in mentioning the sentence of life imprisonment, interprets it as in

---

[1] Letter of Duke Ercole to Ruggeri, p. 129, n. 3, above; Lancellotti, *Cronaca*, pp. 419 f.; Casadei, "Fileno," p. 372.

[2] These special provisions coming at the end of the abjuration are to be found in Tassoni, "Cronaca," pp. 331 f.; Casadei, "Fileno," pp. 374 f.; cf. "Apologia," folio 5 A.

[3] Lancellotti, *Cronaca*, p. 420 f.; Casadei, "Fileno," p. 373. This report is based on one Andrea Barco Cancelero of Modena who happened to be in Ferrara on the day of the solemn sentence, having gone there to present the duke with some fine pigs. Andrea is reported to have described the punishment as that of Phileno's being bound for life in the galley (*galea*), but this is probably a misreading for prison (*galera*).

[4] Letter of Duke Ercole, to Ruggieri, n. 1 above.

itself the act of clemency secured by him in recognition of the fact that the penitent heretic was a man "di tale qualitade."

It is possible that the duke himself chose to interpret the sentence of confinement more liberally than the inquisitors. Phileno was at some point after the trial taken from Ferrara to a prison in Bologna, as we learn from an entry in the Modenese chronicle under date of 11 May 1541.[1] The same source reports that Phileno "was said to have accused many persons of heresy," as indeed he had promised he would in the Abjuration forced from him in Ferrara.

There is, however, no evidence that his alleged delations affected his following in Modena, Bologna, and presumably Ferrara. At least his ideas remained a potent influence. One Modenese chronicler observed that "the evil seed sown by him had, in the meantime, taken deep root"; another, that the doctrine of the immortality of the soul was the subject of an important sermon in the cathedral.[2] Moreover, three letters from Martin Bucer in Strassburg, dated 17 August, 10 September, and 23 December 1541,[3] indicate that radical ideas about predestination and the Lord's Supper were agitating the evangelical conventicles of Bologna and Modena at this time. These evangelicals, whom Bucer addressed as brothers, were exercised by the question "whether God is the author of sin"[4] and whether Christ was in any sense present in the elements of the communion. Lacking, as we do, the letters by which or the informants through whom Bucer learned of the controversy in Bologna and Modena, we can only infer from certain locutions that the Strassburg divine was dealing with a doctrinal ferment more radical than he realized, and that the questions posed were precisely those raised by Phileno.

There is, for example, a faint trace in Bucer's coping with the eucharistic problem of sacrament, mystery, and symbol of the ter-

---

[1] Lancellotti, *Cronaca*, VII, 53; Casadei, "Fileno," p. 375.

[2] Tassoni, "Cronaca," quoted by Cantù, *Eretici*, II, 137 f.; Lancellotti, *Cronaca*, VII, 52, under date of 9 May 1541. The Phileno affair was to be remembered as a *cause célèbre* in Modena well into the seventeenth century. See Lodovico Vedriani, *Historia della antichissima città di Modona* (Modena, 1667), II, 528.

[3] Bucer or pseudonymously as Aretius Felinus writes three letters: "to the Italians," "to the brethren in Bologna and Modena," "to the Italians" (perhaps in Lucca). Works of Bucer arranged topically by Konrad Hubert, *Scripta Anglicana* (Basel, 1577), pp. 687-689. It is of interest that the conciliatory work of Contarini at Regensburg (Ratisbon) in 1541 was preceded by that of Martin Bucer and Johann Gropper at Worms in the *Liber Ratisbonensis*, presented at the Colloquy of Regensburg. On Bucer's relations with the Italians, see Jacques Pollet, editor, *Martin Bucer: Études sur la correspondance*, II (Paris, 1962).

[4] A certain Alexander is mentioned in the letter of 23 December. The fact that in this letter Bucer mentions the recent death of Capito (3 November 1541) suggests that one of the mediators of information from Bologna and Modena might have been Francesco Negri, at the time in Chiavenna (whither Phileno would presently flee); for Negri had studied with Bucer and Capito in Strassburg between 1529 and 1531 and would have given currency among the Italian Evangelicals to the name of the otherwise much less widely known Capito. It is, of course, also possible that Calvin had familiarized the Reform-minded circle with the name of Capito, during his stay at the court of Duchess Renata in 1536.

minology known to have been employed by Phileno at least at a later date. There is a bare suggestion in the terms employed by Bucer for the proper conduct of the eucharistic service that the Italians, under Phileno's influence, had already introduced an *agape* before the communion and that in the observation thereof the distinction between the minister and the *plebs* had been programmatically obliterated.[1] Such egalitarianism suggests Phileno's known ecclesiological views, commonly pilloried as subversive.

---

[1] See especially the letter of 10 September wherein Bucer insists that only the scriptural words and not those of the minister should be employed and that the *ministri* were present " ad distribuendum et sumendum; plebs, ad sumendum " and the injunction: " edamus et bibamus, non circumferamus vel includamus. " These words could, to be sure, just as well be used by Bucer to mark off the evangelical from the elaborate Catholic observances; but in the context Bucer seems to be warning against extremes on the left rather than on the right. It should be remarked that not only in the evangelical conventicles but also even in the Cappella of Renata in Ferrara, " la messa di sette punti " was observed, modeled no doubt on the simplified service as observed at the court of Navarre, with communion in both kinds.

Part II

CAMILLO RENATO: RADICAL RHAETIAN REFORMER (1542- ? 1575)[1]

Some time in 1542 Ricci-Phileno escaped from prison in Bologna and appeared in Tirano in the Valtellina, a protectorate of the Rhaetian Republic, itself confederated with the Swiss. From Tirano he addressed a letter under date of 9 November 1542[2] to Heinrich Bullinger in Zurich; and, signing himself perhaps for the first time "Camillo Renato," he began therewith his extraordinary career within and against the Reformed Church of Rhaetia.

By 1548 Ricci-Phileno-Renato and his followers will be anathematized by the chief spokesman of the Italian-speaking Reformed churches of Rhaetia, the ex-Austin Friar, Agostino Mainardo, pastor in Chiavenna. The first of the XXII Anathemas will read: "We damn those who say [like Renato] that the rational soul (*anima rationalis*) is mortal, that it dies along with the body, but that on the Last Day it will be resurrected with the body, and that then the whole man will be made truly immortal."[3]

Renato will be condemned by the Reformed Church of Rhaetia not only for his psychopannychism but also for his Libertine formulation of the doctrine of election; also for his observance of the Eucharist as a nourishing *agape* or fellowship meal for commingled rich and poor, natives and refugees, in the mountainside parish of Caspano under the patronage of the locally powerful Paravicini family; for introducing adult or believers' baptism; and for preaching religious toleration and defending Michael Servetus in another long *carmen*.

---

[1] This chapter originally was delivered as a lecture in Italian at Torre Pellice in August, 1961 at the annual international *Convegno* devoted to Italian "Eretici" sponsored by the Società di Studi Valdesi. I am very grateful to Mrs. Robert Pfeiffer of Cambridge who prepared the translation and to several scholars in attendance at the *Convegno* who brought me into further contact with Italian research projects, notably, Augusto Armand-Hugon, Salvatore Caponetto, Alain Dufour, Luigi Firpo, Giovanni Gonnet, Henri Meylan, and Giorgio Spini. See John Tedeschi's evaluation of the sessions in *Church History*, XXXI (1962), 235-238.

[2] Traugott Schiess, *Bullingers Korrespondenz mit den Graubündern*, three volumes, Quellen zur Schweizer Geschichte, XXIII (1904), XXIV (1905), XXV (1906), henceforth cited I, II, III. Camillo's first letter is I, No. 37, pp. 48-51.

[3] The XXII Anathemas of Mainardo are printed by da Porta, *op. cit.*, 1: 2, pp. 83-86. Cf. Mainardo's letter to Bullinger, 10 December 1548; Schiess, I, No. 104, pp. 139 f.

In the meantime he will have found occasion to share his convictions with a youthful visitor from Siena, Laelius Socinus. The ideas and practices, the strengths and weaknesses, the vision and the vacillation of Ricci-Phileno-Renato were to be perpetuated in Socinianism.

1) CAMILLO RENATO: PROTESTANT HUMANIST (*1542-1546*)

It is here the place to inquire into the origin of Ricci-Phileno's new and obviously programmatic name. Surely as Camillus Renatus he had been miraculously reborn to enter upon a bright new religious career after the darkness of his imprisonment. That this name originally had an Anabaptist implication of baptismal rebirth is unlikely. More likely is the assumption that the two names are to be taken as one and that the defrocked master of Latin literature and rhetoric was *Camillus redivivus*, the restorer, with reference in the *Aeneid*[1] to the hero who brought back to Rome the *signa* captured by the Gauls; for Camillo Renato's main claim to theological achievement in his subsequent correspondence with the Reformed divines of the Swiss Confederation would be that he had been the most consistent of any as a restorer of the intended meaning of the *segni* of baptism and the Lord's Supper. It is also possible that he wished to indicate by the choice of a new name that, as a defrocked friar and priest, he intended to be henceforth only a *camillus*, that is, according to the classical Roman definition " a (young) nobleman qualified to help the priest in the sacred rites. " It is in any event true that he crossed the frontier of the Rhaetian Republic as a prospective tutor, prepared also to " help " the Italian refugee pastors without wishing to assume a ministerial charge.

In addressing Bullinger the first time Camillo did not broach his favorite subject of the sacraments as signs, but contented himself rather with theological generalities, supplying us incidentally with a few faint biographical reminiscences.

Perhaps the most important fact in the letter of 9 November 1542, written two years almost to the day after the transfer of his trial from Modena to Ferrara, was his statement that he had felt emboldened to write to Bullinger because of the encouragement given him by Celio Secondo Curione, " with whom [he was] closely joined no less by friendship than by religion. " Where did Camillo have occasion to make the acquaintance of Curione?

Circumstantial evidence points back to Ferrara. Curione himself had come from Venice to the court of Duke Ercole and Duchess Renata around the time of Camillo's trial. It is of interest that back in Venice, the Reform-minded Austin friar Giulio della Rovere Milanese had stayed in Curione's home. In fact this was one of the charges brought against Giulio in his own judicial hearing (his second), 19 April 1541, the spring

[1] VI, 825. Cf. Church, *Italian Reformers*, p. 132, n. 3.

after Phileno's condemnation in Ferrara. In this Venetian hearing, "Fileno" was mentioned in connection with an incriminating letter of 13 February (1541) from Bologna found in Giulio's possession. Giulio, who after his escape to Rhaetia was destined to be a major opponent of Camillo, remarked to the examining inquisitor that "Fileno," whom he did not (then) know personally, had been imprisoned because of his foolhardiness (*leggerezza*).[1] This court record would indicate only that the affair of "Fileno"-Camillo, known to Giulio in Venice, was presumably also known to Curione. Curione may have left Venice before Giulio's trial; and it is possible, after settling briefly in Ferrara at the invitation of Fulvio Pellegrino Morato (formerly *maestro di scuola*, former *preceptore* of Cardinal Ippolito d'Este), that Curione was drawn to make the acquaintance of the distinguished Franciscan prisoner, with whom he would have had many literary and some religious interests in common. Curione himself did not stay long in Ferrara. Duchess Renata thought it would be safer for him in tolerant Lucca where there was an evangelical conventicle. A letter from Morato indicates that Curione had departed thither by 30 October 1541; but he would have been long enough in Ferrara to have come to know Camillo confined after his abjuration but enjoying, as it would appear from the terms of his submission, a measure of social contact (before removal for a perhaps harsher incarceration in Bologna). It is even possible that the two men, the one slipping away from Lucca, the other escaping from Bologna, each presumptively aided in accordance with the gravity of his situation by Duchess Renata, entered Rhaetia together.[2]

We know that Camillo's esteem for Curione was reciprocated; for from Lausanne in a letter to Bullinger of 10 December 1542 Curione described Camillo as "a man outstanding in letters and religion" and urged Bullinger to write to him; and soon thereafter he wrote again, mentioning Camillo "as above all a good man."[3] As late as the Basel edition (1544) of his *Pasquillus Ecstaticus*, Curione included Camillo, Phileni Siculus, a man of deep piety and learning, among the most illustrious of the Italians who had espoused reformed views.[4]

---

[1] Giuseppe de Leva, "Giulio da Milano," *Rivista Cristiana*, XV (1887), 326; Kutter, *Curione*, p. 32; Casadei, "Fileno," pp. 326, 377.

[2] The letter of Morato to Curione has been discussed and calendared by Kutter, *Curione*, as Brief No. 3, pp. 41 and 296. The surmise that Curione and Camillo fled together is made by Friedrich Trechsel, without supporting evidence. *Die protestantischen Antitrinitarier vor Faustus Socin*, two volumes (Heidelberg, 1844), II, 74. The point is repeated by Schiess, I, p. lxviii. Against the view that Curione may have come to sympathize with Camillo in Ferrara is that precisely after his removal to Lucca in 1541, Curione wrote *De immortalitate animorum* against "Anabaptists" and others. Kutter, *Curione*, p. 44 and above at p. 133, n. 1.

[3] The two unedited letters of Curione to Bullinger, Lausanne 10 December 1542 and 4 March 1543, Zurich: Staatsarchiv E. II-228 and 366-388, are numbered by Kutter, *Curione*, Briefe Nos. 7 and 10, pp. 70 and 296; cf. Cantimori, *Eretici* (German edition), p. 86.

[4] The Geneva edition of *Pasquillus* in 1544 does not mention our Siculus. The Italian translation of 1546 has substituted for Siculus two other Italians: Pietro da Cittadella

Camillo's first letter to Bullinger was, as already remarked, only an introduction to his request to have Bullinger forward an enclosed letter to Curione. For the rest, what Camillo says about himself and his theology is more significant perhaps for what is left out. After speaking about the suffering and turmoil of all the Italian evangelicals in general, Camillo refers to his own experience of the suspicions inspired by Satan, of threats, machinations, prisons, humiliations, tortures, and the greatest of all calamities, the great and painful uncertainty whether by the order of Antichrist he would be placed in prison for life in solitude and perpetual hunger or whether he would be secretly and suddenly brought to an untimely death. This last allusion comes pretty close to describing the very uncertainty we have already noted in connection with the trial and sentence in Ferrara.

As for his theological views, Camillo, of course, on principle assumes, as in a number of letters to follow, that Bullinger and he are in substantial agreement; but he remains in this letter intentionally vague about just how the " order of priests, first of the Jews and then of the Romans " has distorted the truth. Camillo speaks of " that Christian spirit " which is the source of all joy and knowledge among Christians. He suggests that it is the spirit which leads to " the very certain and true reason for immortal life. " Here, of course, he is no doubt cryptically alluding to his doctrine of the provisional death of the righteous soul with the body pending the general resurrection.

Apart from introducing himself and his thoughts and enclosing a letter for Curione, Camillo in his first letter to Bullinger seems to have been principally concerned to secure the concerted effort of the established churches of the Swiss cantons in placing the ever increasing number of Italian clerical refugees from the Roman Inquisition reorganized on a new basis that very year.

Before proceeding further we must briefly characterize the region around Tirano in which Camillo had himself found refuge. The Rhaetian Republic, roughly the modern Swiss Grisons, and coterminous with the bishopric of Chur as it existed then, was a federation of three component Alpine federations: The Upper or Grey League proper with its chief city, Ilanz, often lent its name to the Republic as a whole (Grigioni, Graubünden, Grisons). The other two component federations were the League of the House of God with its capital at Chur and the League of the Ten Jurisdictions with its chief city, Davos. The three federations constituting the Rhaetian Republic were linked closely with the Swiss Confederation. In 1512 the three federations of the Rhaetian Republic had jointly come into possession of subject territory received as indemnification for their joint military service in Italy. This fringe of subject territory, roughly the valleys of the Mera and the Adda from Bormio down to Lake Como, was administered by appointive

---

and Baldo Lupetino of Chersa. The omission of Siculus in the list of 1546 may well be related to Curione's disenchantment with Camillo in Rhaetia.

Rhaetian functionaries. The principal subdivisions of this federal jurisdiction were the district around Bormio, the Valtellina (German: Veltlin), and the district around Chiavenna. Valtellina, the largest region, was subdivided into three main administrative districts: the Lower Valley with Traona as the chief city, the Middle Valley with Sondrio, and the Upper Valley with Teglio and Camillo's city of refuge, Tirano. The whole of the federal jurisdiction was Italian or Ladin in speech, as indeed were many of the valleys within all three of the component federations of the Rhaetian Republic, especially the League of the House of God except for its chief city, Chur (somewhat detached from the rest). Italian, Ladin (Romansh), and German constituted the three official languages of the Republic.

Religiously also the Rhaetian Republic was divided. At the federal diet in Ilanz in 1526 mutual religious toleration of Catholics and Evangelicals (Protestants) had been decreed with the provision that whichever party had the majority in any parish or district would have also the use of the ecclesiastical edifices. Anabaptists had been expressly excluded from the provisions of the edict. The religious rights under the edict of Ilanz were extended to the joint federal territory, which in contrast to the rest of the Rhaetian Republic stood, on the Catholic side, under the jurisdiction of the bishop of Como. But as early as 1523 the inquisitor of the region, Fra Modesto Scrofo, had been driven out and further inquisitorial activities were no longer tolerated by the Republic.

It was, then, into a region of considerable religious and ethnic toleration that Camillo had found his way as a refugee from the Dominican inquisition of Bologna. Tirano, from which he wrote his first letter to Bullinger, 9 November 1542, was an administrative and judicial center near the seat of the powerful and noble family of the Paravicini,[1] headed by Raffaele and Bartolomeo the Elder. Their ancestral seat (*sedes originaria*) was Caspano, a pleasantly situated high village down the Adda Valley from Tirano, over across from Morbegno. Here Camillo was engaged as a tutor. In a letter of 6 July 1544[2] Camillo commended one of his young charges, Bartolomeo Paravicini Junior, to Bullinger, urging the Zurich divine to help the promising young Italian to learn to write and speak German as a pensionary in some appropriate Zurich home. Soon thereafter[3] Camillo thanked Bullinger for his help in getting young Paravicini established and took the occa-

---

[1] The Paravicini were originally called Casapani, then Paravesini, then interchangeably Para- and Pallavicini, and in modern times Parravicini. For the local history of the ancient village of the Paravicini, see Giovanni Libera, *Cronistoria di Caspano e dei paesi limitrofi* (Como, 1928); Cesare Cantù, *Storia della Città o Diocesi di Como*, 2 vols. (Como, 1899); Francesco Saverio Quadrio, *Dissertazioni critico-storiche intorno alla Rezia di qua dalle Alpi, oggi detta Valtellina*, 3 vols. (Milan, 1756; reprinted 1960). I am indebted to Signor Carlo Mauri of Caspano for supplying some of the details.

[2] I, No. 54.

[3] 22 October 1544; I, No. 55.

sion to ask him whether amid his tremendous responsibilities he would find time to inform the Italian brethren in the valley of the progress of the Reformation in the north.

In due course, Bullinger responded to Camillo's request for news of the Reformation by sending a letter accompanied by a copy of his eucharistic *Confessio*.[1] In this letter, Bullinger was apparently under the misapprehension that Camillo was an established preacher living in Tirano, from whence he had addressed his first letter to him. Camillo in his reply of 15 May 1545,[2] written from Chiavenna, where he was presumably on a visit, explained to Bullinger that he was entirely engaged as a teacher and not in Tirano but now in Traona, a town on the same right bank of the Adda as Caspano and about the same distance down from Morbegno as was Caspano up the valley from it. That his real base remained, however, the Paravicini seat of Caspano is indicated by another letter written from there later in the summer.[3] The thermal baths nearby will have been a special resource for the ailing humanist.

Apart from this geographical and professional specification, along with a recommendation of one Peter Finer, the bearer of the letter, and some perfunctory remarks about the council in Trent, the real interest of the letter to Bullinger of 15 May 1545 is that for the first time in the correspondence Camillo broached one of the important theological issues which will in the end completely separate the two men. It concerned the Lord's Supper. Although Camillo somewhat pretentiously remarked that as regards eucharistic doctrine, locally, " the authority of Bullinger and Camillo " were cited as equal and as virtually interchangeable, still Camillo felt obliged to make clear in what this identity of view consisted:

> We acknowledge nothing, indeed, in the Supper which we have recently begun to celebrate [in Caspano] – as it was instituted by Christ and perpetuated by the apostles – except the recollection (*memoriam*) of the death of Christ, by which we have been drawn (*asciti*) from the tyranny of Satan and the power of darkness into the kingdom of light....[4]

In the very next letter, that from Caspano, 10 August 1545,[5] Camillo made quite clear the practice he had instituted in the evangelical

---

[1] Schultess-Richtberg, *H. Bullinger der Nachfolger Zwinglis*, Schriften des Vereins für Reformations-Geschichte, No. 82, 1904. This was on an earlier draft of what would become the *Confessio Helvetica posterior*. Heinold Fast, *Heinrich Bullinger und die Täufer* (Weierhof, 1959) deals with Bullinger's relation to Camillo, pp. 61-63. Augusto Armand-Hugon deals with the relation of Camillo and Mainardo in *Agostino Mainardo: Contributo alla Storia della Riforma in Italia* (Torre Pellice [1943]), pp. 51-74.

[2] I, No. 58.

[3] Caspano, 10 August 1545, on which more below.

[4] I, No. 58, p. 74.

[5] I, No. 59.

church sponsored by the Paravicini family. It was a communion service preceded by an *agape*, which Camillo, with his predilection for classical terms made bold to call a *libatio* preceded by an *epulum*. Camillo based this practice on Paul's claim to have established the eucharist in Corinth (I Corinthians 11: 17-34, particularly v. 23) as it had been transmitted to him from the Lord; and Camillo therefore laid great stress upon the fact that precisely the Pauline communion in Corinth involved a complete meal with the partakers thereof reclining at tables in the Hellenic fashion.[1] He reminded Bullinger that despite the regrettable excesses indulged in by the Corinthian converts, Paul himself showed no intention of altering the basic character of the full Dominical institution of a meal to be followed by the liturgical action and that Paul sought merely to propose safeguards for seemly and truly fraternal conduct. Camillo insisted, moreover, that the ever-recurring meal of the brethren was precisely the occasion and ordained setting for doing that which Jesus asked his followers to do: namely, when breaking bread and taking the cup, to do so in memory of him until he come again in glory. There is evidence that some such practice of " daily communion " was observed in this sense among the Germanic Anabaptists in and around Chur. Something of a eucharistic character was also given to the meals presided over by Waldensian barbs. Moreover, we have already noted that Camillo himself, under the name of Phileno, seems to have gotten something like this under discussion if not into practice in Bologna and Modena, if we press hard certain of the locutions used by Bucer in his letters to the Evangelicals in those two cities in 1541.

As for Camillo's eucharistic theology, as distinguished from the interesting novelties as to its practice in Caspano, Bullinger was informed with satisfactory precision in the same letter. Camillo distinguished sharply between the supper in which the apostles themselves participated before Calvary, and the Supper as they and all other Christians were to observe it after the crucifixion. The difference is expressed in the two terms *manducatio* and *commemoratio*. Before the crucifixion the apostles, seated about their still living Lord, were asked, by eating the bread and drinking the wine, to realize in this tangible way that the body before them would presently be broken on the cross for their salvation. Eating (*manducatio*) was at this moment virtually a substitute for belief or faith because the apostles were almost incredulous before the impending events. In contrast, after the crucifixion and the resurrection, they and all Christians after them, believing as they now could in the crucifixion as an accomplished fact, were henceforth required only to recall (*commemoratio*) in gratitude (*recordatio*) what had been accomplished for the believer's salvation until Christ should come a second time. In this way Camillo detached the dutiful and faithful *manducatio* of the apostles at the Last Supper as a technical

---

[1] I Corinthians 10: 14-22.

term for the once-for-all experience of salvation by faith in Christ's definitive action for the elect:

For eating takes place but once (*semel*), at that moment when you have assented to the gospel for the first time in your heart; but commemoration takes place however often you wish; the one for each in his turn, apart, the other never except in church and assembly; the one in secret, the other openly; the one beyond bread and wine, the other, not properly at least, without bread and wine.... Accordingly, in the first, to receive the body and the blood is none other than to believe and to be persuaded that Christ has died for thee, given his body on the cross and the blood shed for the remission of our sins.[1]

Here for perhaps the only time in the eucharistic discussions of the sixteenth century the whole of a formal eucharistic argumentation is seen to be built up on the tradition preserved by Paul to the exclusion of any important allusions to the eucharistic texts of John vi or the synoptic accounts of the institution. In a subsequent letter[2] Camillo would be making even more explicit his conception of the relationship between faith and inward eating: " Faith precedes that spiritual partaking (*perceptionem*) of the body and blood; and this [experience], the offering of the bread and wine. "

Camillo's conception of an inward eating as a redemptive experience occurring once in a lifetime has affinities with the view and even the terminology of Caspar Schwenckfeld;[3] but the eucharistic theology of this Silesian Spiritualist, which led to his policy of suspending the outward communion service altogether was based primarily upon John vi in a tradition going back by way of medieval eucharistic piety to Augustinian symbolism. Camillo in his eucharistic theology, in contrast, based as it was on Paul's account of the Dominical tradition, not only interiorized the first faithful eating (*manducatio*) as the unique (*semel*) inward appropriation of salvation, as with Schwenckfeld, but also, and unlike Schwenckfeld, stressed the importance of the outward, corporate *commemoratio*; he even insisted on a full meal to be followed by the eucharistic action, which was at once a grateful recollection (*recordatio*) of what had been done at Calvary and an eschatological anticipation of Christ's imminent return in vindication of his own. " Thus, " it was possible for Camillo to say confidently to Bullinger, " what [Christ] instituted by these very words [*Hoc facite in mei commemorationem*] was not a new kind of eating but a new kind of commemoration, "[4] namely, a loyal and corporate recollection and a solemnly joyful anticipation of Christ's imminent advent in glory.

---

[1] I, No. 59, p. 76. See further on this distinction, below, at p. 155, n. 8.
[2] That of 2 November 1545; I, No. 63, p. 87.
[3] See the discussion of Schwenckfeld's eucharistic theology in my *Radical Reformation*, p. 114.
[4] I, No. 59, p. 76.

The tone of Camillo in his whole letter is theologically confident, and, while he is very respectful of Bullinger's position and authority, he does not hesitate to refer to the usage obtaining in his part of Reformed Christendom — even if that meant only one or at best a few churches under the protection of the Paravicini — as entitled to the same standing in friendly colloquies among Reformed divines; and he firmly but irenically reconstrues whatever suggestion there might have been in Bullinger's communication that the Zurich formulations could bind other Reformed churches, all the time commending Bullinger for his great skill in worsting Luther in the eucharistic treatise of which Bullinger had been so generous as to send him a copy.

The theological forthrightness, seriousness, and confidence of Camillo in this substantial letter to Bullinger of 10 August 1543 — in contrast with the rhetorical evasiveness of some of his other extant writings — confirm the surmise already made that his newly assumed name betokened for Camillo Renato his confidence in having recovered the intended meaning of the bread and wine as eschatological signs and that his own rebirth or redemptive regeneration had been occasioned by the exultant experience of understanding and appropriating the true meaning of the Pauline texts on which he had so long been concentrating. It is easy to see how he will also have linked the Pauline doctrine of election with that once-for-all inner *manducatio*; but in this letter to Bullinger he did not make the point.

It is not necessary to go into the eucharistic arguments of Bullinger's extensive reply in a letter from Zurich 18 September 1545.[1] Suffice it to say, Bullinger did not feel that the *agape* as practiced in Valtellina under Camillo's influence opened up a breach between the two divines; and he in fact exerted himself to show that the differences between the two of them were not too great, nevertheless advancing arguments, notably from John vi, for the conception of the presence of Christ in the eating and the drinking of the eucharistic elements. After deploring any doctrinal formulation or any ecclesiastical observance that would so completely break with the tradition of the centuries as to represent a real discontinuity or schism in the communion of saints, Bullinger commented on what Camillo had said about the council in Trent and asked for further information about the difficulties in getting started there.

It is of interest that from Lausanne, Curione assured Bullinger in a letter of 9 October 1545 that he considered both Camillo and the pastor in Chiavenna, Agostino Mainardo (whom he had come to know in Pavia) as *fratres* and that he had been in regular correspondence with them both.[2] In the meantime, Camillo was apparently engaged in broadening the unusual eucharistic practices countenanced by the Paravicini. His objective was the Reformed community precisely in

---

[1] I, No. 61.

[2] Kutter, *Curione*, Brief No. 23, p. 70.

Chiavenna, by now the most important Italian-speaking congregation in the Rhaetian Republic.

The first bearer of the Protestant gospel there had been Francesco Negri, native of Bassano in the Upper Valtellina, who arrived in Chiavenna in 1531 after following the lectures of Bucer and Capito in Strassburg for three years.[1] In 1539 he turned exclusively to tutoring in and around Chiavenna, making place for Mainardo as the town's evangelical preacher.

Agostino Mainardo (1482-1563) was a native of Saluzzo in the Piedmont. Formerly an Austin Friar, he was destined to become Camillo's principal foe. At first, Mainardo conducted himself with such tact in Chiavenna that the local Catholic majority did not raise any objections to his partial establishment of Protestantism. But as the Reformed community grew, the Catholics appealed to the provisions of the edict of Ilanz, according to which only the majority faith should have the use of the communal buildings consecrated to religion. Presently Mainardo's protectors appealed the case to the federal diet of the Rhaetian Republic meeting in Davos in 1544 and secured the right of donors to make satisfactory provisions for the worship of the religious minority in any given community.[2] A chapel, Santa Maria del Paterino, to which the powerful von Salis family had the right of presentation, was turned over to the growing evangelical community along with a house and garden for the new pastor.

Camillo had arrived in Chiavenna to win Mainardo over to his eucharistic theology and practice. Mainardo was not particularly attracted by the novelty of Camillo's *agape* but apparently went along with Camillo in accepting the use of Caspano. From Chiavenna, Camillo wrote to Bullinger, 2 November 1545,[3] expressing his appreciation for the forthrightness with which his long eucharistic epistle had been dealt with in a constructive spirit. He was particularly concerned to repeat his important thought about faith preceding the inward reception (*perceptio*) of the body and blood and to make clear to Bullinger that he by no means intended to say that faith would thereafter be absent from the observance of the commemorative meal but that the thought of Christ's body broken and of his blood shed was not necessarily any more present at the taking of the elements than when listening to a sermon or praying or conversing devoutly about the life and death of Christ. He repeated his point that the corruption of the supper as a part of the commemoration did not prompt Paul to abandon the meal and he insisted that the very name of the eucharistic action required that there be enough besides bread and wine to constitute a satisfactory *coena*. He noted that the early fathers of the Church up through Tertullian knew of the *epulum libationi coniunctum*.[4]

---

[1] Schiess, *Korrespondenz*, I, lix.
[2] Trechsel, *Antitrinitarier*, II, 74.
[3] 2 November 1545; I, No. 63.
[4] *Ibid.*, p. 88, line 20.

Camillo closed his letter with a greeting from Mainardo, whom he characterized "as a man certainly of learning and of more than ordinary piety," and with a specific request from him to convey his thanks to Bullinger for giving him also a copy of the same tract that Camillo had received. It is of interest that Mainardo was apparently not satisfied to confide the expression of these courtesies to Camillo, for the very next day he himself wrote Bullinger directly, repeating these points in a quite brief note, which no doubt went off with the same courier, and adding only that he had read Bullinger's tract and that he did not feel that "our" Camillo's insistence on the *epulum* was well founded either from the point of view of scripture and tradition or, and especially, from the point of view of practical churchmanship. He wondered what Bullinger had to say.

By December 19 Camillo was up the Mera Valley from Chiavenna where he presumably stayed with Bartolomeo Maturo, formerly Dominican prior in Cremona, the earliest of the Italian refugee preachers in the Rhaetian Republic,[1] from 1530 to 1547 the evangelical pastor of Vicosoprano. From here, Camillo, in the name of both, wrote to Bullinger, asking him to assist a certain Gabriele[2] who had been driven from his church in Morcote and indicating that thereby the spread of the gospel in the whole region of Lugano and Locarno was imperilled.

The next time Bullinger heard from Camillo it was from Chiavenna, 15 August 1546.[3] Camillo was still on good enough terms with Mainardo to feel free to greet the Zurich churchmen in the Lord for Mainardo and the rest of the Chiavenna brethren. Once more he asks Bullinger to send on a letter to Curione, at Lausanne. Camillo expresses some weariness about discussing any further the relatively slight differences between Bullinger's Zurich and Camillo's Chiavenna. He does remark, however, that once tradition is allowed to dictate the usage and practice of the church over and above what is expressly laid down in scripture all kinds of problems arise; and he mentions all the controversy over the words of Augustine, Ambrose, Jerome, and Gregory the Great who had thought that by their words they were solving rather than occasioning further controversy.

2) RADICAL REFORMER (*1547-1551*)

Camillo's interest in sacramental theology seems to have been shifting. When Bullinger next heard from him, Camillo was concerned with baptism. In his letter of 6 July 1547[4] and in a somewhat earlier one referred to therein but lost, Camillo asked Bullinger whether he thought baptism in the names of the triune God was necessary for its validity.

---

[1] He first appeared in 1529. *Ibid.*, p. 74.
[2] The Latin text, of course, is simply Gabriel.
[3] I, No. 73.
[4] I, No. 81.

The question had arisen locally, he said somewhat casually, because when for one reason or another the full triune formula was neglected, some people wondered whether the baptism was not thereby nullified. He asked also that another letter be forwarded to Curione. He closed the letter with a mention not only of Mainardo but also of Francesco Negri, both as sending greetings. Although for the moment Francesco was singled out because he had been quite sick for the past four days, it is likely that Camillo was already conscious of bonds that bound them together against the apparently unimaginative and aging pastor, already under some criticism for his ineptitudes and neglects.

For his part Mainardo, however neglectful of his pastoral charge, was sufficiently alert to the doctrinal restiveness in his congregation to identify Camillo as the source of all his difficulties. At this juncture Johannes Blasius of Chur entered the picture. He had come south for the installation in the church of Caspano of Dr. Bartolomeo de' Paravicini, Camillo's tutee of former days. Bartolomeo, highly qualified by his studies in Zurich, had been named to the ministry of the church of Caspano by Andrea de' Paravicini, of the same noble family. Bartolomeo was apparently involved in a violent episode with the *podestà* when he took the crucifix out of the church by night and broke it up.[1] The case of the needlessly brutal *podestà* (not that of the Renatian iconoclast!) was brought before the federal diet, because his violence controvened the statutes of the Republic, committed to a policy of religious toleration. At the same time, Bartolomeo, not because of the iconoclasm in particular, but more generally because he held strongly to the opinions of Camillo, could not get his nomination synodally approved. Since the federal diet of Chur in 1537, the synod of the Reformed churches of the Rhaetian Republic had in effect gained the right to examine and approve all nominations and elections to local pastorates as a measure for bringing some order into the chaos of the valley parishes, some of them so poor and inexperienced that they had been falling into the hands of impostors as well as of heretics and necessitous refugees. It was Pietro Paolo Vergerio, former bishop of Capodistria, who intervened on behalf of Dr. Bartolomeo de' Paravicini with the synod. This imposing intervention brought Blasius south to solemnize the recognition of the new minister by the general synod and no doubt also to size up on the spot the condition of the churches among the Italians in the lower valleys.

In Chiavenna Blasius found a big controversy in progress between Camillo and Mainardo over the sacraments, as he reported to Bullinger in his letter of 20 September 1547.[2] He remarked the Italian temperament of both contestants as embittering the situation and gave precision to the theological issues between them. Mainardo, he observed, held (in accordance with standard Reformed theology) that the (two)

---

[1] Da Porta, *Historia,* I: 2, pp. 42-44.
[2] I, No. 86.

sacraments confirmed the covenants (*pacta*) of God, while, as we know from his own words, Camillo denied this and felt that great difficulties ensued from this insistence upon externals. When Blasius got back to Chur, he wrote Bullinger more about the discord [1] and, styling Camillo as well as Mainardo a minister, said that he intended to summon them both before the general Rhaetian synod to meet presently, there to answer for causing strife and to give reason for their doctrine. When the synod convened in Chur, only Mainardo showed up with a statement consonant with scripture and Bullinger's known views. Camillo, "led, one knows not by what spirit," did not even acknowledge the summons to the extent of sending a statement, so Blasius reported to Bullinger in his letter of 12 December 1547.[2] Mainardo was encouraged to visit Bullinger personally and, accordingly, was in Zurich in January 1548.

Bullinger will have been reminded of Camillo also in the following month on receiving a letter [3] from Bartolomeo de' Paravicini Junior in Caspano, who had himself once lived in the Bullinger household as a paying guest.[4] Young Dr. Bartolomeo asked Bullinger now to receive into his home the promising thirteen-year old son of Cousin Raffaele. Dr. Bartolomeo incidentally remarks that Camillo, no longer in Caspano, would also be writing a letter of recommendation. From Chiavenna, Camillo wrote to this effect a few days later.[5] In this brief note he did not say a word about what had happened at Chur nor about what he might have been up to during Mainardo's trip to Zurich. But a few days before this in Chur, 28 February 1548, Philipp Gallicius von Salis wrote to Bullinger [6] and supplied him with really fresh news: Camillo Renato had written a whole book, *Adversus baptismum quem sub regno Papae atque Antichristi acceperamus*.[7]

In his *Adversus baptismum* Camillo contended on the one hand that the sacrament as received under the Papacy had no meaning, and on the other that nothing is added by infant baptism beyond what is received from hearing the gospel and, moreover, that it need not be administered except where the church is to be propagated and organized in a formerly un-Christian region. The ambiguity of Camillo's assertions made it possible for some of his followers to stress the inadequacy of the papal and the quasi-papal baptism under the Reformers

---

[1] Letter of 17 October 1547; I, No. 88.
[2] I, No. 92.
[3] I, No. 94; cf. Da Porta, *Historia*, I: 2, p. 41.
[4] See above at p. 143, n. 2.
[5] I, No. 95.
[6] Da Porta, *Historia*, I: 2, p. 88.
[7] Da Porta mentions a work which appeared in Transylvania in 1579, *De regno* Christi with an excursus "Tractatus de paedobaptismo," said to reflect the ideas of Camillo; but we now know that the excursus was by Ferencz Dávid and that it depended primarily on an unpublished work of Michael Servetus. See my *Radical Reformation*, p. 722. Da Porta, *Historia*, 1:2, p. 88 note. Faustus Socinus' grandson, Andreas Wiszowaty, may have come into possession of this document. Cf. Robert Wallace, *Antitrinitarian Biography*, 3 vols. (London, 1850), III, 236, MS No. 32.

and to press for believers' baptism (in effect: anabaptism), while others could with the same sanction infer that children born in Christian households had already undergone a kind of inner baptism — and could therefore reserve water baptism for converts from Judaism, Mohammedanism, and paganism. The latter course was to be taken by Faustus Socinus; the former, by the Italian Anabaptists deriving from Camillo and his associate Tiziano (see below).

There were, to be sure, a number of Italian-speaking Anabaptists in the Rhaetian Republic before Camillo wrote his *Adversus baptismum* sometime in midwinter 1547-48. And the question arises as to whether Camillo derived his baptismal theology from this milieu or whether he himself, expressing himself more openly and fully than in his correspondence with Bullinger (which is the only epistolary exchange that survives) and reformulating the wide range of theological and social topics already taken up in Bologna and Modena, originated a distinctive Italo-Rhaetian Anabaptist movement. It would, in fact, soon be said of him that the whole Anabaptist movement in Italy stemmed from him.[1] But at least the extant documents give two other Italians in the Rhaetian valleys a certain priority.

Both these men claimed to be followers of Bernardino Ochino.[2] The one, Francesco Calabrese, was the evangelical pastor in the small town of Vetto, near Poschiavo. The other was Girolamo Milanese of Lavin.[3] For radical views on baptism as well as on a whole range of institutions and doctrines that remind one of the IX Accusations which were brought against Camillo (Phileno) in Bologna, Francesco and Girolamo were cited in 1544 before a largely Romansh synod in Zuaz (Susa, Süs) in the Engadine Valley. This local synod, which sat for two days on the issues raised by the two refugee Italian preachers, was made up of divines and magistrates, Catholics and Evangelicals. Despite the loyal support of their own congregations the two Italians were excluded from the rights under the edict of Ilanz and removed as Anabaptists.

Without going into the charges against Francesco and Girolamo, we resume our account of Camillo, remarking only that a near-contemporary source says[4] that "two other Italians, called Camillo Renato and Pietro Leone, learned men, are said to have propagated" these ideas at about this time and that in any case almost every one of the charges and others besides appeared in the XXII Anathemas assembled by Mainardo against Camillo and his *asseclae* at the latest in the spring of 1548.

---

[1] See below at p. 160, n. 7.

[2] The principal source is Ulrich Campell, *Historia Raetica*, edited in two volumes by P. Plattner, Quellen zur Schweizer Geschichte, VIII (1887), IX (1890), II, 297-300.

[3] Girolamo Milanese is not the same as Girolamo da Milano (Cavalli Ambrogio) who was received by Renata in Ferrara between 1547 and 1555. Other spellings for Vetto are Vetten, Fettan, Vetonium, Vettis.

[4] Campell, *Historia*, II, 299; but it must be admitted that though Campell was a near contemporary of the events he here describes, his large canvas may have permitted him to generalize in bringing two religious episodes closer together than they actually were.

Precisely in the interest of clarity, we must at this point let enough of the historiographical problem of our sources come to the surface of our general narrative to explain that the XXII Anathemas are but a convenient designation by which we shall henceforth refer to Article X of Mainardo's otherwise lost Confession of XX Articles of Faith. This Confession had conceivably been growing by accretion and emendation for some time. The important point for the career of Camillo is that the XXII Anathemas existed in their present form when Mainardo brought a copy of his whole Confession to Zurich in June, 1548, for he later had occasion to say so in comment on the XXII Anathemas.[1] It is therefore appropriate to deal with these anathemas now, benefiting from Mainardo's later comments, to interpret Camillo's theology, and to place these propositions in their 1548 setting before proceeding with the general narrative of the public disputations that would ordinarily follow at this point.

Mainardo's twenty-two anathemas or charges were directed at a fairly large group of dissidents within and beyond the confines of the Chiavenna congregation. Camillo, however, was said to have held all but one of them; and Mainardo sought to substantiate his claim by specifying (with some inconsistency and overlapping) that some of the points he had personally heard from Camillo's lips;[2] that some had been reported;[3] that one was to be found in an unspecified writing;[4] and that several were summaries from Camillo's *De sacramentis* written expressly against Mainardo. Since this book could not in any case have borne this exact title, in view of Camillo's aversion for the very term "sacrament," and since a book on baptism and the eucharist might well have been written in Italian in the interest of popular suasion, one may conjecture that the "*De sacramentis*" referred to by Mainardo is none other than the unique and now partly edited Bern manuscript of Camillo's *Trattato sul Battesimo e sulla Eucaristia*.[5] In further support of this surmise is the fact that it is directed, in the second person plural, to the "ministri e maistri" of the (Italian) congregations and that almost at the beginning of the tract Camillo warns the readers from supposing that he is "the inventor and the only one professing this [Spiritualist] conception [of the sacraments] which in fact many before me here (*qui*) in the church (*compagnia*) have held and still hold."[6] A preceding reference to "questa controversia" and the

[1] I, No. 104. The XXII Anathemas are printed in Da Porta, *Historia*, I: 2, pp. 83-86.

[2] Anathemas IV, V, VI, VII, VIII, IX, XIII, XIV-XXII.

[3] Anathemas XI, XII, XVII.

[4] Anathema III.

[5] Delio Cantimori and Elisabeth Feist, *Per la storia degli eretici italiani del secolo* XVI *in Europa* (Rome, 1937), pp. 47-54. The portion printed is only about a third of the whole tract, as Cantimori says, in further useful detail, *Eretici* (German edition), p. 429, n. 30.

[6] Cantimori and Feist, *Per la storia*, p. 49. Rotondò holds that the *Trattato*, identical with the *De sacramento*, referred to by Mainardo, e.g. in his letter of 10 December 1548 (I, No. 104, p. 139; cf. above and below n. 5 and p. 171), is the very booklet which was read in Laelius' house by some members of Camillo's circle in Bologna; for one Achille Vizzano was, during a trial in July 1549, charged with having read "il trattato del Phy-

sentence just quoted make it almost certain that the *Trattato* was composed near the beginning of the disputation and for the congregation in Chiavenna and associated *compagnie* in the spring of 1548, and that at this stage Camillo could confidently and cunningly remind the members of the sacramental views of their first pastor, Francesco Negri.

It will be expedient to confine the discussion at first to Camillo's views on baptism and the Supper at this stage. It will be borne in mind that neither the *Trattato* nor the propositions taken from the probably identical "*De sacramentis*," confined as they are to baptism and the eucharist, set forth anything that Camillo could not have claimed to be able to defend as validly Zwinglian even if no longer Bullingerian. Strangely enough, the *epulum* preceding the eucharist is no longer under discussion between the two opponents.

The main issue in Camillo's sacramental theology, both in the *Trattato* and in the pertinent anathemas of Mainardo, is now whether the two sacraments have any confirmatory value. Camillo denies that they do and objects even to the term "sacrament" as unbiblical. He would prefer to use only scriptural terms: "baptism" (or bath of regeneration or renovation of the Spirit) and "Supper of the Lord" (or table of the Lord or the breaking of bread or the company of the body and blood of the Lord). Camillo declared that "brevity and simplicity and clarity are requisite in every science and especially in the science of Christianity if it is to be fruitful and salutary."[1] He was convinced that much of the misunderstanding in the life of the churches stemmed from the persistence in Reformed circles of "the perversity" of papal and scholastic terminology, in this case the misleading use of *one* word — and that unbiblical and with the unscriptural implication of a binding pledge or oath — for *two* different actions. And if, to be sure for convenience, a single term is to be used, it should be the unequivocal *signa*, *segni*. These signs, he argued, have no utility for the recipient; for they were instituted merely as tokens by which Christians are distinguished from non-Christians and whereby believers testify publicly that they believe in Christ. God effects nothing through the signs in those who make use of them. Instead, they betoken what he has already accomplished.[2] In fact, the Word of God and his authorized signs strengthen only those hearing and attending, not the person who speaks the Word nor the person who actually receives the signs.[3] For the fact is that justifying faith has no need of any sacramental or outward confirmation.[4] Just as the baptism at Jordan added nothing to the

---

leno" in the Bolognese residence of the Sozzini. "Bologna," pp. 136-154 with plate 6, a section entitled "Un episodio bolognese della giovinezza di Lelio Sozzini," esp. at n. 1. For other references to Camillo, see Johann Heinrich Ott, *Annales Anabaptistici* (Basel, 1672).

[1] *Ibid.*, p. 50.

[2] Anathemas VII and IX.

[3] Anathema XV.

[4] Anathema XVI.

divine or human nature of Jesus, so its repetition for his followers adds nothing essential but is only a token or public manifestation.[1]

As for the sacraments considered separately, we learn from the *Trattato* and from the succinct anathemas that baptism is not to be considered as the Christian successor or equivalent of circumcision;[2] that it is probably not for infants;[3] that in any event it is to be preceded by faith, which if it is true faith, that is, characterized by that *fermezza* and *certezza* "as Paul says[4] of things hoped for and which are not seen," does not need any external "confirmation or certification." Except as a sign to others, baptism would thus be dispensable. Camillo, according to Mainardo,[5] was also indifferent to the triune formula in baptism or thought rather that instruction in the meaning of the phrase should precede baptism. We know from an earlier letter from Camillo[6] that he had indeed asked Bullinger about precisely this problem as one having arisen in the community; and there is some evidence that it was Francesco Negri who was the most concerned with it.[7]

As for the Supper, neither the *Trattato* nor the two Anathemas XIV and XXII bring anything new; but never before had Camillo distinguished so distinctly between the last *cena con i suoi* and the *cena* which Christ instituted for the *posterità de' suoi*.[8]

So much for the "sacramental" theology of Camillo as we can make it out around 1548 from his own *Trattato* and Mainardo's anathemas against him and his followers. Much more revolutionary were the doctrines ascribed to Camillo by Mainardo in the remaining anathemas. These remind us at once of the charges against Francesco Calabrese and Girolamo Milanese condemned at Zuaz in 1544, and against Camillo Renato himself, condemned under the name of Lisia Phileno *alias* Paolo Ricci in Ferrara in 1540. It will now be expedient to take up these other anathemas which, dealing precisely with eschatology, must quickly remind us of the items in the trial and Abjuration in Ferrara and which, now heading the list in Chiavenna, were obviously

---

[1] One of the anathemas, XXI, suggests a view that on the surface seems to be at variance with what we know Camillo to have said earlier to Bullinger. According to Mainardo's transcription, Camillo was now saying that baptism and the eucharist were signs of things past only and in no case of things future. Mainardo could have misunderstood Camillo at this point, for Camillo did believe earlier that participation, for example, in the *epulum* and *eucharistia* very definitely testify to a hope in Christ's second (future) advent. Thus "past" may here very well refer to the experienced past of the inward *manducatio* and presumably also the inner *renatio*, and "things future" would then be only a faulty transcription of sacramental confirmation, which we know Camillo opposed.

[2] Anathema XIV.

[3] *Trattato*; Cantimori and Feist, *Per la storia*, p. 49.

[4] The reference is to Hebrews 11: 1.

[5] Anathema XIII.

[6] I, No. 81.

[7] See Mainardo's letter of 22 September 1548; I, No. 102, p. 133. Here he describes how he refused to baptize Negri's infant in *his* (Negri's) conception of faith.

[8] Cantimori and Feist, *Per la storia*, p. 54.

the most grievous in the eyes of Mainardo and his supporters. We have already quoted the first anathema by way of transition from Part I to Part II of our narrative.[1]

Camillo at some point in his Rhaetian career had made bold to avow again his view that the rational soul is mortal and his thnetopsychist conviction that though that soul dies with the body, it will be resuscitated with a new body at the last judgment.[2] Mainardo reported that Camillo was maintaining his position with such passion and violence that it was impossible to listen to him and that, when listeners would express their horror, he would express his dismay that they should take offense and would thereupon retreat to the extent of saying that he was pressing the point only for the sake of argument and that, of course, he could not claim to know for sure whether his construction of the texts was correct. Mainardo sought to prevail upon him to confess publicly his belief in the general immortality of the soul (or, if Mainardo were pressed to be more precise: comprehensive individual immortality by grace), if he wished to be considered a Christian and a member of the church. [3]

Mainardo was aware of a related eschatological view, less distasteful perhaps, which he also condemned as it was held by a number of Italians, but which he expressly said was not the view of Camillo, namely, that the souls of the dead *sleep* until the last judgment and then will be awakened as from a dream.[4]

Apparently Camillo believed, as did Paul, that the resurrection body would be a spiritual body, different from the present in substance and nature.[5] Mainardo objects to this view on the ground that it would not then be a matter of a true resurrection but of a new creation.

Camillo held that death, despite the disobedience of Adam, would have entered into the world.[6] Going beyond his views as expressed or reported at Ferrara, Camillo now held that the souls of the wicked, being evil, would never again be called into being, that this indeed was their punishment.[7] Not reborn in the course of their earthly life, they remain irrational like the brutes and will never be transferred to the kingdom of Christ.[8]

---

[1] Above at p. 139, n. 3.

[2] Anathema I: "Damnamus eos qui dicunt quod anima rationalis sit mortalis, moriatur una cum corpore: sed in novissimo die resuscitetur una cum corpore, et quod tunc demum totus homo fiat immortalis."

[3] I, No. 104, pp. 139 f.

[4] Anathema II: "Damnamus eos qui dicunt quod animae defunctorum utut vivant, dormiant usque ad novissimum diem, et tunc suscitentur a somno." That this, alone of the XXII Anathemas, was not held by Camillo is stated by Mainardo; I, No. 104, p. 139.

[5] Anathema III: "Item eos damnamus qui dicunt quod homines non resuscitentur in eadem ipsa natura et substantia in qua prius fuerunt, sed in alia, quia corpus animale et corpus spirituale differunt et substantia et natura."

[6] Anathema VI.

[7] Anathema XII.

[8] Anathema XVII.

Such a position leads logically to Camillo's assertion of the bondage of the will with respect to salvation. With some details going beyond the acts of the trial at Ferrara, Camillo gives expression to a combination of fatalism and libertinism which he could have claimed was purely Pauline, namely, that there is no natural law in man in the light of which can be discerned the things that should be done and the things which should not be done;[1] and, at the same time, that reborn believers, for their part, not being any longer under the Law, have no need of natural law or even of the Ten Commandments, "for pious men have no need of any other law than [that of] the Spirit."[2]

If this is true of pious men in general, what about Jesus the man in particular? Camillo's christological views were also radical, although he did not go so far as Francesco and Girolamo are reported to have gone at Zuaz. According to Mainardo, Camillo, who in any case had managed to avoid all trinitarian formulas in his correspondence with Bullinger, declared that Christ bore the sinful flesh of Adam, and that he saved mankind precisely because he accomplished what he did, eschewing sin, though conceived in sin and himself capable of sin and concupiscence.[3] Even Christ's steadfastness did not prevent his despairing cry on the cross.[4] Mainardo said that Camillo withdrew from this position under attack. As to how Christ saved, Camillo was never very precise; but he attacked the last vestige of the medieval merit system surviving in Reformed Protestantism, when he observed that there was nothing of the principle of merit in Christ's action, for even the word is not found in the scripture.[5]

Clearly Camillo had become the spokesman in the Italian and perhaps also Ladin sections of Rhaetia of a Spiritualism tending towards conventicular Anabaptism on the one flank and toward evangelical rationalist Antitrinitarianism and even Spiritual Libertinism on the other — a Spiritualism, moreover, which embraced a large company of zealous Italian dissidents throughout the valley of the Po and Adige, and the whole Italian diaspora.

There is no doubt that Mainardo, for all his defects as a pastor, was at grips with a very considerable threat to Reformed orthodoxy in Rhaetia, and one must add that he was not getting from abroad the clear counsel that he needed in the mounting crisis. As of June 1548, the date of our next extant documents, there is still no indication that the orthodox Reformed divines of Chur, Zurich, Basel, or Bern realized the full extent to which the turmoil between Mainardo and Camillo had already approached enmity and a dangerous polarization of doc-

---

[1] Anathema IV.

[2] Anathema V.

[3] Anathema VIII. There can be no doubt but that Camillo should be classed with the Spiritual Libertines, against whom Calvin directed his shafts. See Giorgio Spini, *Ricerca dei Libertini* (Rome, 1960), Part I, and my *Radical Reformation*, pp. 577-579; 598-605.

[4] Anathema XI.

[5] Anathema X. See also the *Professio* under remission of sins.

trine and discipline among the Reformed Italians. For example, Blasius and Johannes Comander (1484-5–1557), the latter the chief spokesman for the Reformation in the whole of the Rhaetian Republic, in letters written respectively 1 and 3 June 1548, were content to report to Bullinger that the two antagonists of Chiavenna had been advised to betake themselves to Zurich and to get the personal judgment of Bullinger and his colleagues with whom both antagonists had up to this time maintained friendly relations by correspondence.[1]

Mainardo was glad to go again to Zurich. Camillo chose not to. It was Francesco Stancaro, formerly of Mantua, who represented Camillo and the other dissidents of the Chiavenna church. Although Stancaro did not agree with Camillo on the theological points at issue — indeed it was not in his nature to be in accord with anyone — he was in a position to speak for a large number of religious refugees in Chiavenna, including Camillo and Negri, all of whom had become in varying degrees restive under Mainardo's pastorate and were opposed to his campaign to impose his own Confession of XX Articles of Faith. Apparently Stancaro managed to keep the attention of the Zurich divines from the XXII Anathemas of Article X. In any event, after hearing all aspects of the parochial and confessional problem, the divines of Zurich, headed by Bullinger, signed 7 June 1548 the *Acta ministrorum Tigurinae ecclesiae*,[2] which was notable for the reserve manifested in not condemning Camillo outright and in declining to approve Mainardo's Confession for *general* subscription. Only Oswald Myconius of Basel was willing to go this far in his sharp letter of 16 June[3] to the congregation of Chiavenna and which he directed against the dissidents led and incited by such "intrusive teachers and fanatics" as Camillo. The day after, as it happened, Camillo's old correspondent Curione, wrote, also from Basel, saying to Bullinger that he had been personally responsible for certain changes Mainardo had made in his Confession and now urged Bullinger to approve it wholeheartedly. This is our first clear indication that Curione and Camillo were moving in different directions.[4]

In the course of the summer, if not during the discussions with Mainardo and Stancaro in June, Bullinger altered his view of Camillo completely. His original respect, changing into anxious reserve, was suddenly transformed into enmity. Stancaro told Camillo on returning to Chiavenna that Bullinger had even characterized Camillo as "the worst of heretics." Camillo was deeply hurt by this accusation; and, writing to Bullinger 21 September 1548,[5] he professed ignorance of the reasons that might have prompted Bullinger to make such an adverse

---

[1] Da Porta, *Historia*, I: 2, p. 93; Trechsel, *Antitrinitarier*, II, p. 102, n. 3.

[2] Trechsel, *Antitrinitarier*, II, p. 102, n. 4.

[3] *Ibid.*, p. 103, n. 4.

[4] 17 June 1548. *Ibid.*; Kutter, *Curione*, Brief, No. 45. That Curione's estimate of Camillo (Phileno) had been already considerably downgraded, see above, p. 141, n. 4.

[5] I, No. 101.

judgment after all the friendly correspondence between themselves and their mutual professions of learned esteem and Christian fraternity. After a few lines about the still confused situation in Chiavenna and his bafflement that things should be in such a turmoil among Christians, Camillo closed his letter in the confidence that Bullinger would surely oblige him with a full accounting for the sake of the Italian's honor and their mutual friendship. With greetings to the Zurich brethren, especially Theodorus Bibliander, from the brethren in Chiavenna, Camillo signed his letter somewhat dubiously, "Thine as always."

Bullinger had apparently not at first realized that the XXII Anathemas embedded in Mainardo's Confession were almost entirely concerned with Camillo; for he now requested of Mainardo a full list of specific errors in order to reply to Camillo. Thereupon, in a letter of 10 December 1548,[1] Mainardo had to point out to Bullinger that Camillo's heretical articles were in fact contained in Article X of Mainardo's Confession as already submitted to the Zurich divines the preceding June. Bullinger had obviously not been very attentive to the list of heretical propositions at the time. (It is from Mainardo's comment on them that we in part drew in presenting Camillo's theological views as of 1548).

In this letter of 10 December and in an earlier one of 22 September 1548,[2] when Mainardo was writing to Bullinger for the first time after the visit to Zurich in June, the troubled pastor of Chiavenna found occasion to relieve himself of the smart of an old man charged with lack of close pastoral attention to his flock (*incuria*), by insisting once again that the cause of the local schism lay deeper than that. He also told Bullinger how he had read from the pulpit the endorsements he had received from Basel, Zurich, and Chur, how he was proceeding to impose his Confession on the Church, and how he had refused to baptize Negri's baby on Negri's terms. He expressed the hope that Camillo would beget himself somewhere else "in peace"; and, after noting that Stancaro had left for an unknown destination, he quoted with evident relish from a sheaf of letters which he had received from people in Venice who had known Stancaro there and were willing to describe his unpleasant traits. Mainardo may have thought that in sharing all this with Bullinger, his problems were drawing to a close. But there was more bitterness ahead.

As late as 12 May 1549[3] Camillo, still in Chiavenna, made bold to write Bullinger again, insisting still more urgently than before that a full explanation be given why Bullinger should, as Stancaro reported it, be calling him "the most heretical of all." He closed his letter on a firm but still irenic note, saying that with such a response, however hard to take, he would for that very reason be able to continue to think of Bullinger as "a friend and a Christian."

---

[1] I, No. 104, p. 139.
[2] I, No. 102.
[3] I, No. 108.

Three days after this, Mainardo likewise wrote to Bullinger[1] telling, among many other things this time, that Camillo was really " the coryphaeus and shipowner " of an ever-widening fleet of Spiritualist Anabaptists. In substantiation, he described a certain surgeon, Pietro Bresciano, formerly of Casalmaggiore[2] (between Parma and Mantua), who at the dinner table in the presence of Vergerio told about his recent conversion, his renunciation of his baptism as received under the Papacy, of his becoming a new man, renewed by the Spirit and filled with God, and about his rebaptism. Using Camillo's language about the worthlessness of baptism under Antichrist, the surgeon made bold to call Mainardo a wolf, a false prophet, and a deceiver. It is possible that Vergerio had taken the conversational initiative in exploring the revolutionary possibilities of the radical attack Camillo had mounted against all the institutions of papal Christianity. It is clear from his subsequent career, at all events, that the former bishop was trying to find a place for himself at the head of something bigger than a local Reformed parish under the emerging " episcopates " of the Zurich and Genevan divines. Mainardo, who was at dinner with Vergerio, admitted that Camillo himself would not have gone so far toward revolutionary Anabaptism, perhaps out of fear, but that there could be no doubt about Camillo's being the driving force behind the radical movement; and already[3] Baldassare Altieri, who would be carrying two of Mainardo's letters to Bullinger, and who had been himself in Caspano as late as July 6, had written to Bullinger[4] calling Camillo " anabaptistarum patronus. "

By the midsummer, dissidents were meeting apart from the main church of Chiavenna. And in the next letter, 7 August 1549,[5] Mainardo said that a certain Tiziano,[6] a friend of Camillo and his followers, was recently expelled from synod " by the secular arm. "[7] Tiziano, destined to be a major leader of Anabaptism in Italy, had once served in the court of a cardinal in Rome and had gone to Geneva where he may first have come into contact with Anabaptism before meeting Camillo.

---

[1] Letter of 15 May 1549, I, No. 109.

[2] The name comes out only in a subsequent recital; I, No. 110.

[3] Letter of Altieri to Bullinger, I, Anhang, p. 474.

[4] Letter of 3 August 1549 from Poschiavo; I, p. 475.

[5] I, No. 110.

[6] Mainardo does not say where and by whom, though presumably locally. It would appear from this that Tiziano may have served somewhere in Rhaetia as a Reformed pastor. He is known also to have maintained one son in Rovigo and another near Vicenza.

[7] The fullest accounts of Tiziano (identical with Lorenzo Tizzano ?) are by Henry A. De Wind, *Mennonite Encyclopedia*, IV, 729 f.; III, 455. See below p. 165, n. 3. and Emilio Comba, *I Nostri Protestanti*, 2 vols (Florence, 1895-1897), II, 477-517. Lemmi prints Tizzano's confession, *op. cit.*, pp. 68 ff. It is possible that Tizzano, *alias* Benedetto Florio, derived his extreme views in what he called his third or " diabolical " phase from Camillo Renato; but in his testimony he says from Francesco Renato. On Judaizing liberalism in a Tiziano convert, see M. E. Pommier, *l'itinereire religieux d'un moine vagabond italien*. Ecole Française de Rome, *Mélanges*, LXVI (1954), 293-322.

In the same letter to Bullinger, Mainardo reported that Francesco Negri who had, among the dissidents, stood until recently more with Stancaro than with Camillo, was now in the absence of Stancaro rallying completely to the side of Camillo — though again more out of weakness than out of explicit theological involvement, so Mainardo surmised.

Mainardo describes further his difficult position. If he did not react to "the lacerations" of his Confession and the open criticism of his pastorate, truth itself would be endangered. At the same time, if he did enter the fray, they would say it was the bitterness of a morose old man, stubborn and bull-headed. He never completely understood that many of his opponents were more opposed to his project to impose uniformity by means of subscription to his Confession than to the specific points of doctrine contained therein. Once again he decided to enter the lists for truth. He was disconcerted, however, by the fact that Camillo declined to prepare a formal confession of faith or to participate in the public disputation to which Mainardo invited him and his allies. In the meantime Camillo had malevolently drawn up *Errores, ineptiae, scandala, contradictiones Augustini Maynardi a 45. anno citra* in 125 articles,[1] which he circulated with a prefatory epistle to the reader, so mean and vainglorious that, as Mainardo hopefully reported, no one could read it through without sickening.

Mainardo closed his letter filled with a sense of misery and professional failure, observing that he was very much tempted to accept the invitation arranged for him by Ochino to go to Edwardian England. But for the moment he knew he had to stay in his storm-tossed bark. His practical suggestion was that Bullinger urge Comander and Blasius to make a personal visitation of the disaffected region, and he implored Bullinger to advise them or their representatives to conduct their investigations before the whole church, never in private conferences either with the dissidents or with himself.

The bearer of the first of the two letters which we have now summarized was Baldassare Altieri, formerly the representative in Venice of the elector of Saxony and the landgrave of Hesse, before that the secretary of the English ambassador. He had been the lay head of the evangelical community of Venice until he was forced to leave in 1549, repairing to the Rhaetian Republic with the hope of finding a comparable position. More than Mainardo realized, perhaps, the bearer of his letter had sojourned in Chiavenna long enough to see that part of the local schism was due to the temperament and the age of the pastor himself. Altieri so reported when he reached Zurich on personal business.[2]

Bullinger acted on the advice of Altieri, of course, and on the request of Mainardo himself. Four official visitors to the Chiavenna church

---

[1] I, No. 110, p. 147; Da Porta, *Historia*, I, 2, p. 99.

[2] For the correspondence of Altieri with Bullinger, especially his adverse judgment on Camillo from Caspano, 28 July 1549, and his suggestion for a conclave from Poschiavo, 3 August 1549, see I, Anhang.

were appointed: Philipp Gallicius von Salis as chairman, at the time pastor in Lavin and no doubt well acquainted with the Anabaptist and psychopannychist views of his ousted predecessor (Girolamo Milanese); Johannes Blasius, pastor in Chur; Andreas Fabritius, pastor in Davos; and Conrad Jäcklin, " the learned and even distinguished " pastor in Thusis. From Chiavenna nobleman Francesco Pestalozzi sent a warm letter inviting the announced visitors to stay at his residence; and the presbyteral chapter of the Chiavenna church, for its part, sent also a letter, filled with scriptural allusions, expressing their willingness to be investigated.[1]

At first Camillo, so it is reported of him hostilely, was filled with alarm at the thought of four evangelical pastors coming to ferret out his " warrens " and he considered leaving Chiavenna to escape the Protestant " inquisition. "[2] But he then decided that a sudden and secret flight would compromise his cause throughout the Grigioni and he resolved to stand his ground and prepare his defenses. It was undoubtedly at this juncture that he discreetly complied with Mainardo's earlier request to draw up a confession of faith by resorting to verse, as a hostile commentator observed, the better to conceal behind his classical flourishes his heretical alteration of the Apostles' Creed, which as a *Professio* in Latin verse he dedicated to one of the most powerful of the Protestant statesmen of the Rhaetian Republic, Friedrich von Salis.[3] It is true that the sharpness of his theological points are rounded off; but Camillo does not in the *Professio* conceal his (Servetian) conception of the Holy Spirit as a force rather than as a person, nor his preference for *signa* instead of *sacramenta*. He suggests baptism by immersion and alludes to the *agape* as part of the eucharistic action during which men and women, the rich and the poor, masters and servants are one. He speaks of the communion of saints among whom force does not reign, an allusion perhaps to his growing interest in the ban as the sole means of exercising discipline in the community of faith. As for the death of the soul and the resurrection of the just, this basic conviction of Camillo is all there in veiled language. We do not know what effect this credal poem had upon the patron " honored " in the dedication.

---

[1] Campell, *Historia*, II, ch. 62, pp. 329 ff.; Da Porta, *Historia*, 1: 2, pp. 99 ff.; Trechsel, *Antitrinitarier*, II, 105.

[2] Da Porta, *Historia*, I: 2, p. 98.

[3] The versified *Professio* is printed by Da Porta, *Historia*, I: 2, pp. 113-117. Stanislaus Dunin Borkowski purports to find an echo of Camillo's proto-Socinian formulations respecting the doctrine of the Trinity in the mordantly anti-Trinitarian diptychs of Ferencz Dávid entitled *Dehortatio, et Descriptio Dei Tripersonati*. Dávid's poem is printed in the appendix of Elek Jakab, *Dávid Ferencz Emléke* (Budapest, 1879), pp. 55-59. For Dunin Borkowsky's observation (which I do not find clearly substantiated on inspection of Dávid's text), see *idem*, " Untersuchungen zum Schrifttum der Unitarier vor Faustus Socini, " *75 Jahre Stella Matutina, Festschrift*, II (Feldkirch, Austria, 1931), 114 f. Rotondò picks out of the *Professio* the stress upon the church as the community of love in mystical solidarity endowed with the gifts of the Spirit. " Bologna, " pp. 120 f.

It is clear, however, that at the beginning of the investigation, as it unfolded in the Pestalozzi residence, Camillo was confident that he could count on support in high places. But his conduct was so tempestuous, that sympathies in the examining panel and among the attendants shifted to the aged Mainardo, who replied with gentleness and piety to the bitter reproaches of his assailants. Moreover, Mainardo was able to quote incriminating passages from two of Camillo's works, *De paedobaptismo* (possibly identical with *Adversus baptismum*) and an otherwise unknown *De coena Domini*, and all the more effectively because these books had been rather widely circulated and were known by all.

After deliberation, Gallicius summarized the views of the visiting divines, bringing together XXI Points of Agreement.[1] The four visitors were not without some appreciation for the more moderate of the points made by Camillo and his faction and they, no doubt, sincerely believed that they had taken due heed of Camillo's sensibilities in their final formulations. In paraphrasing the account of these XXI Points, we shall omit the numbers which in any event were not a part of the original version. Some of the points, for example those dealing with tombs, have not entered into the discussion up to this moment but are presumably related to Camillo's conviction about the death of the soul with the body and his concern, already expressed back in Modena, to reduce by all outward signs the social differences between the rich and the poor within the fellowship of the Christian community. The most notable shift in emphasis in the XXI Points (December 1549) in contrast to the IX Accusations of Ferrara (December 1540) and Mainardo's XXII Anathemas (c. June 1548) was the prominence of the problem of baptism.

According to the findings of four synodally appointed visitors, it is Christian to baptize the infants of church members; no one who has been once baptized, even by a papal priest, in the triune name should be rebaptized; only God knows when and how the Holy Spirit is imparted to infants at baptism; and, though infant baptism is the order of the church, it should not be said that infants dying unbaptized are damned. There were three points respecting the sacraments as a whole: that they may be called sacraments, that the term is admittedly inappropriate if either the ancient Roman or scholastic meanings are allowed to cling to it; but that these sacraments, however defined, do confirm one's faith and do ratify the ancient promises.[2] There was

---

[1] Printed by Da Porta, *Historia*, 1:2, pp. 101-103.

[2] The three points as paraphrased are in the source: V, VII and VI respectively. The wording of VII takes up the most space of any of the XXI points, which would suggest that the visitors were trying not only to accomodate Camillo but also to bring order into the somewhat contradictory action and assertion of Comander, who had earlier assented to both Stancaro's and Mainardo's confessions without having noted the discrepancy on precisely this issue of signs, seals, and sacraments. See the letter to Bullinger on what Comander had inadvertently done, 22 September 1548; I, No. 102, p. 134.

only one point on the Lord's Supper. It was agreed also that the church should proceed to the catechetical instruction of the baptized children and that it was desirable that excommunication or the ban be exercised in the church assembled. This may have been a concession to Camillo, who later, at least, would be expressing himself against resort to the secular arm[1] and in favor of the congregationally agreed upon ban (excommunication) as the only kind of discipline allowable for Christians.

There were five eschatological and related propositions[2] which, though directed against Camillo's affirmations, betray in their wording something of a concession to his sensibilities; for it was agreed that it was not possible to know where the souls of the deceased are[3] and that the saints in heaven[4] do not make intercession, only Christ; but it was also agreed, and directly against Camillo, that wherever they are, the souls after the first death of the body live and are capable of feeling; that it is not improper to take thought during one's lifetime of tombs and sepulchral monuments, although admittedly pride and vainglory unfortunately often attend such preoccupations; and that it is not against the evangelical faith (for the rich) to leave legacies for the benefit of the poor. Conceivably Camillo objected to such wills because of the possible implication that the grateful legatees might be expected to pray for the souls of the departed benefactors.

This leads us to that cluster of points which have little to do with Camillo's career or central thought but which reveal perhaps more than the principal points of doctrine the intellectual and social milieu of the synodal investigation. It was agreed, for example, that it was not a sin to visit the graves or to make a pilgrimage to the Holy Land (to see the Holy Sepulchre);[5] that a person who had recently departed from a monastery as an evangelical convert might, for a while, continue to wear his habit without being censured as insufficiently converted; that, although for the most part Evangelicals felt free with respect to the traditional days of fasting, those who for one reason or another observed them were not to be violently criticized; and that it was not improper for an evangelical teacher to make use of logical arguments and inferences in the tradition befitting learned theological discussion.[6] This last point may well have been directed against Camillo's insistence that only scriptural language should be used. The final point was that

---

[1] See the several references to the ban in Camillo's *Carmen* against Calvin, printed elsewhere in this volume, p. 191 . There is a not entirely clear constitutional statement about calling the church together, Point XVIII.

[2] Contained in Points XI, XIV, XV and XVI.

[3] Point XIV. Da Porta perhaps misprinted Campell's *animas* as *animos*; but it is quite possible that there was such a distinction. See below on Gianandrea Paravicini at p. 169, n. 2. Cf. p. 141, n. 2.

[4] The reference to heaven is somewhat in conflict with the foregoing expression of ignorance as to the place of the provisional sojourn of the souls of the deceased.

[5] Cf. Question XVIII in 1561, below at p. 180, n. 3.

[6] Point XVII.

if there should be any further disputation between the pastor and his flock, the issues should be carried before a duly convened synod to which all would be invited.

It is reported that Camillo was prohibited henceforth from interpreting scriptures either in public or in private,[1] that most of the participants seemed to go along wholeheartedly with the XXI Points, and that the visitors could therefore leave Chiavenna buoyed by a widespread feeling that at long last the schism had been ended.

Camillo could not, however, restrain himself. It was not long after the departure of the four ecclesiastical visitors that he resumed his agitation. Accordingly, he was formally excommunicated before the whole church, 6 July 1550. Thereupon he proceeded to organize "a church of the Anabaptists." The principal tenets of this conventicle, as reported hostilely, were that baptism under the papacy was invalid and that the soul dies with the body. Among others whom Camillo converted at about this time to his views was the antitrinitarian Anabaptist pastor in Gardone near Brescia, Girolamo Allegretti.[2]

We have reached the end of another phase in the shifting career of Camillo Renato. It is clear from Mainardo's hostile remark — "Utinam Deo renatus fuit!" — that by this time the preacher of the Italian-speaking *ecclesia anabaptistarum* of Chiavenna had probably come to connect his name with rebaptism, although there is no direct reference anywhere to his having actually submitted to the rite himself.

It was, however, precisely two months later, in September 1550, that the most important conclave of Italian Anabaptists took place in Venice under the direction of Pietro Manelfi and of his converter Tiziano who, as of 7 August 1549, was reported by Mainardo to have been recently — as a friend of Camillo and an Anabaptist — expelled "by the secular arm," presumably from Chiavenna. There is no evidence that Camillo himself attended the Venetian synod; but it has long been conjectured that "il Nero" listed among the distinguished delegates from afar was Francesco Negri.[3] The X Heads of Agreement set forth by the Venetian synod, reproduced precisely the

[1] We learn of the suspension of Camillo's preaching only from a subsequent letter of Mainardo to Bullinger, 4 August 1550; I, No. 130, p. 174. The impression given by Campell and Da Porta is that even Camillo went along with the XXI Points at first.

[2] The evidence for the material of this paragraph is supplied by two letters: that of Mainardo to Bullinger, 4 August 1550; I, No. 130; and that of Giulio Milanese to Girolamo Allegretti, antitrinitarian Anabaptist minister in Gardone near Brescia, 14 June 1550. In the latter Giulio exhorts Girolamo to turn away from the influence of one whose voice he had heeded in Chiavenna (Camillo). Archivio Veneto, Sant'Uffizio, Busta 8, printed by Comba, *Protestanti*, II, 177-179.

[3] The principal accounts of the Venetian synod are Karl Benrath. "Wiedertäufer im Venetianischen um die Mitte des 16. Jahrhunderts, " *Theologische Studien und Kritiken*, LVIII (1885), 9-67; Emilio Comba, "Un sinodo Anabattista a Venezia, anno 1550," *Rivista Cristiana*, XIII (1885), 21-24; 83-87; and Henry A. De Wind, "Anabaptism and Italy," *Church History*, XXI (1952), 20-38. As for Negri, both Benrath and Comba think that "il Nero" was he. Schiess, *Korrespondenz*, I, p. lxi thinks that more proof is needed.

christological, the eschatological, and the predestinarian views of Francesco Calabrese and Girolamo Milanese condemned by the mixed Evangelical-Catholic synod of Zuaz in 1544 and of Camillo and his associates as contained in the XXII Anathemas of Chiavenna, c. June 1548. Absent from the Venetian synod were any articles on baptism or the Lord's Supper, which were apparently not under dispute; and we are hence unable to ascertain whether a distinctively Renatian view of the sacraments had likewise entered into the mainstream of Italian Anabaptism. However Camillo's contribution to the important synod of Venice is assessed, the event itself coincides with the climax of Camillo's emergence as a Spiritualist Anabaptist.

Thereafter we follow a career that seems to have lost its sense of direction and to a certain extent its integrity, for once again Camillo was to recant, this time formally disavowing his "sectarian" doctrines in order thereby to regain his place within the company of Reformed churches in Rhaetia.

3) CAMILLO'S SECOND RECANTATION AND SECOND RELAPSE (*1551-1554*)

On 19 January 1551 Camillo signed a long orthodox Reformed confession of faith in Italian in the presence of Mainardo, several members of the Chiavenna chapter of elders, and Vergerio, now, for a season, pastor of the little church in Vicosoprano.

It is of some interest that the former bishop first settled as Protestant pastor in precisely the parish where Camillo's friend Bartolomeo Maturo had presumably introduced, among other things, Camillo's *agape*.[1] Vergerio was now signing himself as "the visitor of the synod of preachers." This title appears to be one to which the ambitious ex-bishop aspired rather than one to which he had been duly appointed. His presiding over the recantation of Camillo must be seen as a move in a concerted effort.[2]

Camillo's ample recantation of 1551 differs from that in Ferrara a decade earlier in that there was in Chiavenna no threat of death or coercion even under the terms of the edict of Ilanz. Unaccountable on the surface therefore is Camillo's willingness to sign a document in which even what might be called the still optional or, from the point of view of Protestant orthodoxy, discussible elements of his theology were disavowed with the same firmness as with the more controversial propositions. Among many other things, he affirmed his belief in the triune God; he reappropriated the term "sacrament" and its full Bullingerian connotation; he vigorously repudiated "diabolic" Anabaptism at many points and then also specifically avowed that infant

---

[1] To be sure, Maturo had been succeeded by Camillo's critic, Giulio Milanese. Da Porta, *Historia*, I: 2, p. 30.

[2] The Recantation is printed by Trechsel, *Antitrinitarier*, II, Beilage II, 409; reprinted by Casadei, "Fileno," pp. 411-416.

baptism under the papacy was valid, that Christians might serve as magistrates, and that a Christian magistracy could be properly charged with the external affairs of the church; and, when it came to last things, instead of at least shifting to a belief in the mere sleep of the soul (with the early Luther, for example, and William Tyndale), he avowed his belief in the natural immortality of the souls of the good and the wicked.

There are instances of Germanic Anabaptist leaders, especially those of a spiritualizing trend and of an irenic temperament, who recanted or abandoned their " narrow " sectarianism in conforming to the established Protestant churches. One thinks of Hans Denck's so-called recantation in Basel, of Balthasar Hubmaier's provisional recantation in Zurich, and of Obbe Philip's despairing *Confession* in the Netherlands. [1] But these three northern radicals had had to experience severe persecution at the hands even of Protestants and had been long and perilously acquainted with martyrdom. Moreover, their disavowals of certain excesses of fellow Anabaptists were made with palpable sadness and want of rancor; and they still managed to preserve, in modified form, something of their old convictions. Camillo's Recantation, in contrast, in exceedingly tolerant Evangelical-Catholic Valtellina along with his Abjuration in inquisitorial Ferrara, points again to that major defect of character which Giulio Milanese once agreed to call *leggerezza*.

The only plausible explanation of Camillo's second Recantation is that it was a calculated concession to Vergerio who was ambitious for a role in tolerant and powerful Rhaetia, consonant with his dignity as a former bishop of noble birth who had once been charged with important diplomatic missions of the Holy See. It is possible that Vergerio, who had but recently left his episcopal crosier in Capodistria (1549), was at work on a plan to become the head of the Italian Evangelicals of the Rhaetian Republic centered in Chiavenna in order to counterbalance the Germanic synod centered in Chur; and that Camillo was willing to support him in the assurance, or perhaps even with an explicit promise, that the proposed Italian Church in Rhaetia, though formally orthodox, would under Vergerio be latitudinarian in the interpretation of the Confession. It is also possible that Vergerio had known of Camillo's life and thought even before either had left Italy and that he had a basic sympathy with the vigorous radical. For a moment, Camillo will have given up a radical solution to the problem, however appropriate in a Catholic environment, beguiled by the hope that a comprehensive territorial-magisterial reformation might still become a reality in this Germanically protected Italian-speaking region. He had presumably become convinced that Vergerio could be compliant in the interest of a united Italian Evangelical front. To be sure, we lack any documentation for such a tactical agreement between Camillo and Vergerio. We know only that Vergerio a few days after Camillo's Recantation, in a letter to Rudolf Gualther in Zurich,[1] claimed that

---

[1] Williams, *Radical Reformation*, pp. 140, 179, 359.

[2] Letter of 21 January from Vicosoprano; Da Porta, *Historia*, I: 2, p. 158.

it was he who had done all to bring about the reconciliation of Camillo with Mainardo.[1] It was of course in the interest of Vergerio to demonstrate to the authorities in Chur his local success as a mediator and " overseer. "

Having been reconciled locally with the church of Chiavenna, Camillo now sought reinstatement by the general Rhaetian synod as a teacher in good standing. Mainardo himself, together with one of the elders who had with him witnessed Camillo's Recantation, wrote to Gallicius, as the chairman of the synodal committee of inquiry, asking him to endorse the new measure of rehabilitation in the name of the general synod. In the meantime Camillo himself apparently went to Chur to present his case. Comander and Gallicius, probably with others, heard Camillo and talked with him about his Recantation and also about his book *De Baptismo* (perhaps this was the older *Adversus Baptismum*); but they were far from being satisfied that Camillo had really changed at heart and so wrote the brethren of the church of Chiavenna, 29 May 1551.[2]

Even if Renato was himself pursuing a policy of " comprehension, " Renatian Anabaptism was at this very moment widespread in Rhaetia and Italy and consistently radical. For example, 24 May 1551,[3] Camillo's enemy, Giulio Milanese, wrote from Poschiavo to a " sister " in Venice, bringing together the X Heads of Agreement of the antitrinitarian Anabaptist Creed in XII Articles. Heresy, he said to her, was no less dangerous to the apostolic reformed Church than Catholic persecution. Since the XII Articles are not expressly a transcript of Camillo's theology, we shall not here enumerate them. Suffice it to say that this synthetic Anabaptist Creed testifies to the potency of Camillo's influence among the separatists despite his strategic Recantation.

Just a year after Camillo's Recantation attested by (? the self-styled) " authorized visitor of the synod, " Vergerio himself appeared in Chur on his way to Zurich, as we learn from three letters addressed to Bullinger, one by Comander, 21 January 1552, and two by Gallicius about a month later.[4] With Vergerio came a young minister of the Paravicini family. We have already encountered young Dr. Bartolomeo Paravicini.[5] This time it was his elected or nominated successor in Caspano, presumably a cousin, Gianandrea Paravicini, likewise a follower and no doubt also a tutee of Camillo. Gianandrea had accompanied Vergerio to Chur in order to be examined and approved by the chief divines of the Rhaetian synod concentrated in and around Chur. Despite Gianandrea's avowed aberrations from Reformed ortho-

---

[1] On Vergerio's interest in using the Camillo case, see Cantimori, *Eretici* (German edition), p. 86.

[2] Printed by Trechsel, *Antitrinitarier*, II, 107, n. 2; Casadei, " Fileno, " p. 418.

[3] Printed by Comba, *Protestanti*, II, 498-506.

[4] I, No. 174, p. 234; I, No. 177; No. 179.

[5] See above at p. 143, n. 2; p. 150, n. 1.

doxy, Vergerio was fully prepared to sponsor him on the ground that he belonged to the powerful Paravicini family.[1]

Vergerio's protegé and Camillo's tutee acknowledged that he had indeed received Camillo into the fellowship of the church of Caspano after his teacher had been excommunicated by the church of Chiavenna. Gianandrea told Comander and Gallicius that he held that the Father, the Son, and the Holy Spirit were one (*unum*, not *unus*) as the scripture testified but that the same scripture nowhere indicated that they were three distinct Persons. The two probing divines characterized this view quite correctly as Sabellian. Gianandrea, Vergerio presumably listening, said also that he did not believe in the virginity of Mary after the birth of Jesus. The critical divines characterized this view as Helvidian, although Gianandrea is not reported to have gone on to add either that Jesus was the son of Joseph or that Mary had other offspring besides Jesus (as did the Anabaptists at the synod of Venice in 1550). Also, and for the first time in our sources bearing on the thought of Camillo and his circle, Gianandrea in answering the question about immortality distinguished between the *anima* and the *animus*. He said that the *animus*, presumably the rational soul (or universal intellect) present in the (intellectually) reborn elect, animated by the *Spiritus sanctus*, was (in a sense) immortal but that the ordinary *anima*, that of brutes and unenlightened men, was mortal.[2] Gianandrea did not say, with Camillo, that the *animus* (or the *anima*) was to be rejoined with the body of the elect at the resurrection. Perhaps he was more narrowly Averroistic than Camillo, but this seems scarcely possible in view of his tutor's known convictions. It is more likely that we have here our sole indication of what the full eschatology of Camillo must have been, for on this crucial element in his theology we have otherwise only the transcripts of his opponents.[3]

It will therefore not be amiss to insist again that it may well have been the great originality of Camillo to have constructed a fully New Testament eschatology within the framework of medical-humanistic Averroism (endemic in the Italian university towns where he had sojourned), by identifying the world soul or the rational soul with the human *ratio* purified or endowed by the visitation of the Holy Spirit to the thus reborn elect and by then going beyond a purely

---

[1] See Trechsel's extremely critical account of Vergerio's conduct, *Antitrinitarier*, II, 108-125.

[2] This important datum is to be found in Gallicius' report of the conversation, I, No. 177, p. 237. " Nondum finis: animas nostras post hanc corporis mortem vivere fateri nolebat [Gianandrea], etsi hic certi quippiam non ita potuerimus [Gallicius and Comander] extorquere ex eo; rogatus enim rogabat et ipse nusquam non subinde quaerens, quasi clavum clavo retundere volens, quid esset anima. Distinguebat nescio quid inter animam et animum. Hunc quidem non interire, animam vero nescire se, quid esset; non posse ergo quid affirmare de ea. "

[3] Namely, the IX Accusations of Ferrara, the XXII Anathemas, the XXI Points. The XXVI Questions of 1561 (see below at p. 180, n. 3) and the X Heads of Agreement of the Venetian synod, though not hostile records, cannot serve directly for the reconstruction of Camillo's personal views; and they are in any event also summary.

Averroistic conception of an impersonal immortality of absorption in the world soul to reaffirm the Pauline hope of the resurrection in spiritual bodies of all the elect insofar as they have been once regenerated by the Holy Spirit. The *renati* are the elect who have been reborn in the Spirit and who await the resurrection of the just. Camillo's evangelically re-interpreted Averroism may be put down as one of the very important impulses in what we have called Evangelical Rationalism (Socinianism).

But for the moment we are with Camillo's tutee, Gianandrea, and Vergerio in Chur. Gianandrea's application for standing in the synod was turned down. In fact, he was, and no doubt rightly from the point of view of the synodal spokesmen, dealt with as had been Camillo " in the traces of Paul, " which would mean that he was excommunicated.[1] Gallicius was especially irked by Vergerio for so light-heartedly endorsing the " purified " Camillo and for sponsoring his still guileless tutee.[2]

Comander also turned down Vergerio's request made at this time that he be appointed official visitor or superintendent for the Italian congregations with the right to visit them and to examine, to depose, and to install the ministers as deputy of the general Rhaetian Reformed synod. Comander did not add, what he later wrote to Bullinger, that the magnates in Graubünden were getting to dislike all the Italian refugees heartily, and on all counts.[3]

The disappointed and vexed Italian noblemen complained in Zurich of their treatment in Chur at the hands of divines who wished to concentrate all the Protestant power of the Rhaetian Republic in Germanic hands. But young Paravicini took the precaution of writing back to Chur, saying that he had by no means intended to deny the doctrine of the Trinity.[4]

Back in his parish of Vicosoprano, Vergerio, still smarting from his frustration in Chur and in the meantime further vexed by word received from friends that Comander and Gallicius had written critically of him to Bullinger (as we, too, know from the above-cited correspondence), sought to defend himself in Bullinger's eyes by pointing out that since his Italian confrères were all excitable and temperamentally prone to sudden exaggeration, his remedy for the fissures opened up in the body of the church was to cover over the wounds with healing ointment instead of inflicting more surgery. There was, of course, no debate, he said in this letter of 3 March 1552,[5] that Anabaptists (insofar as they were programmatic separatists) could not be endured; but, he added, it was far better to act moderately with a view to curing them rather than acting precipitately. He hoped that Rhaetia might earn

---

[1] " Cum Camillo et Paravicino agemus in nundinis Paulinis. " I, No. 174, p. 234; the equivalent is to be found in I, No. 177, p. 237.

[2] The letter to Bullinger of 29 February 1552; I, No. 241, pp. 242 f.

[3] Comander reports the request to Bullinger in the letter of 5 April 1552; I, No. 181.

[4] Reported by Comander, *ibid.*, p. 247.

[5] I, No. 180: 1.

thereby a reputation in the world for proceeding prudently and with great gentleness and love, " as indeed God our Lord deals with us. " Since, however, Camillo had apparently already gone back on his Recantation and rejoined the overt separatists, Vergerio was quite eager to dissociate himself from him for the sake of the larger plan for a comprehensive (latitudinarian) Italo-Rhaetian synod; and, in his note of 13 March, he was willing to use Bullinger's own word for Camillo, " a poisonous skin, " and remarked incidentally that the magistrates had recently forced Camillo to leave (presumably as a crypto-Anabaptist) like Tiziano before him.

In another letter of 20 June, Vergerio said that he and Laelius Socinus (who had left just four days before for Siena) had finished a tour of the whole Valtellina together and found that it, like the region around Chiavenna, had been infected by " the poisonous skin. "[1] On the same day, Vergerio wrote to the Zurich Hebraist Konrad Pellikan, commending the bearer of his message (an Italian evangelical refugee) as a worthy friend, and took occasion to remark that " our Laelius has been staying with me for three weeks, since then departing for a visit to his father but amidst many perils.... — may God snatch him from them! "[2] Later writers, both pro and anti-Socinian, will see in the sojourn of Laelius in the Valtellina at this time one more occasion for him to have become closely acquainted with the thought of Camillo and even to adduce evidence that on this perilous journey to his birthplace he may have carried some of Camillo's writings for distribution among the evangelical conventicles in Tuscany and Emilia. Laelius had lived in Bologna (whither, it should be recalled, his father had brought him as a youth in 1542 when Mariano became a professor in the *Studium*). It is now known from the transcript of a Bolognese trial held in July, 1549 that one Achille Vizzano and others of his circle were charged with receiving six letters from Laelius, after his departure from Bologna, with having met in the Sozzini residence for evangelical discussions, and with having read " il trattato del Phyleno. " This writing was presumably Camillo's *Trattato del Battesimo e della Santa Cena*, shared by members of his old circle in Bologna and by new recruits, thanks to the good offices of Professor Sozzini's peregrinating son.[3]

To return to Rhaetia, in another letter to Bullinger of 22 August 1552,[4] still trying to ingratiate himself and offset the aspersions from Chur,

---

[1] I, No. 185, p. 253. Giulio Milanese was under the impression that Vergerio accompanied Laelius to Bologna to visit the latter's father. Letter to Bullinger of 23 June 1552: I, No. 186. It is the view of Da Porta that Laelius, though under the influence of Camillo since 1547, did not share all of Camillo's doctrine and would therefore with Vergerio have deplored the excesses. *Historia,* I: 2, p. 86. Cf. C. Illgen, *Vita Laelii Socini* (Leipzig, 1826), 35, n. 11.

[2] Da Porta, *Historia,* I:2, p. 86.

[3] See above at p. 153, n. 6 and Rotondò, " Bologna, " p. 144 f. on the Bolognese trial of Ulisse Aldrovandi. For the Vicentine "Collegia," see my *Radical Reformation,* pp. 561, 569 and 572.

[4] I, No. 189: 1.

Vergerio tells about his translating one of Bullinger's writings into Italian and remarks in connection with the efforts of the divines of Chur to implicate him willy-nilly in Camillo's heresies that Camillo seems to have quieted down. Vergerio had to clear himself of such an association in order to avoid what he as a latitudinarian considered the greatest calamity that could befall Protestantism in the Rhaetian Republic, namely, the imposition of a binding confession of faith, which is exactly what the autumn synod was to decree.

It was with relief that Vergerio could write Bullinger 15 September 1552 [1] that he had just heard that Camillo had ventured outside the Rhaetian asylum into Bergamo possibly on his way to Vicenza and had been immediately apprehended by the constables. Vergerio took malicious satisfaction in the thought that his former collaborator in latitudinarianism would probably never return alive.

By 24 September 1552 [2] Cardinal Innocenzo del Monte, secretary of Pope Julius III, was in possession of the information that this " Sicilian heresiarch " had just been captured in Bergamo; for on that day he wrote Bishop Lodovico Beccadelli, formerly a secretary of Contarini (who had concerned himself with Fileno) and now the papal

---

[1] I, No. 191: 1. The conjecture that Camillo might have been on his way to Vicenza is based solely on the fact that a Socinian tradition associates Camillo with a liberal academy there of some forty members. It is here the place to put down what can be said about Camillo and Vicenza.

The Socinian list of participants in the academy of Vicenza includes Laelius Socinus, Bernardino Ochino, Francesco Negri, along with two Italian Anabaptists who became Hutterites in Moravia. The most ample version of this account is that of Stanislas Lubieniecki, *Historia Reformationis Polonicae* (Amsterdam [Freistadius], 1685), pp. 38-40. It is based upon two now lost manuscripts, a history by Stanislas Budziński and a life of Laelius Socinus. This most ample version of the academy, which allegedly broke up in 1546 (the year of Laelius' departure for Basel), does not mention the name of Camillo among the forty participants, nor does that of Andreas Wiszowaty, " Narratio compendiosa, " most readily available in Christopher Sandius' *Bibliotheca Antitrinitariorum* (Amsterdam, 1684), pp. 209 f., nor that of Sandius himself in his brief reference to the academy under Socinus, *ibid.*, pp. 18 f. Modern scholarship has completely dissolved this phantom academy of proto-Socinians and has discovered instead a typical Italian Renaissance academy and a cluster of radical Anabaptist conventicles in and around Vicenza deriving from the mission there of Lorenzo Tizzano. Bernardo Morsolin, " L'academia de' Sociniani in Vicenza, " *Atti del regio istituto veneto di scienze, lettere ed arti*, V, serie 5 (1879), 473-475. Earl M. Wilbur reviews the arguments in *A History of Unitarianism* (Cambridge, 1947), pp. 80-84 and correctly refrains from mentioning Camillo among the forty participants. There can be no doubt about the radical character of the Anabaptist conventicles in and around Vicenza, but they did not date from before c. 1550. Morsolin surmises that the story of the Vicenza meeting found its way into the Socinian records by way of the two Italian Hutterites, Giulio di Treviso and Francesco di Ruego. Undoubtedly at least one or two proto-Socinians were associated with these conventicles, otherwise the account would not have been perpetuated among the Socinians. Both Church and Cantimori accept as probable the attendance of Camillo at a meeting in Vicenza c. 1547. Church, *I Riformatori*, I, 289. But after careful scrutiny of the data, we can see nothing more than a possible interest of Camillo in the Vicenza group c. 1552.

But see now the forthcoming rehabilitation of the " Vicenza Academy " by Aldo Stella of Padua.

[2] Casadei, " Fileno, " pp. 426 f.

nuncio to Venice (1550-1554) in charge also of Bergamo (because of the recent suspension of its bishop for involvement in heresy), to send the captive to Rome. Del Monte added more details about the prisoner, " an apostate Sicilian " who had already once abjured his heresy, " a very great heresiarch " who had been living " nel paese de Grisoni. " He gave further instructions for getting the prisoner to Rome. In his impatience he followed this letter with still another on 1 October.

On that very day in Venice Beccadelli, who had in the meantime received direct word from the new administrator of the diocese of Bergamo (Nicolò Durante), had to inform Del Monte that, alas, the administrator and *rettori* of Bergamo had released the prisoner because of the threat of reprisals against all Catholic Venetians resident in the Rhaetian Republic.[1] Then in his second response to Del Monte,[2] Beccadelli named the thus favored prisoner *Fileno*, and Del Monte in his (third) letter of 18 October spoke resignedly of the failure of "the Fileno affair. "[3] We have become accustomed to calling the heresiarch by his programmatic Rhaetian name. There can be no doubt, however, that the Sicilian-Rhaetian heresiarch protected by some powerful influence from within Rhaetia was Camillo under his old name, the one preserved in the inquisitorial acts. And one may conjecture that the protective influence was that of the Paravicini family operating from their ancestral seat in Caspano. Two weeks after Beccadelli wrote to Rome about the failure of his mission in Bergamo, Vergerio from Vicosoprano informed Bullinger that Camillo had escaped from Bergamo (as Bullinger had apparently at one time anticipated) — not, however, without denying again all the articles that he had been spreading![4]

On 1 November 1552[5] Vergerio, again referring to the tour of the Valtellina with Laelius, reported to Bullinger that the valley they had traversed was very much affected by the Anabaptist infection; that Camillo more insolent than ever, now that he had made good his escape from Bergamo, was at it again; and he implied that Bullinger might do no better than persuade the negligent overseers in Chur that there was after all only one person, already on the spot, who could handle the situation. Writing a fortnight later from Chur[6] where Vergerio attended the autumn general synod, he told Bullinger that the urgent problem was to remove " the poisonous skin " once for all from Rhaetia. Five days later[7] he added another note, urging Bullinger to do some-

---

[1] Beccadellis' response of 1 October 1552 is found in its original in Biblioteca Vaticana, Lat. 6752, f. 169 r.; the register form in Biblioteca Palatina, Parma, Codex 1011; it is excerpted by Casadei, " Fileno, " p. 427, and by Pio Paschini, *Venezia e l'Inquisizione Romana da Giulio III a Pio IV* (Padua, 1959), pp. 95 f.

[2] Excerpted by Casadei, " Fileno, " p. 428; by Paschini, *op. cit.*, p. 96.

[3] Excerpted by Casadei, " Fileno, " p. 428.

[4] Letter of 15 October 1552; I, No. 193:1.

[5] I, No. 195: 1.

[6] I, No. 195: 2.

[7] I, No. 195: 3.

thing drastic lest "Camillo infect for us the whole of Rhaetia with his poison." Still more desperately he wrote again at the end of the month, adding this time that Camillo would soon triumph throughout the Italian sections of Rhaetia, "for he has powerful supporters who are able to use shields of gold," while at the same time, Vergerio added, his own position was being undermined by the machinations of the papists. "The devil cannot endure it that the Valtellina be opened up by the gospel," he concluded, "but the Lord is more powerful; in him I trust."[1]

In his next letter to Bullinger, 11 December, Vergerio announced that Camillo had made bold to seek the headship of the evangelical school in Sondrio, even though the valley magistrates had recently warned that nobody might be so appointed without the authorization of the Rhaetian general synod. "Camillo knows this," he added, and asked, perhaps rhetorically: "With what protectors do you think he dares such a thing?" Vergerio may have known or surmised that his protectors were the Paravicini, whose favor he himself may have lost. In the meantime, the federal diet of the Rhaetian Republic had restored to private benefactors the right to maintain their religion in the community where it was a minority view — a privilege first established in 1544 in extension of the decree of Ilanz but temporarily rescinded. Thus Camillo's "powerful supporters" were again confirmed in their rights.

Camillo's success was so great in the Valtellina that Comander and Gallicius again occupied themselves with the problem and went so far in their joint communication of 12 December 1552 as to enclose excerpts from Camillo's "book written in Italian," the one which had presumably featured in the two-day investigation conducted by Gallicius and the three other visitors in Chiavenna. They called these gleanings the sheaves or ears of Camillo's wild oats.

Although it has not been said expressly by any of the correspondents whose letters we have been leafing through since the Recantation of 19 January 1551, it is clear from this effort to supply Bullinger with fresh condensations from a pre-Recantation writing that Camillo had, in fact, resumed his old Spiritualist Anabaptist position and that the many references to Camillo's contamination of the Valtellina with the Anabaptist plague or malady must be taken as a clear indication that he had indeed after his escape from Bergamo resumed the propagation of his peculiar form of spiritualizing, psychopannychist, anti-Nicene Anabaptism. That the whole of Italian Anabaptism south of the Rhaetian frontier had also stemmed from Renato was asseverated by two refugees from the inquisition in the Italian states who had themselves submitted to rebaptism in Italy and had now turned to "the purity of our doctrine," wrote Vergerio 10 January 1553.[2] He also reminded Bullinger of his suspicion shared while with him in Zurich that

---

[1] Letter of 30 November 1552; I, No. 195: 4.

[2] I, No. 199: 2.

someone very well known to him and in the first ranks of Reformed society in Basel had recently embraced rebaptism.[1] One month later Vergerio repeated his signal of alarm: "Here Camillo reigns!."[2]

It is not hard to imagine that all these bulletins from Vergerio on the spiritual climate in Rhaetia are building up into another huge storm, but one would not expect it to strike again at the same place and at the same person. It was, rather, Camillo's friend and convert, Tiziano, who was struck; and it was in Chur and not in the Valtellina that the sentence was pronounced. His case was heard, Tiziano defended himself, and then recanted his heresies; he was driven by rods from the town, and was exiled from the Rhaetian Republic. Gallicius described the proceedings in a few crisp phrases to Bullinger 2 June1554.[3]

That was the summer after the ominous burning of Servetus in Geneva. The burning and drowning and beheading of thousands of Anabaptists within the borders of the Holy Roman Empire had somehow never gripped the imaginations of the Italian Evangelicals in Italy and in the diaspora, orthodox and latitudinarian alike, with such anguish and with such foreboding as did Calvin's burning of the always incalculable Spanish anti-Nicene, anabaptist, psychopannychist physician (so much like many of the Italians themselves). Gallicius in Rhaetia was more aware of Italian sensibilities than Bullinger; and in his letter to him of 25 June[4] he felt obliged to justify his relative leniency in the treatment of Tiziano, whose views were not unlike those which had brought Servetus to the flames. Gallicius pointed out that Tiziano's recantation was demoralizing for his followers, whereas another martyrdom would have raised their devotion to a new pitch.

In Tiziano's recantation the doctrine of the Trinity, Christology, and the perpetual virginity of Mary, including the defense of the received scriptural texts by which these doctrines are biblically grounded, featured to the complete neglect of such distinctively Renatian ideas as the death of the soul.[5] Tiziano, a friend and possibly a convert of Camillo, may have, like him, stood also under the direct or indirect influence of Servetus.

---

[1] *Ibid.*, pp. 279 f. Schiess in a footnote conjectures that it was Curione who accepted rebaptism. It is known that Curione was in Rhaetia, presumably with Giulio Milanese, in the summer of 1553 in connection with the publication of his *De Amplitudine Beati Regni Dei* (Poschiavo, September 1554). Cantimori accepts this surmise, *Eretici* (German edition), p. 86. But this is unlikely in view of the fact that on 22 August 1553 Curione from Chiavenna wrote to Bullinger, taking the side of Mainardo against Camillo. Kutter, *Curione*, Brief, No. 91. Moreover, the hero of the dialogues of *De Amplitudine* is an idealized Mainardo in his Pavia setting where Curione first made his acquaintance around 1535. *Ibid.*, pp. 21, L 88. It is possible that the convert in Basel was Girolamo Allegretti who, having been in Basel, was an antitrinitarian Anabaptist pastor in Gardone. See letter of Giulio Milanese to him 14 June 1550, above, p. 165, n. 2.

[2] Letter of 10 March 1553; I, No. 207: 1.

[3] I, No. 261: 1.

[4] I, No. 261: 2.

[5] The full text of the recantation is given *ibid.* Tiziano would not be the same as Lorenzo Tizzano, whose principal deposition was made before the inquisition in Venice in October 1553. See above, p. 160 n. 6, 7; p. 172, n. 1.

Surely Camillo himself will have had some contact with the writings of Servetus. Their ideas and even their lives offer parallels. And when Camillo came to write his long *Carmen* against Calvin for burning Servetus,[1] he was clearly acquainted with certain traits and episodes which would indicate more than a reading knowledge of the Spanish heretic.

In Traona, in September 1554, on the anniversary of Servetus' martyrdom, Camillo signed his name to a long, passionate, and flamboyant indictment of Calvin in 357 lines of verse. The *Carmen*, mingling biblical and mythological allusions in a highly mannered humanistic Latin, belongs with Sebastian Castellio's *De haereticis* and Curione's *Apologia*[2] to the considerable literature of protest against the use of force in the realm of conscience.[3] It was addressed to the select company of humanists, humane divines, and their noble patrons. One can imagine the satisfaction with which it was first read aloud and received in the cultured Paravicini residence in Caspano. The poem recounts near the beginning the great hope that all Italian Evangelicals had in the temples set by God upon the top of the mountains in the latter days (Isaiah 2: 2), how the Italians fleeing from persecution streamed with the nations into this protective sanctuary, looking forward to " the golden age about to be restored under the fair auspices of Christ, " when suddenly, in a shudder of revulsion, they learned that the prophet of the Reformed people had burned a fellow-Christian.

Camillo distinguishes between two dispensations, that of the old covenant and that of the new. He associates the Roman priesthood with that of the Hebraic covenant and its stress on law and sacrifice, and he appeals for a gentler conception of religion as proclaimed by Jesus who healed, who forgave, who was slow to anger.

Nowhere else do we have in Camillo's surviving writings such a stress upon the apostolic ban as the only means of force allowable to Christians. As far as Camillo's theology is concerned, this is perhaps the one *novum* in the document. It is, in fact, the one distinctively Anabaptist institution that has thus far been almost missing in our

---

[1] The full critical edition of the " Accusation et procès de Michel Servet " is published by Robert M. Kingdon, *Registres de la Compagnie des Pasteurs de Genève*, II (Geneva, 1962). It might be added that Camillo had never come to know Calvin personally, as had Laelius Socinus. The editor's references to Camillo Renato in two of Calvin's letters are false identifications. Calvin, *Opera*, XI, letter No. 431 to Viret, col. 458. The suspect Giulio Camillo whom Calvin " has " with him in Geneva is not our Renato, as the editor suggests in n. 9, but the creator of a curious wooden contraption conceived as a Theater of Knowledge. See Elizabeth Hajós, " References to Giulio Camillo, " *Bibliothèque d'Humanisme et Renaissance*, XXV (1963), 207.

[2] Edited and translated elsewhere in the Volume by David Pingree. It will be noted that there are several phrases and scriptural allusions in common which might suggest that Curione and Camillo, old allies, might have been drawn together in mutual horror at what had happened to Servetus. The work of Dr. Pingree now supersedes my earlier conjecture that the pseudonymous *Apologia* might belong to Matteo Gribaldi. See *Radical Reformation*, p. 624.

[3] The *Carmen* has been translated by Dorothy Rounds and edited elsewhere in this Volume as the closest thing we have to a portrait of Camillo: a self-portrait in verse.

account of Camillo's thought and practice. An allusion to believers' baptism is not discoverable in the poem, barely one to the death and ultimate resurrection of the soul. But the *epulum* and the *commemoratio* are there behind the mythological language of classical Rome. On the doctrine of the Trinity Camillo does not here profess to be Servetian. For perhaps tactical reasons he hopes, by admitting that Servetus might well have been in error, that he can be more effective in his appeal for toleration within civil society and in his recommendation that long prayers, instruction, and as a last resort the ban, administered in love and with a readiness to readmit the truly penitent, become the only instruments of ecclesiastical policy.

The *Carmen* was to be the last important expression of Camillo's thought. After a tempestuous career of radical preaching, of at least two recantations, of three arrests and five extraordinary escapes from the inquisition, of great dreams and petty projects, Camillo was no doubt vaguely aware of the great difference between himself and the physician-theologian whose martyrdom he had besung. In fact, what he chose to stress in verse, significantly, was not the steadfastness of Servetus to the end nor his passion for Christian truth, as he had come to formulate it as a lay theologian, but rather the cruelty of his oppressor. For now the defrocked Franciscan, the excommunicated Bullingerian, the relapsed Anabaptist no longer insisted on truth with sharpened edges but upon a policy of latitudinarian toleration in church and state which, like a sheath, would keep the two-edged sword of dogma from hurting anybody for life. In the *Carmen* he, the would-be Spiritualist, came very close to identifying the "gentle Christ" with that sheath rather than with the wielder of the "sword of the Spirit".

The remainder of Camillo's story after 1554 can be fairly briefly told. Since his correspondence with established Reformed churchmen, like Bullinger, had long since been broken off, we have much less about him and nothing more from him in the surviving documentation, except the notice of a letter circa 1554 from Chiavenna, directed to Duchess Renata of Ferrara. In it he asked his (presumed) former protectress to send aid to the (evangelical) brethren in exile.[1]

We may picture Camillo now largely withdrawn to the precincts of the Paravicini family. As he grew older and age prevented his restless spirit from expressing itself in travel, he was probably invited to settle down in one of the Paravicini homes in or near Caspano. Insofar as he was in fact the source of a major current in Italian Anabaptism, and still had sympathies with it, he will have learned by frequent bulletins of the inquisitorial ravages among the Italian Anabaptists as a consequence of the disastrous defection of Pietro Manelfi. As for his eschatological Spiritualism, it would survive only as it was absorbed into Evangelical Rationalism, notably when it came to find

[1] Fontana, *op. cit.*, III, p. xxxiv paraphrases the letter not otherwise located with reference to a document of 1554: " Eretici che erano in Ferrara al tempo di Madama Renea. "

expression in Socinianism. Indeed it was in Socinianism that his most distinctive ideas were to be perpetuated in organized form: his rationalist exegesis, his conception of election and of the eventual resuscitation of the extinguished soul of the elect alone, his conception of the Lord's Supper, and again with modification his conception of the person and office of Christ in salvation. It was through the mediation of Laelius Socinus and others that Camillo's ideas and practices were to be transmuted and transmitted in areas and eras that were to be aware of him only vaguely as "a gentle mystic."[1] What remains therefore to be recounted in completing our biography of Camillo Renato is to mention one or two episodes connected with men who during his lifetime transmitted his ideas.

4) EPILOGUE (*1554-? 1575*)

The most important "Renatian" was Laelius Socinus (1525-1562), whom Camillo, though older by a quarter of a century, was to outlive by a decade. Laelius first came in contact with Camillo (and Mainardo) in 1547 when he passed through Chiavenna on his way to matriculate at the university of Basel. Like the older Camillo, young Laelius had considerable contact with Curione and with Bullinger. The latter could scarcely believe, as the more discerning and also more irascible Calvin came to avow, that Laelius was really implicated in the heresies and the propaganda for toleration which were every once in a while reported of him. For example, in the early summer of 1555 Giulio Milanese, since c. 1547 the pastor in Poschiavo (after having made way for Vergerio in Vicosoprano) wrote to Bullinger, charging Laelius with an inclination towards Arianism and a sympathy for Servetus. It will be recalled that back in Venice with Curione this same Giulio had spoken of Camillo, but recently tried at Ferrara, as a man of *leggerezza*. During Curione's visit to Poschiavo he will have filled in for his old acquaintance what he knew from his vantage point in Basel about Camillo and Laelius.

Bullinger replied to Giulio in an undated letter of July 1555.[2] He had taken Giulio's warning with sufficient seriousness, incredulous though he was, to ask Laelius in and to present the problem to him

---

[1] Faustus Socinus, the nephew of Laelius, held precisely Camillo's views; but the Socinians yielded to the influence of the indigenous Polish immersionist antitrinitarian Anabaptists insofar as "Socinian" baptismal practice was concerned. See my *Radical Reformation* and the therein cited Polish literature.

[2] I, No. 290. The general surmise that Laelius had considerable Christian contact with Camillo back in 1547 when he was on his way to Basel stems from Illgen, *Vita*, p. 17. Illgen in turn cites Da Porta, I: 2, p. 86, who in turn cites only Vergerio's letter of 1552, above, p. 171, n. 1. Illgen himself makes this the tenuous basis for presupposing close acquaintance between Camillo and Laelius in 1547, but it is a major theme of his small book that Laelius was theologically dependent on Camillo, *Vita*, pp. 8, 11, 17, 35, 39, 44. See, most recently, at p. 108, n. 3.

frankly. Laelius said that he could not understand what the basis of the charges might be except that in Geneva he had indeed expressed himself against the execution of Servetus and still held that it was better to liberate the man from his error by argumentation than by cremation — a turn of phrase found, incidentally, also in the *Carmen*. For good measure Laelius proceeded to sign a Confession [1] in which he avowed all the proper things and disavowed all the heresies of Camillo and Servetus, the latter by name.

Giulio remained unconvinced. After a trip to Sondrio where he received in fact Bullinger's letter with Laelius' Confession of Faith and disclaimer of heresy, and after a stop in Tirano (whence Camillo had directed his first letter to Bullinger just thirteen years before) Giulio wrote again to Bullinger, still very uneasy about Camillo's activities and his influence on Laelius. Writing from Poschiavo, 4 November 1555, he remarked that he had found out "that what they have once absorbed, Servetians and Anabaptists can never really eliminate," whatever their protestations and however earnest they profess to be; for they almost perfidiously blow hot, then cold. Surely, says Giulio, this was true of Camillo, whose sly and calculating manner of thought and behavior are now well known. He is in fact like a slippery snake in his twists and turns which has to be stepped on hard or it gets away. And changing the image a bit further on, Giulio says that Laelius, for all his protestations, may well be simulating, and that the mask must be torn off from all these wolfish pretenders for the sake of the safety of the church, "because a hypocritical friend is more dangerous than a public enemy."

After this exchange the sources are silent about Camillo until the year before Laelius' death, though the next episode does not concern Laelius but rather Mainardo again. It was the final fight between Camillo's allies and the now aged pastor of Chiavenna. It will be recalled that Mainardo had long sought to have his Confession of Faith imposed upon his church in Chiavenna and that there was a sentiment widespread among the defenders of Reformed orthodoxy that something like it should be imposed on all the Italian churches in addition to the Rhaetian Confession, a credal statement that would be subscribed not only by the pastors, elders, and deacons, but also *by everyone* wishing to become a member. This was the so-called *Definitio* of the church of Chiavenna.[2] It was Pietro Leone in Chiavenna, Girolamo Turriani in Piur, and especially Michelangelo Florio in Soglio, all of them self-confessed Servetians and Renatians, who led the attack against Mai-

---

[1] See the remarks by John Tedeschi elsewhere in this Volume concerning the Confession.

[2] The *Definitio* is printed by Trechsel, *Antitrinitarier*, II, 426. For the larger setting of the problem see Peter Dalbert, *Die Reformation in den italienischen Talschaften Graubündens nach dem Briefwechsel Bullingers* (Zurich, 1948), pp. 120 ff. and Emil Camenisch, *Geschichte der Reformation und Gegenreformation in der italienischen Südtälern Graubündens* (Chur, 1950; Italian version Samedan, 1950).

nardo. Mainardo wrote Bullinger, 4 August 1561,[1] saying that Michelangelo was conducting himself even more outrageously than Camillo. He reported that Michelangelo with a second preacher had prepared an attack on him drawn from a writing by Camillo (presumably the mordantly introduced *Errores, ineptiae, scandala, contradictiones Augustini Maynardi*, which had already been used against Mainardo during the two-day investigation by the four synodal visitors) and that an excommunicated member of the Chiavenna church bore the expense and made the arrangements for its being printed in Milan and circulated in order to defame the old man in the eyes of his colleagues in Zurich and Bern.

The new agitation against Mainardo aroused enough support from different kinds of people to warrant the dispatch of Michelangelo as the spokesman for five established Italian pastors who opposed the imposition of a binding formula, namely, besides Michelangelo, the already mentioned Girolamo, Agostino of Cremona at the time pastor in Tirano, Francesco Cellario of Morbegno, and the pastors of Mese and Casaccia.[2] The five wished to ascertain whether their somewhat latitudinarian ideas and Renatian sensibilities would be sanctioned in Zurich.

Their XXVI Questions[3] were presented to the Zurich ministers 24 May 1561. It is evident from the prominence and the number of questions (the first three and several others indirectly) that the overriding concern of the five Italian ministers and of the others, lay and clerical, whose sentiments they reflected, was to prevent any confession of faith from being imposed upon the Rhaetian churches as a condition either of initial membership or of participation in the offices and ministrations of the churches. It is further evident that the doctrine concerning which the most uncertainty prevailed was that of the Trinity (Questions IV through VIII and XX). The ministers were opposed to any formal subscription to the creeds insisted upon by Mainardo, namely, the Nicene, the so-called Athanasian Creed, and the Tome of Pope Damasus (c. 380). They wished to have no binding statement to go beyond the Apostles' Creed. For in two questions notably (IX, X) and in many others indirectly, they were at great pains to defend the rights of conscience and reason. In all the questions about the two accepted sacraments and the related actions and institutions with a Roman sacramental tradition like marriage, ordination, and excommunication they were greatly concerned lest false conceptions and practices be perpetuated (such as the nuptial sermon) and also lest the Reformed minister deprive any layman or another minister of the ministrations of the church as a means of forcing a particular theological view. At the same time, they themselves, needless to say, had their own par-

---

[1] II, No. 360; cf. the letter of Johann Fabricius to Bullinger, 24 May 1561; II, No. 346.

[2] The pastor of Mese (Mess) near Chiavenna was Hieronymus Tryphernus; the pastor of Casaccia, Georgius Stephanus.

[3] Printed by Trechsel, *Antitrinitarier*, II, Beilage V, pp. 417-419.

ticular views, notably about baptism; and it is in these questions (XI, XII, XV, XXVI) that their Renatian proclivities are clearest; for the five protesters wonder, on the one hand, whether baptism should be administered to infants in arms when parents still believe that the sacrament actually effectuates (or confirms — but the word is not used) salvation, and on the other, whether baptism should be administered to the infants of excommunicated parents. The several questions about the Lord's Supper (XIV, XVI, XVII, XIX) do not suggest the persistence of Camillo's special interest in the *epulum*. Almost all the questions may be said to be based upon the tenacious conviction that each congregation, duly constituted of officers and faithful laymen, is an organic, autonomous community upon which neither its single pastor nor its pastor with his elders and deacons (XIX), nor other churches acting through synods of visitors may impose any order or doctrine without the consent of the whole congregation in meeting duly assembled.[1]

The efforts of the five latitudinarian pastors was doomed to failure. In fact their *démarche* precipitated an action, abetted by Bullinger and the Zurich divines, of the general synod at Chur, which obliged the five recalcitrant pastors to sign a confession, no longer to be called "that of Mainardo but rather that of the Rhaetian Church!"[2]

Mainardo died in 1563, to be succeeded by Girolamo Zanchi, equally vigorous in the defense of Reformed orthodoxy. Camillo lived on, less and less noticed. The man he had molded the most significantly as far as later influence was concerned, Laelius Socinus, had died the year before in Zurich.

Camillo, who took no part directly in the struggle against the imposition of the new Rhaetian creed, was no doubt living quietly with the Paravicini at Caspano. A Genoese merchant, one Nicolò Camulio, on his way back from Antwerp, in three letters written in December 1563 to two of the five antisubscriptionist pastors, Michelangelo Florio and Girolamo Turriani, remarked, in connection with the woes of Bernardino Ochino, that Camillo Renato, though likewise surrounded by powerful foes, was able to live peacefully in Rhaetia.[3] Camillo's two followers continued their restless careers, Michelangelo still in Soglio and Turriani now in Teglio. The orthodox Reformed Scipio Lentulo, at the time pastor in Sondrio where Camillo had once tried to head the school, remarked discerningly in a letter of 19 October 1566 that once these

---

[1] This insistence upon full congregationalism in the XXVI Questions should be brought into relation with Point XVIII of 1549. See above at p. 164, n. 1.

[2] The letter of Fabricius to Bullinger of 6 June 1561, II, No. 349, p. 303.

[3] The three letters of Camulio are dated 1, 3 and 29 December 1563. They are to be found in Bern, Stadtbibliothek, MS. A 93. They are discussed by Cantimori, *Eretici* (German edition), p. 467, n. 14 and by Roland Bainton, *Bernardino Ochino, Esule e Riformatore Senese del Cinquecento 1487-1563* (Florence, 1940), pp. 180, 188 ff. It is of interest that Ochino wrote 4 June 1558 to Friedrich von Salis, asking for protection, the same Rhaetian statesman to whom Camillo dedicated his versified *Credo* or *Professio*, c. December 1549. See above at p. 162, n. 3.

Italians had begun to turn from Catholicism, no religion could really please them.[1]

There was at this time a good deal of trouble fomented from the outside in this region, especially in and around Morbegno. For example, a violent effort was being made to strengthen the monastery there. The Reformed pastor of the town, Camillo's follower, Francesco Cellario, one of the five antisubscriptionist pastors, was waylaid in a Catholic ambuscade and carried bound over the Rhaetian frontier to Como.[2] From Como he was taken to Milan and then, to be burned, to Rome. Somewhat before this episode Antonio (Aonio) Paleario, poet and rhetorician and professor at both Lucca and Milan, stood trial in 1567 for heresy. In the course of the inquisition, a certain Luigi Fontana of Como testified 10 December 1567 that the minister of Morbegno (Francesco Cellario) or Camillo himself, once told him that the two heretical poets had for some time exchanged letters and sonnets until at length Paleario asked "Camillo Renato napolitano" whom he or Luigi knew as "Fileno Eretico, old and blind" to desist for fear of the inquisition. Though Paleario denied this correspondence during the trial, the fact that he was also in correspondence with Curione, with Laelius Socinus' father, with the Florentine historian Giovanni Michele Bruto, and with others suspected of heresy, makes the inquisitional record entirely plausible that Phileno-Renato and Paleario had for some time been friends.[3]

The last certain notice of Camillo Renato comes from 1572, the date of Ulrich Campell's topographical *Descriptio*, wherein he remarks that Camillo, "old and blind," was at the time living at Caspano.[4]

---

[1] Da Porta, *Historia*, I: 2, p. 496; Cantimori, *Eretici* (German edition), p. 290.

[2] Letter of Tobias Egli to Bullinger, 9 June 1568; III, No. 96. Another version from the perspective of 7 January 1572, *ibid.*, Beilage, especially pp. 531, 534.

[3] B. Fontana, "Sommario del Processo di Aonio Paleario," *Archivio della Società Romana di Storia Patria*, XIX (1896), 167 f. This is a summary of the Roman Inquisitorial records prepared by Giacomo Laderchi for apologetical purposes. Cf. *Annales Ecclesiastici*, II (Rome, 1733), 22-25. Laderchi's source is explicit on the identification of Camillo and "Fileno." Luigi Fontana may have derived his information from Camillo directly, but it is possible that his information came from the kidnapped pastor of Morbegno, Cellario. It was on this eighteenth century summary that Church, *Italian Reformers*, first ventured among modern scholars upon the identification of Camillo and Phileno (Italian edition), I, p. 85, n. 2. But he was unnecessarily hesitant. Cf. Casadei, "Fileno," p. 357. Ernesto Mattone-Vezzi in his serialized biography of Paleario accepts the identification but minimizes its significance in keeping with the general trend of the study which is a substantial vindication of the orthodoxy of Paleario. "Aonio Paleario e la Riforma Religiosa in Italia," *Miscellanea Storica della Valdelsa*, esp. LIX (1948), 52-54. Mattone-Vezzi, in stressing what he considers the basically different temperaments and theologies of the two poets, overlooks the humanistic ties that could have bound the two men together along with their common interest in religious toleration.

[4] *Raetiae Alpestris Topographica Descriptio* (Chur, 1572), p. 427. The relevant passage is excerpted *in toto* by Casadei, "Fileno," pp. 432 f., where he is at pains to show that the phrase "Hic jam diu oculorum usu captus ibi *vivit*" belongs to the draft of 1572 and not to the revision of 1581. As for the blindness, it will be recalled that Camillo, as Ricci-Phileno, already in Modena suffered from impending blindness. See above at p. 126, n. 2. In October 1594 the last known follower of Camillo in Rhaetia, Fabrizio

It is just possible that Camillo thereafter left Caspano to join the Italian evangelical church which had migrated from Locarno to Zurich. In the records of this parish under date of 30 October 1575 we note the expenses incurred for the burial of a certain "Camillo Modenese che habitava qua et è morto di peste."[1]

Camillo's influence long survived him in Caspano. When in 1578 the nuncio from Como under the direction of Archbishop Carlo Borromeo made a pastoral visitation of the Valtellina, he found that half of the five hundred families of Caspano were Evangelical, which in this mountainside seat of the Paravicini would have meant Renatian.[2]

Pestalozza, after an absence of seventeen years from his *patria*, is said to have returned to Chiavenna and to have been tolerated. Da Porta, *Historia*, 1:2, p. 632.

[1] Ferdinand Meyer, *Die evangelische Gemeinde in Locarno*, II (Zurich, 1836), p. 32, n. 109.

[2] Carl Camenisch, *Carlo Borromeo und die Gegenreformation in Veltlin* (Chur, 1901), p. 116. The Evangelical Church was destroyed in the "sacred massacre" of 1620. One of the Paravicini was burned alive in Morbegno for refusing to recant. To this day the Catholic Church in Caspano and in several neighboring communities like Morbegno keeps permanently an empty, black-shrouded coffin in the center of the church, a constant reminder of hell and purgatory. This usage may well be a surviving testimony to the influence of the eloquent evangelical psychopannychist, Camillo Renato, in this region.

CAMILLO RENATO

CARMEN[1]

AGAINST JOHN CALVIN
ON THE UNJUST BURNING OF MICHAEL SERVETUS

Traona, September 1554

TRANSLATED BY DOROTHY ROUNDS

[1] The Latin text is printed by Friedrich Trechsel, *Die Protestantischen Antitrinitarier vor Faustus Socin*, 2 Vols. (Heidelberg, 1839-1844), I, 321-328, and in Calvin, *Opera Omnia*, XV (Corpus Reformatorum XLVIII), No. 2017, coll. 239-245. There are a few emendations in the second text. See below pp. 189, 193.

Are you not aware at all, O Calvin, that you have consigned to future generations a disgraceful deed and proof of a demented state while you were ordering Servetus, undeserving though he was, to be sent to the consuming flames? What spirit or reason compelled you to such a dire crime, or what revelation of God's will prompted you to enter upon such a profanation, or what desire befitting heavenly peace? Fleeing in exile through a thousand perils from the enraged Gauls,[1] driven to seek foreign lands, and calling on the names of the true Christ and God in heaven, reconciled with the human race, by what laws, alas, did you learn to cast down the wandering one to Orcus and to burn with fierce flames the bodies of the followers of Christ and learned men sincerely preaching both justifying faith and sure salvation, [gained] not as once by the blood of a bull or a vile-smelling goat, but by the pure blood of the Lamb whom God had chosen from eternity, and not by Ceres either, as now, and overflowing Lyaeus.[2] Nay more, if anyone should say he believes in Christ as God's Offspring which nature joins to the divine Parent and which no attribute peculiar to it separates from the same, and if this conviction should remain firmly fixed in his heart, how can you allow him, O Calvin, to be shut up in the dark shades of prison (walls) grieving, crying aloud, and at last, consumed, to fall in the midst of flames, — a dreadful deed that no age would forgive! What God would suffer this offense, and ordain that it be left unpunished, Heaven defiled by such a wicked act? (It does no good to defend dark plans by publishing tracts,[3] executing the dire counsel of Satan!) Will you, a minister of the celestial flock of Christ and God, a proclaimer of the good news that the wrath of God toward the human race has long since been appeased, that the punishment oft deserved by our sin from the beginning has been suspended, that we have been snatched from Stygian fires, and that the everlasting wrath of God has ceased, to be followed by the return of the Golden Age under the fair auspices of Christ with untroubled lands

---

[1] The Catholic inquisitors in Vienne and Lyons.

[2] The eucharistic bread and wine. With these mythological terms Camillo suggests his opposition to any deification of the elements, whether Catholic or Protestant. Lyaeus is an epithet of Dionysus. Cf. Plut. de ir. coh. 462 B, quaest. conv. 613 C, Anth. Pal. VI 154, 1; Anacreontica *passim;* Aeneid IV 58; Ovid, Met. IV 11, Amor, III 15, 17.

[3] The reference is to Calvin's defense of his action in publishing the acts of the trial. *Opera,* VIII, coll. 453-644.

enjoying peace, — will you (I say) present this outrage to the devotees of Christ and exhort them in their hearts to crime and with cruel words incite them to the death of a brother who freely listened to you as you preached divine decrees and followed you at the time with a light heart as you prayed in the midst of the blessed congregation of the devotees of Christ and who called on our common God and Christ in prayer?[1]

38 He, with impiety, was not preparing plots against your life and that of the brethren, considerate as he was of both time and place. He did not stop you if you expressed controversial opinions to the people and to the congregation; aroused by anger, he did not upbraid the assembly, filling it with noisy shouts, but whatever you were pleased to say, he received with quiet mind and considered it in his heart. Saying nothing, he sought refuge from the temples on mountain tops.[2] Recognized by chance through information from certain worshippers whom, so the story goes, he had once helped at some time by his skill in healing,[3] he was suddenly seized by your design and your desire and held in the jail for common criminals; without help, he was enclosed in gloomy shades. Here considering many things, he wore himself out with consuming cares, nor did he close his eyes in peaceful sleep. Nay more, fires would often come to mind, and he would think in his misfortune of being led between lictors with his hands bound behind his back, the crowd following; of the funeral pyre built of straw; of his body about to burn; before long, of his pallid neck bound by chains to the stake that is up-raised, as he is consigned to the mounting flames.

56 You, O Christians, children of God, you who are most worthy of heaven, whose hearts a Spirit within compels, a spirit more merciful than any in heaven or hell, more peaceful than any in the world. 'Tis you I address. How could you behold this sight in your land: a brother being burned, and giving up his life in the midst of flames, calling for help with pious lips upon both Christ and God, begging with devout prayers that the followers of Christ be merciful and like unto the gentle Christ? And you especially, the highest hope of the holy church, noble souls, examples of piety! Alas, with what hatred did you plot these flames, staring with dry eyes on the agony and the death of this man? For shame! O crime unforgettable in time to come! Whither has forsaken piety, worthy only of heavenly souls and to be hoped for by the reborn (*renatis*) alone, taken flight?

---

[1] An idealization of Servetus' participation in the Genevan church service, 13 August 1553.

[2] This seems to be an allusion to the eschatological role of the Reformed churches of the Alpine Confederation in fulfilment of Isaiah 2: 2. Later this reference to all nations flowing to Jehovah's temple in the top of the mountain was transferred to the Carpathians by the Unitarians of Transylvania.

[3] Certain Protestant refugees from Lyons recognized Servetus during the service and denounced him.

69 May I now talk with you and seek out the reasons for the deed and hear just accusations. Let no suspicion, no ire arouse you, nor be you ashamed to lend your hands, though shackled by this crime. We are here, alike children of God and adorers of Christ; and our many dangers have made our faith certain. For this reason we departed from the Ausonian shore,[1] embracing exile, to live in foreign lands. Poverty is our only companion. Our condition in life is hard. Work cheats us on some days, but constant labor yields our tutor's fees,[2] worn though we be. We ourselves brought the gospel whenever occasion offered, prompted by no ambition for advancement nor adequately recompensed. Advancing through the usual dangers of life, where the divine impels us, where a blessed hope calls us ever willing, with mighty force we have laid low the opposing foes. Those whom providence predestined and whom the Spirit drove from within, we have snatched from Satan and joined as new souls to Christ.

84 What cause prompts you to this crime? Pray tell, O prophets and captains of the Christian people! Was it that impious error of his that rightly carried off Servetus in consuming flames, or was it a driving fear that sharpened your concern lest error, creeping far under a fair name, should entice your brothers from your midst whilst they were off their guard and in the holy congregation stir up hatred and disorder and disruption and destruction?

91 If, among Christians, he had the name and the outward appearances all the while impounding[3] wickedness and Stygian poison in his heart, still he was a brother [and] he ought not to have been shut up in dark prison walls and attacked by dire evils and burned by fire. Rather, if there was any love, if there was any compassion, if there was any thought or feeling for the heavenly Father, then he ought to have been withdrawn (*excipiendus*)[4] with the unstaunched tears and groans of his sorrowing brethren; and then they, at once with prayers and supplications by day and night, should have besought both God and Christ that the miserable one be freed from his error and that he himself eject the virulent infection from his heart and thereupon, restored to his right mind and [readmitted to the church and] longed for salvation, attain the merited blessings in the congregation.

104 Like one whom a spirit of Tartarus has snatched away while suspecting nothing of the sort, and twists the wretch now this way and now that; or as when a loathsome disease and fever attacks and wears out the sufferer and, with the infection, takes away his mind

---

[1] The Italian states.

[2] A reference to Camillo's own service as a tutor of classical languages to the children of the Paravicini in Caspano and elsewhere.

[3] Reading *Servantemque* rather than a conjectured *Servatumque*.

[4] Excommunicated.

and senses, so he was in need of great pity and should have been relieved of the disease and restored to himself, the frenzy driven from his heart. So it became ministers with a compassion imitative of Christ's to struggle earnestly by means of pious ministries and to leave no place for sleep by day and night, nor any time. Such should have been the reasoning of your faith. Such was the care that should have been exercised for your brother whom Satan had enviously led (astray) by guile. When such befalls any one of ours there is need for that solicitude which Christ once enjoined[1] on our unlettered fathers and apostles before whom an only son, dear to his father, beset with terrible demons and evil spirits, had been brought and by whom he had at length been dismissed uncured along with his saddened parent since he could not be helped by their ministrations and emerge from such confusion. Thereupon the good Christ said rebukingly: "Rather must ye choose long fasting and silent prayers before a man in such a grievous plight be turned away."[2]

124 If care of your flock, if some other concern for your brethren moved you, brethren whom he had corrupted by his erroneous ideas or previously published books, or if it seemed best to look ahead to future dangers and to be inflamed with such anger, certainly zeal deceived you and preposterous anxiety for the heavenly flock. Not by that craft is the honor of doctrine kept pure and the souls of the pious. It was not Christ who pointed out that way, nor did Paul take these steps. Here may be seen the exemplars for the servant, the precepts of the Lord. Are your counsels to be considered better than His? By this practice will you be permitted to establish justice and rule in the holy congregations?

135 It was first requisite that a man be reprimanded once or twice. Whereupon only if he were unresponsive in spirit or unwilling to abandon his wilful deeds, should he be expelled from the congregation and kept from the fellowship of Christians.[3] Whatever there is beyond this (if there be any true faith) is added injury. It was right for you to hand over bodies to Satan,[4] scarcely to destroy a soul forever by committing it to flames. This is the cruelty worthy of Roman beasts[5] and of wild bears. Such deeds do not become the pious nor those thoughts, Christ. God did not teach such things, nor did the gentler Spirit. Christ, while he lived, did not leave examples of such wrath against the erring; but, on the contrary, when he recognized one time that two,[6] with unworthy hearts, would call down fire from heaven on Samaria because the people did not receive them, straightway he

[1] Cf. Matthew 17: 14-20; Mark 9: 14-29; Luke 9: 37-43.
[2] Mark 9: 2-29.
[3] Cf. Matthew 18: 15-18.
[4] Cf. I Corinthians 5: 5.
[5] The Roman Inquisition.
[6] James and John; Luke 9: 51-56.

rebuked them and burned with just anger; and, calling on his unlettered followers, certain both of the facts and of his own nature, he said: "O what spirit kindles your hearts, is it mine or is it Satan's that arouses such frenzy in your breast? Although you have been warned many times, have you not yet perceived the thought of the divine Master? Come, turn your minds to this and learn in what ways it becomes you to follow henceforth if it please you to be mine and to rely on proper prayers. Surely I, sent from heaven, did not come to destroy the nations or, as an avenger, to punish evils by the rod; but I bring rest for the weary, and health for the sick, pardon for wickedness and light for darkness. O my companions, my Spirit directs these concerns from the heart, a Spirit prone to help the wretched with aid and resources, bearing the gift of God the Father, who gives light with his sun when it rises from the eastern lands, for the just and the unjust, and fructifies with rain from heaven the fields of both, good alike to all."[1]

164 Nay more, expelled from the congregation, he ought not to have been considered an enemy, if now we have any faith in Paul;[2] but it behove the followers of Christ and the leaders of the congregation to counsel the ailing brother oft with admonitions and to administer in turn to the wound he had received both oil and wine, and to apply our hands and anger gently. For although purgation[3] was allowed to the [apostolic] fathers as harsh medicine for disease, it was not [considered] a punishment. Nor did it then, as now, bring deadly wrath and destruction on brethren who are ill. Now indeed, the [apostolic] ban, repulsed and despised by your [Reformed] church (so the report is) retires to older conventicles[4] and the place of the banned [ban] is taken either by luxuriating license or by the savage anger of the magistracy with harsh laws reaching bodies and not souls in their righteous indignation. What prophet could endure these things? Who will not see the troubles destined to fall on the congregations of the faithful and the followers of Christ? Alas, unworthy prophets hear the disaster! May you repent the deed. May it not be vainglory, prompting you, that urges you on or pride with puffed up scorn!

182 Why vaunt of your places of refuge and your fair retreats, whither the brethren may cross over from the Ausonia they have left behind in order that the divine countenance can be seen in your congregation which they ought to be questing for wholeheartedly? What a reflection of Deity!, to burn with flames the wandering one who avowed Christ to be the Offspring of God and God the Parent of Christ,[5]

---

[1] Matthew 5: 45.
[2] Cf. I Corinthians 5: 5.
[3] Excommunication.
[4] The Anabaptists. Camillo here personifies the wholesome apostolic practice of the ban and plays with the image of the ban as itself banned.
[5] A poetic version that sacrifices the theological precision of Servetus' final words.

and, confident even in the midst of flames would commend himself and his soul to Christ, raising his face to heaven, and would beg pardon for the erring ones? Keep wickedness and cruel deeds from the realm of Ausonia, O pious brethren, and cease your wicked attempts. Win back the wandering one, not by fire, but by devout solicitude. It is better to take a stand albeit fearfully in the land of Ausonia, than to gaze with silent eyes on monstrous deeds. Unless by chance the stranger approve of these acts, one word of his will make him an accomplice of the crime; and straightway prison will snatch him away and shut him up in gloomy shades, never to emerge from this place unless either his lips, reformed, recant their evil, or heeding the decrees of the unanimous Senate, sent into exile from the land [temporarily] opened to him, he goes sadly away. A disturber of the sacred congregation and of the civil peace, he departs as one of many whom the heedless wave casts up, a hated breed rejected by all the world. Barbarity, unworthy of the pious and the faithful congregation! When Christ wished to appear the Head and Lord than whom nothing is more merciful or more gentle in all the world, he much preferred to die for others and to undergo alone the suffering work and, although he merited it not, to sustain in his innocent body our punishment and in his heart sore troubles, rather than to have any other subjected to that peril, albeit warranted, or to stir up rumor with malice or, as an avenger, to attack a person with criminal charges and render him odious in all the world, wherever he might go and wherever he might tarry, placing him trembling before a thousand perils. To sustain these burdens and the congregations and the rulers of the congregations with heavenly courage, it would have been fitting to have the mind [of Christ] in so great a crisis for the trembling world. By such an expression the divine face could be seen in us, [Protestants] authenticated by these traits, painted in this hue.

218 Do the words you have so often heard, of Christ and God and the vain murmurs in the churches help you after all? What does the frequent communion profit, of what use the wave poured once upon the head with a Christian name bestowed if there is no love among the followers of Christ, no mutual pardon of the faithful for error, and if piety has no power to pacify?

224 Not words, not sacraments, although most pure, establish churches and a people pleasing to Christ; but rather virtue, embracing the heart and reshaping the moral life, certain in its strength, dwelling deep within, which, set against all vice, bursts forth in pious deeds, wherein zeal for the right may flourish, wherein love for our brethren may abound, wherein we may follow the examples of our heavenly Father and of Christ, wherever the plight of the miserable beckons, wherever fortune calls us: for of the one are we the body, of the other are we the sons.

233 Piety does not consist in a fair appearance or an outward show; but, relying on its divine duties, it rises to Olympus where it assumes the true traits and the countenance of God which — heed well this prophet — pious Ausonians seek and look for everywhere in the midst of Christendom.

238 For truly, the face of God is twofold, one known in olden times and wont to be seen in holy assemblies and in the liturgy of the ancient temple, when Jerusalem stood, and the ark of the covenant was a refuge of the people, and the altar was stained with the sprinkled blood of bullocks slain amid the approving throng, while the insignia and robes of the priests of old flashed far, gleaming with gold and gems.

244 The other [aspect] is known alone in the hearts to men reborn (*renatis*) from heaven — that countenance which cannot be approached by mortal eyes, neither in loftily built churches, nor in liturgical processions, nor in the midst of the festival exuberance of the surrounding throng. Therefore, both because it is the religion for you and because it is Christ who is the true image of God and the aspect most gracious for the children [1] of God, to have withheld your heart and hand from capital punishment would have been more appropriate that to commit a brother to devouring flames.

253 But perchance personal anxieties and the oft incurable wound of the followers of Christ moved you, the leaders of the Church. The sword of God by which alone error can be cut out [2] with its reliable blade, could have cured the stricken one — not prison, not devouring fire, not the avenger with death. But if fear gripped your hearts in sight of judgments yet to come and it seemed best to check the Hydra with Herculean hand and envelop it in flames lest it crawl away (horrible deed, atrocity, cruel and dreadful expiation), nevertheless solicitude should have rushed to the aid of your fear, as reformed Christendom trembled, not punishment, not the death of a brother. For by what decree, by what law would the fathers [3] have punished offenses to come and have summoned offenders who had, up to that time, accomplished no wickedness, to endure such a blow?

266 "But, Servetus, you brought disaster to the church by your writing and by the books which you published." [4] But what obstacle to such (farflung) attempts is the fiery wrath of men or their swift-

---

[1] The children or the reborn, presumably in contrast to the servants or slaves of God under the old covenant.

[2] Reading *exciditur* for *excinditur*. Cf. Hebrews 4: 2.

[3] The apostles.

[4] Here formulates the general charge against Servetus as it might be stated by Calvin defending the imperiled Reformed church.

consuming fire? It availed nought. The impious error[1] binds Christian minds. Writings abound, learned men approve them; they are worn out by the eager hand of both the Germans and the Italians. The error is defended and worse fires arise from your fires. Vain was the hope of such counsel, vain the attempt of wrath, vain the glory of your vow, God all the more certainly condemning cruel acts by his progeny and wrath blasphemous to the heavenly beings.

276 Go now, Calvin, keep in published books the indicted error and the fury which amounts to nothing in the light. They have been exposed by the judgment of God and by the moral sense of the devout. For you see the man has perished and his error has survived; and far and wide the infection creeps stealthily through all lands. Learn therefore to serve mankind and to remove error from captive minds. Learn that a surviving man can frequently be changed, never a surviving error with its oft attendant impiety. Not zealous works, but decrees of election (*fata*), Calvin, bring the salvation of Christ, preordained before all time for the chosen races. Therefore the man should be spared and credence be given to Paul.[2] Decreed salvation might perchance have come to apply to him in the course of the revolving years had he repented and been freed from the bonds of Satan.

289 But you will deny that you have consigned a *brother* to the flames. You will say that he was burned, ignorant and a rebel against Christ, and one who knew not God, a disgrace as well to our era, from whose wicked zeal there has descended upon us, hardly deserving of it, an enormous shame and source of catastrophe.[3] But does the Spirit descending to you from heaven rouse such anxieties as these in the human heart? It was not fitting, was it, unless the mind proposed cruel deeds, to base the judgment not on sacred [scripture] but rather on [Roman imperial] laws?[4] O ignorant priests and proud spirits! Leave us the possibility that truth-telling liberty may now also have her prophets. For the Muses do not with equanimity allow crimes to be defended, nor venom to creep into the sacred rank. This Spirit is in Paul. To defer to Paul you consider right. This is his precise injunction, when he prescribes laws for faithful Corinth and when an extraordinary sin pervades the obscurity of their minds. Thus he speaks:[5]

---

[1] For the sake of his basic pleas of toleration and humaneness, Camillo is prepared to grant that Servetus' trinitarian formulation was defective. It will be observed, however, throughout the *Carmen*, that the triune formula is never used.

[2] See above p. 190, n. 4.

[3] Camillo ascribes to Calvin the argument that Servetus' grave deviation from orthodoxy threatens the whole of the Reformation by discrediting it in the eyes of the Catholics.

[4] The judicial basis for the condemnation of Servetus was the law of Justinian. See Roland Bainton, *Hunted Heretic: The Life and Death of Michael Servetus 1511-1553* (Boston, 1953), p. 210.

[5] A paraphrase of I Corinthians 5: 2-6: 11.

It is not right to bring under your judgment, O Christians, men who are without or know not Christ; in no way is our judgment exercised over the unbelievers. These the fashioner of heaven and earth commands to be submitted to his judgment when on the last day, as awesome avenger, he may well call the wretches to everlasting punishments.[1] At the same time it behooves us to watch over the brothers with zeal; and thus should we judge the life of fellow Christians.

311 Just as when a father who had a daughter, fair of face, marriageable in years, whom suitors seek out at evening, lechers by day, and, though placing watchmen around the house, does not as some avenger plot punishment or death for the suitors, but wisely watches over his daughter with warning and with threats that, yielding to their importuning, she not precipitate herself into their embrace, so may the church and the followers of God and Christ protect the entrusted flocks with devout care, keep mad wolves from their counsels, fierce lions from their abode. Put aside, O guardians, the wrath, appropriate only to beasts of the wilds, and may wisdom enfold the enrolled members in heaven.

322 Therefore, it is your responsibility to remove the pestilence, if there be any, from the midst of the congregation and to close the doors to dangers. You must avoid frenzy and injury to fellow men. Thus have the heavenly Muses sung their song. No false Apollo he who gripped my heart and filled me with these words.

Camillo Renato of Rhaetia composed this in Traona in the month of September, 1554.

---

[1] This view, reported as Paul's, is somewhat at variance with Camillo's more characteristic view of the death of the soul with the body and the resurrection of the righteous only for eternal life.

It is not lawful to bring under your judgment, O Christians, men who are without or know not Christ; in no way is our judgment exercised over the unbelievers. These the Teacher of heaven and earth commands to be brought to his judgment when on the last day [illegible] may well call the wretches [illegible] punishments. At the same time it behoves us to watch over the brothers with zeal and diligence, amending the life of [illegible] Christians.

411. Just as when a father who has a daughter, [illegible] marriageable in years, which suitors seek, [illegible] day, and, though placing watchmen around the house, does not [illegible] some severe [illegible] punishment or death for the suitors, but wisely watches over his daughter with warning and with threats that, yielding to their importuning, she not [illegible] herself into their embraces, so must the church and the followers of God and Christ protect the [illegible] flocks with devout care, keep mad wolves from their [illegible], [illegible] the wrath appropriate only to beasts of the wilds, and may [illegible] members in heaven.

412. Therefore it is your responsibility to remove the pestilence, if there be any, from the midst of the congregation and to close the doors to dangers. You must avoid frenzy and injury to fellow men. Thus have the heavenly Muses sung their song. No false Apollo, he who gripped my heart, has filled me with these words.

[illegible] Rewards of [illegible] composed
this [illegible]
[illegible], 1534

[illegible]

THE *APOLOGIA* OF ALPHONSUS LYNCURIUS

TRANSLATED WITH AN INTRODUCTION BY

DAVID PINGREE

C. S. C. per Christum Servatorem S. D.

Ex literis tuis proximis te domicilium mutasse
intellexi. quod si ex sententia tua factum est,
gaudeo. Vidi etiam quae ea de re ad patrem
scripsisti, a casa, a camera, et a dozena: qua
in re video te in lingua Italica proficere, qui
tam belle voces illas moremque, et rationem singula-
tim explicaveris. parum abfuit, quin ad te hasce
lingua ista Italica perscripserim; nisi scirem tuas esse
partes, ad me prius Italice scribere, qui in aliena
lingua versaris, ut mihi ad id faciendum aperias
viam, et invites, ne errem, ad eum ita scribens quem
nesciam, eius linguae gnarum esse. Fac ut igitur
primo quoque tempore ut intelligam, quantum profeceris
Praeceptori tuo D. Erbaldo te subinde commendo
ne patiatur te quicquam nec in ratione pecuniaria
nec ulla alia in re, desiderare: quanquam eum
per se id facturum non dubito. Horatius noster si
nescis, est magna cum laude Medica Laurea
donatus Pisis: et speramus eum mense Junio
affuturum, sicuti spem ipse nobis facit. Hoc
tibi, quia scio te nos amare, et nostris secundis rebus
gaudere, quae tua bonitas, immo pietas est
scripsi. Expecto iam ad binas meas alte, responsum.
Gener meus eius uxor Violanthis, quae propediem futura
est mater: atque Angela quae sunt Argentorati bene va-
lent, teque resalutant. Uxor mea, Augustinus, filii
quique domi sumus te complectimur, osculamur tanquam
filium, et fratrem. Leo est in Galliis, valet. De
statu nostrarum rerum audies ab Antonio Francisco
Pigafetta viro, qui domum revertitur: et literas ad
patris, tibi reddet, et misisset. Vale mi carissime
Basili, et pietate religioneque sinceriore cole, quae
te beatum faciet. Basileae VIII. Cal. Junii 1554.
Tu mihi amicos istic saluta quaeso, atque in primis
Robortellum virum optimum et eruditissimum mihique carum
non dubito quin meas literas consorori ut ego tuas.

12

Letter of Curione to Basil Amerbach, May 25, 1554.

et detectus eo ipso die coprehensus et carceri comedatus
fuit, Res sic habet, Accititius quida minister, aut ministri
puer Immo ut pleriq aiut ipsius ecclesiastæ coquus magistra=
tu adijt, expones adesse illhic hæresiarchā Seruetū qui sacti=
ssimā trinitatem pregaret et cerberu tricipite appellaret
in ipsa Geneua et eius ministros ppetuo cotumeliosu et ple=
raq alia de homine magistratui psuadens Viatoris sibi copiā
fieri postulans ut confestim detineretur ne ullo pacto elabi
posset se cū illo carceribus offeres donec utriq ius fieret, sic
enim illhic nescio quo more receptū est ut quicūq pegrinus
et aduena illhac transiens possit p quevis aliū de quovis facto
etiā apud indos patrato postulari et reus fieri dūmodo accusator
se talioni subijciens offerat se unà cū ~~acc~~ accusato iudicatu et
censurā dicti magistratus se in carceribus subituru Donec utriq
vel alteruter sibi sponsore inueniat de iuri stado vel iudicato
parendo Nuc audite tragediā probus minister, utroque postulato reo co=
festim sponsore adinuenit: paup Seruetus nullo ~~capto~~ repto fideiussore in
carceres male detruditur illhinc no exiturus donec de pelle sua
iudinatio pagatur, accusator psonatus facto liber et securus eva=
sit ~~Rejiciens~~ Nūc qualis scenę introitus dispicite (queso vos pij et
nullo affectu polluti) si accusator in capitali causa debuit fideiusso=
ribus liberari? si talioni obstrictus iure dimitti potuit? reo car=
ceribus mācipato, Quid si ~~nūc~~ Michael ~~equi~~ equiores et rectos
Iudices nactus universalis ~~fuit~~ Cocilij ~~iudicio~~ sententia absoluēdus fuisset,
et accusator talionis pœna feriendus? nunqd et fideiussor ad capitale
pœnā vocatus esset? nunqd sponsor ad flāmas deductus? alienū
facinus suo corpore luiturus. at q natura ratio, eqtas et iuris
censura huic ordini refragatur. Constat enim pro accusatore

19

A page from the *Apologia* of Alphonsus Lyncurius.

54.

Ego Lelius Sozinus a pueris unũ sỹbolũ didici et
nũc scio et agnosco quod Apostolorum dicitur esse antiquissimũ
omnibus tẽporibus in ecclesia receptũ tametsi uariis scripturis
Sed nuper legi etiã alia et honorẽ tribuo. quẽ possũ
et debeo symbolis uetustissimis nyceno et constantinopo-
litano. Praeterea quod ignari homines pertinaciter infi-
ciantur ego Trinitatis personarũ ὁμοούσιος con-
substantialitatis unionis distinctionis et alias similes
uoces agnosco nõ recens excogitatas sed a uiris illustribus
300 annis inde usque a tẽporibus Justini Martyris in toto fere christiano orbe fuisse usitatas
et quidem maximis grauissimisque de causis.
Veruntamẽ libere dicam quod sentio ego. malis
omnibus probare si adhuc uerbis christi Apostolorum
et euangelistarum christiana Apostolica et euangelica
fides nobis explicaretur nec ideo illa uocabula
nego patribus necessaria fuisse ad ea splendi-
dius efferenda que iam catholice nota traduntur
ac sanẽ tanta in ueneratione ab ecclesijs recipiuntur
multo minus in dubiũ uerto christianae religionis
fũdamẽta que singulis orthodoxis certissima debẽt
esse ac utinam mihi redderentur certiora quia
nõ credo patrẽ esse eundem qui filius et spiritus sanctus
nõ imaginor tres Jouas deos nõs coessentiales non

The first page of Lelio Sozzini's *Confession*.

INTRODUCTION

The *Apologia pro Michaele Serveto* is preserved in a single manuscript copy at the Universitätsbibliothek in Basel (Ki. Ar. 26 a, ff. 18-25); it was edited from this codex in the collected works of Calvin.[1] The text was copied by a professional scribe soon after its composition in 1554,[2] but is corrected throughout by a different, though contemporary hand. These corrections are, by and large, introduced for stylistic reasons; the inappropriateness of the last one (immo Christo ipso) indicates that the author and the corrector are different persons. A note in a nineteenth century hand in the upper left-hand corner of f. 18 states, "Correcta manu Curionis."

This identification of the hand of the corrector has been accepted by many scholars, including, most recently, Kot,[3] Kutter,[4] and Dufour.[5] But Cantimori[6] claims that the hand is that of Lelio Sozzini. In fact, it appears that neither identification is correct.

As an example of Curione's handwriting I reproduce here his letter to Basil Amerbach, written on 25 May 1554 (Basel, Universitätsbibliothek G. I. 18. 12). If one compares the "sententia" in line 3 of that letter with the same word written above "iudicio" in line 24 of f. 19 of the manuscript of the *Apologia*, also reproduced here, one immediately recognizes that these are two different hands, even after giving due consideration to the fact that one document was written more hastily than the other. Note especially the ways in which the *e*'s are formed and that in which a *t* is connected to a following vowel. It should also be observed that Curione's *c*'s are joined to succeeding letters at the bottom, the corrector's at the top.

For Sozzini's hand I refer to the reproduction of the first page of the manuscript of his *Confession* (St. A. Zürich. E II 367, pp. 54-57), which is signed: "Idem Lelius manu propria." The word "sentio"

---

[1] *Ioannis Calvini Opera quae supersunt omnia* ed. W. Baum, E. Cunitz and E. Reuss, vol. 15 (Brunsvigae, 1876), cc. 52-63.

[2] Shortly after 15 January of that year; see G. H. Williams, *The Radical Reformation* (Philadelphia, 1962), p. 623.

[3] S. Kot in *Autour de Michel Servet et de Sebastien Castellion*, ed. B. Becker, (Haarlem, 1953), p. 92, fn. 44.

[4] M. Kutter, *Caelio Secondo Curione: Sein Leben und sein Werk (1503-1569)*, *Basler Beiträge zur Geschichtswissenschaft* 54 (Basel-Stuttgart, 1955), p. 184.

[5] A. Dufour in *Mélanges offerts à M. Paul-E. Martin* (Genève, 1961), p. 490.

[6] D. Cantimori in *Religio*, 12 (1936), 418, fn. 1.

will be found in line 13, again in a hand differing from that of the corrector. As well as for connecting his *c*'s and his *t*'s as did Curione, Lelio is distinguishable from the corrector for his initial *s*'s, which are consistently lower-case. It is not necessary to go further to substantiate the inaccuracy of Cantimori's observation. One must conclude that both hands in the manuscript of the *Apologia* have not yet been identified.

A more serious problem than the foregoing is that of the authorship of the *Apologia*. The same nineteenth century annotator who claimed that the corrector was Curione wrote in the upper righthand margin of f. 18, " Pseudonymus "; he was referring to the name of the apologist as given in the title of the work, Alphonsus Lyncurius Tarraconensis. It was proposed by Cantimori[1] that Lyncurius is a pseudonym for Lelio Sozzini, and suggested by Williams[2] that the author might be Matteo Gribaldi. Both theories must be rejected on stylistic grounds.

Lelio's style is unimaginative and frequently unclear; he does not enjoy writing in Latin, a language with which he is not completely familiar. A careful reading of his *Confession* or of his letters[3] will confirm this assessment. The apologist, on the other hand, is a brilliant Latinist, whose enormous delight in Classical rhetoric is evident in his every sentence. Gribaldi's style is indeed more lucid and straightforward than Lelio's, but it lacks suppleness and fire and enthusiasm. As an example of his rather pedestrian prose I quote a passage from the preface to his *Subtiles atque perutiles interpretationes in difficillimam l. ii. C. commu. de lega. et in l. Verbis legis de Verbo. signifi.*[4]

Neque tamen id cuiquam de humano genere mirum videri debet, quandoquidem scire solius Dei est, qui solus eorum omnium, quae sunt, veras causas, et principia novit: homines vero solis opinionibus agitari perspicuum est, quippe qui arbitrariis causis, et rationibus sibi ipsis singuli blandiuntur. Atque id plane efficit, ut ab orbe condito in supremum usque diem crebrae in omni disciplinarum genere dissensiones, mireque definitionum varietates inter homines, et fuerint, et futurae sint semper. Haud tamen propterea non liberum cuique esse debet promere, quid sentiat, suumque de re quacunque proferre iuditium; ut legentes varietate ingeniorum excitati, quid sequendum, fugiendumve sit, alieno labore perdiscant. Ego igitur, ornatissime Antistes, inter tot Doctorum opiniones, inter tot sensuum ἑλώρια,

---

[1] D. Cantimori, " Serveto e Lelio Sozzini, " *Religio*, 12 (1936), 414-438, and *Eretici italiani del Cinquecento* (Firenze, 1939), p. 175; see also Kutter, p. 183.

[2] Williams, pp. 623-626; his argument based on Blandrata's omission of Gribaldi's name applies with equal force to Curione.

[3] The *Confession* was published by J. H. Hottingerus, *Historiae Ecclesiasticae Novi Testamenti*, vol. 9 (Zürich, 1667), pp. 421-427; see Tedeschi's critical notes elsewhere in this volume. Samples of his epistolary style will be found in *Calvini Opera omnia*. The attribution to Lelio of the two texts published in D. Cantimori and E. Feist, *Per la storia degli eretici italiani del secolo XVI in Europa, Reale Accademia d'Italia, Studi e documenti*, 7 (Roma, 1937), pp. 55-78, is questionable.

[4] Venice, 1553.

seu (ut Iustiniani verbo utor) lacerationes, iuditium quoque meum sub tuo amplissimo nomine publicare non dubitavi,...

How far is this from the vigor of the apologist!

The true identity of Alphonsus Lyncurius was proved a decade ago by Kot in a strangely neglected article.[1] He showed that Vergerio had discovered among the papers of the unfortunate Pole, Michael Zaleski, who was murdered at Tübingen in early 1559, definite indications that the real name of the man who called himself Lyncurius was Caelius Secundus Curio.[2] As Kot points out, the style of Curione is exactly that of the apologist; as evidence of his talent I quote from one of his magniloquent orations.[3]

Plenum insolentiae videatur, si quis eloquentiae laudes vel conetur attingere, quae immensae sunt: vel recensere, quae sunt innumerae: vel demonstrare, quarum laudum lumen et splendor omnium oculos mentesque perstringit. Sentit fulgorem tuum, Eloquentia, tenebris immersum mortale genus. Nemo te, nisi tu, exprimere recte valet. Tu in alto solio sedes, ignorantiae tenebras illustrans. Tu tuos tibi similes, claros et admirabiles facis. Tu Platonem, tu Demosthenem, tu Ciceronem, tu Homerum, atque Virgilium: tu denique Herodotum, Thucydidem, Livium, Sallustium, aliosque innumeros ad divinos prope honores evexisti, immortalitateque donasti. Te reges invicti, te tyranni saevissimi reformidant: et qui nullis telis vinci potuere, tua divina vi victi subactique sunt. Tantam vim habet, o Adolescentes, illa *πειθώ*, quae recte dicta est suada, vel flexanima, atque omnium regina rerum, Oratio: ut non modo inclinantem erigere, aut stantem inclinare, sed etiam adversantem et repugnantem, ut imperator bonus et fortis, capere possit. Hanc igitur tam eximiam, tam necessariam, tamque utilem facultatem ut cognoscatis, Ciceronis De Oratore libros in manum sumpsimus.

Here surely speaks Alfonso!

---

[1] S. Kot, " L'influence de Michel Servet sur le mouvement antitrinitarien en Pologne et en Transylvanie, " *Autour de Michel Servet et de Sebastien Castellion*, ed. B. Becker, (Haarlem, 1953), pp. 72-115; see especially pp. 86-94 and 113-115.

[2] A. Dufour, " Vers latins pour Servet, contre Calvin et contre Genève, " *Mélanges offerts à M. Paul-E. Martin* (Genève, 1961), pp. 483-496, thinks that some wretched verses entitled *Epitaphium Michaelis Serveti Villanovi Lusitani ad pios Christi fratres loquentis* may have been written by Curione. It is difficult to believe that he would be so incompetent a poet.

[3] Caelii Secundi Curionis, *Selectarum Epistolarum Libri Duo. Eiusdem Orationum .... Liber unus* (Basel, 1553), pp. 190-191.

APOLOGIA FOR MICHAEL [a] SERVETUS.

BY ALPHONSUS LYNCURIUS OF TARRAGONA [1]

Finally have you obtained from your prostrate foe an eminent victory and a noteworthy triumph. Behold, at last he lies defeated who was so hostile and troublesome to you when he attacked your doctrines and traditions. So great an adversary, like a second Trojan Hector finally vanquished by the Greeks, has passed to ashes and cinders. Erect your trophies that the memory of so glorious a crime may never be eradicated. Print books; disburse and distribute them throughout the world that all churches may know of your consulate, and may give thanks for a task so well performed and for a religion so well preserved! Now deservedly shall all recognize and praise you as the mightiest protectors, protagonists, and avengers of the evangelical faith and of the Christian republic against all the prodigies of heretics. But the reward for the deed seems to be now to expose the whole course of the affair so that they may know the outstanding justice of your procedure. [b] I shall not here recite in detail the reasons of private hatred, dissension, and jealousy, which I think are familiar enough to all; but as briefly and truthfully as I can I shall narrate the arrest and trial of the man.

Michael Servetus of Villanova in the territory of Tarragona, a man most learned in the art of medicine, an imitator of that physician, Luke (whose praise is frequent in the Gospel), since he was endowed with great genius, and perceived, bitterly enough, that the world is in tumult concerning the truth of religion and is stuffed with the writings and volumes of many authors, turned his attention from medicine to sacred literature, and put all his zeal and genius into these studies. And when he realized that the Lutherans and Zwinglians and Papists

---

[a] M. ed.

[b] insignem iustitiam vestri progressus: insignem vestri progressus aequitatem m 2 ed.

[1] The following translation is based on the original text as preserved in the manuscript of the *Apologia*. The corrections in the manuscript (m 2) and the variant readings of the printed edition (ed) are recorded in the lettered footnotes. I wish to thank Prof. Williams for having read the typescript of this translation, and for having improved the style of some particularly cumbersome passages and identified the Scriptural references. For a recent account of Servetus' arrest and trial, see R. H. Bainton, *Hunted Heretic* (Boston, 1953), pp. 168-215.

fight duels over external ceremonies and rites and over primacy, but agree at the same time falsely and impiously on the knowledge, substance, and mysteries of the true and highest God and of our Lord Jesus Christ, his only-begotten Son, he began to investigate the matter more diligently and to consider more maturely, from the fountain of Scripture, everything which concerns the true God and his Son. Finally, when he thought that he had acquired something which would be useful to the whole Christian flock, he published a book, *On the Errors of the Trinity*, in which he freely expressed his opinion [a] about God and God's Son, teaching that there is only one, most simple God, who is neither triune non trinonymous, neither divided nor composite, namely that eternal Father and Monarch who is the author of all things and who dispenses all things through his Word and Spirit; and that there is a unique Son of God himself, that Jesus Christ who was born of the Davidian Virgin, and that no other, invisible Son of God is demonstrated from the Scriptures; and he treated of many other matters as well, affirming things which were most displeasing to modern [b] writers, especially to those of Geneva whom he attacked by name. Disturbed and irritated at this, and not being able to bear such a spirit any longer, they did not desist from persecuting him with hatreds, calumnies, conspiracies. When he observed that he was under too much pressure in France and that the treacheries of the envious had left him no place where he could dwell in security, he at last determined to go to Italy [c] and there to spend the remainder of his life. And so, having collected his few belongings and got together a little money from his effects and labors, the unfortunate one girded himself for the journey, and first came incognito to Geneva. For he doubted not their evil intent toward him, but, strengthened by some hope of evangelical piety and gentleness and believing that he travelled without being openly recognized, unhappily enough he began his journey there in order that he might pass as quickly as possible through the land of the Sedunians [1] to Italy. Yet, while he was in Geneva, he paused to listen to a preacher's harangue, covering himself with his cloak and cap and remaining standing on his feet. But, recognized and detected by some, he was arrested on the same day and thrown into prison. This is the story.

A certain minister,[2] or the servant of a minister — rather, as some say, the cook of the Ecclesiast himself — went to the magistrate and disclosed that the heresiarch Servetus was there, he who denied the most holy Trinity and called it a three-headed Cerberus, and who was continuously contemptuous of Geneva and of its ministers. He per-

[a] suam after sententiam: om. ed.
[b] modernis: recentibus m 2 ed.
[c] libere after Italiam: crossed out in MS, om. ed.

[1] The present Canton of Valais.
[2] The obscure word Accititius is not translated.

suaded the magistrate of many other things about the man, demanding that he be given the office of summoner that Servetus might be immediately arrested lest he be able by any means to escape; and he offered himself to be sent to prison with him until judgment should be passed on each. For it was an accepted practice there — I know not by what custom — that any traveller or foreigner passing through the city could be accosted by anyone and accused of any crime, even one committed in India, and be made a defendant, while the accuser, subjecting himself to similar punishment if his charge proved false (*talio*), offers himself to undergo in prison together with the accused the judgment and decision of the said magistrate until one or the other finds a sponsor for his standing trial or obeying the court's decree.

Now hear the tragedy. The upright minister,[a] having accosted the defendant, quickly found a sponsor; poor Servetus, having discovered[b] no pledge, is rudely thrust into prison, not to emerge till the bickering over his skin is completed. The accuser, having spoken, departed in freedom and security. Good Gods![c] See of what sort was the beginning of the scene! I ask you — you who are pious and polluted by no prejudice — ought the accuser in a capital case be freed to his pledges? Being bound to the *talio*, can he justly be allowed to leave while the defendant has been committed to prison? What if Michael had found more just and upright judges, and should have been absolved in the judgment[d] of the whole council, while the accuser should have been punished with the penalty of the *talio*: would the pledge have been summoned to capital punishment? would the sponsor have been led to the flames, to wipe out another man's crime with his own body? But natural reason, equity, and the decision of law are opposed to this consequence. For it is agreed that one should not accept a sponsor or a pledge for the accuser in a capital case, but the accuser himself should be detained in person with the accused until one knows clearly about the guilt or innocence of each. Therefore you see what was the nature of the beginning of the trial of Servetus, how great was the observance of equity and justice. Already, I think, you are turning this over in your minds[e] and almost grasp the course and conclusion of the tragedy. Indeed, who might not have guessed the ending that is equal to such a beginning? For naturally almost all things are inclined by a certain flaw in nature towards the worse, so that (as the proverb says) whatever begins ill cannot end well.[1]

See now what you have done![f] So foully and ignominiously have you betrayed a helpless man, a sojourner and a pilgrim who trusted

---

[a] vel coquus added m 2 ed.
[b] comperto: reperto m 2 ed.
[c] Dii boni: Nunc m 2 ed.
[d] iudicio: sententia m 2 ed.
[e] vobiscum before animo: om. ed.
[f] viri evangelici added in margin m 2, accepted ed.

[1] Unidentified.

your evangelical profession and Christian charity, so woefully and awfully have you extinguished his life. You have accused one who had faith [a] in you, who came without tumult, without sedition, without injury. By deceit you detained him. You have thrust him in prison and tried him; and finally, you have ordered him, with all humanity and compassion, to be burned alive in blazing flames.[b] Oh outstanding crime, never to be obliterated! Is this that Christian charity, is this your evangelical profession of which you were so eager to persuade the entire world? Did our Lord and Redeemer, Jesus Christ, teach you to proceed thus in the case of heretics, He who warned that the heretic is to be driven from the Church and considered a Gentile (Matt. 18: 17)? Did you learn this from Paul, the vessel of election, who preached that a heretic must always be warned and avoided (I Cor. 5: 2)? Did Ignatius, Irenaeus, Augustine, and the other orthodox Fathers hand down this custom as a tradition to you, they who said that they were not accustomed to permit the true Church of God to persecute, and that one must pray for heretics in the hope that they may perhaps be restored to their senses and brought to repentance through the grace and kindness of God? But that wise lawyer Gamaliel,[1] one of the chiefs of the Synagogue, ought to have instructed you, he who ordered his followers to forbear from spilling the blood of the Apostles who were promulgating the new doctrine, and who commanded that the whole matter, which would dissolve itself if it were evil, be entrusted to God. Did it [c] become you, even if you were not gentler, to be meaner or crueler than the Scribes and Pharisees? But what did you do? A poor little man, destitute of all, who was given into your hands, you treated first with all shame and ignominy, and then burned with a blazing fire. What has the Gospel to do with flames? Did you perchance think that one in so great anguish and tribulation [d] of mind, in so much ignominy of the world, opprobrium, fierceness, and aggressiveness, had been abandoned by most merciful God?

Enough of this! Let us unfold the cause of his death. He said that there is only one God, the Father of our Lord Jesus Christ from whom come all things. The Son himself confesses this, and Paul clearly testifies to it. He laughed at your name of Trinity. Deservedly so: since the name is imaginary and of the feminine gender, and indeed is most insulting to God, who is called neither a *sancta* nor a *dea* Trinity, and who is neither triple nor trinonymous, neither divided nor composite, as you could have learned from the Holy Book. He recognized only one Son of the one highest God, Jesus Christ, born from the Virgin and [e] crucified by the Jews, the Redeemer of the human race. But

---

[a] fidentemque: fidentem ed.
[b] coniectum after flammis crossed out in MS, om. ed.
[c] Num: Nonne ed.
[d] tribulatione: horrore m 2 ed.
[e] et crossed out in MS, om. ed.

[1] Acts 5: 34.

this is the foundation of the whole Christian religion. The Prophets, Apostles, and holy Church bear witness to nothing else. What, then? What else can we say but that pagan line:[1] "Every vice stood on the precipice"? Oh, if only you had wished to soothe the seething of your wrath with some tempering of leniency, if you had permitted that heat boiling in your brains to cool off in the course of time, if you had not given free rein to so vengeful a passion, how distant you would now seem from that rage or belief that a man must be killed! Did that poor man deny the true God to whom alone he looked? Did he prefer the seducer, Muhammad, to the Son of God, this man who recognized only the crucified Jesus Christ, who had Him always in his heart and on his lips, preached Him alone, in Him alone placed all his hope and faith? But if he conceived of an opinion concerning that name of Trinity and an interpretation and explanation of the word different from the common opinion of the learned which is also accepted and approved by you, a conception which he hoped that he could and ought to defend by Scripture and arguments, was he to be condemned by so hasty and precipitous a judgment, and to be handed over so cruelly and ignominiously to the horrible penalty of flames, especially in an evangelical and free city? At a place where a council was convoked of the fathers and leading citizens that they might maturely deliberate about so difficult and serious a matter, controlling all hatred and human emotions, or (to use a more vulgar phrase) passions of the mind? You yourselves were the accusers and scribes, the judges and executors for the death of a solitary soul. Tell me, I beg you, what advocate or defender did you decide upon for him who was shut up in prison? What liberty of speaking freely and of setting forth his arguments did you grant him? But you will say: "He was bound by no chains when he argued; he spoke freely; he said what he wished; all the proceedings were faithfully recorded and sent to the other churches; the defendant was condemned to death. It is well. The tragedy was acted out according to law." As if he might in fact freely have pled his cause who was continuously detained in jail, who was aided by the assistance of no advocate or confidant, who was tried by suspect judges — rather by judges who pursued him with mortal hatred and wrote the records as they pleased with no one on behalf of the prisoner assisting or interceding in their writing — who leaned on the support of no friend or defender with whom this pitiable man might have discussed his feelings and the reasonings of his mind. What shall I say? Briefly I repeat: Did he speak his case freely who had the same men as mortal

---

[1] Juvenal, *Satires* 1, 147-150:

> Nil erit ulterius, quod nostris moribus addat
> posteritas; eadem facient cupientque minores.
> Omne in praecipiti vitium stetit; utere velis,
> totos pande sinus!

enemies, accusers, scribes, judges, and executors? Who will still doubt that, under the appearance and pretence of divine zeal and public vindication, a private revenge was exacted? What other evangelical city or church would have with such perfidy arrested a foreigner and traveller who, even though he was an heresiarch, yet was causing no trouble in that city; would have condemned him with so precipitous a judgment; would have inflicted on him so dire and unchristian a punishment? Indeed, your city has contained, has seen and recognized many men passing through who despised God and true religion, who were impious, blasphemous, and open contemnors of the Gospel — indeed, its persecutors — whom, however, it allowed to depart free, secure, and unharmed. But this one head was so offensive to your minds, so troublesome to your eyes, so hostile to your ears; this one head was besieged by so many nooses and snares, sought by so many weapons, cursed by so many dire imprecations: when [a] finally the prey fell into the trap, it could not escape the nooses and snares. At last he paid the penalty for his courage and boldness. Rejoice, Anthony, rejoice and be satisfied! Behold the head and right hand of the man who so keenly took up his pen against you and your ways, who so freely and unrestrainedly inveighed against your errors and vices![1] "The Ithacan wishes this, and the sons of Atreus would pay a great price"![2]

But if with a calmer mind we consider the laws of justice, how much injustice, how much cruelty will soon appear. For no one is punished with death who has not committed a crime of stealth. But how can he be accused of stealth who was prepared to defend with the Scriptures and with arguments the opinion he had conceived in his mind as being true and evangelical, and even to die for it? I think no one is of so dull an intelligence, with so slow an understanding, so lacking in common sense that he could have the idea that a man would wish openly and to his own loss to defend what he knew to be false, and for the sake of this to seek not just temporal, but eternal death. For although there are found very many who, for the sake of temporary conveniences, may oppose for a time what they recognize to be true or who may in dissimulation favor falsehood, yet none has ever been discovered who,

---

[a] cum: sic m 2 ed.

[1] The head and hand belonged to Curione's most admired predecessor, that Tullius whom Marc Anthony proscribed in 43 B. C. Valerius Maximus (5, 3, 4) relates the story thus: Sed ut ad alium consentaneum huic ingrati animi actum transgrediar, M. Cicero C. Popilium Laenatem Picenae regionis rogatu M. Caeli non minore cura quam eloquentia defendit eumque causa admodum dubia fluctuantem salvum ad penates suos remisit. Hic Popilius postea nec re nec verbo a Cicerone laesus ultro M. Antonium rogavit ut ad illum proscriptum persequendum et iugulandum mitteretur, impetratisque detestabilis ministerii partibus gaudio exultans Caietam cucurrit et virum, mitto quod amplissimae dignitatis, certe salubritate studio praestantis officii privatim sibi venerandum, iugulum praebere iussit ac protinus caput Romanae eloquentiae et pacis clarissimam dexteram per summum et securum otium amputavit eaque sarcina tamquam opimis spoliis alacer in urbem reversus est.

[2] The last line of Sinon's speech to the Trojans in *Aeneid* 2, 77-104.

being a prudent and wise man, has wished to die for a false opinion and to lead his soul freely and voluntarily to eternal death. Besides, since we cannot be in any way searchers of hearts (which matter is reserved to God alone), we ought not rashly to judge about another's conscience nor accept another's faith at a lower value: but the simplicity and the charity of a good mind persuade us to believe that one who thinks or feels wrongly sins more by error than by deceit, and that he falls by imprudence rather than that he betrays himself knowingly and binds himself with the chains of eternal death. For faith and the knowledge of truth are the gift of God, and are not granted to all all the time. Therefore does the Spirit judge all things, but is judged by none save itself.[1] Wherefore is it most wicked to wish to constrain erring spirits with corporal punishments and to adjudge with the ultimate penalty men who fall imprudently and who are deceived by false opinion.

Now let us add examples. The spirit of Martin Luther, when God so wished, was so aroused that he not only called into question many opinions in the Christian religion which had already been commonly and universally accepted by the public consent of all the Fathers for one thousand and three hundred years, especially — to omit an almost infinite number of others — those concerning the transmutation and adoration of the symbolic bread, concerning purgatory, the invocation of the saints, celibacy, free will, and the primacy of the Roman See, but he also completely destroyed and rescinded them by his published works, and persuaded many people that they were false. If this is so, and yet there is now found none among those professing the Gospel who would say that he had acted wrongly or would think that he deserved flaming punishments for having dared with his spirit to rescind so many Catholic opinions which had been confirmed for so many centuries, and to disturb the whole Church with new dogmas and to split the ancient and long-enduring religion with open schism: if so much, I say, was permitted to one German monk in peaceful times, while the Roman See was flourishing, why was it not permitted to the Spaniard Servetus, a man very learned and diligently versed and exercised in the sacred letters, when the times had become disturbed and schisms added to schisms, and when new opinions, interpretations, and decisions of men were appearing every day, to call into doubt just one opinion, that concerning this imaginary name of Trinity, about which not even a syllable is found in the Scriptures, which was first introduced by pagan philosophers, and of which neither the Apostles nor their disciples ever had any idea, and to show on the authority of Scripture and by clear arguments that it is erroneous, impious, and absurd? No spirit is to be despised, but all things are to be tested, as Paul says (cf. I John 4: 1), and whatever is good is to be embraced. Daily God arouses new spirits to the revelation of truth and of his judgments,

---

[1] Cf. I Cor. 2: 15.

and equally shall he arouse them till [a] the end of the world, lest any of men should be able to flatter himself that he alone shines above all, that to him alone is all the truth made clear: nay, rather is every man a liar, and God has imprisoned all in lies and sin [b] in order that he might pity all, and he alone may be justified as true and truthful in his pronouncements.

But to return to the examples. Did not [c] Ulrich Zwingli, a pious and learned man, refute with a new, fervent spirit Martin's opinion about the sacrament of the eucharist, which had already been accepted in various places by almost all of Germany, which had been approved and confirmed by the assent of the most learned men, by means of a new interpretation of the Scriptures, and try to show that this was more probable, though Martin kept more to the literal meaning of the words, while Ulrich recognized the imagery and figurative sense of Scripture? This controversy was waged between the churches of evangelical profession with so much zeal on both sides, with so many darts, and is waged up to the present day with so many contentions and well-known tracts that not unless God the Most High puts his hand to it will there be any hope that so great a conflict will be laid to rest before the Day of Judgment: so persistent a defender of his reputation and zeal is each. But they — namely Luther and Zwingli [d] — had the greatest princes as their supporters and as the protectors of their bodies, so that they could freely promulgate whatever they wished without fear of persecution and torture. And thus was it brought about that they filled the world with their books and their opinions, and excited many churches with divergent enthusiasms: and though these churches attacked each other with rather immodest writings, wounded each other, and charged each other with heresy, yet was none of their [e] members burned or condemned to the unchristian punishment of flames.

But indeed, that poor man Servetus, a sojourner and a pilgrim, destitute of every aid of friends and of leading citizens, a man who had no place where he could lay his head,[1] but was everywhere harassed by treacheries and persecution, could scarcely publish one booklet on the error of the Trinity. Although we may grant that he sometimes went too far in this and was not entirely free from error (a condition which is peculiar to all mankind), yet he was carried along by righteous zeal and by eagerness for divine truth; and, although in promoting this he could not while alive attain that which he especially strove for, yet he spoke of many things from his assessment of Scripture and disclosed very many things which are most worthy of note, but which

---

[a] usque in: usque ad ed.
[b] mendacio et peccato: peccato et mendacio ed.
[c] An num: annon ed.
[d] illi Lutherus scilicet et Zuinglius: illi and scilicet crossed out in MS, om. ed.
[e] illarum: earum ed.

[1] Cf. Matt. 8: 20.

previously had seemed to be hidden here and there, or certainly neglected. In the end he will be said to have done a good job in this and will be praised by posterity for rousing tepid and dormant spirits to seek more diligently the knowledge of the one true and highest God and of his only-begotten Son. Surely recent theologians who protest that they are evangelical and who preach that they are the protagonists of the true doctrine, have put almost all their studies on the rear of religion. About inferior elements they valiantly and diligently elaborate the long-accepted opinions concerning the primacy of the Roman Pontiff, whom they testify to be the true Antichrist, concerning mass, purgatory, the sacraments, confession, penitence, satisfaction, the enjoyment of food, the invocation of the saints, images, monastic vows, celibacy, free will, and predestination, concerning which matters they have not yet reached agreement among themselves. And they strongly oppose the other ceremonies of the Church,[a] but (as I said) they labor about the rear, desiring only to subvert the cause of Popery, but, completely neglecting the head, they have given no study, work, and diligence at all to the knowledge of the true God and of his only-begotten Son, but have traversed with the Papists their false and erroneous path, following those sophistic and imaginary chimeras concerning the Trinity, and unanimously approving of them; and in such philosophy they did not consider the Pope and his adherents as Antichrist, but conceded that thus far they were inspired by the Holy Spirit. When they were asked about the articles of the rear, why they so vigorously opposed and uprooted all the received Catholic opinions, they answered that whatever was handed down by or accepted from the Popes and their scholastic followers contained nothing of the truth, but that everything was false, corrupted, and depraved; and that nothing which is good, holy, true, or pure can come out of the Roman Church, which they call the See of Antichrist and the Synagogue of Satan, since it has no spark of the Holy Ghost, but is most obviously governed in and through all things by the spirit of the Devil. Then, presently, when attention turned to the head and when God aroused the spirit of Daniel to correct the errors and sins of the elders and to shake the lethargy from their minds by teaching that they were negligently instructed in the knowledge of the true God and of his Son, Jesus Christ, and that they were seriously hallucinated by the Papists and had strayed far from the path of truth; good God! what rumblings, what commotions, what fires! Instantly they shouted "heresiarch," swore to slay him, stretched out snares and nooses, persecuting this poor man in fantastic ways; and finally, when he had fallen into their hands,[b] even as he called on Jesus, the Son of God, they burned him alive in blazing flames. They asserted that the opinion of the Papists was correct on this point and that they taught the truth; and that they themselves did well to agree with them in this matter. Behold

[a] Romanae added m 2 ed.
[b] manus: manum ed.

how suddenly they change their words! The doctrine of the church of Antichrist is the best there is concerning the Holy[a] Trinity, and also concerning the burning of heretics. Therefore, as they unanimously agreed on the article of the Trinity, so also did they concur on the use of the punishment of flames on heretics; except that the evangelicals are somewhat gentler in that they do not strangle the heretic before burning him as the Papists do, but snuff out his life with the flames; thus they not only imitate the savagery[b] of Perillus and Phalaris,[1] but far surpass it.

This is their Christian piety, this their evangelical charity and religious profession! As they imitated the humility of our Lord Jesus Christ, and his patience, kindness, magnanimity, and compassion, infallible Truth and the best Teacher should have been powerful enough to warn them and exclaim: Learn from me that I am gentle and lowly of heart.[2] Learn what this is: I desire mercy, not sacrifice;[3] allow the tares to grow till the day of reaping, lest perchance you uproot the wheat as well;[4] if anyone refuses to listen to you and to the Church, let him be as a Gentile and Publican to you;[5] avoid a heretic, after you have frequently warned him, only don't kill anyone;[6] the Son of Man did not come to destroy anyone, but to save;[7] and Most High God does not desire the death of a sinner, but rather his conversion and life;[8] love your enemies, pray for those who persecute you and do them well;[c][9] vengeance is mine;[10] if any should say, "I love God," and should hate his brother, he is a liar; for whoever does not love the brother whom he sees, how can he love God whom he does not see?[11] Love comes from God, and everyone who loves comes from God: whoever does not truly love does not know God.[12] These are the words of Christ, these the sayings of the Holy Spirit, which ought to be fixed in your evangelical hearts: not to embrace the dogma and the ritual of the impious to the perdition of your neighbor, not to agree with antichristians on the punishment of believers.

---

[a] sancta om. ed.
[b] sevitiam: exemplum m 2 ed.
[c] eisque benefacite added between the lines.

[1] See, inter alia, Pliny, *Natural History* 34, 89: Perillum nemo laudet saeviorem Phalaride tyranno, cui taurum fecit mugitus inclusi hominis pollicitus igni subdito et primus expertus cruciatum eum iustiore saevitia.
[2] Matt. 11: 29.
[3] Hosea 6: 8.
[4] Matt. 13: 29. See R. H. Bainton, "The Parable of the Tares as the Proof Text for Religious Liberty to the End of the Sixteenth Century," *Church History*, 1 (1932), 67-89.
[5] Cf. Matt. 18: 18.
[6] Cf. I Cor. 5: 2.
[7] Cf. Luke 9: 56.
[8] Cf. Mark 2: 17 and Luke 5: 32.
[9] Matt. 5: 44.
[10] Rom. 12: 19.
[11] I John 4: 20.
[12] I John 4: 7-8.

But already I see the cavils with which you twist in a depraved manner the opinions [a] recorded above. But you accomplish nothing. For you cannot impose on pious spirits endowed with charity and you strive in vain to persuade them that you were not eager to betray to the extent of your ability the body and soul of your neighbor who was baptized in Jesus Christ, the Son of God, and who confessed wholeheartedly the evangelical faith, one for whose life and salvation Christ wished to die. If you knew that he had lapsed into error, you ought not to have destroyed his body; if you knew he was sinning deceitfully — a matter which is far from probable — much less ought you to have betrayed him for the sake of faith, killing his body and his soul, because the most merciful God is benign, patient, and magnanimous, and has great compassion; nor does he wish the death of a sinner, but that he be called to repentance.[1] Do you not know that faith is a gift of God? that there are twelve hours in a day, and the man who errs can be corrected in a single moment, the sinner converted, the blind man made to see, the infidel led back, the heretic reunited,[b] the publican justified, and the thief glorified? These are the admirable works and judgments of omnipotent God, all of whose ways are full of compassion and whose hand for upraising is not at all drawn back. Yet how have you wanted with your precipitous decision and avenging plan and rash daring to hasten and to anticipate,[c] following the examples of truculent and harsh judges who precipitate to the penalty a defendant who is hateful to them for some private reason and who is condemned to death with the greatest possible speed [d] lest, perchance, the clemency of the king intervene, free that defendant from their hands, and restore him to safety and life. But surely it was Christian, it was evangelical and in accordance with religious profession humanely to warn a pilgrim who had fallen into your hands, to convince him with the Scriptures, to lead him back to union in love; and, if he persisted, either to cast him forth or, for working on him a longer time, to keep him in prison; [e] and to pray to God for him, in the hope that he could perhaps be led back to sanity and penitence. This is the more to be expected if there were truth and charity on your part.

Thus are souls gained for the Lord, thus is the cultivation of true religion increased and the unity of the holy Church preserved. These things are so plain and clear from the Scriptures and the testimony of the inner spirit that they cannot be concealed except by persistent cavil and uncontrolled malice; and however you try to persuade by publishing pamphlets, which are composed more with verbal pomp and

---

[a] flammas: sententias m 2 ed.
[b] reuniri: revocari m 2 ed.
[c] praescindere: perscindere ed.
[d] claritate: corrected to celeritate.
[e] carceribus: honesta custodia m 2 ed.

[1] Cf. Mark 2: 17 and Luke 5: 32.

eloquence[a] than with truthful simplicity, and to excuse so great a crime, you accomplish nothing. Rather you give greater offense to the minds of pious men, and more impiously strengthen the opinion of tyrants concerning the burning of heretics.

But could you have done otherwise? You who never knew the true God nor the true Son of God, whom you always considered to be some imaginary relations. Did not Christ predict accurately (Matt. 5: 11; Luke 21: 12) that the pious would suffer persecution and be afflicted by those who knew neither his Father nor himself? What spirit of God would ever have impelled you to so monstrous a crime? When will you ever persuade posterity or the Church which is reborn in the Gospel that you have acted in a Christian, evangelical, and religious manner, when they read or hear that you with such cruel revenge girt with the arms of the impious, busy, in fact, in a private cause, hastening as quickly as you could to slay body and soul, have so cruelly and wickedly destroyed a pilgrim who trusted in your piety, who came to you of his own accord, alone and defenseless, who was destitute of every aid, who was tossed about at your will — that is to say, at the will of his mortal enemies; who was torn to pieces and treated with undying hatred, ignominy, and shame? Dare to deny, if you can, that you were his worst enemies and were attacked by name in his writings, that you sought his blood with all your heart, that you brought every plan and deed to bear on removing your adversary and affecting him with the most serious punishments, that you looked on his death and disgrace with laughing eyes, that you insulted him with ridiculing words as he went to his penalty. "Why do you grieve? Why do you groan? Why do you sigh? If your opinion is true, why do you not depart happy and joyful"? Such were the words of those who betrayed the Son of God:[1] "If you are the Son of God, come down from the cross, and we shall believe in you." Oh Christian piety! Oh evangelical charity! Oh glorious crime, conceived for the protection and peace of the Church! Who is so iron and Neronian that he is not horrified when he hears it? Who so Busiric[2] and adamantine that he reads it with dry eyes?

But so far the spectacle has lacked a dirge. At once a pamphlet[3] was published which investigated the whole trial and judgment. It was that funeral oration which commended the ashes of the deceased. Light the flames, oh tyrants! Split, tear, roast the heretics whom you judge, scatter their ashes and stabilize peace for your empires and abodes! Why do you hesitate? Why do you delay? Why do you cease?

---

[a] pompa et eloquentia: pompa quadam m 2 ed.

[1] Matt. 27: 40.

[2] The story of Busiris' inhospitality was very popular in antiquity; for references see H. von Gaertringen, *RE*, 3 (Stuttgart, 1899), cc. 1074-1077.

[3] The *Defensio orthodoxae fidei de sacra trinitate contra prodigiosos errores Michaelis Serveti Hispani* of Calvin will be found in *Calvini Opera omnia*, vol. 8 (Brunsvigae, 1870), cc. 453-644.

Betray, sacrifice, devour! It is right by human and divine law. You have [a] evangelical churchmen and most splendid theologians to praise you. Thus, thus is the liturgy fittingly performed for the greatest God, thus is the Gospel properly propagated, thus the peace and union [b] of the Church preserved: namely, through removing hostile heretics by iron and fire. A dead man does not fight. Now at last will heretics know that the Gospel does not lack swords and flames: now at last is the Church wise which has learned how to extirpate heretics from the land of the living and to uproot tares from the midst of the wheat. Christ was too gentle, Gamaliel too stupid, Paul, Ignatius, and Augustine too foolish when they wished heretics to be sent away and tares to grow. You are much more clever than Gamaliel, than Paul, than Ignatius, and than Augustine,[c] much wiser, endowed with greater spirit and judgment, you who have learned to give such good counsel to your church. Therefore all churches will unitedly imitate you as the restorers of evangelical peace and quiet: they will praise you and celebrate you, and erect memorials to elevate you to the stars! I have spoken.

---

[a] habetis added m 2 ed.
[b] et unio: concordiaque m 2 ed.
[c] immo Christo ipso added m 2 ed.

FOUR LETTERS FROM THE SOCINUS–CALVIN CORRESPONDENCE (1549)

TRANSLATED AND EDITED BY
RALPH LAZZARO

I. – Lelius Socinus to Calvin [1]

[*Zurich, May 14, 1549*]

To the most distinguished John Calvin, the very vigilant and ever cherished pastor of the Church at Geneva.

The Lord Jesus, who in his prayers has always (in mind) the glory of God the Father and our salvation, has distinguished you with such excellent endowments, most learned Calvin, that whoever would not love, respect and admire you and, at the same time, would not perceive Christ himself speaking in you, must necessarily be an unwitting hater of the true and the good, and obviously stupid. That I am not mincing words in this respect is attested to by the thousands upon thousands of the sons of God whom the heavenly Father willed to be brought back to Him after they had been recalled by you from the cult of images.

In this regard, as in many others, the whole Church is not a little in your debt. I will confess, quite ingenuously, that even though up to now I have been quite convinced by a number of your writings, nevertheless one booklet, *On the Avoidance of Superstitions*,[2] has bound me to you by new and so much tighter bonds that I couldn't be more devoted to you. For drawn totally and irresistibly to a love and admiration for you, I praise God, [who abides] in you in a certain wondrous way.

But you will say, to what purpose is all this? That in so deeply satisfying me you may have my own most eloquent testimony, declaring

---

[1] Epistle § 1191, *Calvini Opera*, ed. Baum, Cunitz, Reuss, XIII, coll. 272-274 (Corpus Reformatorum, XLI).

This and the following letters are studied by D. Cantimori, *Eretici Italiani del Cinquecento* (Florence, 1939), p. 133 f. For a subsequent exchange in 1555 between Calvin and Socinus dealing with the doctrine of Christ's merits, see the article by Dr. David Willis, elsewhere in this Volume.

[2] It had just been published with the title *De vitandis superstitionibus, quae cum sincera fidei confessione pugnant libellus J. Caluini, Eiusdem excusatio, ad Pseudonicodemos Philippi Melancthonis, Martini Buceri, Petri Martyris responsa de eadem re....* (Geneuae: Per J. Girardum, 1549). A second expanded edition " quibus accessit responsum pastorum Tigurinae ecclesiae " appeared, also in Geneva, in 1550. An Italian translation entitled *Del fuggir le superstizioni che ripugnano a la vera e sincera confessione de la fede* was published (probably in Geneva) in 1553. The only known copies of the latter edition are in the British Museum and in the Guicciardini Collection in Florence.

myself to be immersed in all the matters which to God's glory work to the salvation of the elect. And why should I not also wish, indeed with my whole heart, to find esteem in your eyes, and to be [considered] one brought to this light not entirely in vain.

For the rest, inasmuch as you have so far proved yourself to be a healthful physician to these our fellowmen who are still afflicted with the bestial disease, I wish to entreat and prevail upon you not to refuse, with some antidote from that well supplied laboratory of yours, to prescribe for certain ones who, as they have not yet fully regained their health, are in a terrible quandary as to whether they are to avoid marriage as much with Papists as with Jews. For on the one hand there is the person who thinks it to be all right to wed a woman who places her whole righteousness in Christ, and who is not unreasonable, but who is nevertheless held back by other superstitions and falls kneeling before the saints, etc. Then there is another person, who maintains that it is not possible to marry such a one, even though she be in complete agreement in all the elements of doctrine, until she be united to the [true] Church of Christ either by public confession or some other manifest acceptance of the truth, Antichrist having been abjured, just as it is forbidden to contract marriage with a Jewess, even though she holds the right [Christian] opinion in all matters, until she makes this evident through baptism.

Yet another person, granted that he in other respects lives piously [Reformed], is greatly perplexed as to whether, because he is compelled to baptize his infant [within the Roman Church], everything else must be abandoned, or whether instead he is allowed to meet the needs of his offspring and the rest of the family with a certain amount of contamination of himself, — especially since Melanchthon, of whom you approve, would have it so and since Peter Martyr [1] also allows the same, — given, of course, that the abomination be abominated, because if this person will do otherwise, the child will doubtless be deprived not so much of baptism as of life itself.

Next, [I ask] whether you consider valid even that baptism which is administered in mockery, for you are acquainted with the [so considered] efficacious baptism of the Papists, who believe that there can be true baptism both in mockery and in blasphemy, as well as with their exorcisms and incantations rather than with the power of God or by the Word, unless, perhaps, they dream that some special power is contained in their words. To these words [themselves], I have no doubt at all of this, you attribute no such power; otherwise you would scarcely rebaptize one who had once been baptized with these same words most simply and in good faith at home by a friend or by his parents. For you say, and quite rightly do you say it, that the [baptismal] act should be solemnized before the eyes of the congregation.

---

[1] Socinus is undoubtedly referring to the *responsa* of Melanchthon and Peter Martyr Vermigli in Calvin's *De vitandis*.... See above, p. 217, n. 2.

And if you deny the Church to be present in the house of a [Reformed Christian] no matter how faithful, how much less will it be found amid the assembly of idolaters!

As for the Mass, first of all certain persons [the Nicodemites] say that the assent which is [allegedly] betokened by our presence is not censurable, unless you would also censure anybody who, to be sure, does not frequent Mass and yet lives so guardedly that he is considered among its approvers, and unless you would have it that as often as talk arises about it [the Mass], it should forthwith be execrated openly, not only with the possibility of grave danger but also without a single remnant ray of hope. But as for the stumbling-block [1] which you so greatly press (once this had been removed, Paul even seemd to have allowed the eating of food sacrificed to idols), — they [the Nicodemites] reply, and thus they think to have got out of it handsomely: "Look," they say, "I most assuredly know that there is not a single weakling anywhere who could by my example be misled to worshiping idols; to the contrary, indeed, there is not a single person who would not suppose that I had gone [to attend Mass] only to satisfy the mind, that I might find some persons with whom I might stroll a bit, etc. (and this indeed is evidently quite common among us), or to whom it would occur that I had, somehow, finally come to approve of what the largest part of them believe; but it is for the sake of exercise that they thus convene once a week and caper. Indeed, my good friends would laugh to notice how very little faith I have in such nonsense. So well instructed are they that few there are who are even convinced that God exists!" It is alleged that attendance of this kind ought not to be permitted as a special case to travelers who, although they have professed their [Reformed] faith in more than one place, are compelled in a strange land to be present again and again at the spectacle of abomination; of necessity, as these fellows [who have been compelled] indeed pretend, but of a necessity really by which they may serve their own ends rather than Christ's.

Now, there would be no need of so many questions if (as should be) we had the least bit of legislation that a person should undergo some sort of punishment rather than give offense to the most beneficent Father. May 14, 1549, at Zurich.

I pray that you extend my greetings to Anthony de Paré [2] and take diligent care that the enclosed get to Budé.[3]

Yours most respectfully,

Lelius Sozinus

---

[1] I Cor. 8: 9.

[2] The name of this mysterious figure occurs occasionally in the Calvin correspondence. especially in the communications to M. de Falais. Cf. *C.O.*, xxii, col. 416.

[3] Louis Budé, son of the celebrated Classicist Guillaume (1467-1540), traveled in Italy from 1546-1549. He served briefly as Professor of Hebrew at Geneva before his death in May, 1551.

II. – Calvin to Lelius Socinus [1]

[*Undated*] [2]

I got your letter [3] a few days after my return; from that time a catarrh has plagued me greatly, nor does it leave off giving me trouble.

Let me reply briefly to your questions. Since a Christian man must marry a woman under no other rubric than that she prove herself to him in respect to all the requirements of a pious life a helpmeet and companion, when there is even the slightest variance from this purpose, I have no doubt but that the marriage is sinful. Furthermore, whoever takes in marriage a woman who is still involved in the impious superstitions of the papacy, what else does he take into his home than profanation? For if the wife is the body of the man, there can be no apology for the man who unites himself to a woman daily prostituting herself to perverse cults so that he becomes defiled in half of himself. I will not go so far as to say that, if anyone take unto himself such a wife, he will be forced to consecrate his marriage under magic auspices. Besides, I should not certainly venture to compare with an enemy of religion a girl of otherwise right opinions who nevertheless is by fear of the flesh detained by the sham of idolatry. For the farther a person is from Christ, the more it behooves us to shrink from that person's company. But the sort of woman you describe to me is certainly quite far from belonging to the class of professed enemies.

Whoever offers his children for papal baptism, sullied with so many perverse superstitions, is not free from guilt. And that, if I am not mistaken, I count among the anomalies which surely ought to spur pious men to migrate. To be sure, Melanchthon and [Peter] Martyr [4] do not prohibit [such a baptism], just so long as the things which war against Christ's institution are spurned. I would have no quarrel with this position just so long as the man who is to undergo such baptism has to be made ready for certain death. However, I approve of the opinions of those you name, without subscribing to every single item. I hold that a derisive imitation of baptism ought to be considered as unadulterated mockery. Nevertheless, the baptism of the papists, however much it may abound with a thousand mockeries, retains its efficacy, inasmuch as it is administered to this end, that the children of the faithful in accordance with the mandate of Christ receive the sign of adoption. For I see that circumcision, though corrupted with many superstitions, has nonetheless been held as a symbol of grace. Your objection that baptism must be performed in the presence of the congregated pious nonetheless does not stand in the way of its validity when it is administered in the congregation of idolaters. For

[1] Epistle § 1212, in *C.O.*, XIII, coll. 307-311.
[2] Written at a time late in June or early in July, 1549.
[3] Presumably epistle § 1191.
[4] See above, p. 218, n. 1.

when we teach what must fittingly be done to make baptism pure and free of any stain, we do not abolish the institution of God, even if idolaters do corrupt it. Further, in and among those corruptions of papal baptism there still remains something of God's very own. Then, when we deny the name of Church to papists, we do it in such wise that we nevertheless do not deny that there still abide among them certain remnants of the Church. Certainly when Josiah [1] and Hezekiah [2] gathered from all Israel those who had defected from the Lord, they did in no sense call them to a second circumcision. And when the temple itself was defiled with a variety of sacrilege, the circumcision did not nevertheless cease to have validity. Therefore, whenever I say that they sin who offer their children to baptism in that place [the Roman Church], I nevertheless consider that to be a valid baptism, if in it some marks of the divine institution appear, even though it be otherwise defiled with many blemishes.

Those who do not keep from an external profession of idolatry I do not dare to condemn without reserve, even if they conceal their faith for fear of reprisals. For when we see that the pious who went into hiding during the persecutions were approved of God, it is not right that more should be asked by us. Yet, I am not such a one as would look favorably upon their listlessness. No, I will rather urge that they eagerly seize every opportunity to profess their faith, and that they not listen to the open blasphemies of the impious against God in such silence that they seem to assent. Nevertheless, I dare not lay down a rule as to how far they must go. But those, meanwhile, who wander about in the shrines to satisfy the mind and who pretend certain outward appearances while services are in progress, — deserve no excusing. For beside the fact that the very amusement they derive from this sort of spectacle points to their being little affected by these insults to God, in the mind of many they heedlessly fall into this kind of discredit, as that they do this out of contempt rather of religion than of superstition. And for this reason I duly disapprove of such license to do as they please; since it appears to be not far removed from idolatry, it smacks of something more profane than Christian.

The last question,[3] concerning the resurrection of the flesh, which you so eagerly wish me to unfold for you, although it presents no great difficulty in my mind, nevertheless requires more time and effort. For a good number of scriptural passages would have to be gathered and carefully explicated, if I were to undertake a thorough discussion of the evidence. But I, not so much for the sake of escaping painstaking effort but because the question seems to require more labor than its

---

[1] II Kings 23.
[2] II Chron. 29.
[3] This question is not found in Socinus' epistle § 1191, but seems to have been asked either in a letter which has not been preserved or in conversation with Calvin. For evidence supporting the latter possibility see p. 224, n. 6. Lelius repeated his doubts on the resurrection in Epistle § 1231 below. Calvin's summary reply is in § 1323.

usefulness warrants, prefer by this very brevity to go on record that nothing more than a reasonable treatment of it would be my pleasure. Offhand, the madness of the Manichees must be refuted, for they deny that the flesh will rise up again, inasmuch as it is unclean. That the resurrection of this flesh seems to you an incredible thing is of little wonder.[1] However, that you should, because of this prejudice, have decided it to be enough simply to believe that one day in the future we shall be clad in new bodies, is inconsistent with the teaching of Scripture. In the first place, the very word "resurrection," especially when in reference to the flesh, has a different ring [from that of your interpretation]. For this is the promise: "He who hath raised up Christ from death will vivify your mortal bodies also, on account of the Spirit of Christ that dwelleth in you."[2] And thus elsewhere: "Christ will shape up again our lowly body that it may conform with his own glorious body."[3] Without question immortality is promised expressly for these very bodies which are now subject to decay. These words are pointless otherwise: "This corruptible will put on incorruption."[4] He could not have spoken more pointedly, says Tertullian,[5] without holding his own skin in his hands! Here is the proof from logical conclusions: If the death of this flesh is from Adam, then from Christ is the resurrection of that same flesh, because he restores us from corruption. The passage in Ezekiel[6] which contains the figure of the resurrection must be cited. God kills and restores to life: what, except that which was dead? From the fact that the Athenians scoffed at the resurrection preached by Paul we gather what kind of thing he preached.[7] The fact of their scoffing is to the pious the confirmation of a sound understanding. "Fear him who is able to destroy both soul and body in hell."[8] What body? Why, none other than that which the tyrants slay. The resurrection of the flesh is proved ritually by the use of the sacraments. Baptism sanctifies not only the soul but the body as well. Partaking of the Supper, which invites us to belief in a heavenly life, is aimed at our bodily senses also. The passage in the eighth chapter of the Epistle to the Romans will be fitting, especially where it speaks of the redemption of the body.[9] "Bearing about the dying of Christ, that the life also of Christ may be made manifest in our body."[10] Tertullian has it: "He has brought the earnest of

---

[1] Here, one is tempted to add, "in view of your associations with Camillo Renato." On this Sicilian psychopannychist and his influence on Socinus, cf. the study by George H. Williams elsewhere in this Volume.

[2] Rom. 8: 11.

[3] Philipp. 3: 21.

[4] I Cor. 15: 53.

[5] Tertullian, *Against Marcion*, Bk. V, Ch. xii, in A. Roberts and J. Donaldson, ed. *The Ante-Nicene Fathers* (Buffalo, 1885), III, 455.

[6] Ch. 37.

[7] Acts 17: 32.

[8] Mt. 10: 28.

[9] Rom. 8: 23.

[10] II Cor. 4: 10.

our resurrection into heaven."[1] Therefore, those who deny that we shall be raised up likewise deny that He is in heaven. Unless God raise us up in body, he does not raise up the dead. Tertullian calls Enoch and Elias, preserved in body and soul, representatives of the immortality to be.[2] Further, not only are the faithful called "temples of God," but even their bodies are distinguished with this honor.[3] Likewise are they called even "members of Christ." Moreover, it is exceedingly incongruous that "temples of the Spirit" and "members of Christ" vanish into decay without hope of restoration. Yes, indeed, in that same passage Paul makes it sufficiently clear that it is these present bodies for which God has destined celestial and eternal glory. Furthermore, men are summoned before the judgment seat of Christ, that each may receive in accordance with what things he has done in the body.[4] And besides, it makes very little sense that we be repaid the reward of our works [clad] in strange bodies, when in the performance of these works the present bodies with which we are now clad were the instruments. That is to say, shall Paul's body in which God's name was made renowned[5] be deprived of honor, and a body got up [for him] from some other source be crowned with the glory of martyrdom? To this is added the fact that Christ, in whom we have not only a lively image of our future resurrection but its pledge as well, took on again the body which he had laid aside. In that fashion are we to be reshaped. Otherwise he could not properly be called, as he is called, "the first fruits of those who are to rise again."[6] And to be sure, whomever that day shall find still surviving, these shall rise up again with a sudden change in their same bodies. And if you object that our reasoning is conflicting, I throw back at you that statement of Paul's: "Indeed, we shall not all sleep, but we shall all be changed."[7] If a change happens unto all, then certainly this very flesh will be renewed. And what could you want more clear than these words? "This corruptible must put on incorruption."[8] Nor is it a contradiction that Paul in that same passage teaches that the flesh will be different, — for that is in reference to its quality. And he does not mean anything else than what he later proposes in other words: "that what is mortal may be swallowed up in life."[9] Therefore are the bodies of the saints said to have risen up out of their graves.[10] In the same manner that they came forth from their tombs, so also without any doubt will the Lord

---

[1] Tertullian, *On the Resurrection of the Flesh*, Ch. li (*Ante-Nicene Fathers*, III, 584).
[2] Tertullian, *On the Resurrection of the Flesh*, Ch. lviii (*Ante-Nicene Fathers*, III, 591).
[3] I Cor. 6: 19.
[4] II Cor. 5: 10.
[5] Philipp. 1: 20.
[6] I Cor. 15: 20, where he is called "the first fruits of those who have fallen asleep."
[7] I Cor. 15: 51.
[8] I Cor. 15: 53.
[9] I Cor. 15: 54, "Death is swallowed up in victory."
[10] Mt. 27: 52.

bring us forth. For that reason does Isaiah, when he depicts the restoration of the people under the figure of the resurrection, say: "Awake, ye that dwell in dust."[1] Nor for any other reason does Christ say: "The dead who are in their graves shall hear the voice of the Son of God."[2] And that could not be, unless they rose again with their corpses resumed. This Isaiah also expresses at that point where he says: "Thy dead shall live, and my corpse shall rise up again."[3] Whence also the noun "sleep" has sprung, which would have no significance unless the bodies were to be reawakened as from sleep. For it is a falsehood [to say] that bodies made of earth sleep, if new bodies are to be created for those that have been consumed. Surely, if the bodies in which we are now encompassed do not rise again, the ritual of burial from the beginning of the world has been a matter of superstition; but that it has been divinely transmitted to serve as a symbol of the future resurrection ought to be beyond dispute. And indeed, if the creation of a new body were to be hoped for rather than the restoration of this present body which we inhabit, Paul could wish in vain that the spirit and soul as well as the body be blameless unto the day of the Lord.[4] Yet another exhortation pertains to this, — "that we cleanse ourselves from all filthiness of the flesh and spirit."[5] For if this flesh is defiled with the squalors of sin, it must needs sustain the punishment of its squalors. With such testimonies I am so satisfied that no door is left open for contrary thoughts to shake my faith.

And so I hope that these words will satisfy you, unless they find your mind too set, — a thing far removed from your piety and sobriety. But nevertheless for our friendship's sake I have deemed it wise to apprise you of the fact that recently, when I listened to you,[6] I was somewhat apprehensive that this opinion had struck within you roots too deep for you to cast it off with ease. Besides, deeply confident of your fine abilities, I have thought it sufficient to point a finger at those things which with a man less astute or versed I should have had to pursue further. Farewell, distinguished gentleman and friend most dear to me in Christ the Lord. Lovingly greet in my name your host, Master Pellicanus,[7] and the rest. May the Lord Jesus be ever with you and direct you with his Spirit.

---

[1] Isaiah 26: 19.
[2] John 5: 28.
[3] Isaiah 26: 19.
[4] I Thess. 5: 23.
[5] II Cor. 7: 1.
[6] This passage supports the idea that Socinus had first proposed his doubts on the resurrection to Calvin orally. See above p. 221, n. 3.
[7] Konrad Pellikan (1478-1556). It was in the home of this former Franciscan, who became professor of Hebrew at Zwingli's invitation, that Lelius resided during a part of his sojourn in Zurich, from October, 1548 to June, 1550.

III. – Lelius Socinus to Calvin[1]

[*Basel, July 25, 1549*]

To that most distinguished person, Master John Calvin, the very vigilant honorable bishop at Geneva.

In am enormously grateful that you have not yet written in reply. I would have been very pleased to have it, but now its arrival will be all the more pleasant for the sharper desire with which I burn to read yours. For, impelled by that desire, I am now forced to entreat and beseech you by all means to favor me with an immediate reply, at your earliest convenience in the midst of your so busy schedule. Otherwise, since my desires cannot increase further, I shall consequently fall prey to some serious illness. I know that you would very gladly deliver me and all others of any affliction, should occasion arise, and you have the power to prevent any affliction from striking me; so, you see, I shall be in constant doubt as to whether you shall be coming to my aid. Your affection is so extensive and so broad that it embraces in great kindness not only friends who are near and are fellow-countrymen but also foreigners who are at a great distance, enemies even, and it gives encouragement to all for the good of mankind. And I, although not present in your company, yet not too far, a foreigner indeed but a friend, assuredly most devoted to you, — shall I not even once after many entreaties obtain help from you or the promise of such? I altogether hope, therefore, that, as in many other matters, in this also you will exceed my expectation. But that you may do so with increased pleasure to me, I trust that you will very kindly reply not only to my previous questions (of which you have a copy elsewhere in this letter, in case that first copy has somehow got lost) but as well to these which I shall submit below. For although we must treat all matters of this kind unceasingly and reverently, we must yet treat them primarily for God's greater glory (and how, I ask, is that glory made brighter than if, taking deeper notice of God's works and oracles, we arrive at a more exact notion of what he has most magnificently promised us); yet what can be of greater importance (and that a thing which is impossible in this life!), than that at some time in our most blessed [future] state we may render eternal glory to the author of us and indeed of every good thing?

But the question asked now is, Who are we? or rather, What shall we become and of what shall we consist? Will there exist only our soul in that blessedness of which it becomes a partaker very soon after it has flown out of this workhouse, or will this present body, too, although it is endowed with a different kind of nature, exist likewise at some future time? For, a good number of scriptural passages seem to confirm this latter proposition, while reason readily grants the former.

---

[1] Epistle § 1231, in *C.O.*, XIII, coll. 336-340.

Not that I am of that school of thought which considers nothing believable that is contrary to reason! But as in many other matters, in this also may the inexpert be assisted. It is a difficult thing, I admit, especially in the way of the Lord, not to place one's faith outright on the authoritatively established word of God. And yet, on the other hand, it is no less difficult to persuade oneself that impossible things can come to pass, and to force one's will to aspire to something which the intellect hopelessly suggests can never be. Not that I would not like to think so and would wish to disparage the divine power in any way! But what I really think is that Scripture, when it so munificently promises the resurrection of bodies and with other anthropopathies sets our hope right before our eyes, has intended nothing more than, by the use of some physical terms, to make easily understandable to our senses, as it were, not only that ineffable blessedness but even our own selves, who would otherwise be invisible and incomprehensible to ourselves, until such time as, endowed with a more perfect light, we may truly and not darkly [1] behold God Himself in Christ as he is, — bodily, that is. For this reason also is that statement made: "And I appoint unto you a kingdom, [as my Father has appointed unto me;] that ye may eat and drink [at my table in my kingdom,] and sit on thrones, etc." [2] And what absurdity would there be in our believing that we would have no more need of bodies than that those bodies would have no more need of food and drink and other similarly promised conditions, for those bodies to be thoroughly imbued with all happiness? Trembling, I ponder all these things; just as they are uncertain and dubious, if not actually terrifying to me, so are they submitted to you alone, wisest of men. Please make me fairly definite and careful reply and show clearly in what way at one and the same time it is possible and profitable for me and others, who have been and will be the subject under concern, that there be restored [after death] the stuff of this very hand by the operation of which I am writing to you, and of this entire body to which this arm is attached; or whether from some other source a body will be fitted to us. Point out when the divine judgment will be, when the resurrection, when that transformation of this lowly body. For, unless I am mistaken, we should have to expect an alteration of the body, not of its qualities, and a certain kind of passing of the soul, not a return to its old tabernacle.

If such is the case, I beg and implore you again and again to guide me through to the truth. Farewell, and my best wishes.

Basel, in the house of Münster,[3] July 25, 1549.

Your most respectful

Laelius Sozinus.

---

[1] I Cor. 13: 12.

[2] Luke 22: 29-30.

[3] Sebastian Münster, 1489-1552. Socinus, who when in Basel was enrolled at the University, resided in the home of this celebrated German Hebraist and cosmographer.

Addendum [1]

To which I add this one thing: (Addition) You would not argue, would you, that if a Turk has been christened, his whole household must also be baptized, and if it is not right for circumcision to be construed as a baptism in the father's case, why would it be right in the case of sons who had not been circumcised by the higher rite ? [2]

IV. - Calvin to Lelius Socinus [3]

[*Geneva, Dec. 7, 1549*]

I reply more tardily than I wished for the reason that I am unwillingly, to tell the truth, being drawn forth whither your letter bids me. I see that you are least happy [with my notions] concerning the resurrection of the flesh. And so, if you want more of me, [let me say that] I have no desire indeed to have greater knowledge than I have provided. If I should plead by way of excuse that no more has been given me by the Lord, it would not be right for me to be pressed further. For we must hold to the formula: " I have believed, therefore I speak. " Indeed, I state that I find such satisfaction in this faith which I have set forth to you that I do not think it right for me to reach out further. I can hear your objection: Since this is the chief fundamental principle of our faith, since on it rests all of our happiness, research into it seems not to be pointless. And this is indeed attractive bait. But because the Spirit of God through the mouth of John advises us that it is put off until the last day [of judgment],[4] I feel that a restriction is laid upon me. The things that I have written you are so powerful in my mind and so sanctioned by the word of God that no doubt vexes me. Further, they are so sufficient to me that with their assurance I unconcernedly have no fear of death. If you want more arguments, they must be sought elsewhere, for you shall never get me to exceed the limits set by God in an effort to comply with your request.

In the other matters also, if I am briefer than you would wish, forgive me. On the matter of taking a wife, if anyone ask my advice, I shall recommend nothing more than that he marry such a woman as is prepared to follow Christ with her husband. And this she should not only profess with her lips but give evidence of in fact. For whatever man shall take unto wife a woman of otherwise right opinion who is

---

[1] At this point Lelius repeats his questions in Epistle § 1191, verbatim, with a few very slight word changes that do not alter the translation, beginning at p. 218: " Quaeritur an ex aequo a papisticis nuptiis abstinendum, atque a Iudaicis ? etc. "

[2] This is the only question which Lelius adds to those of Epistle § 1191. It is inserted just before the discussion on attendance at Mass.

[3] Epistle § 1323, in *C.O.*, XIII, coll. 484-487.

[4] John 16: 12.

nevertheless unwilling to renounce the profession of impiety will put upon himself the worst kind of halter. Too often have I seen, in many cases, how far those who have become involved in marriages of this sort withdraw from Christ.

But let me reply to you point by point. You ask whether one ought not to abstain from papal marriage just as much as from Turkish marriage: I myself would not be so rash as to place on the same level with the Turks those who still inwardly hold on to the superstitions of the papacy in which they have been brought up. For they come somewhat nearer to us. But leaving the comparison aside, I say that it is not right for a Christian man to be joined to a wife who is estranged from Christ. We know that papists are in that category. Whoever thinks it is all right for him to marry a woman (though she is still considered to be involved in many errors) just so long as she seeks her righteousness in Christ, is heedless of the many matters in which he will be in disagreement with her. No one, therefore, by my advice, will submit to such danger; indeed, it is rather my belief that whoever takes unto himself any other woman for wife than one who has previously separated herself from the pope contracts a marriage that is neither pious nor in the Lord. I realize that the choice is not always given in accordance with the wish; but difficulty does not wash away the guilt. If a solemn abnegation of the papacy occur, it will indeed be considered praiseworthy; but I should not dare to require it as being necessary, just as I should not dare to define a stipulated limit to which any intended wife must have progressed in the instruction of piety, except that, having abandoned the enemy of Christ and having bid farewell to her manifest impiety, she shall have professed Christ. You ask whether the Church ought to consider valid or invalid marriage of that sort, — I do not understand to what end this relates. For inasmuch as the mutual consent of both parties is required for the marriage to be consecrated ritually in the name and under the auspices of God, if any person shun his duty, the bond of marriage, by which one person is locked to another, does not nevertheless cease to be legitimate. Such a person will with good cause indeed make reproachable the lightness of purpose, but he does not dissolve the troth plighted.

If one were to choose the lesser of two evils, I think that a man who lives in papal lands cannot do otherwise than to present his children for baptism, even though it be adulterated. If he detest the corruptions which do battle with God's commandment, he will be acting piously and dutifully as a Christian man. Indeed, the danger of death is ever at hand; but steadfastness [to the Reformed faith] will be all the more praiseworthy for the reason that any man [who adheres to it] will not be deterred by any fear from declaring a confession worthy of his piety. If a man deprive his children of baptism, he will produce a more than double offense. Therefore I should not advise this. Now, since weakness of spirit keeps almost all of those who live under the tyranny of Antichrist from attesting freely that they are estranged from the pollutions of the papists, they are therefore to be advised, as I do advise them, how wretched and how overwhelmed in a maze are those who cannot ward off an offense to God except by committing another offense. That indeed is to be pressed, as the saying goes, between the victim and the knife,[1] that they cannot offer their children to Christ without prostituting themselves to the pollutions of Antichrist; and yet they cannot abandon the practice of baptism without taking upon themselves the stigma of contempt for Christianity. This is the goad I apply to those who delude themselves in that respect, — that they see the signs of their unhappiness in their own children as well. When I make a distinction between the baptism of papists and an invalid one, you fashion a reply for yourself to attack as though it had been given by me. You will not find it in my writing, I know, that the power of baptism depends upon the intention of the officiant. Unless I am mistaken, I have said that it is efficacious only to the extent that it is administered to this end, namely that it introduce us into the body of Christ, or that it be the symbol of our renewal. Now, it makes no difference to me whether the man who baptizes is a Lucianist,[2] or whether the baptizer is the devil. For only the institution must be respected and its continued use, which began from Christ's mandate as from a spring. Certainly the rite of baptism did not start yesterday. Neither the papists nor other idolaters thought it up. You size it up incorrectly, unless you go back to its beginning. However, no matter how tainted it has become with many perverse additions, this nevertheless has always remained fixed, that one be baptized by the mandate of Christ in the name of the Father, the Son, and the Holy Spirit, as a witness of regeneration. This in my teaching is the goal that must be considered. And there was no other reason why long ago God, in the midst of man's profanation of all sacred institutions, considered circumcision valid, than that it was still directed to that original end, namely, that it be the sign of the divine covenant: "I shall be your God, and of your seed after you."[3] Therefore, when the people under Josiah[4] made a covenant afresh and did solemn penance for its defection, there was nevertheless no repetition of the circumcision, which had been defiled not only by their infidelity but by many impious superstitions. For a holy institution of God is of such dimension that in spite of the manifold corruptions of mankind it is quite capable of retaining its potency. There is no reciprocal argument that you can twist against me. It is not by the identification of baptism [with circumcision], as you would have it, that corruptions were introduced into]circumcision by] God's people; but by the [repeated] observance of

---

[1] "That indeed is to be pressed, as they say, in great straits." The idiom is *inter sacrum saxumque stare* [*premi* (here in Calvin)], Plautus, *Capt.* 3, 4, 84, or colloquially, today, "to be between the devil and the deep."

[2] From Lucian of Samosata, martyred 312, who had attacked the absolute divinity of Christ. In his school at Antioch, Arius received his early theological education, and later called himself boastfully a "Lucianist."

[3] Gen. 17: 7.

[4] II Kings 23: 3.

the rite divinely handed down.[1] And yet the sons who had violated the covenant upon which they had entered together with their fathers were degenerate. When I say that in the papacy there are remnants of the Church, I do not restrict it to the elect who are scattered therein; but I imply that the ruins of the dispersed Church are visible there. However, lest I have to go into a discussion with long argumentations, it is proper that we rest content with the authority of Paul, who proclaims that the Antichrist will sit in the temple of God.[2] Although I believe that I have proved even this with sufficiently valid arguments, namely, that some aspect of the Church, though half broken, — indeed, if you will, shattered and shapeless, — yet remains in the papacy, still I do not allow that in the private home of a pious man baptism can be administered purely, in accordance with Christ's rule. One could easily retort: "But I would more easily tolerate a baptism of this sort, which is not permitted among us and indeed is legally forbidden us, than that papal baptism which is stained with so many pollutions." But here it is not a matter of my having the burden of proof. That you think, however, that I would consider as worthless a baptism which some one of my brethren has perchance administered within private walls, I call God and man to witness that this has never entered my mind! For it is one thing to prescribe what is correct and genuine, and quite another thing to prescribe what is residual from God's institutions among foreign additions.

If a Turk is received into the Church by a solemn profession of faith, I have no doubt but that his children must also be baptized. For that promise is still vital: "I shall be your God and the God of your children." It is not mine to condemn outright that fear by which it happens that certain people live so cautiously as not to fall under the suspicion of tyrants. For there is but one lawgiver and one judge, and in his words I see no condemnation [of such fear]. There are those who believe that their astute pretence in going to Mass is a useful resource for advancing God's glory. Oh that they would consider that God is not so resourceless as to need our falsehoods! A sure thing it is indeed that by such an opportunity certain people are occasionally won over to Christ. Whenever this happens, like Paul, I rejoice.[3] For howsoever the kingdom of God may be propagated, we must count it gain. But now the question is whether such is an approved service to God, — which he himself denies.[4]

Dec. 7, 1549.[5]

---

[1] "Neque enim lusoria baptismi imitatio, ut credis, in populum Dei inserebat: sed instituti divinitus traditi observatio."

[2] II Thess. 2: 4.

[3] Philipp. 1: 18.

[4] Rom. 12: 1 f.

[5] The closing salutation normally found in Calvin's letters has apparently dropped out.

DAVID WILLIS

THE INFLUENCE OF LAELIUS SOCINUS ON CALVIN'S DOCTRINES OF THE MERITS OF CHRIST AND THE ASSURANCE OF FAITH

In the course of his brief yet richly varied life, Laelius Socinus carried on a correspondence with John Calvin which is as instructive about the Genevan reformer as it is about the Italian pilgrim. In 1549 the two men discussed issues such as the resurrection of the flesh, and problems facing an evangelical minority with respect to marriage with Roman Catholics, baptism within the Roman communion and attendance at Roman ceremonies.[1] Socinus apparently reproved Calvin in 1551 for banishing Jerome Hermes Bolsec because of his dissent on the doctrine of predestination; the following January the Genevan Reformer paternally admonished Socinus against the dangers of an unbridled curiosity in theological matters.[2] In 1555 Calvin gave his opinion on four questions directed to him by Laelius concerning the merits of Christ and the assurance of faith.[3] In 1558 Calvin recommended the disinherited Italian to Prince Radziwill,[4] and the following year, after his Eastern journey, Socinus reported to Calvin on the state of the Polish churches.[5]

Most of this correspondence, especially the exchange of 1549, has been thoroughly examined.[6] However, Calvin's responses of 1555 have curiously not received the attention they deserve,[7] despite their accessibility in the *Institutes*, in the final edition of which Calvin incorpo-

---

[1] *Ioannis Calvini Opera Quae Supersunt Omnia*, ed. G. Baum, E. Cunitz, E. Reuss (Brunsvigae, 1863-1900) [henceforth designated by " CO "], 13: 272-274, 307-311, 336-340, 484-487.

[2] CO 14: 229-230.

[3] " Responsio ad aliquot Laelii Socini Senensis Quaestiones, " CO 10 a: 160-165.

[4] CO 17: 181-182.

[5] CO 17: 604-605.

[6] Cf., C. F. Illgen, *Vita Laelii Socini* (Lipsiae, 1814), pp. 20-22, 39-40; F. Trechsel, *Die Protestantischen Antitrinitarier vor Faustus Socin*, II (Heidelberg, 1844), pp. 144-151, 156-157, 166-169; Otto Fock, *Der Socinianismus* (Kiel, 1847), pp. 134-137; E. Doumergue, *Jean Calvin*, VI (Neuilly-sur-Seine, 1926), 458-465; Delio Cantimori, *Eretici Italiani del Cinquecento* (Firenze, 1939), pp. 128-142, 172 ff.; George H. Williams, *The Radical Reformation* (Philadelphia, 1962), pp. 568-569; F. C. Church, *The Italian Reformers* (New York, 1932), pp. 163, 270, 286.

[7] When he comes to this exchange of 1555, Doumergue merely notes that Socinus questioned Calvin on grace, *op. cit.*, p. 464. Cf. also J. T. McNeill, *The History and Character of Calvinism* (New York, 1954), p. 183; Fock, *loc. cit.*; Cantimori, *op. cit.*, p. 174. The exceptions are Illgen and Trechsel who briefly summarize the responses of 1555, and François Wendel who summarizes the responses and raises critical questions about the implication of Calvin's view of the merit of Christ for the doctrine of the humanity of Christ. François Wendel, *Calvin, Sources et évolution de sa pensée religieuse* (Paris, 1950), pp. 94, 171.

rated them almost without alteration. There the response to question one exists as Book II, 17, 1-5 and the responses to the three remaining questions comprise most of Book III, 2, 11 and over half of Book III, 2, 12.[1] Socinus' questions unfortunately are not extant so we are dependent upon Calvin's responses to disclose the nature of Socinus' concern and to provide the basis for judgments about the influence he may have had on Calvin's theological development.

The first response deals with the merit of Christ and the latter three with the assurance, or certainty, of faith. Both matters are joined by the central question which, at least in this particular portion of the Calvin-Socinus correspondence, preoccupies the Italian: can God's fidelity be counted on if his will is mutable as would seem to be implied by a doctrine of the merits of Christ and by a doctrine which admits that God sometimes removes faith once apparently given.

The first question might be paraphrased, " If the justification of men depends on the sheer mercy of God, how is it necessary that Christ's merit should at the same time intervene? How can one say both that God freely forgives and that Christ merits our forgiveness? "[2]

Calvin answers that it is by Christ's merits that the Father who has always loved us and who is now reconciled to us embraces us and discloses his love. " In some inexpressible way, God loved us and yet was angry toward us at the same time until he became reconciled to us in Christ. "[3] " How did God begin to embrace with his favor those whom he had loved before the creation of the world, if not because he showed his love where he was reconciled to us by Christ's blood. "[4] Calvin's reply is best summarized when he says, " Both God's free favor and Christ's obedience, each in its own degree, are correctly opposed to our works. Apart from God's good pleasure, Christ could not merit anything; but he did merit because he had been appointed to appease God's anger with his sacrifice and to blot out our transgressions with his obedience. "[5]

---

[1] *Ioannis Calvini Opera Selecta*, ed. P. Barth, G. Niesel (München, 1926-1936) [henceforth designated as " OS "] III, 509, note c; OS IV, 20, note c; OS IV, 21, note h; and OS IV, 22, note d. Jean Calvin, *Institution de la Religion Chrestienne*, ed. J.-D. Benoit (Paris, 1957 ff.), vol. II, 304, note 3; vol. III, 28, note 5. *Institutes of the Christian Religion*, ed. J. T. McNeill, trans. F. L. Battles (Philadelphia, 1960) refers to the 1555 responses (vol. I, 528, note 1) but does not indicate that these sections of the *Institutes are these responses.*

[2] Illgen offers this reconstruction of the Socinian perplexity: " .... Si iustificatio hominum ex mera Dei misericordia pendeat, num necesse fuerit, ut Christi meritum simul interveniret, *nam utrumque inter se putat pugnare,* etenim si Deus ex libero arbitrio homines iustos reddere sibi constituerit, commoveri eum non potuisse merito Christi. " *Op. cit.*, p. 39.

[3] CO 10 a: 160; Inst. II, 17, 2, OS III: 510.

[4] CO 10 a: 161; Inst. II, 17, 2, OS III: 510.

[5] Atque ideo nostris operibus apte tam gratuitus Dei favor quam Christi obedientia opponitur, utrumque suo ordine. Nam Christus nonnisi ex Dei beneplacito quidquam mereri potuit, sed quia ad hoc ordinatus est, ut iram Dei sacrificio suo placaret, suaque obedientia deleret transgressiones nostras. " CO 10 a: 160; cf. Inst. II, 17, 1, OS III: 509.

According to this answer the basic opposition is not between God's free favor and Christ's obedience, but between God's saving action, including his free favor and Christ's obedience, and our works. Men cannot merit what flows freely from Christ's obedience. Such a doctrine of Christ's merits is based on a refusal to take seriously an abstract notion of God's freedom apart from its manifestation in the Redeemer's fulfillment of the will of the Father in an obedience which eventually meant the death on the cross. It is God's love, Calvin says, that is the highest cause or origin of our salvation whereas faith in Christ is the second or proximate cause. By this Calvin means that the matter of our salvation is in Christ, so that he is not merely its formal cause. Our faith is, Calvin seems to be saying, a dependent and created cause and so can only specify the kind and not the being of our salvation.

The resemblance between Calvin's argument on the merits of Christ and that of Duns Scotus on the same subject has been noted and is indisputable.[1] Both argue that apart from God's good pleasure, Christ could not merit anything. Scotus says that Christ's work and especially his willing was meritorious because of the *acceptatio* of God. If it had pleased God, a good angel could have made satisfaction by an offering which God could have accepted as sufficient for all sins. For every created offering is worth exactly what God accepts it for and no more. [2]

Although on this point Calvin's and Scotus' views are similar, it would be a mistake to over-emphasize the Scotistic element here. Scotus, in the traditional fashion of Lombard, St. Thomas, and Bonaventura, considers both what Christ merited for himself and what he merited for others.[3] Calvin restricts himself to what Christ merits for others.[4] Scotus says that Christ's superabundant merit is indispensable,

---

[1] Wendel, *op. cit.*, pp. 94, 171; Alexander Gordon, " The Sozzini and their School, " I, *The Theological Review*, 65 (July, 1879), 293-322, esp. 315.

[2] "Dico, quod sicut omne aliud a Deo, ideo est bonum, quia a Deo volitum, et non est converso: sic meritum illud tantum bonum erat, pro quanto acceptabatur. " *Comment. sent. Lib.* III. Dist. 19, Quaest. I, 7 (ed. Antwerp, J. Keerberg, 1620: 140).

[3] All three agree that "meruit autem inquantum viator non inquantum comprehensor " (St. Bonaventura, *Compendium Theologicae Veritatis* Lib. IV, c. 16, " De merito Christi, " Lugduni ed., 1648, *Opera*, T. VI, p. 746, a distinction which guards against an adoptionist Christology being brought in with the doctrine of Christ's merits. According to Bonaventura, " .... meruit sibi vitam aeternam iam habitam et nobis habendam, " (*ibid.*). For us he merited " veniam, gratiam, et gloriam, stolam quoque carnis, et apertionem ianuae caelestis " (*ibid.*), and for himself he merited not " glorificationem mentis, quam iam habebat, meruit tamen sibi per humilitatem passionis accelerationem resurrectionis, glorificationem sui nominis, et dignitatem iudiciariae potestatis.... " (*ibid.*). Cf. St. Thomas, *Summae Theologicae Pars Tertia*, Q. 46, Art. 3 (Migne ed., Paris, 1858, Tomus IV: 417), Q. 48, Art. 1 (Migne ed., IV: 444), and Q. 49, Art. 3 (Migne ed., IV: 455). Scotus, " pie sentiendo cum Magistro (who taught that Christ merited for himself impassibility of body and soul) et pie glossando, " maintains that although Christ did not merit directly the impassibility of both, still he merited the cessation of the miracle by which the divine glory had been kept from overflowing completely his soul and body. *Comment. Sent. Lib.* III, dist. 18, Quaest. unica, 15 (ed. Antwerp, J. Keerberg, 1620: 134).

[4] In the 1555 response Calvin does not consider the question of whether Christ merited anything for himself, and in 1559 he adds Inst. II, 17, 6 a note why such a question is unprofitable: " Quid enim opus fuit descendere unicum Dei Filium ut sibi acquireret quicquam novi ? ", OS III: 514.

but not entirely sufficient for our salvation.[1] For Calvin, Christ's merit means exactly that no merit is required or can be offered to supplement or complete Christ's deserving. Above all, Calvin and Scotus are interested in slightly different things in the way they relate Christ's merits and the will of God. Scotus is especially careful to emphasize the fact that unless favorably accepted by God, Christ's work would not be meritorious. Calvin's interest is more positive. He makes it absolutely clear that Christ's work is meritorious for us because God has in fact so ordained it. Scotus leaves more room, at least hypothetically, for the satisfaction of God by another offering. Calvin says such consideration is limited by the fact that God had ordained the fitting sacrifice of obedience in place of the offense of disobedience.

As a result of Laelius' question, Calvin was forced to give expanded clarification to the doctrine of the merit of Christ.[2] The question had this effect on Calvin because of its urgency and form, not because the concern which it reflected was original with Socinus.[3] If[4] behind Laelius' first question there is the conviction that the doctrine of the merits of Christ is incompatible with the free grace of God, we are in touch with one of the many forms of the dissolution of the medieval synthesis on the basis, not of the neglect of theology, but of the outworking of one aspect of the *potentia absoluta-potentia ordinata* distinction so cha-

---

[1] Scotus says Christ, by his merit, took away the obstacle which blocked way to heaven; he gained first grace for all, so that the human will on its own cannot merit that which is given only in baptism. With the exception of baptised infants, no one actually enters heaven who, if he has fallen into actual sin after his baptism, does not supply a *meritum de congruo*, thus cooperating with God by making use of the first fruit which Christ merited for us. *Comm. Sent. Lib.* III, dist. 19, 8 (edition *op. cit.*, 140). Gabriel Biel can even go so far as to say that if we do not add our merits to those of Christ, his merits will be not only insufficient but non-existent. See Heiko A. Oberman, *The Harvest of Medieval Theology* (Cambridge, Mass., 1963), pp. 268, 84.

[2] Through the 1554 Latin edition of the Institutes the doctrine of the merit of Christ was assumed rather than explicated and was only briefly, if clearly, treated: " Huius obedientiae merito factum est, ut reconciliaretur generi humano coelestis pater, quod ante toto animo aversabatur " (VII, 18, CO 1: 523). " Nam Dei benevolentiam, in qua potissima vitae arrha fiduciaque consistit, Christum sacrificii sui virtute nobis esse promeritum toties scriptura docet, ut nihil frequentius.... " (VII, 18, CO 1: 524).

[3] We find the difficulty recognized in one of St. Thomas' objections: " .... in psal. 24: 10 dicitur: *Universae viae Domini misericordia et ver et veritas.* Sed non videtur necessarium quod pateretur ex parte misericordiae divinae, quae sicut gratis dona tribuit, ita videtur quod gratis debita relaxet absque satisfactione...., " St. Thomas, *Summa Theologica*, Pars III, Q. 46, Art. 1, obj. 3 (Migne ed., Tomus IV: 413). Socinus was apparently alerted to the perplexing aspects of the traditional doctrine by Camillo Renato (cf. the article in this volume on Camillo Renato by George H. Williams; cf. also Illgen, *op. cit.*, pp. 35, 39-40); and his inquiry may have been further sharpened, as some have suggested, by his reading of Bullinger's *De Gratia Dei Justificante Libri IV* (Trechsel, *op. cit.*, 166-167, 436-437; Gordon, *op. cit.*, 315).

[4] We do not know whether this question was only the form by which Socinus meant to argue a theological position he had worked out or whether it was genuinely designed to gain aid in solving a difficulty with which he was confronted. For an especially ambitious attempt to discern the intent behind Laelius' public expression, see Edward M. Hulme, " Lelio Sozzini's Confession of Faith, " *Persecution and Liberty: Essays in Honor of George Lincoln Burr*, New York, Century, pp. 221-224.

racteristic of late medieval nominalism.[1] If Laelius' question actually registers a dissatisfaction, it is not with the conviction that our salvation should be assigned to God's absolute will; it implies only dissatisfaction with the conviction that within this absolute will there can be a holy anger with men which needs appeasement by propitiatory oblation. There is a continuity of speculation about the absolute power of God on the part both of the "evangelical rationalists" of the Radical Reformation[2] and the late medieval nominalists.[3] This continuum of theorizing accounts in one way for the similarity of the criticism which the classical Reformers directed against both groups: both were judged to be given over to idle speculation. The warning Calvin speaks about the schoolmen he also directs to Socinus. His words to him, although written about the questions on the resurrection of the flesh, apply to what the Genevan Reformer considered Socinus' overly curious bent of mind: "If you want more (than I have given in my response) you will have to look elsewhere. For you will never get me, as a favor to you, to overstep the limits laid down by the Lord."[4]

---

[1] Heiko A. Oberman, "Some Notes on the Theology of Nominalism with Attention to its Relation to the Renaissance," *Harvard Theological Review*, 53 (1960), 47-76, especially 50-51. For an alternative view see that of George Lindbeck who considers that which unites the diverse currents of nominalism to be a preoccupation with the question of meaning and evidence: "Nominalism and the Problem of Meaning as Illustrated by Pierre d'Ailly on Predestination and Justification," *HTR*, 52 (1959), 43-60. Francis Oakley concludes that at least so far as d'Ailly is concerned the issue of meaning and evidence is not the motivating force of his thought but that to which his theological reflection forces him. Thus it is the *potentia-absoluta-ordinata* distinction which generates the distinction d'Ailly draws between *evidentia absoluta* and *evidentia conditionata vel secundum quis*. Francis Oakley, "Pierre d'Ailly and the Absolute Power of God: Another Note on the Theology of Nominalism," *HTR*, 56 (1963), 59-73.

[2] To use, for the moment, George H. Williams' terminology: *Spiritual and Anabaptist Writers*, ed. G. H. Williams and A. M. Mergal (Library of Christian Classics, XXV, Philadelphia, 1957), 23-24.

[3] The nominalist theologians felt free to speculate about what might have been provided for according to God's absolute power (Could the Word have become incarnate in an ass or a stone? Could God have been satisfied with an offering made by an angel? Could men be justified before God without contributing any merits of their own?) They remained loyal sons of Rome in the midst of this speculation because they maintained an obedient stance before the decrees of the Church's infallible *magisterium*. Although God might have done things otherwise *de potentia absoluta*, he did, in fact, ordain those ways which the Church infallibly teaches that he did. When, however, ecclesiastical positivism falls away, a restraining force and the same speculation about the absolute power of God remains; human reason is viewed as freely capable of sounding the depths of the mystery of God's dealing with men and even of passing final judgment on the Biblical traditional account of God's economy. Applied to soteriology, this confidence in speculation can mean that the entire concept of merits is subjected to rapid erosion: Could God have freely forgiven sinners apart from Christ's death and obedience which merited forgiveness for us? Although the Church teaches that we are dependent on the merits of Christ, and although the Scriptures contain many suggestions of God's being propitiated by Christ's sacrifice and his deserving life for us, it does not seem reasonable that God should require such meritorious sacrifice on Christ's part.

[4] "Si plura desideras, aliunde petenda sunt. Quoniam nunquam a me impetrabis, ut sibi studio fines a Domino positos transsiliam," Dec. 7, 1549, CO 13: 485. Even Socinus' usual defender, Bullinger, felt called upon to instruct him on the limits of specu-

The limits which, according to Calvin, God laid down as those within which theological inquiry could legitimately occur were those permitting His children to know of Him and His ways through his revelation witnessed to by the Scriptures illumined by the testimony of the Holy Spirit in the body of the faithful, the Church. Quite clearly Socinus considered his questions to be Biblically motivated, and quite clearly most of his questions, especially those of 1549, had a practical impulse behind them. He saw less sharply, however, than Calvin the separation between God's ways and thoughts and human ways and thoughts. He had a more exalted view of the power of human reason to encompass and render into a rationally coherent whole the various Biblical testimonies and their various traditional interpretations. Calvin intended, by contrast, to confine his discussion and thought to activity which God has in fact ordained. With regard to redemption this entailed a conviction that Christ was obedient to the will of the Father, and that this obedience led him to the cross as the way God took for redemption. Such a disciplined view of salvation holds to God's benevolence and justice without defining them in such a way that "the force and power of Christ's death,"[1] as Calvin spoke of it, is dissipated for us.

The concept of Christ's merits seemed to pose obstacles for the tenet of the full sufficiency of God's will and his faithfulness for salvation. However, the same realities seemed to be vulnerable on another flank, namely that of the observable data of the feeling and behaviour of persons who, having come in contact with the Gospel, feel that they are elect although in reality they may not be. It is plain that many who claim to have genuine faith may be among the reprobate, and it is equally plain that many true believers are often beset with doubt and grave uncertainty.

It is to these tensions that Calvin is pressed to address himself in the remaining three responses. The three questions seem to be somewhat as follows: Question two: If one begins with the affirmation that only the predestined have saving faith and feel the efficacy of the Gospel, then how can one assign faith to the reprobate without implying that God is one who takes back what he has once given and therefore cannot be counted on? Question three: if faith, which is understood as knowledge of the divine will towards us and a certain conviction of its truth, disappears, how does one avoid the implication that both God's will and his truth are changeable? Question four: If it is necessary to stir up a mutual love in the hearts of the reprobate,

---

lation: "Video te studiosissimum esse sacrarum literarum et negotii salutis nostrae verae, sed simul etiam valde curiosum, qui multos subinde quaestionum nodos flectis et reflectis, implicas item et dissolvi postulas.... Nostra religio non est infinita, sed in compendium redacta. Haec recte intellecta simplicem quoque scripturae sensum sufficit, nihil admittit alienum, omnia refert ad pietatem, nihil curat quaestiones varias et implicatas. Non probat Apostolus eos, qui semper discunt, nunquam ad cognitionem veritatum, ut in ea acquiescant, perveniunt." Trechsel, II, 450.

[1] CO 10 a, 161; Inst. II, 17, 4, OS III, 512.

how can one say that they are affected with a certain sense of divine grace?[1]

Responding to these, Calvin draws a basic distinction between awareness of divine grace and saving faith. The reprobate, as well as the predestined, may, and indeed do, have a sense of divine grace, or, which is the same thing, a persuasion of divine love as being paternal. But, in the reprobate, this sense of divine grace is accompanied by a faith which passes away and bears no lasting fruit, whereas in the predestined, it is accompanied by genuine faith which is confidence in God that may grow weak and deficient but will never disappear from their hearts.[2] Properly speaking, what distinguishes the elect and the reprobate on this level is not the continuous existence of a sense of divine grace, but the testimony of the Holy Spirit which is the one sure guarantee and seal of adoption.[3] The Spirit of adoption assures us that we are judged by God, not on the basis of our own power and condition, which would leave us damned before his righteousness, but as covered by Christ's righteousness and as participants in his benefits. If one wants to be certain of his election, he should gaze on Christ, not on his own spiritual condition. It can, however, still be asked: how does one differentiate the true from a counterfeit Spirit of adoption? And if one cannot do so, what happens to the assurance of faith?[4]

Calvin's answers will come as a surprise to those expecting from him a fearless and coldly rational *syllogismus practicus*, i.e., an argument from one's outward conduct, and especially from one's evident peace and prosperity, to the conclusion that one is of the elect company.[5] Calvin explicitly combats the false and misleading security which may abound in the reprobate and which is not a sign of the gift of the Spirit of adoption. The elect are taught to examine themselves carefully and humbly lest "the security of the flesh creep in and replace assurance of faith."[6] A well developed *syllogismus practicus* would

---

[1] Cf. Illgen, *op. cit.*, p. 40.

[2] CO 10 a, 165; Inst. III, 2, 12, OS IV, 22.

[3] CO 10 a, 163-164; Inst. III, 2, 11, OS IV, 21 (for the elect, faith never finally or totally disappears: cf. Jürgen Moltmann, *Prädestination und Perseveranz* (Neukirchen, 1961), p. 56.

[4] Cf. Sermon on Deut. 12: 1-2, CO 42: 127; Comm. Acts 13:48. CO 48: 314; and "Quod si in eum sumus electi, non in nobis ipsis reperiemus electionis nostrae certitudinem: ac ne in Deo quidem Patre, si nudum illum absque Filio imaginamur. Christo ergo *speculum* est in quo electionem nostram imaginamur." Inst. III, 24, 5, OS IV, 415-416. (According to Calvin), "Unüberwindlich ist der Glaubende nicht in sich selber, sondern allein in Christus. Aber nicht in einem personal von seinen Gleidern Separierten Christus an sich, nicht in dem Christus, 'der in weiter Ferne stünde,' sondern in dem Christus, 'der in uns wohnt'." Moltmann, *op. cit.*, p. 55.

[5] Moltmann, *op. cit.*, p. 49; W. Niesel, *The Theology of Calvin*, trans. H. Knight (Philadelphia, 1956), pp. 169-181; W. Knusche, *Das Wirken des Heiligen Geister nach Calvin* (Göttingen, 1957), pp. 244-245. The latter clearly shows that for Calvin we know of our election from the testimony of the Spirit and by looking to Christ, but also that we can discern signs of it in our sanctification.

[6] CO 10 a, 164; Inst. III, 2, 11, OS IV, 21.

be more consonant with "confidence of the flesh" than with "assurance of faith." The latter does not exclude the faithfuls' being subject to doubts, uncertainties, and fear. Indeed the faithful still discern a certain "wondrous" anger of God, not because God, of himself, hates them, but because he wants, one might say by way of accommodation,[1] to "frighten them by the feeling of his wrath in order to humble their fleshly pride, shake off their sluggishness, and arouse them to repentance."[2] In short, part of the God-given assurance of faith is the continual testing and movement to repentance God saves for the elect by which they are assured that God has not abandoned them to the false security and fleshly confidence to which they would otherwise incline.

In evaluating Calvin's response to this difficult problem, one must say that it is a great strength that he does not exempt the elect from the doubts, trials and uncertainties which are common to all men.

What is unique to the elect is that God, while never allowing the sense of divine mercy to degenerate into false security, never permits faith to be erased; even in the midst of deepest doubt and severest anguish the Spirit of adoption continues to cry "Abba, Father" for them.

On the other hand, this doctrine of the assurance of faith is open to criticism such as assaulted it in the sixteenth century. One criticism attacks the very presupposition that there are two classes of people, the elect and the reprobate, around which such a distinction can revolve. Even within the framework of a doctrine of predestination, one may object to the uncertainty in this doctrine of the assurance of faith, or perhaps that such assurance as there is cannot possibly be explained to one who has not genuinely sensed the Spirit of adoption. Presumably, only one who has had this sense can distinguish between God's damning wrath and that wondrous anger by which he upholds the elect in the way of salvation. As a second generation Reformer, Calvin had to delineate the evangelical assurance of faith against two alternatives: the first so enthusiastically took one's salvation for granted that it presumed on God's grace and disdained and neglected the ordinances for life in this world; the second placed assurance finally on the declaration of a sacerdotal system which feared, above all, antinomianism and indifference towards sacramental grace.[3]

---

[1] For a discussion of the theme of accommodation in Calvin's thought, see E. A. Dowey, *The Knowledge of God in Calvin's Theology* (New York, Columbia, 1952), pp. 1-18.

[2] "Dico etiam Deum mirabiliter irasci filiis suis quos amare non desinit: non quod apud se eos oderit, sed quia eos terrere vult irae suae sensu, ut superbiam carnis humiliet, torporem excutiat, ad poenitentiam sollicitet." CO 10 a, 165; Inst. III, 2, 12, OS IV, 22-23.

[3] See the Council of Trent's *Decretum de justificatione* (Sess. VI), Cap. 9, "Contra inanem haereticorum fiduciam"; Henry Denzinger et C. Rahner, *Enchiridion Symbolorum*, ed. 31 (Barcellona, 1960), p. 289. There was consensus at the Sixth Session of the Tridentine Council that what should be condemned was the certainty of faith in

Calvin was not attempting, obviously, to steer a course between two contemporary extremes; but his central contentions and the extremes on either side were identified as such, according to Calvin's interpretation of the matter, by Biblical testimony.

In what, then, consisted the particular Laelian contribution to the development of Calvin's thought on the doctrines of the merits of Christ and the assurance of faith? Socinus did not contribute to Calvin's development of these doctrines by maintaining a clearly enunciated position which the latter incorporated in some form into his own thinking and writing. But out of his encounter, Calvin was moved more carefully and fully to work out both doctrines. The ripe expression Calvin gave to them takes into consideration the difficulties which are met in the doctrines and of which Laelius' questions were insistent reminders. It is this urgent demand to confront the ambiguities and to attempt to deal with them more satisfactorily that was the Laelian influence on Calvin's thought. It is a tribute both to the stubborness of the inquiring mind and to the faithfulness with which the theologian sought new ways of expressing evangelical doctrine, that these questions, posed by Socinus, found their way into Calvin's mature theological expression.

---

the Lutheran sense, i.e. in the sense in which it was condemned at Paris, April 15, 1521. But the Council engaged in lively discussion as it attempted to go beyond condemning the " heterical " view to speaking on the " Catholic " view. At least two different impulses were present in those discussions, representing Saint Thomas' view (that one could not be sure he was in a state of grace unless he knows " *ex revelatione* " and " *ex conjecturis* " (from the fact that he rejoices in God, despises worldly things, and similar indications) and representing Scotus' views (which, although variously interpreted at Trent, argued for the possibility of a certainty of grace as based on one's ability to rely on the unfailing efficacy of Baptism). Costacciari, the General of the Conventuals, felt it necessary to defend Scotus by poiting out that whereas for Luther, certainty of faith is based on the divine promise, with Duns, certainty is based on the preparations which precede and upon the power of the sacrament *ex opere operato*. The issue was not clearly settled at Trent, which chose the ambiguous wording to describe what kind of certainty was being rejected: " .... cum nullus scire valeat certitudine fidei, cui non potest subesse falsum, se gratiam Dei esse consecutum. " (Denziger, *op. cit.*, p. 289) (CT V, 484) (*Concilium Tridentinum*, vol. V, ed. S. Ehses, Freiburg, 1911, p. 484).

JOHN A. TEDESCHI AND JOSEPHINE VON HENNEBERG

" CONTRA PETRUM ANTONIUM A CERVIA RELAPSUM ET BONONIAE CONCREMATUM "

INTRODUCTION[1]

On the seventh of June, 1567, Fra Domenico da Imola, the trusted agent of Cardinal Morone, Bishop of Modena, reported to his absent superior on the progress achieved against the spread of the Protestant heresy in his diocese:

Last week I went to the Inquisitor in Bologna to see if, among so many prisoners, there were any Modenese; and he replied no, except for that Cervia, whom Your Excellency knows how I pursued to have in my hands; he has confessed certain accomplices who in part are dead and in part have recanted....[2]

The revelations made by Pietro Antonio da Cervia, sometime soldier, painter,[3] farm steward, and indigent evangelical proselytizer before the Inquisition in Bologna dealt a serious blow to the fortunes of the reformed movement in the Modenese.[4] A pliant, talkative, and fearful prisoner who did not hesitate to implicate his wife in his heresy, Cervia through his testimony has provided us with a rich source for understanding the doctrines, rudimentary "institutions,"[5] and even the social mores of certain reformed Italians at the mid-mark of the sixteenth century.

The proceedings of the first trial instituted against Cervia in Modena on 22 December, 1563, at the instigation of Fra Bonifacio of

---

[1] It is a pleasure to aknowledge our debt to Prof. Antonio Rotondò of Modena, who generously brought the existence of this trial to our attention. It is preserved in manuscript in the Archivio di Stato of Modena, Inquisizione, busta: *Processi 1550-1565*. It has survived in the original for the two hearings dated 1563 and 1564; for the last three sessions, all of 1567, we have a copy.

[2] A. Mercati, *Il Sommario del Processo di Giordano Bruno con Appendice di Documenti sull'eresia e l'Inquisizione a Modena nel secolo XVI* (Città del Vaticano, 1942), p. 141.

[3] He is called a painter by A. Battistella, *Il Sant Officio e la Riforma Religiosa in Bologna* (Bologna, 1905), p. 99.

[4] There is no comprehensive modern study of this phenomenon. The existing literature and work in progress are cited by Prof. Williams in his study on Camillo Renato elsewhere in this volume.

[5] In their connection, one should note Delio Cantimori's important distinction between a "religious community" (consisting of an actual ecclesiastical organization within which cultic rites are performed) and the "conventicle," composed of laymen who, with or without the assistance of pastors met to discuss religious issues, read from Scripture, or listen to reports brought by brethren from Geneva and the Grisons. Under this criterion, the only Italian religious community recognized by Cantimori is the one that flourished in Cremona *c.* 1550. *Prospettive di storia ereticale italiana del Cinquecento* (Bari, 1960), pp. 57 ff.

Mantova, Vicar to the Inquisitor of Modena, have only been preserved for two sessions, the latter ending, 2 January, 1564. Apparently, Cervia was persuaded to recant and reembrace the Catholic faith. After almost three years of freedom, he was seized in Bologna as a relapsed heretic and again placed on trial on the sixth day of February, 1567. In contrast to many Inquisitorial ordeals which often spanned entire years, his second trial under the presidency of Fra Antonio Balduzzi, Inquisitor of Bologna, terminated in June.

The policy of the Roman Church was to deal severely with the twice-fallen. Cervia's melancholy end is briefly narrated in a contemporary document:

.... and on the fifth day of September (1567), six ounces of wax were consumed for the accompaniment to justice of M. Pellegrino Righetti, painter of Bologna, and Pietro Antonio da Cervia, Lutherans; and they were hanged and burned in the square.... They died, so far as one could tell, in the state of grace and in the knowledge of the true faith.[1]

IN THE NAME OF CHRIST, AMEN.

The 22nd day of December in the year of the Lord, 1563

Since I, Fra Bonifacio of Mantua of the Order of Preachers, Vicar to the Reverend Father Fra Camillo of Pavia, Inquisitor General of all the dominion of Ferrara, have heard from people worthy of faith that a certain Pelegrino de Varanis of Fiorano[2] had said that in the city of Modena there dwelled a certain man, called Cervia, who spoke and thought erroneously about those matters which pertain to the holy Catholic faith, and about the sacrifice of the Mass and things of that sort; and moreover that he had heard from the aforenamed Cervia that in the city of Modena there existed a certain congregation of more than thirty men who read heretical books and who held erroneous opinions about the Catholic faith; therefore desiring to learn the truth about this matter, I summoned the abovenamed Pelegrino by order of the office of the most holy Inquisition on the day as above at the 19th hour. He appeared and I, having administered to him the oath to speak the truth, interrogated him as appears below:

Having been asked firstly whether he knew that he was bound both by the precept of God and by the command of the Church to reveal to the Inquisitor or his Vicar if he knew any man who was a heretic or suspected of heresy, he replied: "I believe one is allowed to denounce them." Interrogated if he knew any heretic or suspect of heresy, he replied: "I know one who is called Pietro Antonio da

[1] A. Battistella, *op. cit.*, p. 99, n. 2 who cites from the Archivio dell'Ospedale di S. M. della Morte: *Libro dei Morti*, vol. I, f. 169.

[2] unidentified

Cervia who, while in my house, said that it was not good to go to Mass or to say so many *Pater Nosters* or *Ave Marias*, because these are the inventions of the friars of San Domenico." Similarly he testified that he had heard him say that "priests and friars are all of the devil's household for all the masses and vespers they say."

Interrogated "As to when and where he had said the above-mentioned things," he replied "that he had said these things in the home of Borello,[1] near San Giacobo," which is where said Pelegrino dwelled. Interrogated "As to who had been present," he replied "that his wife had been present."

Interrogated "As to whether he had heard Cervia say that in the city of Modena there existed a congregation of men who read heretical books," he replied "that he had heard it from the very mouth of Pietro Antonio Cervia that there were almost thirty who called themselves brothers and who met in the home of Mr. Gratian,[2] and read to each other." Also, "he had seen a book in Cervia's possession, of which Cervia said, 'if this should be found on me, I would be burned at once'."

Also, he testified "that when Cervia was ill, he was cured by that group called the brothers and this" he says "I heard from the mouth of Cervia." He also testified that "the aforenamed Mr. Gratian used to come to talk with this Cervia, and beseeched said Pellegrino to give him (Cervia) work."

Interrogated "whether he had ever heard Cervia himself say by name that he had others either as brothers or as accomplices," he replied that he had not.

He testified also that when he was once in a certain inn, located beyond the river called Samoza,[3] he saw a certain booklet, which was called the indulgence of the Lutherans,[4] and contained many blasphemous words against the faith, in the hands of Cervia, who read it before them, namely the host and one who is called...,[3] and who stays in the home of a Bolognese gentleman.

---

[1] unidentified

[2] He was one of the central figures in the Modenese heretical movement. In the unpublished trial before the Inquisition of the Modenese printer and bookseller, Antonio Gadaldino (1557-1560), Gratiani is mentioned as one who frequented his shop. See "Contra Magistrum Antonium Gadaldinum," Archivio di Stato di Modena, Inquisizione, busta 3, *Processi 1550-1565*, f. 12. He appears in the records of the Roman Inquisition published by C. Corvisieri, "Compendio dei processi del Santo Uffizio di Roma (da Paolo III a Paolo IV)," *Archivio della Società Romana di Storia Patria*, III (1880), 278: "Iacobus Gratianus mutinensis suspectus." After his flight, he was burned in effigy with other Modenese "luterani," Giovanni Conselice, Pietro and Antonio Biancolini. Cf. the manuscript "Cronaca Carandina" under date 28 January, 1570 cited by T. Sandonnini, *Lodovico Castelvetro e la sua famiglia* (Bologna, 1882), p. 227.

[3] The river Samoggia intersects the Bologna road *c.* 20 kilometers from Modena.

[4] It is possible that this curious title refers to the printed edition of Luther's 95 Theses first published in Wittenberg in 1517 as the *Disputatio D. Martini Luther Theologi, pro declaratione virtutis indulgentiarum.* Several editions are listed in the *British Museum, General Catalogue of Printed Books* (London, 1962), v. 146, col. 652.

[5] Text unclear.

Interrogated "As to whether he knew the surname and parentage of that Gratiani and in what street he lived," he replied "that he did not know the parentage, but that he dwelled by San Giacobo."

Interrogated "As to whether he had said the preceding things out of hate or love," he replied: "I have said them because they appeared to me obnoxious things, and not because of any hate or malevolence that I bear against him."

This done by me, Fra Paolo Vallato of Mantua, of the Order of Preachers, Notary of the Sacred Inquisition in the city of Modena, present the reverend Fathers, Fra Nicodemo of Modena and Fra Leandro of Bologna, in the chamber of the Reverend Father of the Order of Preachers, Fra Bonifacio of Mantua, Vicar of the Reverend Inquisitor of Modena; this interrogation having been recorded by the aforesaid Vicar himself.

The second day of January, 1564

There appeared before the Reverend Father Fra Camillo of Pavia, Inquisitor of Ferrara, Modena, and Reggio, Urselina, wife of Peregrino de' Varrani, an inhabitant of Modena in the section of St. Agatha, summoned by order of the Holy Office so that certain information might be received from her. After she had been warned and had been administered the oath about telling the truth, when interrogated she replied as appears below:

Interrogated "As to whether she knew anybody who was a heretic or a follower of the doctrine of heretics," she replied, "I know of none other besides one called Cervia who used to reproach me because I went to mass, saying that to stay at home and recite *Paternostri* with one's heart turned to God was of as much value as going to Mass. And he used to exhort my husband not to permit me to go, and this with many Latin words that I did not understand."

Interrogated "As to whether he said such things to her often," she replied, "He spoke to me thus on more than one occasion."

Interrogated "As to the place and time," she replied, "In the house where we dwelled by San Giacomo, and it was a year ago in the season of the masks." [2]

Interrogated "As to who was present," she replied, "There was no one else besides my husband."

Interrogated "Whether he had urged her not to go to Mass because he said that the mass is a human invention and not a sacrifice, and that the true body of Christ is not immolated in it," she replied, "He did not tell me other than what I have said."

Interrogated "Whether she had heard him say that those who celebrated the mass were damned," she replied, "Father, no."

Interrogated "Whether she had heard him boasting about his

---

[1] The period of several weeks known as Carnevale, celebrated with balls and masquerades, preceding Lent.

accomplices and brothers," she replied, "He used to say a multitude of things, but I paid no attention and I do not remember anything other than this."

Interrogated "Whether she had testified or kept silent from hate or love or any human consideration," she replied, "Father no, I have told the truth."

Done in the Church of San Domenico in the city of Modena, present the Reverend Father Fra Bonifacio of Mantua of the Order of Preachers, and reverend Vicar of the Inquisitor, and Fra Cirillo of Lugo of the Order of Preachers, witnesses having been requested and summoned. And I fra Nicolò of Reggio was Notary by Apostolic authority.

The sixth day of February, 1567

Pietro Antonio di Blasio de' Carundii de' Cervia having been arraigned personally before the Reverend Father Fra Antonio Balduccio[1] of Forlì, Inquisitor of the city of Bologna, assisted by the Magnificent Lord the Fiscal Advocate,[2] in the torrone[3] of said city; having been administered the oath in the form and interrogated and examined both against himself as a principal, and against others as witness, responded, spoke, confessed, and testified as follows:

"In Modena I am known as a Lutheran because I had constant dealings with the aforenamed, and I have known M. Giovanni Rangoni,[4] a Paolo Soperchio,[5] a M. Francesco Camurando;[6] the latter two

---

[1] The Dominican Balduzzi served as Inquisitor of Bologna from 1560-1572. He was Bishop of Trevico from 1576 until his death in 1580. J. Quetif, *Scriptores Ordinis Praedicatorum.... Tomus Secundus, Pars I 1499-1639* (Lutetiae Parisiorum, 1721), 256 ascribes two works to him: "Tractatus de auctoritate summi pontificis," and "Tractatus alter de fide."

[2] The public accuser.

[3] The *criminale* or criminal court of Bologna.

[4] Rangone, the bearer of a distinguished Modenese name, fled Italy when summoned to appear before the Inquisition in Rome. The sentence pronounced *in absentia* against "Johannes Rangonum Mutinensem" on 7 September, 1566 is in K. Benrath, "Atti originali dell'Inquisizione Romana," *La Rivista Cristiana*, VIII (1880), 11-12. He is condemned to bear the stigma of eternal infamy and the confiscation of his property. In January, 1552 he established a silk shop in partnership with M. Pelegrino de' Sette, who is named by Cervia as one of his heretical companions in Modena (see below p. 251). The event is recorded by Tommasino de' Bianchi detto de' Lancellotti, *Cronaca Modenese*, Monumenti di storia patria delle provincie Modenesi, Serie delle cronache, 17 vols. (Parma, 1861-1919), XI, 112. It is possible that the document entitled "1554 - Eretici che erano in Ferrara al tempo di Madama Renea," published by B. Fontana, *Renata di Francia*, 3 vols. (Rome, 1889-1899), III, xliv refers to our man: "Ludovico Palavicino in bagnacavallo for his letter of 23 May, [15]49; and one can also entertain doubts concerning Gio. Batista Rangone...."

[5] A Pietro Paolo Superchio appears in 1547 as a supplicant in a civil case. Recorded by Lancellotti, *Cronaca*, X, 72. In 1548 he is one of the *conservatori* of Modena, *ibid.*, p. 267.

[6] Francesco Camurando (also Camorana, Camerone, Camerona) was a prominent student of Greek and Latin in the suspected "Academy" of Giovanni Grillenzone in Modena. Cf. M. Maylender, *Storia delle Accademie d'Italia*, 5 vols. (Bologna, 1926-1930),

are dead; also Gasparo di Rocco Calzolaro,[1] another called 'the Cathaldo',[2] Gemignano Tamburino,[3] Claudio Carandino[4] who is dead; and I have not known others to be heretics and Lutherans in Modena. All these used charity towards me, and gave me bread and wine and money[5] and wood to live and sustain my small family.

III, 123-128; G. Tiraboschi, *Biblioteca Modenese*, 6 vols. (Modena, 1781-1786), I, 7. See also the excerpt from the 1568 trial against Geminiano Calegari published by T. Sandonnini, *op. cit.*, p. 169. The accused testified that "It was in his home, where he had been teaching these heresies for about twenty-four years, that Francesco Camurana converted me; and in this house, in my presence, various people discussed these heresies, namely Messer Ludovico Castelvetro, a physician of the Grillenzoni family now dead, Master Tommaso Bavellino, Giovanni Antonio de' Rossi, Machella the physician, and several others." Lodovico Castelvetro in his testament dated November, 1553 specified that Camorana, and a few others, should always have access to the library which he would someday leave in his brothers' care. The document is published by L. A. Muratori in *Opere varie critiche di Lodovico Castelvetro.... non più stampate* (Lyons, 1727), p. 76. C. Cantù, *Gli Eretici d'Italia*, 3 vols. (Turin, 1866-1868), II, 20, on the basis of A. Caracciolo's ms. Life of Paul IV, includes him in that notorious group active in the Modenese area which, "used to send aid to the heretics in Germany." The name of "Franciscus Camerona mutinensis haereticus," appears in the fragmentary list of those tried by the Roman Inquisition published by Corvisieri, *op. cit.*, p. 275.

[1] unidentified

[2] Fra Domenico da Imola, the trusted agent in Modena of Cardinal Bishop Morone, reported to his superior on 7 June, 1567 that his (Imola's) policy of leniency towards penitent heretics was generally disapproved. He admitted that occasionally his trust had been misplaced: "having seen that some had betrayed me, I began to go after them; for this, a certain Cataldo who later recanted, twice sought to cause me displeasure with arms." The letter is published by A. Mercati, *op. cit.*, p. 141. He may be the Cataldo Bozzale who in September, 1566 was languishing in Modena, a prisoner of the Inquisition. His advocate, a Ser Marsilio Seghizzo, petitioned the city authorities to indemnify his client for the costly expenses of his imprisonment which the Inquisitor was seeking to extract from him. The itemized list of expenses is in T. Sandonnini, *op. cit.*, p. 341.

[3] Tamburino, a Modenese heretic of modest birth, appears frequently in Mercati's documents, first as a suspect and later, thanks to Cervia's disclosures, as prisoner of the Inquisition. Fra Domenico's letter (see above, p. 245) relates that our Cervia "has confessed the names of certain accomplices, some of whom are dead and some of whom have recanted; and of one other who, although under suspicion, has not yet been questioned, a certain *tamborino* in Modena." A subsequent letter to Morone from Fra Domenico, dated the day of Saint Francis, 1567 reports that, "we are about to imprison three others; a Geminiano Taborino and a Giovanni Padovano, both Modenese and of low condition, for old errors; and a certain Albert.... who a while back was in Modena; but I am waiting for the Governor, who has gone to Montefestino to provide the secular arm (il brazo)." Mercati, *op. cit.*, p. 142. Lastly, in a document entitled "1568 - Suspecti in fide," *ibid.*, p. 144 we read the following entry: "Pietro Madonina: we must interrogate the imprisoned *tamburino* if he had him as an accomplice, and if he holds erroneous opinions concerning the faith. Should he testify nothing against him, it will become necessary to summon him and administer a sound warning." A marginal note in another hand informs that, "Tamburino says that he doesn't know anything."

[4] The marriage in February, 1549 of a Claudio Carandino with a Madama Dalida, widow of M. Julio Castelvetro, is reported by Lancellotti, *Cronaca*, XI, 22; he may be the same Claudio Carandino who in 1551 was a supervisor of victuals in Modena, *ibid.*, p. 50.

[5] T. Sandonnini, *op. cit.*, p. 198 serves himself of precisely this passage to support his statement that, "The Academy, following Castelvetro's example, made propaganda with the assistance of money, when words were not enough."

Those who taught me and were my masters were the above named Modenese who used to meet in the shop of M. Piergiovanni;[1] and there we used to discuss and treat the things mentioned previously, and read books in the vulgar tongue, such as the New Testament translated by Antonio Brucciolo,[2] and a certain book of Calvin's which discussed the Mass."[3]

(This testimony) accepted.

The last day of February, 1567

Led from prison, the aforenamed Pietro Antonio di Blasio de' Carundii de' Cervia was arraigned against himself as principal and against others as witness in the presence of the Reverend Father Inquisitor and his assistant, the Magnificent Father Sebastian, the Fiscal Advocate, in the upper chamber of examinations.[4] After they had administered the oath, and he had received it, and after he was interrogated and examined, he responded, spoke, confessed, and testified as follows:

Interrogated "As to whether he wished to add anything, or to cancel from that which he had said and confessed in the other session," he replied, "I would like to add this in regard to my companions, namely that I have known a Mr. Vincenzo Quistello of Mirandola,[5] and Mr. Iacomo Cavazza of Modena,[6] and a M. Gio. Battista Magnano[7] as heretics. And of these three, Cavazza and Magnano are dead, and Pelegrino di Sette[8] also is dead. Mr. Vincenzo Quistello is

---

[1] Pier Giovanni Biancolino's name appears frequently in the trial. He was burned in effigy as a *luterano*. See above p. 247, n. 2.

[2] The Florentine Brucioli's Italian translation of the Old and New Testaments, many times revised by other hands outside of Italy, served as the Bible of the Italian Reformation until it was supplanted by Giovanni Diodati's published in Geneva in 1607. The first edition of Brucioli's New Testament issued in Venice from the presses of Lucantonio Giunti in 1530. See G. Spini, "Bibliografia delle opere di Antonio Brucioli," *Bibliofilia*, XLII (1940), 129-180, and the model biography, *Tra Rinascimento e Riforma: Antonio Brucioli* (Florence, 1940). The records of Brucioli's trial for heresy are conserved in Venice, Archivio dei Frari, S. Uffizio Busta 51, Anni 1555-1558.

[3] Undoubtedly the BREVE E RI- / SOLUTO TRA- / tato de la Cena del Signore com / posto da M. Gio Cal. e tradotto / nuouamente in lingua volgare / Italiana. / I. COR. XI. / *Proui l'huomo se stesso, e cosi mangi di / questo Pane, & beua di que- / sto Calice. / Appresso Francesco Durone. / M.D.LXI.* This anonymous Italian translation of Calvin's *Petite traicté de la Sainte Cene* (first published in Geneva in 1541) is unknown to A. Erichson, *Bibliographia Calviniana* (Berlin, 1900). A copy is conserved in the Biblioteca Casanatense in Rome (Miscellanea 2402, int. 2).

[4] The Bolognese Inquisition occupied a few rooms attached to the monastery of San Domenico. One of them in an upper floor served for the examinations conducted under torture. Cf. A. Battistella, *op. cit.*, p. 31.

[5] unidentified

[6] In the already cited document, "1568 - Suspecti in fide" (Mercati, *op. cit.*, p. 144), under the entry for Giulio Sadoletti, there is a probable reference to our man: "we should summon Cavazza, formerly his steward, to see if he will confirm the testimony which he has already given against him (Sadoleto) when they were enemies; it should be in the files of the Holy Office of the Inquisition and shall be found...."

[7] Lancellotti, *Cronaca*, X, 30 recalls that a Zan Battista Magnanino was a co-owner of large parcels of land with a certain Bernabe Thofanino, who died in February, 1547.

[8] For his association with Giovanni Rangoni, see above, p. 249, n. 4.

alive, and so is Mr. Giovanni Conselso,[1] who has departed with Mr. Giovanni Rangoni and with Maranello[2] and with Jacomo Gratiani, this past May. All these fled as heretics, and when they were summoned they did not want to appear."

Interrogated "That for the sake of truth he, the arraigned, should tell, omitting any mendacity, from what date he had begun to listen and adhere to heretical words and heretical propositions against the Catholic faith."

He replied, "It is going on eleven years that I have been in Modena, and I had been there about three years, before I began to hear heretical talk; so it is about seven or eight years since I began to listen and discuss.

And the first to speak to me about it was a Mr. Piergiovanni Biancalino[3] who has left Modena together with Mr. Giovanni Rangone and the others; the first occasion was when I asked him for a book to read for entertainment while they were on guard duty, and he gave me one which is the *Dialogo di Caronte e Mercurio*;[4] and he said that when I had read it, he would give me another even more beautiful. Thus, when I had finished reading that one, he gave me another one which

---

[1] He appears in Sandonnini's list (see above, p. 247) among the Modenese burned in effigy as *luterani*. Lancellotti, *Cronaca*, XI, 27 may be referring to our man in the entry dated 27 March, 1550: "Zohano Conselexe, citizen of Modena, has been conducted to prison this morning.... It is said that he was taken for suspicion of debt...." A later entry (*ibid.*, XII, 3) under the date 3 August, 1553 reports that Zohano Conselexe has become seriously ill in the home of his friend, M. Gerardino Molza, who had also been stricken with a serious fever.

[2] Giovanni Maria Tagliadi, originally from the neighboring town of Maranello, obtained Modenese citizenship in 1535 and died in his adopted city in 1574 after a long career as teacher of Latin and Greek. Two treatises on grammar are ascribed to his pen by G. Tiraboschi, *Biblioteca*, V, 163. In the already cited trial against Antonio Gadaldino (see p. 247, n. 2), he is named, together with Jacomo Gratiani, as one of the "suspecti de fide" who had frequented Gadaldino's book shop. Maranello seems to have brushed with the Inquisition on more than one occasion. In 1548-1550, he was tried in Modena and admitted that he had read a treatise by Servetus. Almost two decades later he reappears before the Modenese Inquisition. Writing to Cardinal Morone on 29 January, 1567, Fra Domenico da Imola reports that "this week Maranello who had shown reticence (quale stato in se stesso) during the first examinations.... has confessed the errors which he has held up to now, and I truly believe that he has resolved to be an honest man (homo da bene)." See Mercati, *op. cit.*, p. 140. To this good news, Morone replied, "I am indeed pleased that Maranello is becoming a good man, and the others also," *Ibid.*

[3] See p. 247, n. 2.

[4] This celebrated anti-Roman satire was, first published in Spanish, *c.* 1529. It's author, Alfonse de' Valdés (d. 1532), was secretary to the Emperor Charles V. The first Italian translation, dated 1546, was probably printed in Venice with the title: "Due dialoghi, / l'uno di Mercurio, et Caronte: / nel quale, oltre molte cose belle, gratiose, / et di bona dottrina, si racconta quel, che / accade nella guerra dopo l'anno, / MDXXI. / L'altro di Lattantio, et di uno / archidiacono: / nel quale puntualmente si trattano le cose / auenute in Roma nell'anno / MDXXVII. / Di Spagnuolo in Italiano con molta ac-/curatezza et tradotti, et reuisti. / MDXLVI / Con gratia, et privilegio, / per anni dieci. /" Edward Boehmer, *Bibliotheca Wiffeniana. Spanish reformers of two centuries*, 3 vols. (Strassburg, 1874-1904), I, 107-111, describes seven Italian editions in the 16th century. That the author was Alfonse rather than his brother Juan was proved by

is called the *Tragedia del libero arbitrio et delle religioni*,[1] that is, how they are founded and other things; and having finished reading this tragedy, he gave me another book which is called Agostino Mainardo Piedmontese[2] on the unique and perfect satisfaction of Jesus Christ, which affirmed that there was no other justification for our sins, besides Jesus Christ, both for the guilt or the penalty, whether temporal or eternal.

This Piergiovanni did not give me any other books; but when I eventually went to his shop, to which others also came, I made the acquaintance of Mr. Jacomo Gratiani who used to read there the epistles of St. Paul in the vulgar tongue.[3] And this Mr. Jacomo Gratiani brought

---

M. Bataillon, " Alonso de Valdés auteur du ' Dialogo de Mercurio y Caron, ' " *Homenaje ofrecido a Menendez Pidal* (Madrid, 1925), I, 403-415.

[1] The famous " DELLA TRAGE-/DIA DI M. FRANCESCO / NEGRO BASSA-NESE, / INTITOLATA / LIBERO AR-/BITRIO, / *Editione Seconda, / Con accrescimento.* / Dell'anno M.D.L. " In this second expanded edition, perhaps printed in Poschiavo (Grisons) by the Landolfi, this booklet became one of the most popular and widely diffused writings of the Italian Reformation. The *Tragedia*, in five acts, takes place in Rome in the course of a few hours with " Free Will " who has been selected by the Pope king of the Roman Catholic world as the protagonist; the disintegration of Papal authority commences from this event. Much rarer is the first edition of this work (1546); a copy is conserved in the Vatican Library (Capponi IV, 474). A Latin translation by Negri himself, dedicated to the Polish Prince Nicolas Radzivill, was published by Jean Crespin in Geneva in 1559, who a year earlier had already issued a French edition. Finally, in 1589 an English translation appeared in London under the imprint of J. Charlewood. The poet and former Benedictine, Francesco Negri of Bassano (b. 1500), was one of the first Italians to abandon his native land (1525) for reasons of religion. His wanderings led him from Strassburg to the Grisons and finally to Poland where he died in Cracow (1563). The most comprehensive study of Negri remains, G. Zonta, " Francesco Negri l'eretico e la sua tragedia, ' Il libero arbitrio '," *Giornale Storico della Letteratura Italiana*, 47 (1916), 264-324, 48 (1917), 108-160.

[2] " Trattato Dell'/Unica, Et Perfetta Sa/tisfattione di Christo, nel qual si dichi-/ara, & manifestamente per la parola di / Dio si proua, che sol Christo ha satis-/fatto per gli peccati del mondo, ne / quanto à Dio c'è altra satisfattione che / la sua, o sia per la colpa, o sia per la pe-/na, composto per *M. AGO.-/STINO MAINAR-/DO PIAMON/TESE. / M.D.LI.* This booklet, a staunch defense of the doctrine of justification by faith, by the former Augustinian Mainardo (1482-1563) who from 1541 served the reformed community of Chiavenna (Grisons) as its pastor, is today extremely rare. Two copies are conserved in the Zentralbibliothek, Zurich and in the Biblioteca Nazionale in Florence (Guicciardini 2-4²-37). It has been studied by Augusto Armand-Hugon, " Il Trattato della soddisfazione di Cristo di A. Mainardo, " *Bollettino della Società di Studi Valdesi*, LVIII (1939), 69-77; and *Agostino Mainardo, contributo alla storia della Riforma in Italia* (Torre Pellice, [1943]), especially pp. 93 ff.

[3] Italian editions of Paul's letters were available in different forms. Although they were most frequently read in New Testaments such as Brucioli's, Bernardino Ochino's commentaries on *Romans* and *Galatians* also circulated widely. It is also quite possible that the following rare booklet, dedicated to the Duchess Renata of Ferrara, enjoyed a certain success: " Le dotte e pie / PARAFRASI, SOPRA / le Pistole di Paolo à / Romani, Galati ed / Ebrei: non mai / piu vedute / in luce. / *Di M. Gian Francesco Virginio / Bresciano. / IN LIONE. / M.D.LI.*

Now very rare, copies survive in the National Library, Florence (Guicciardini, 1-4²-22) and in the Angelica of Rome (G. 9.15*). A second expanded edition was printed in Geneva by G. L. Paschale in 1555. A copy survives in the Guicciardini (2-4²-46). The *Parafrasi* on " Romans " (without " Galatians " and " Hebrews ") was reprinted by E. Comba in the *Biblioteca della Riforma Italiana*, 6 vols. (Florence, 1886), VI, 43-156. We lack biographical data about the author, Gian Francesco Virginio of Brescia.

me a book by Martin Luther which spoke of the sacrament of the eucharist,[1] saying that the mass was not a sacrifice but a commemoration, and that to want to institute another sacrifice was to despise the first which was Christ, and to make of Christ a liar since he had said that he was the true priest, and had sacrificed himself once and for all.

Likewise, in the shop of the same Piergiovanni, I struck up friendship with Jacomo Cavazza, because he too used to come to this shop together with those named above, and others still, to discuss and read on matters of heresy against the Catholic faith and the Roman church. This Cavazza gave me a book by John Calvin on the Mass, Indulgences, and similar things;[2] and I had many other books which these men, whom I have mentioned, gave to me, but I do not remember their titles.

I heard heretical matters discussed in the shop of Mr. Piergiovanni on numerous occasions. And I also took part in the discussions held there both with these men, and with the others whom I have named to you already; and not only did I listen and myself take part in these discussions of heretical matters against the Catholic faith in that shop, but also in the very homes of the individuals mentioned, meeting once in the house of one, another time in the house of a second. And frequently we even discussed in the squares and in the streets, but of course among ourselves. And the homes where we met on various occasions were the house of Piergiovanni, which is by San Giorgio, and the house of Jacomo Cavazza, which is on the Grand Canal. I have also been in the house of Jacomo Gratiani, but we were alone. Since Mr. Giovanni Rangoni, Maranello, and Iacomo Gratiani were important people, it never happened that I was where they met. They all came to the shop of Piergiovanni, and I saw them, and I found myself in their presence, and I heard them discuss heretical subjects, but I never went to visit them, nor do I know of any special place where they met.

I have been to the homes of all those mentioned above, namely Mr. Giovanni, Maranello, Gio. Jacomo Cavazza, and Gratiani, who were rich, for flour and other things I needed to support my family. They used to provide me with these things, because they knew me as one of their sect and company."

Interrogated "As to whether he had other accomplices and allies besides those named so far, either in Modena, Reggio Bologna, or elsewhere,"

He replied, "I have not known or heard of others being heretics and suspect of heresy, except those whom I have named: Mr. Giovanni Rangoni, Mr. Gio. Maria Maranello Mr. Gio. Jacomo Cavazza,

---

[1] The reference could be to the: "Libellus Doc. Martini Lutheri, de Sacramento Eucharistiae, ad Valdenses fratres, e Germanico translatus per I. Ionam. Apud. Iohannem Lufft, Wittembergae, 1526." It is listed in the *British Museum Catalogue of Printed Books* (London, 1962), v. 146, col. 758.

[2] See p. 251, n. 3.

Jacomo Gratiani, Piergiovanni Biancolini, Mr. Claudio Carandini, Mr. Francesco Camaranando, Mr. Marco Caula,[1] Gio. Battista Magnanino, Peregrino di Sette, Gemignano Tamburino, Paulo Soperchio, Mr. Giovanni Conselice,[2] Gasparo di Rocco Calzolare, Cathaldo, a velvet weaver, Mr. Vincenzo Quistello of Mirandola. All these I have known as heretics in Modena from the dealings I have had with them, from the declarations I have heard them make, and because some of them gave me charity because I was a heretic like them."

Interrogated "As to whether, besides the aforementioned, he had information, dealings, and conversation about and with Giovanni Bergomuccio,[3] Leonardo Scandiano,[4] both silk merchants, Julio Sadoleto,[5] Thoma. Capellina, Gaspare Chiavenna, Giovanni Padovano,[6] Bartolomeo Ingone, and Christophoro Rampono,"[7]

---

[1] The *acta* of Marco Caula's two interrogations before the Inquisition, 29 March and 1 April, 1541 are in Mercati, *op. cit.*, pp. 137-139. They reveal that he had attended the discussions of doubtful orthodoxy which took place in the home of the Grillenzoni. In his first brush with the Inquisition, he is released with light penalties. But he could not have mended his ways altogether. A letter from Fra Domenico to Morone of 7 June, 1567 reports that, "We have sent Marco Caulla to Ferrara because the Inquisitor's Vicar had said that he could not come to Modena; he [Caula] was eager to put his affairs in order and so has gone. We gladly allowed him to go, to escape this burden, thinking also that the matter would go more smoothly in this way," *ibid.*, p. 142.

[2] See p. 252, n. 1.

[3] C. Corvisieri, *op. cit.*, p. 277, indicates his trial before the Inquisition: "Iohannes Bergomozzo Mutinensis haereticus"; and C. Cantù, *op. cit.*, II, 201 lists him, together with Francesco Camorana (see above p. 249, n. 6), as one of the heretics from the Modenese area who sent assistance to their brethren in Germany.

[4] Fra Domenico's letter of 29 January, 1567, reports to Morone that "we have also imprisoned one Lionardo Scandiano against whom there was certain evidence," Mercati, *op. cit.*, p. 140.

[5] A "Giulio Sadoleti" is mentioned among the Modenese erudites associated with the teaching of Greek, *c.* 1536 by L. Vedriani, *Historia dell'antichissima città di Modona* (Modena, 1667), p. 520. It is uncertain if our Sadoleto was the protagonist in the clamorous affair recorded by Lancellotti, *Cronaca*, XI, 250 for 3 June, 1552: "Since a son of Carlo Piatese, by the name of Hercule, was wounded a few days ago, the blame was laid to Julio, son of M. Lodovico Sadoleto; and while he was being detained in the castle by Sig. Batistino Strozo, who is substituting for the absent governor..., he raised 1000 Scudi as surety that he would not leave Modena and would appear each time summoned. Now, the aforenamed (Sadoleto) has fled Modena....". In a slightly different version, we learn that although guilty, Giulio "did not suffer great damage, made his peace with the wounded party, and with a trivial fine settled his account with the law." See T. Sandonnini, "Un famoso bandito Modenese," *Atti e Memorie delle RR. Deputazioni di Storia Patria per le Provincie Modenesi e Parmensi*, Serie III, Vol. IV, Parte II (1887), 433. See p. 251, n. 6 for Giacomo Cavazza's testimony against our Sadoleto before the Inquisition. "A G. Sadoleto from Modena of the house of the eminent Cardinal Jacopo" is listed as a refugee in Geneva by J. Galiffe, *Le refuge Italien de Genève aux XVIme et XVIIme siècles* (Geneva, 1881), p. 148. The presence of a Sadoleto, not further identifiable, one of the Italian heretics at the Synod of Coira (Grisons) in 1571 is noted by R. Da Porta, *Historia Reformationis Ecclesiarum Raeticarum*, 2 vols. (Curiae Raetorum, 1772-1777), I, 543; F. Trechsel, *Die Protestantischen Antitrinitarier vor Faustus Socin*, 2 vols. (Heidelberg, 1839-1844), II, 135; D. Cantimori, *Eretici Italiani del Cinquecento* (Florence, 1939), p. 317.

[6] He was imprisoned with Geminiano Tamburino in 1567. See above p. 250, n. 3.

[7] Thomaso Capellina, Gaspare Chiavenna, Bartolomeo Ingone and Christophoro Rampono have not been identified.

He replied, "I neither know or have heard of Giovanni Bergomuccio, and Lionardo Scandiano. I know Mr. Julio Sadoleto, but not as a heretic because I have never heard him voice his sentiments in this matter. I do not know Thomaso Capellina; nor do I know Gasparo Chiavenna, unless he is that Gasparo di Rocco whom I have named before. Giovanni Padovano I do know. He is the one with the red beard who has a shop on the canal Chiaro by San Francesco; and I know him as a heretic, because he too participated in our discussions. I am not acquainted with Bartholomeo Ingoni and Christophoro Ramponi, nor have I heard of them."

And warned that he should be careful to tell the truth about each and every associate and ally whom he had, and about whom he knew in the dominion of the most Illustrious Lord the Duke of Ferrara, or in the city of Bologna, or elsewhere, since otherwise it would be necessary that further suitable provisions of the law be brought to bear against him in order to have the truth in this matter,

He replied, "I do not know any heretical person, or anyone suspect of heresy except those whom I have already named to you Reverend Fathers; and if it shall be found that I know others, do of me what you will. You can be certain that I do not want to suffer for them. And as I have talked about myself and those who have been my benefactors, I would certainly also tell you about others if I knew them or had heard about them."

Interrogated and diligently warned to openly, wholly, faithfully, and sincerely explain all the errors and heresies which the aforesaid held among themselves, as did he himself the arraigned, and about which they spoke and treated against the holy Catholic faith, and the Roman church,

He replied, "As to the sacraments of the church, we held and believed in the sacrament of Baptism without any difference from what the Holy Roman Church holds, except that we only esteemed to be minister of the Baptism him who had been ordained by the people to preach and baptize. The sacrament of Confirmation we denied and considered worthless. The sacrament of the Eucharist we interpreted in this way, namely, that the consacrated host was only a commemoration of the Passion and death of our Lord Jesus Christ. As for the Mass, we deemed it good to attend it out of respect for the gospels and epistles which are recited, and also for the *credo* and the *pater noster*, but not out of respect for the sacrament. In fact, we held that the adoration of the sacrament was idolatry. As for Penance, we believed that confession to the priest is not necessary, and that one could do without it; that actually while it was of no utility, it also produced no harm: confession to God was all that was required. Of justification, we used to say and believed, that since Christ the Lord had sacrificed himself for us both for the guilt and the penalty, whether temporal or spiritual, our satisfactions consisting of fasts, alms, pilgrimages, and similar works are neither capable of justifying, nor meritorious. But we are strongly obliged to do good works; and because we do that which is our duty, we do not merit anything from God, whose debtors we are for such works.

As for the sacraments of Orders and of Extreme Unction, we denied them, and didn't believe in them in any way. We accepted the sacrament of Matrimony.

As for the Church, we used to say and hold that the Church was the congregation of the faithful and the believers; that is, of those who trust that they are saved through the death and passion of Christ. That was the true Church; but those who thought they were saved by indulgences, pardons, vows, pilgrimages, and other similar works did not have a true belief and therefore were not of the Church.

Of the Pope, we believed that he had the authority from Christ to enforce the observance of what God had ordained and decreed, but not to add new laws and precepts as he does, and to make an insupportable burden of the Christian commandments. Consequently, we used to declare and hold that the laws, decrees, and precepts of the Pope could not oblige anybody into sin because they were positive laws made by a man; and that a human being could not compel another human being into mortal sin, since only the law of God obliges to mortal sin.

Nor did we accept the precepts of the Pope about the observance of feast days, fast days, and similar matters; or that they could be a cause for sin. We did not believe in Indulgences, nor that the Pope or other prelate in the Church could so decree a case that man could not be absolved before God. We also did not believe that the Pope or any prelate could excommunicate anybody; for only they are excommunicated who do not believe in the Son of God.

As for the invocation and intercession of saints, and the cult of images of Christ and the saints, I have always believed that the saints pray for us. But the others whom I have named, said and held that we were not to invoke or appeal to the saints, but only to God and to Christ who said, *Venite ad me omnes qui laboratis*, etc.; and as for images, we were not to revere them, because they were works produced by the hand of man, and to revere them would be idolatry. This of the images, I held in the same manner as did the forenamed, because they made me see it expressly in Exodus.[1]

Of saints' relics, we held and believed that no reverence at all was due to them, because they possessed no holy quality.

Of Purgatory, we believed that there was no other Purgatory besides Jesus Christ, which is how St. Paul puts it;[2] consequently, we denied prayers for the dead.

As for the vows of the Orders and of monastic life, we censured them, and considered them misdeeds, because there is no other religion besides the Christian religion, and these particular religions were sects.

---

[1] Cf. Exodus 20: 4.
[2] Cf. Hebrews 1: 3.

The vows which are made to the Virgin Mary and to other images, we reputed of no account.

Of the *libero arbitrio*, we held and believed that we did not possess it, except to do evil, and that we could not do good without the grace of God. We believed that God's supravenient grace was that which operated the good in us, and not our own doing. And if within us there was a thing of worth, it was from God, and the evil was from us.

Concerning salvation, we held that we were justified solely by faith in Jesus Christ, and not by any works of ours; such works in no way could contribute to our justification, which is solely by the grace of God.

These are the only errors which I remember holding and believing up to now, and which all my aforenamed accomplices and companions in Modena held and believed; and if I recall anything more, I will tell it to your Reverences during another examination."

And falling to his knees, he sought pardon saying, "I seek your pardon, and I beg you for the passion of Christ to have mercy on me."

Having received this in each and every part, "I Pier Antonio affirm the foregoing."

The second day of June, 1567

The aforementioned Pietro Antonio de' Cervia, having been led from prison and personally arraigned before the Reverend Fathers, the Lord Vicar General of the episcopal curia of Bologna, and the Vicar of the Reverend Father Inquisitor of the same city, in the upper chamber of examinations; and the oath having been administered and received by him about speaking the truth both against himself and against others; interrogated and examined, he said, answered, confessed and testified as follows:

Interrogated, "Whether he had anything further to add to what had been confessed and testified by him in his previous examinations. or whether he had anything to declare,"

He replied, "Fathers, no. I have nothing further to add or declare, because in my previous examinations I confessed and testified all that which I have known as the truth."

And when the presiding Reverend Fathers said that there were more things that he had kept silent about, both concerning himself and others, and that he ought to tell the truth which he had so far neglected,

He replied, "If there is anything which I do not remember, and which can be recalled to me, I will confess it candidly as true."

Interrogated, "That for truth's sake, he should reveal who it had been who had warned him by letters to depart from the Inn of the *Fossa* where he had been staying,"

He replied, "About this I can not say anything, except that when I was lodged at the inn of the *Fossa*, which is two miles from Modena on the road to Bologna, there was brought to me there, it could have been two at night, and it was raining, it was the month of December last, there was brought to me a message written in the name of my wife Laura, in which she said that I must set out at once, and go with God because the guards were on their way to seize me. I neither know in whose hand the message was written, nor did I know the person who brought it. But my wife, who is informed about both matters, can be examined. And I also remember that the innkeeper, Giovanni Rapaiolo [1] by name, told me that he knew the peasant who had brought the message to me; and he too can be examined, and will confirm this.

I did not learn anything more because I did not return home again, but as soon as I had received the warning, I departed and went to the house of laborers in the employ of a certain Mr. Molza,[2] who dwell below the street almost facing the inn. I remained there that night, and then early the next morning I set out for Stansello, where I remained in the home of the Cavalier Molza for three days. When I left there, I headed for another possession of the same Cavalier Guido Molza, where a certain laborer of his, named Alessandro, dwells; and I remained in that place for eight days. Then I went to different towns to see if I could find an employer, namely to Parma, Reggio, Borgo and Fiorenzuola. Later I took the Bologna road and reached Samoza.... and that was for about fourteen days.[3]

There I joined up with Pier Bordino,[4] on his way to Reggio to run an inn there, and he sent me to Bologna to get certain goods of his. And it was there that I was taken by the court, and finally led here to the prison of the Inquisition."

Interrogated, "As to whether the knights de' Molzis knew of his flight, and that he had hidden himself in and among their possessions at their peasants',"

He replied, "I don't believe that they knew a thing, because none of them ever came in that season. It was winter, and there was snow and rain, but it is always possible that the laborers have told them something that I am not aware of."

---

[1] unidentified

[2] A Messer Guido Molza, together with Giulio Cesare Codebò (see below p. 265), accepted on 16 September, 1566 the delicate office, after several candidates had declined, of presenting to Cardinal Ippolito of Ferrara grievances drawn up by the Modenese authorities against the Vice-Inquisitor of Modena, Fra Nicolò del Finale. The pertinent documents, including the memorandum drawn up by the Modenese as a guide for their two ambassadors and the petition for the Cardinal, are in T. Sandonnini, *Lodovico*, pp. 334-339. A Guido Molza who died on 29 April, 1569 at the age of thirty-nine, a compo ser of sonnets, is remembered by Tiraboschi, *Biblioteca*, III, 244. Undoubtedly not to be confused with our first Guido Molza but who could be identified with Cervia's former master is that Cavalier Guido Molza who in 1546 was banished from Modena for the killing of a certain Scocera. Cf. Lancellotti, *Cronaca*, X, 240. After his return, he was the passionate organizer of jousts (a skill acquired during his Bolognese exile) and other knightly diversions, *ibid.*, XI, 13 ff.

[3] Tex unclear.

[4] unidentified.

Then of his free will he added, "The laborers I have mentioned did not mind when I went to them, because I had been the steward of Cavalier Guido."

Interrogated, "As to how long he had been in the service of the knight Guido,"

He replied, "I worked for him about four or five months."

And at the specific question, he said, "My lords no. In that period I was not in the errors and did not hold the heretical opinions which I held later. In the home of Cavalier Guido one did not speak of these things, and we lived religiously and as Christians, meaning by Christian, according to the rule of the Holy Roman Church."

Interrogated, "From what date he began to serve the aforenamed knight Guido and to dwell in his house, and at his service,"

He replied, "In that year in which there was such a great famine [1] and just after the harvest, which may be five or six years ago."

Interrogated, "As to whether he had or has information about any soldiers who were and perchance still are in the same, or similar errors and heretical opinions,"

He replied, "I know that in the entire squad of soldiers where I was stationed at the gate, which might have consisted of eighteen soldiers, we used to discuss publicly and privately matters pertaining to Scripture and to these heresies. But I can not tell you exactly who was of one opinion, and who of another. I know that we all participated [in the discussions] because we used to go in the morning to hear the sermon, following which, each one spoke his mind.

But, as I have said, I can not name the particular opinions held by any one of the soldiers."

And when the Reverend Fathers said that it was unlikely that he did not know, and that he was informed, he replied that all the soldiers were of the same kind as he, since they had treated him so familiarly and domestically, and had discussed with him Lutheran errors and heretical opinions. And having been further warned to desist from ambiguities and similitudes, and to embrace the pure and sincere truth, by naming all those whom he had seen and known to have been, and still perchance to be found in such errors and opinions,

He replied, "I tell you that we discussed these heretical opinions thus in a general manner in my squad when we were on guard, and I was the one who infected everybody. And when I argued, they listened to me, and some of them supported my opinions, and others rejected them, and others still remained undecided. Those who supported and accepted my opinions were a Gian Lodovico of Fiorano,[2] who used to say, 'to me it appears, to the best of my judgment, that it is so,' and

---

[1] Cf. A. Tassoni, "Cronaca di Modena," *Monumenti di Storia Patria delle Provincie Modenesi: Serie delle Cronache* (Modena, 1888), XV, 331 who describes the great procession organized in Modena on 14 April, 1560 by the Bishop Egidio Foscarari to raise funds for the "rusticis" who were starving due to the serious famine.

[2] It has not been possible to identify Fiorano or the other members of the squad.

Alessandro of Parma, the younger. I do not recall any others who approved. As to those who were undecided, I think that everybody else in the squad was undecided, because they allowed themselves to be persuaded first by one side, and then by the other, neither accepting these errors and opinions nor those of the Roman Church.

It was Captain Giacomo who rebuked these opinions of mine; and he upbraided me several times in the presence of the whole squad, warning me not to discuss these things with the soldiers. And I discussed them so much that finally the Captain was forced to remove me; nor do I recall that any other of those soldiers rebuked me. The names of the soldiers who were in the squad, and with whom I discussed these errors and opinions many times are these:

Squad

Antonio Maria of Nonantola, Sergeant
Origene of Modena, Lance
Giovanni of Solera, Corporal
Giovanni of Carpi
Girolamo of Carpi
The Florentine from Carpi
Lorenzo of Luca
Alessandro of Parma
Gian Lodovico of Fiorano
Francesco Maria of Reggio
Nicolò Butelli of Modena
Giovan Battista Bachino of Modena
Francesco of Lugo
Piergiovanni of Reggio

One from Senigaglia who played the lyre and one from Urbino played the lute and sang, but I don't remember their names."

And at the specific question, he said,

"I also used to read to the soldiers of that squad certain books which I had in the vulgar tongue, treating such errors and opinions, as John Calvin,[1] *Il Dialogo di Mercurio et Cheronte*,[2] *Pasquino in estasi*,[3]

---

[1] See above p. 251, n. 3.

[2] See above p. 252, n. 4.

[3] The first Italian edition of the Piedmontese Curione's (d. Basel 1569) anti-Roman satire is entitled simply, *Pasquino in estasi*. The frontispiece in jest has Rome as the place of publication. The date suggested by the British Museum *Catalogue* (vol. 46, col. 42) is 1545. It was translated from the original Latin version, published slightly earlier in Basel with the title *Pasquilli Extatici*, by Bernardino Ochino, the former General of the Capuchins, then in Geneva. In this extremely popular booklet which was many times revised and translated into French, English and German, Pasquino recounts to his friend Marphorio his experiences during a journey to Paradise, Purgatory and Hell. For the various editions see the bibliography appended to M. Kutter, *Celio Secondo Curione, sein Leben und sein Werk* (*1503-1569*) (Basel and Stuttgart, 1955). The best study of Curione's thought remains D. Cantimori, *op. cit.*, *passim.* For a good study on Pasquinades as a contemporary form of satire see, M. Dell Arco, *Pasquino e le pasquinate* (Milan, [1957]).

dealing with Paradise, Purgatory and Hell. I don't remember that I read from other books to the soldiers at the gate because Pier Giovanni Limatore [1] and Mr. Giovanni Gratiani did not give me other than these three books to read to the soldiers. Moreover, they gave them to me one at a time, intending that when I had finished reading one, I should return it."

Interrogated, "As to whether he had any information, dealings, and conversation with any soldiers in the city of Modena or outside whom he saw and knew to have been involved in such errors and opinions,"

He replied, "No."

Interrogated, "As to whether he had any information, dealings, and conversation about and with Captain Camillo Caula,[2] Jacobo his nephew,[3] and Alphonso Roveta,[4] and in what opinion he held these persons or any one of them in the matter of faith and religion,"

He replied, "Fathers, yes. I have known and had dealings with them, but I don't know of what opinion they are regarding the faith and religion, because we never discussed these matters together. It is true that it is said, and publicly accepted in Modena, that Captain Camillo Caula and Captain Giacomo his nephew are Lutherans and heretics, and that Captain Camillo gave the lie to a friar who was preach ingfrom a pulpit in Modena according to the manner and order of the Roman Church. But about Alfonso Roveta, I can not tell you anything, because we never discussed these things together, nor have I heard it said that he holds heretical opinions."

Interrogated, "As to whether he had information, dealings, and conversation in the city of Modena or outside, about or with certain doctors and other persons of rank whom he knew to be infected and weakened by and with errors of this sort and heretical opinions,"

He replied, "My lords, no. And if I had known any doctor or other person of rank who had been or was presently in these errors and opinions, I would have named them."

---

[1] Text uncertain.

[2] He is the almost legendary soldier-author who died in 1571. Captured by the Turks at Zara on 28 October, 1538, he was ransomed by his wife and reentered Modena almost a year later in the habit of a Franciscan friar. This colorful episode is narrated by Lancellotti, *Cronaca*, VII, 65, 130, 203. In July, 1547 he was appointed Captain of the Duke of Ferrara's troop of Light Horse, *ibid.*, IX, 118. His friendship with Lodovico Domenichi (a familiar of the Duchess Renata of Ferrara who suffered a trial for heresy in Florence as an alleged translator of Calvin) earned him the dedication of Domenichi's Italian edition of Polybius. From his erudite friend, Caula also received as a gift, his Italian translation of Augustine. Cf. G. Tiraboschi, *Biblioteca*, II, 14 ff. For Caula's own literary compositions, *ibid.*, p. 19. The printer Andrea Arrivabene dedicated to him Giuseppe Betussi's *Dialogo Amoroso* published in Venice in 1543. See M. E. Cosenza, *Biographical and Bibliographical Dictionary of the Italian Humanists*, 5 vols. (Boston, 1962), II, 950. Fra Domenico da Imola, writing to Cardinal Morone " the day of St. Francis " 1567 (already cited, see p. 250, n. 3) ends with the note that " Captain Camillo Caula kisses Your Illustrious Excellency's hand; he is very upset because of the death of his only son. "

[3] unidentified.

[4] unidentified.

Interrogated, "If especially he had any information about or acquaintance with Philippo Vignola,[1] Giovanni Calorio,[2] Antonio Tanarisio,[3] Simone Castro vitreo,[4] Sigismondo called Ronchino,[5] and Marco Caula,"

He replied affirmatively, saying, "I know Mr. Filippo Vignola because he is my uncle[6] and also that Ronchino who plays ball and Marco Caula. But I don't know the others named by you at all. I have never had dealings with them, nor do I know who are Mr. Giovanni Calora, Mr. Simone Castelvetro, or Mr. Antonio Tanariso."

Interrogated, "In what opinion he held Mr. Philippo Vignola, Marco Caula, and Ronchino, concerning matters of faith and religion,"

He replied, "As to my uncle and Ronchino, I do not know of what kind they are, because we have never discussed such matters together. But as for Marco, I have already stated in previous examinations that I have heard and gathered that he is a Lutheran, and that he has gone with God as a heretic."

Interrogated, "As to whether he had information, dealings, or acquaintance with Lady Bartholomea della Porta,"[7]

---

[1] A Filippo Vignola is remembered in Modenese records as a prominent advocate and city councillor. Cf., for example, Lancellotti, *Cronaca*, XI, 381 where under the date 29 March, 1553 it is recorded that he was elected to the *conservatori*. In the year 1550 a M. Filippo Vignoli is numbered among the "most excellent procuratori who practiced in this time and year" in Modena. See L. Vedriani, *Dottori Modonesi di Teologia, Filosofia, Legge Canonica e Civile* (Modena, 1665), p. 128 ff., where he is named among those "who for the sake of public order drew up the statutes." In 1566 he is one of the city authorities who approves the anti-Inquisitorial embassy to the Cardinal of Ferrara. See above p. 259, n. 2.

[2] Lancellotti's *Cronaca* (cf. especially the indices of vols. XI and XII) frequently refers to a Giovanni Calora who served several terms as a *conservatore*. Especially interesting is Lancellotti's entry for 9 July, 1545 which relates that when the Pope demanded that the Duke of Ferrara send Filippo Valentini, a prominent member of the Grillenzoni Academy under heavy suspicion of heresy, to Rome, as a preliminary step, the Duke summoned Valentini to Ferrara. Already on route to Ferrara, the latter halts his journey to petition the *conservatori* of Modena for a letter that would recommend him to the high authority awaiting him. A Giovanni Calora is one of the city officials who acceded to Valentini's request. For this generous gesture, the responsible authorities are soundly berated by our conservative chronicler. Lancellotti, *Cronaca*, IX, 38.

[3] unidentified.

[4] Simone, seventh son of Giovanni Castelvetro and Maria Rangoni, studied medicine in Padova from 1538-1546. After having served as physician to Pope Gregory XIV, he returned to his native Modena in 1591 and died the following year at the age of sixty-eight. One of his sonnets in praise of a Lucia Bertana is in *Parte IV delle rime di diversi eccellentissimi autori* (Bologna, 1551). Cf. G. Tiraboschi, *Biblioteca*, I, 485-487. Anonymous verses dedicated "Ad excelsos viros Simonem Castrovitreum et Ioanem Baptistam Paccianum," are published by Gio. Batt. Spaccini, *Cronaca Modenese* (1588-1636). *Monumenti di Storia Patria delle Provincie Modenesi* (Modena, 1911), XVI, 272-278.

[5] The death of a M. Sismondo Ronco at the age of forty-five on 6 September, 1552 is recorded by Lancellotti, *Cronaca*, XI, 293. Under the date 30 September of the same year, he notes the election as a *conservatore* of "Sisismondo Roncho son of M. Sisimondo (sic)," *ibid.*, p. 298.

[6] The text reads "barba" which can be translated either "uncle" or "Godfather."

[7] Among the names in the already cited "1568 Suspecti in fide" in Mercati, *op. cit.*, p. 145 we read: "Bartholomea Porta: the Vicar will examine her diligently and if any-

He replied, "No sirs, I do not know this woman." Adding of his own accord, "I have neither dealt or spoken of these opinions with any woman, except with the sister of Panzachio, [1] and with the women of his household in which I was staying, and with Laura my wife, all of whom are in the errors and opinions in which I have been, and which we discussed many times together."

Interrogated, "As to whether he had had dealings or conversation about and with Mr. Julio Sadoleto, and Mr. Giovanni of Castro Vitro," [2]

He replied, "Fathers, I have no knowledge whatsoever of this Mr. Giovanni Castelvetro. But this Mr. Julio Sadoleto, I have certainly known, but never for a heretic."

Interrogated, "As to whether he had read any lessons outside the city of Modena, concerning faith and religion,"

He replied, "My lords, no. In fact, I never brought a single book outside of Modena, except one to Alessandro Panzachia [3] here in Bologna."

Interrogated, "As to whether and how often he attended in Modena the Lord's Supper celebrated in the Lutheran manner,"

He replied, "My lords, I never attended a single celebration of the Lord's Supper in Modena. Nor did they invite me to these mockeries because they did not trust me."

Interrogated, "Whom did he have in mind, and whom does he have in mind when he said, 'they didn't trust me, and they didn't invite me to these mockeries',"

He replied, "I mean those who performed these Suppers, if they actually took place, because I know nothing about them; although I became aware that they did not trust me, because once, when I was conducted by that Piergiovanni (Biancolino) to read the epistles of Saint Paul in the home of Gian Giacomo Cavazza — as I have told you in my other examinations — I noticed that the master of the house, Gian Giacomo, called Piergiovanni aside, and told him that he was

---

thing should be found, we shall proceed against her; otherwise we shall administer a sound warning."

[1] The merchant Alessandro Panzachia was hanged and then burned in Bologna on 8 October, 1567 as a follower of the "Lutheran heresy." His death is recorded in the Ms. "Libro dei giustiziati in Bologna dal 1540 al 1792," conserved in the Biblioteca dell'Archiginnasio of Bologna (B. 311), f. 20. A. Battistella, *op. cit.*, p. 99 notes that Bianchetti in his ms. "Annali di Bologna" calls Panzachia a *notaro*; he is remembered in Bolognese Inquisitorial records as late as 8 May, 1604, *ibid.*

[2] The reference is probably to that nephew of the famous Lodovico who figures in our often cited "1568 Suspecti in fide" in Mercati, *op. cit.*, p. 145: "Nicolo Castelvetro: it is necessary to summon him with his sons and administer a sound warning, interrogating him especially on Images and on the observance of the feast, about which matters we have suspicions.... and we shall also interrogate again Giovanni, his son, as to whether he has ever given forbidden books." Another Giovanni Castelvetro (d. 1557), a third cousin to Lodovico, a jurist and several times a *conservatore* of Modena, subscribed to the famous confession of orthodoxy imposed by Rome on Modena's leading citizens and members of the Grillenzoni Academy on 1 September, 1542, *ibid.*, p. 134. He was the father of that Simone about whom Cervia was questioned (see p. 263, n. 4).

[3] See above, n. 1.

never to bring me there again. Which he did. And from this I inferred that I was so suspect that they did not trust me, perhaps thinking that if ever I should be seized, I would reveal them. Therefore, if there were any infected persons who performed the Lord's Supper, they did not trust me, and did not invite me to their meals."

Interrogated, "As to whether he had in the past or then any information, dealings, and conversation about and with Don Francesco Cavalo[1] in the villa Baluaria, and since when,"

He replied, "Fathers, yes. It has been within the past three years that I have been acquainted with Don Francesco, and had some dealings with him. But I am of the opinion that this Don Francesco is a good Christian and a good religious."

Interrogated, "From what time had he not seen or talked with Don Francesco,"

He replied, "The last time was during my flight, and in the month of November last, when, departing from the inn of the Fossa, I went one morning to eat with Don Francesco."

And warned for the sake of truth to relate what discussions he had had with the aforementioned Don Francesco regarding religion, the faith, and his flight,

He replied, "I told Don Francesco that I was in flight because of the Inquisition, and that I had left behind me three gentlemen in Modena entrusted with communicating to the Father Inquisitor my desire to present myself and to tell him the truth about all matters. In fact, I had charged Mr. Girolamo Rubico,[2] Mr. Lodovico delle Ere,[3] and Mr. Giulio Cesare Chodebò,[4] doctor, to intercede for me with the Father Inquisitor of Modena, and to ask him to receive me because I was ready to present myself to the Inquisition."

Warned that for the sake of truth he should reveal everything which he had said to the aforementioned Don Francesco from whom the court had learnt that he [Cervia] had stated in his presence that he would never expose in the office of the most Holy Inquisition the accomplices, instructors, allies, and companions whom he had had, and

---

[1] unidentified.

[2] unidentified.

[3] He was elevated to the position of apostolic and imperial notary on 14 March, 1547. Lancellotti, *Cronaca*, X, 71.

[4] A celebrated jurist remembered in several contemporary sources. On 6 March, 1553, he appeared, together with other doctors of law, before the city authorities to discuss "important matters regarding the observance of statutes and the officials who did not observe them." Lancellotti, *Cronaca*, XI, 362. In September, 1566 he was elected with M. Guido Molza to represent the city before Cardinal Ippolito d'Este in Ferrara. See above p. 259, n. 2. In 1579, Codebo was one of the four ambassadors selected to represent Modena at the marriage of the Duke of Ferrara with Margherita, daughter of the Duke of Mantua. Vedriani, *op. cit.*, p. 581. On 5 January, 1585 he publicly defended the controversial decree, which had been passed three years earlier, requiring advocates to be draped in their long doctoral gowns during the performance of their legal functions. Cf. G. della Fontana, "Il collegio degli avvocati di Modena, 1337-1797," *Accademia Nazionale di Scienze, Lettere e Arti, Modena: Atti e Memorie*, Serie VI, Vol. II (1960), 60.

was having in the matter of heresy, except those who were dead or fugitive,

He replied, " My lords, this is not the truth, and if Don Francesco wants to say this, he is wrong, because he knows well that he encouraged me to present myself to the Holy Office, and to confess candidly and purely the truth in everything. He exhorted me, in the most excellent manner possible, to confess all my errors, and also all my associates. " Adding of his own accord, " I marvel at all this, because I have considered Don Francesco a good man and trustworthy, and it is possible that while conversing, as can happen, I did tell him such a thing. But the truth is that in this and other examinations, I have always told the truth about all the opinions and errors which I have held and the associates I have known, all of whom I have named. And I have kept back nothing which I was supposed to tell about the truth. "

And when the Reverend Fathers and the Lord Judges declared that for the sake of further truth against himself and his accomplices, he should speak and frankly tell his other errors, if he had and held any besides those which he had already confessed, and equally that he should name his other accomplices if he had any besides those whom he had already disclosed in matters of heresy and religion,

He replied, " No Sirs, I have not held other opinions and other errors outside of those which I have already confessed to you in my other examinations. Nor have I known any other associates or participants in such opinions and errors, even slightly suspect of heresy, except those whom I have named in this and other examinations."

And further warned with the threat that he would have to tell such truth under torture,

He replied, " What would it be for me to confess other opinions if I held them and believed them, when I have already talked about and confessed those which I consider the principal; nor would I let myself be crippled for others if I knew that they were heretics or suspect of heresy. Nevertheless, I am here to receive these torments, since my sins merit these and more. I beseech you to have compassion and mercy on me. "

And falling on his knees to the ground, he begged and demanded mercy. And the Reverend Fathers and the Lord Judges having received the preceding in each and every part, under request of the Magnificent Lord the Fiscal Advocate, after the oath had again been administered to the arraigned about speaking the truth both against himself and against others; they ordered that the arraigned be subjected to the *taxillorum*,[1] and that therefore one foot be bared, and that he

---

[1] Also known as the *Stanghetta*, it was administered in cases where the prisoner " either because of serious physical defects, or because of obvious youth was incapable of receiving the torment of the cord. " Cf. the Inquisitor's manual compiled by E. Masini, *Sacro Arsenale, overo Prattica dell'Officio della S. Inquisizione* (Rome, 1693), p. 216. This coincides with Cervia's testimony that he was " infermo. " This torture consisted of prostrating the victim on the ground and exerting pressure on his ankles which had been placed in a concave vise-like apparatus, *ibid.*, p. 217.

be subjected to the aforementioned torture and interrogated in it about the matters mentioned above, in order to have further truth both against himself and against his companions; yet with the premise always repeated that they did not wish or intend to interrogate him concerning things which he had already confessed, but only for the sake of further truth, and concerning the other accomplices and beyond any prejudice and derogation of persons who had already testified before any office or court. Accordingly his right foot was bared, and subjected and put under the aforesaid torture, being in which torture and being interrogated he began to shout out with loud cries, " Oh Jesus, Oh Jesus, I have said everything that I know and I have said the truth; and everything that I have told you in my conscience is the truth, " many times crying out, " Oh Jesus Christ I have spoken the truth and affirm as much. Oh, do you wish me to speak against my conscience. And as for those soldiers, as much is true as I have told you in my examinations. Jesus help me. Our Lady help me. I have told you the truth. What do you want to do tormenting me so ? "

Interrogated, he replied, " Sirs, no, I am not a priest and never have I been ordained to any of the sacred orders. Nor do I have any of the four minor orders: [1] what would it be for me to say it. Wouldn't it be better for me, as I wouldn't have committed idolatry by celebrating mass as many times as I did. Religion would have more compassion on me, and also your lordships, because much graver is this error of having celebrated (the mass) without being ordained, than if I had been a priest and had taken a wife. Jesus Christ mercy, I have told the truth. I have named all my accomplices. "

And more and more often warned to speak the truth about the above things,

He replied " My lords, I have told you the truth. I have told it to you, and I have nothing more to tell you, and if I knew that the whole world was in this opinion, I would say it; and all that which I have said about myself and the others whom I have named, be fully certain that I have told the truth, and I confirm and ratify it. And of these soldiers, it is true that those two, that is Ludovico of Fiorano and Alessandro of Parma, agreed with me and said that in their judgment the truth lay with what I was saying, while the others reproached me, and remained in doubt just as I have told you, and I assure you all this. "

And while he was saying these things, he was shouting with great cries and lamenting greatly for the pain of the tortures with which he was affected. And as he had been under torture for a notable length of time, at the will of the aforesaid Reverend Lord Judges, and since he had confessed nothing more, but only said and repeated to the frequent questions of the Lord Judges,

---

[1] The four minor orders in the Western Church are porters, lectors, exorcists and acolytes who, while entitled to ecclesiastical privileges, are not bound to celibacy. Cf. F. L. Cross, ed., *The Oxford Dictionary of the Christian Church* (London, 1958), p. 904.

"I have told you the truth about everything that I know, both about myself and the others, and everything that I have told you is the truth and I confirm and ratify it, and if I knew more I would tell it to you without respect for any person in the world,"

They ordered the arraigned to be removed from the torture and to be returned to his own place, the proceedings having been accepted by the Magnificent Lord the Fiscal Advocate in each and every part, and his subscription having been obtained as follows: I Pietro Antonio da Cervia affirm, ratify and approve what I have said and confessed.

Present as witnesses, Fra Alexio tertiary of the Order of Preachers and Lorenzo Pensabene, citizen and Notary of Bologna, and Sebastian Trentino, public executor of Bologna. This copy was taken from the originals by me, Fra Pietro Poncinio of Modena, of the Order of Preachers, Notary of the most Holy Inquisition in Bologna.

I, the same Fra Pietro Poncinio.

JOSEPHINE VON HENNEBERG

FAUSTUS SOCINUS' COMMENT ON ARISTOTLE'S *RHETORIC*

In a still unpublished document,[1] Fausto Sozzini criticizes the interpretation that Alessandro Piccolomini (1508-1578)[2] had given to the words "probability" and "fallible sign" in his commentary on the first book of Aristotle's *Rhetoric*.

The *Copiosissima Parafrase di M. Alessandro Piccolomini nel primo libro della Retorica d'Aristotele* had been printed in Venice in 1565, followed in 1569 and in 1572 by two more commentaries on the second and third books, and in 1572 by the Italian translation of the complete text of the *Rhetoric*.

Sozzini wrote his essay as *Il Frastagliato Intronato*, under which name he belonged to the *Accademia degli Intronati* of Siena, probably in the years between 1565 and 1568. It seems likely that – for a work well within the frame of translations, criticisms and literary discussions that constituted the main activity of the Academy – he used his name of *Intronato* while the Academy was still active. Although there are differences of opinion about the year in which the *Accademia degli Intronati* was closed for the second time, it did certainly come to a temporary end in 1568, when all the academies of Siena were dissolved by a decree of Cosimo de' Medici.[3]

Sozzini wants to "demonstrate how obviously false is the opinion of M. Alessandro, not only because this has not yet been done by anybody, but also because.... his opinion is, more than any other, damaging to the truth."

Piccolomini had affirmed that the only difference existing between a probability and a fallible sign was that probability meant the whole probable proposition, while fallible sign was the subject contained in that same proposition, considered in relation to its predicate: so that

---

[1] "Breuissima dichiaratione della differenza ch' e' tra 'l segno non necessario, il quale è come l'uniuersale uerso il particolare, e 'l uerisimile, di cui parla Aristotile nel secondo capo del primo libro della sua Retorica. Del Frastagliato Intronato." A copy, numbering 20 ff., is preserved in Siena, Biblioteca Comunale degli Intronati, MS, P.V. 15 (2). Its existence has been thoughtfully brought to our attention by Signor Nello Cortigiani of that library. A typescript of the transliteration has been deposited with the Andover-Harvard Theological Library, Cambridge, Massachusetts.

[2] On this interesting Sienese literary figure who became Archbishop of Patrasso in 1574, cf. F. Cerreta, *Alessandro Piccolomini, letterato e filosofo Senese del Cinquecento* (Siena, 1960). Sozzini refers to him in his essay only as "M. Aless. Picc." or "M. Alessandro."

[3] It was reopened in a solemn ceremony almost a half century later on 14 December, 1603. Cf. F. Iacometti, *L'Accademia Senese degli Intronati* (Siena, 1950), p. 7.

the proposition " the pale persons are ill " was for him a probability, and the fact of being pale — as the subject considered in relation to its predicate, the illness — was a sign.

But, Sozzini argues, Aristotle himself before stating what is a probability, and what is a sign, had clearly said that the materials of enthymemes are probabilities and signs, and these he considered as separate and distinct sources. How can this be true, then, if, according to Piccolomini, where the probability is, there the sign will necessarily be found? In such a case, every enthymeme formed by a probability could be considered formed by a sign, which would be against Aristotle's teachings.

Further, probability may not always mean the whole probable proposition. Indeed, in this very place Aristotle meant by probability the subject considered in relation to its predicate, because he wrote, " A probability is a thing that usually happens,... and that bears the same relation to that in respect of which it is probable, as the universal bears to the particular. "

On the other hand, sign is not always the subject of a proposition considered in relation to its predicate, but is sometimes the whole proposition. In fact, the Prior Analytics state (II, 27, 70 A) that " a sign means a demonstrative proposition, necessary or generally approved. "

Therefore, what Piccolomini calls sign, or thing of the sign, is Aristotle's probability, or attributed to probability; and what he calls probability, or thing of probability, is Aristotle's sign, or attributed to sign. Probability and sign are distinct and separate, and an enthymeme derived from a probability is different from one derived from a sign.

But there is another, and more important difference between the two terms. In a probability, the thing that is sign of another (or the subject considered in relation to its predicate) always precedes — as cause near or far — the thing of which it is indicative; while in a sign, the subject, as effect near or far, always follows the predicate, or the cause near or far of such predicate. For instance, the proposition " the old are misers " is a proposition of probability, because old age does not follow avarice, but avarice follows old age; while the proposition " a pale person is ill " is a proposition of sign, because being pale follows an illness, and not an illness the fact of being pale.

In propositions of signs, this definition is true also when there are signs that indicate a thing still to come, and — consequently — the subject does not follow the predicate: this can be seen from the example, taken from the Introduction to Boccaccio's Decameron, that " black spots were signs of future death ": black spots did in fact follow the cause of death, that is, the illness of which they were the real effect.

This is, then, the true and principal difference between probability and sign; and if Aristotle didn't explicitly dwell on it, it was simply because he tried to remain as close as possible to everyday language, and thought that anybody familiar with it would understand his meaning.

There are clearly many probable things that in our daily language are not called signs, nor are said to contain any sign in themselves. But even if a sign may be commonly called probability (as when we say that it is probable that a pale man be ill), this does not mean that Aristotle did not consider probability and sign as different things. Actually, there are not many signs that can be argued as probabilities: had there been, Aristotle wouldn't have tried to conform to our common language, as he wanted the sign to differ from the probability.

There is something more to be observed, and nobody has noticed it yet: a probability, according to Aristotle's definition, is usually true. A usually false probability is not considered, while among the signs which we are now discussing (fallible signs that bear the same relation to the statement they support as the universal bears to the particular) there are signs that are usually false, and signs that are usually true. If a probability were both true and apparent, why would Aristotle have omitted to consider here the probability that is apparent, so easy to find, when in the discussion of the sources of enthymemes he includes those that are both true and false? when he mentions the signs from which apparent enthymemes derive, and when he writes, in the second book of the Rhetoric, about enthymemes true and apparent as pertinent to this art?

In conclusion, although probability and fallible sign seem to be the same thing, because they are similar in many respects (i.e., neither of them constitutes a complete proof; both of them can be usually true; both of them are of a thing that contains more in respect to another that contains less; in both of them there is something that in some way gives sign of another), they are, however, different for one principal reason: in a probability, the thing that is sign of another precedes that other thing, of which it is sign; while in a sign, the thing that is sign of another, follows the other, or its cause.

There are clearly many probable things that in our daily language are not called such, since they are said to contain any sign in themselves. But even if a sign may be commonly called probability, as when we say that it is probable that a pale man be ill, this does not mean that Aristotle did not consider probability and sign as different things. Actually, there are not many signs that can be argued as probabilities, and there been, Aristotle would not have tried to conform to our common language, as he wanted the sign to differ from the probability.

There is something more to be observed, and nobody has noticed yet. A probability, according to Aristotle's definition, is usually true. A usually false probability is not considered, while among the signs which we are now discussing (fallible signs that bear the same relation to the statement they support as the universal bears to the particular) there are signs that are usually false and signs that are usually true. If probability were both true and apparent, why would Aristotle have omitted to consider here the probability that is apparent, so easy to find, when in the discussion of the sources of enthymemes he considers those that are both true and false, when he mentions the signs from which apparent enthymemes derive, and when he writes in the second book of the Rhetoric about enthymemes true and apparent as pertinent to the art?

In conclusion, although probability and fallible sign seem to be the same thing, because they are similar in many respects (i.e., neither of them constitutes a complete proof; both of them can be usually true; both of them are of a thing that contains more in respect of another that contains less; in both of them there is something that in some way gives sign of another), they are, however, different for one principal reason: in a probability the thing that is sign of another precedes that other thing, of which it is sign, while in a sign, the thing that is sign of another follows the other, or its cause.

JOHN A. TEDESCHI

NOTES TOWARD A GENEALOGY OF THE SOZZINI FAMILY

INTRODUCTION

" De Mariano et Bartholomaeo Socinis:
Socinos venerare sacri duo lumina Iuris,
Ius geminum illustrant filius atque pater."

Matteo Gribaldi, *De Methodo ac ratione studendi libri tres* (Venice, 1559), f. 97 v. (Catalogus aliquot interpretum iuris civilis).

The notes that follow, although they do not constitute a complete account of the Sozzini family, may be useful to its future historians. We have contented ourselves with touching upon those details which appeared to be the most important, the least known and even, in a few instances, new. This is especially so in the cases of Lelio and Fausto, whose histories have often been told. It has also been thought unnecessary to trace the descent of other branches of the Sozzini family in Siena. This has already been partially done by Cesare Cantù, *Gli Eretici d'Italia*, 3 vols. (Turin, 1865-1867), II, 510-515. Nor did we seek to follow the fortunes of the Sozzini merchants who settled in Switzerland in the mid-fifteenth century. (See " I Sozzini di Siena a Bellinzona e a Lugano, " in *Bollettino Storico della Svizzera Italiana*, XXV [1903], 41). Our intention has been to trace the family line to Lelio and Fausto.

This study suffers from obvious defects. For the earlier decades of the family's history, it has been necessary to rely heavily on Cantù's genealogy and, unfortunately, he rarely cites the sources which underly his assertions. Nevertheless, it has been preferrable to preserve Cantù's notice of an individual rather than allow him to drop into oblivion.

In the latter part of our genealogy, it has proven difficult to untangle the maze of references concerning the brothers of Lelio Sozzini. Their movements are too obscure and the available information is too scanty to permit a clear chronological pattern. Instead of attempting to offer hypotheses which might add to the confusion, we have generally limited ourselves to collecting the available data. Perhaps Professor Aldo Stella in the course of his *Ricerche sul Socinianesimo*, of which a first installment devoted to Cornelio has already been published (and which we cite below), will have new information to report also for other members of the family.

GENEALOGY OF THE SOZZINI FAMILY

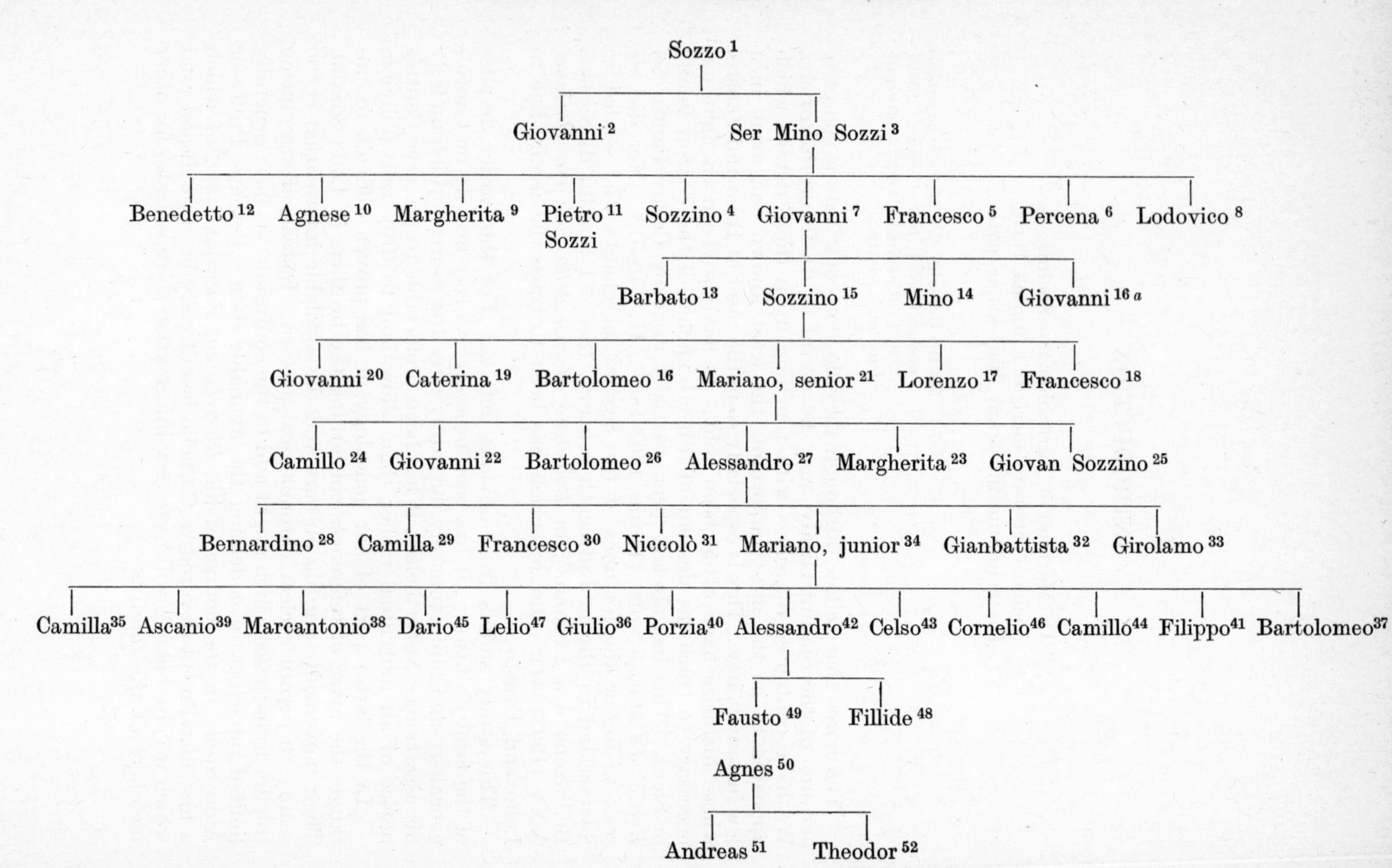

NOTES

1. (Sozzo).

Banker of Percena, the son of Martinello da Percena. He was still living in 1294. C. Cantù, *op. cit.*, II, 506.

2. (Giovanni).

Registered in the *Libro delle Gabelle* as a citizen of Siena in 1304. His wife, Margherita, survived him and died in 1345. Of their two sons, Checco and Minuccio, the latter was *Gonfaloniere* for the *Terzo* of San Martino in 1368. Cantù, *op. cit.*, II, 506.

3. (Mino).

d. 1340. Notary from Castello di Percena, near Buonconvento. He transferred his family to Siena where he was registered in the *Libro delle Gabelle* in 1304. His wife, Gherarda, died in 1348. Cantù, II, 506; G. Gigli, *Diario Sanese.... seconda edizione*, 2 vols. (Siena, 1854), II, 246.

A notarial act from his hand, dated August 19, 1306 is published in G. Milanesi, *Documenti per la storia dell'arte senese*, 3 vols. (Siena, 1854-1856), I, 165. It is signed, " Ego Minus olim Sozzi notarius, et nunc scriba et notarius dictorum dominorum novem...," and pertains to architectural improvements that will be effected in the cathedral square.

4. (Sozzino).

d. 1355 according to Cantù, II, 506. A different date (1372) is furnished by Donato di Neri, " Cronaca Senese, " in L. A. Muratori, *Rerum Italicarum Scriptores* (Città di Castello, 1939), XV, Part 6^2, p. 650. He was a merchant who had served as Ambassador to Aquila in 1349 and as *Capitano del Popolo* in 1355. On June 29 of the latter year, he was one of the Sienese citizens entrusted with full authority to negotiate the surrender of the rebel city of Casole. O. Malavolti, *Dell'historia di Siena* (Venice, 1599), T. II, Bk. VI, f. 114 r. Of his several sons, one Mariano, a " famosus mercator " died on February 12, 1402. Donato di Neri in his " Cronaca ," p. 647, relates that " a son of Sozino of Ser Mino " was taken prisoner with other adherents of the *Dodici* faction after it was discovered that in October, 1372 they had plotted with Florence to subvert the existing government of Siena, at that time in the hands of the rival *Riformatori*.

His definitive death date is contained in the *Necrologio dei laici* of the church of S. Domenico, Siena: " Sozzinus ser Mini de Percena sepultus est die XII iunii 1355. " H. Laurent and F. Valli, *Fontes vitae S. Catharinae Senensis historici. Vol. XX: I necrologi di San Domenico in Camporeggio*. (Florence, 1937), p. 81. The death of his son, Pietro, is entered under the date June 12, 1363. *Ibid*, p. 95.

5. (Francesco).

d. 1398. In 1362 he was appointed the first *castellano* of the *Rocca* (fortress) of Montalcino. Ms. Passerini 227, n. 36. Collezione Genealogica Passerini, Biblioteca Nazionale, Firenze. On 10 October, 1368, " Franceschinus Soczini capitaneus et vexillifer Masse terzerii dicti, " is listed as a member of the *Consiglio Generale* of

Siena. G. Luchaire, *Documenti per la storia dei rivolgimenti politici del Comune di Siena dal 1354 al 1369* (Lyon and Paris, 1906), p. 155. He was a member of the *Signoria* in 1377 and Ambassador to Florence in 1381. Cantù, II, 506. According to Gigli, II, 248, he served on embassies for Siena on five occasions. In 1380 he was a middle-man or *mezano* when Siena indemnified Guglielmo di Giurino (Bishop from 1371-1377) for damages he had sustained at Crevole. Donato di Neri, *Cronaca*, p. 680. On 26 May, 1385 he was elected one of the ten *Priori* from the *Terzo* of San Martino for a term of three months. Paolo di Tommaso Montauri, " Cronaca Senese " in L. A. Muratori, *op. cit.*, XV, Part 6^2, p. 711. After he died in Mantova, a memorial service was held in the church of S. Domenico in Siena (the traditional resting-place of the Sozzini), on the last day of August, 1398.

" Francischinus Sozzini ser Mini de Percena mortuus est Mantue et factum est hic in conventu officium pro anima sua die ultima augusti (1398). " *Necrologio*, p. 167.

6. (Percena).

d. 1376 and buried in S. Domenico. Cantù, II, 506.

" Percena ser Mini de Percena sepultus (sic) est die XXV februarii sub testudinibus iuxta primam moram in ingressu versus ortus ad manum dextram. " *Necrologio*, p. 120.

7. (Giovanni).

Married (Lodovica ?) Bargagli. He was *Capitano del Popolo* in 1351 and 1356; of the *Dodici* in 1361, 1363 and 1367. Cantù, II, 506. However, he is listed as *Capitano* and *Gonfaloniere* only for the period from January 1, to February 29, 1356 in the *Archivio del Concistoro del Comune di Siena* (Rome, 1952), p. 5. He was *Capitano del Popolo* also in 1361 at the time of the hostilities with Montalcino according to the " Kalendarium Ecclesiae Metropolitanae Senensis, " L. A. Muratori, *op. cit.*, XV, Part 6^1, p. 30. He served Siena on several embassies: to Cortona in 1350, to Florence in 1359, to the count of Montefeltro in 1362, and again to Florence in 1364 to negotiate peace with Pisa. Cf. Giovanni Vincenzio Coresi del Bruno's manuscript, " Descrizione et armi gentilizie delle famiglie di Siena, che hanno goduto il Supremo Magistrato, " II, 494. Biblioteca Nazionale, Firenze, II. I. 209. When Cardinal Aegidius, the Legate to Italy of Innocent VI, sought to end the strife raging among the Tuscan states, " Giovanni di Ser Mino di Sozzo " was one of the citizens selected on April 21, 1359, to settle Siena's differences with neighboring Perugia. Malavolti, *op. cit.*, T. II, Bk. VII, f. 119 v. When Siena promised 27,000 florins in October, 1364 to the marauding English mercenary company of " Messer Alberetto " if the latter would abandon her territory, six citizens, including Giovanni, were surrendered as security for payment; they were eventually released upon the fulfilment of the agreement. *Ibid*, f. 126 r. and Donato di Neri, " Cronaca Senese, " *op. cit.*, XV, Part 6^2, pp. 607-608.

As a member of the *Concistoro* his recommendation was approved on April 25, 1368 that a certain Franciscan friar should be compelled to reveal everything that he knew about a plot to overthrow the government of the *Dodici*. Luchaire, *op. cit.*, p. 125 f. An unnamed daughter (perhaps an infant) died on May 2, 1363. *Necrologio*, p. 91. Giovanni's own death occurred in 1374: " Johannes ser Mini de Percena sepultus est die XII augusti. " *Ibid*, p. 115.

8. (Lodovico).

Cited by Cantù, II, 506 as mentioned in a document preserved in the *Spedale di Santa Maria della Scala* (1335).

9. (Margherita).

d. 1360 and buried in San Domenico. Cantù, II, 506.

" Domina Margherita filia olim ser Mini de Percena sepulta est in XXVII mensis iunii (1360). " *Necrologio*, p. 86.

10. (Agnese).

Married a certain Filippo di Lapo who died in 1397. Cantù, II, 506.
"Domina Agnes soror Iohannis et Benedicti ser Mini de Percena sepulta est die 27 Augusti in sepulcrum patrum suorum." *Necrologio*, p. 165.

11. (Pietro).

Dominican who became Master of Theology at Paris. Subsequently he was appointed Inquisitor of Siena by Bishop Donusdeo Malavolti. I. Ugurgieri, *Le Pompe Sanesi*, 2 vols., (Pistoia, 1649), I, 339 records that from Paris he brought many books to enrich the Dominican monastery in Siena. Gigli, II, 246, states that in Paris Pietro had become a Doctor of Theology and gives his death date as 1363. According to Cantù, II, 506, he perished from the plague in 1348.
He accompanied a certain "Giacomo di Guglielmo" on an embassy to Clement VI in Avignon. Their instructions, dated December 3, 1346, are published in M. Chiadauno, "I Rothschild del duecento," *Bullettino Senese di Storia Patria*, VI (1935), 140-142. The mission's goal was the removal of the interdict which had been laid on Siena by Papal envoys on October 26, 1345. The *Necrologio dei Religiosi* of S. Domenico records his passing (p. 5): "Anno Domini 1348, fuit dura pestis. Frater Petrus Sozzii, dum erat actu prior conventus."

12. (Benedetto).

According to Coresi del Bruno, *op. cit.*, II, 494, he is named as the first of his family to hold a position in the supreme magistracy of Siena, in the *Concistoro* (1359). However, Cantù indicates that Giovanni (see above, n. 7) was a *Capitano del Popolo* in 1351.
He was one of the three Sienese ambassadors to Urban V in Avignon, in 1367. On the clamorous sequel to the embassy, resulting from the "slanderous" allegations of one of them, Giovanni Pagliaresi, against the *Dodici*, cf. Malavolti, T. II, Bk. VII, f. 128 r. and Donato di Neri, "Cronaca Senese," *op. cit.*, XV, Part 6², p. 615. He was one of the ambassadors sent from Siena to the Emperor Charles IV, when he entered Lombardy in 1368. Donato di Neri, "Cronaca Senese," *op. cit.*, XV, Part 6², p. 616. In 1385 he was one of the negotiators imposing onerous terms upon the city of Montepulciano. Malavolti, *op. cit.*, T. II, Bk. IX, f. 155 r. In 1391 at the head of a squadron under the Visconti of Milan, he set fire to two of Florence's city gates. Although he had been declared a rebel by Siena, this daring action against the traditional enemy restored him to favor. Coresi del Bruno, *op. cit.*, II, 495.
On January 12, 1369 he is a member of the *Consiglio Generale* debating the reply that should be made to the demand for funds imposed on Siena by Emperor Charles IV. Benedetto's proposal to relegate the matter to the proper financial authorities of the republic (Provisores Biccherne, Executores kabelle, etc.) was approved by 223 to 31 votes. Luchaire, *op. cit.*, p. 211. His death in recorded in the *Necrologio* (p. 163): "Benedictus ser Mini de Percena sepultus est in sepulcro suorum in Claustro die XXIIII aprilis (1395)."

13. (Barbato).

d. 1374. A daughter died in 1363 and was buried in San Domenico. Cantù, II, 507.

14. (Mino).

d. 1419. He served in the *Signoria* in 1389, 1395 and 1399. Cantù, II, 507.
He was one of the witnesses at the canonization trial of Caterina Benincasa in Venice. Mino's testimony given in Siena on March 5, 1415 related a visit of the future saint to two learned Augustinians in Lecceto where she miraculously demonstrated her ability to read and interpret scriptures. R. Fawtier, *Sainte Catherine de Sienne*, 2 vols., (Paris, 1921-1930), II, 5. Although Fawtier is not able to identify Mino, he suggests that he had "fait partie de la *famiglia* de Catherine." (p. 39). A daughter of Mino died in August, 1420. *Necrologio*, p. 222. His own death

occurred earlier in the year, probably caused by the plague that was then ravaging Siena: " Minus Johannis ser Mino obiit die prima aprilis, fuit sepultum corpus eius die 2 dicti mensis (April) in claustro in sepulcro suorum antecessorum iuxta partem conventus. " *Ibid,* p. 220.

15. (Sozzino).

d. 1403. He was a *Priore* in 1389 and 1398 and a *Gonfaloniere* for the *Terzo* of San Martino in 1400. In 1376 he had been ambassador to Arezzo. Cantù, II, 507.

" Sozzinus Iohannis ser Mini de Percena probus et honoratus civis, dilector specialis ordinis et conventus, sepultus est die 10 Maii 1403 in sepulcro paterno in claustro. " *Necrologio,* p. 181. He married Margherita di Francesco Malavolti in 1376 when she was fifteen years of age. On May 30, 1407, a widow for four years, she sued, through her son, Giovanni (N. 20) who was her *procuratore,* for the sum of 1400 florins which had been denied to her at her father's death (1374) by certain of her Malavolti relations. The pertinent document is published in the *Miscellanea Storica Senese,* IV (1876), 166 and by C. Mazzi, *Cose Senesi in Codici Ashburnhamiani,* (Siena, 1897), 76 f.

16. (Bartolomeo).

A son, Girolamo, was a *Priore* in 1499. Cantù, II, 507.

16a. (Giovanni).

" Johannes Sozzini Iohannis Ser Mini de Percena die 22 settembris (1428) sepultus est in claustro in sepulcro paterno. Requiescat in pace clementia Salvatoris. " *Necrologio,* p. 254. He does not appear in Cantù's genealogy.

17. (Lorenzo).

d. 1462. Cantù, II, 507. For a Lorenzo Sozi (?) who was elected to the *Signoria* in December, 1479 from the *Terzo* of San Martino and who was banished to Lucca in the upheaval of 1480, cf. C. Cantoni, " Cronaca, " pp. 881 and 886.

18. (Francesco).

d. 1381. Cantù, II, 507. This date is certainly incorrect.

When his son Lorenzo was captured by soldiers in the hire of Florence, the jurist, Francesco Accolti of Arezzo, wrote to Lorenzo de' Medici begging his release. The letter, dated November, 1478 is published in A. Fabronio, *Laurentii Medicis Magnificii vita,* 2 vols., (Pisa, 1784), II, 135.

19. (Caterina).

Married a Fazio Bellarmati with 450 florins in dowry. Cantù, II, 507. Their son, Sozzino, was created *cavaliere* on 25 June, 1480. Cristoforo Cantoni, " Cronaca Senese, " Muratori, *op. cit.,* XV, Part 6^2, p. 884. Together with his more celebrated cousin, the jurist Bartolomeo (see n. 26 below) he was on the list of thirty-six citizens given the *Balìa* in the uprising of June, 1482. *Ibid.,* p. 896.

20. (Giovanni).

d. 1427. Progenitor of Branch B of the Sozzini family in Cantù's genealogy, II, 512-514.

21. (Mariano senior).

First great jurisconsult in the Sozzini family. He studied law in Padua and Siena, in the latter university under one of the most learned Canonists of the age, Nicolò Tedeschi, who taught there from 1418-1431. Mariano quickly became a doctor and then proceeded to read canon law alongside his former master. On 24 September, 1427, Roberto dei Cavalcanti was hired " ad lecturam Sexti et Clementinarum ad concurrentiam cum Domino Mariano Sozzini. " Archivio di Stato di Siena, *Concistoro*, Vol. 369, f. 16. In 1430, with Fra Pietro of the Order of Hermits of St. Augustine, he was named arbitrator to compose a dispute between Fra Silvestro da Bologna, a miniature painter, and a Florentine student at Siena, Giuliano Nelli, who had not been able to agree on the value of certain miniatures executed by the artist on a codex belonging to the student. G. Milanesi, *Documenti per la storia dell'arte senese*, 3 vols. (Siena, 1854-1856), II, 155. In 1431 he was again hired by the Sienese *Studium* to read the Sixth book of Decretals at the salary of thirty florins. Archivio di Stato di Siena, *Concistoro*, Vol. 393, f. 67 v. But in 1432 he was exiled for political reasons. *Ibid.*, Vol. 399, f. 4 v. Three years later his *condotta* in canon law was renewed at a salary of sixty florins. L. Zdekauer, *Lo Studio di Siena nel Rinascimento* (Milan, 1894), p. 167.

His most celebrated pupil was a Sienese of his own generation, Aeneas Sylvius Piccolomini, later Pius II. The latter's love and esteem for his master were shown in many ways. On various occasions he described him as the closest of his Sienese friends: " Enim namque dum Senis essem, unice dilexi nec diminutus est amor, quamvis separatus est. " Cited from G. Paparelli, *Enea Silvio Piccolomini* (Bari, 1950), p. 23. He also praised him as a great jurist: " Marianus Sozinus per id tempus scientia juris non solum apud Senenses, sed tota Italia late clarus habitus est. " *Aenae Sylvii Piccolominei Senensis.... Opera quae extant omnia* (Basel, 1551), p. 456. He willingly recommended Sozzini to the Austrian Chancellor, Hans Mayrs, for a teaching post in Vienna: " Alloquetur te.... Mariani Sozini Senensis, utriusque iuris doctoris excellentissimi qui libenter in hac temporis tribulatione ad Germaniae partes se transferret, & ius Viennae legeret. " *Opera*, epist. 40, p. 526. An early literary piece by the humanist Pope, the famous *Storia di due amanti* (1444) was written at the urging of Mariano. It recounted with fictional names an amorous adventure of Gaspar Schlick, a high Austrian courtier, in Siena during an Italian journey. A modern writer has attempted to identify the unfaithful matron of the romance, Lucrezia, with the wife of Sozzini, and consequently views the work as a treacherous joke played on Mariano by his friend. G. Zannoni, " Per la storia di una storia d'amore, " *La Cultura*, XI (1890), 85 f. This suggestion is, however, soundly refuted by A. Frugoni, " Enea Silvio Piccolomini e l'avventura senese di Gaspare Schlick, " *Incontri nel Rinascimento* (Brescia, 1954), p. 25 f.

The figure of Mariano has descended to posterity clothed in a legendary reputation for learning and culture. Ugurgieri, I, 430 described him as an " arca di scienze " whose opinions, respected as if they had emanated from the mouth of God, were never opposed or refuted by anyone. He was reputed to have been, together with Piccolomini, a charter member of the *Accademia Grande* (c. 1425), an institutionalization of learned literary discussions which had, according to the tradition, flourished continuously in Siena from as early as the middle of the 12th century. Cf., for example, Gigli, I, 268. For more realistic accounts, see L. P. Costantini, *L'Accademia degli Intronati di Siena e una sua Commedia* (Siena, 1928), p. 64 and A. Della Torre, *Storia dell'Accademia Platonica di Firenze* (Florence, 1902), p. 142 f. Mariano was also credited with having introduced the tradition of Provencal poetry to Siena. Gigli, I, 418. His eulogy by Piccolomini is extremely impressive: " His knowledge of philosophy is akin to Plato's, of geometry to Boethius' and of mathematics to Macrobius. There is no musical instrument which he does not play and he is as expert in agriculture as Virgil.... he sculpts like Praxiteles nor is he unacquainted with the medical arts. " *Opera*, Ep. 112, p. 622.

Sozzini's published writings are listed and evaluated by J. F. von Schulte, *Geschichte der Quellen und Litteratur des Canonischen Rechts*, 3 vols. (Stuttgart, 1875-1880), II, 319: " Seine Schriften konnen auf grossen wissenschaftlichen werth keinen Anspruch machen, geben aber eine Fülle interessanter Notizen für die Literatur bekunden zugleich grossen Fleiss und werden haüfig citirt. " For an earlier and more favorable estimate, cf. G. Panciroli, *De claris legum interpretibus libri quatuor* (Venice, 1637), p. 150 f. Many of his writings, some of which were now published for the first time, were collected in a late edition dedicated to Clement VIII, entitled: *Mariani Socini.... Commentaria Omnia quae extant in jus canonicum.... cum nonnullis additionibus D. Bartholomaei ejus filii* (Venice, Giunti, 1593). His *Repetitio quod si super positi in c. quoniam frequentes ut lite non contestate* (Siena: Heinrich of Cologne and Hendrick of Harlem, 1491) is a bibliographis curiosity, since it is the only book known to have been printed in Siena by the two northern printers in partnership. It had been ordered by Benedetto Ciccolini, a lawyer of Lucca. Seven early editions of his writings are listed in M. Stillwell, *Incunabula in American Libraries* (New York, 1940), p. 46.

In his *Consilia* (I Cons., 13: 16), Mariano attributed the *plenitudo potestatis* to the Pope: " Potest papa dispensare et absolvere a iuramento per quod iurans Deo et homini obligatur.... Papa est vicarius Christi.... Dei, locum gerens in terram.... unde omnia regit et disponit et iudicat, prout sibi placet.... et habet plenitudo potestatis.... in omnibus et per omnia potest dicere quicquid placet.... " Cited from G. Pilati, *Chiesa e Stato nei primi quindici secoli* (Rome, 1961), p. 356.

Manuscript copies of his legal opinions are dispersed in several European libraries: " Consilium de iudiciali confessione, " Biblioteca Vaticana, Cod. Ottob. Lat. 1727, ff. 26 r.-27 v.; " Consilium de pupillari substitutione, " Cod. Ottob. Lat. 1726, ff. 14 r.-147 r.; " Consilium de bonis damnatorum, " *Ibid.*, ff. 168 r.-173 r.; " Tractatus in materia oblationum, " Biblioteca Nazionale, Firenze: *Fondo* Magliabecchiano, F. 20. a. The " Voto legale di Mariano Sozzini (il Vecchio) e di altri giurisperiti, nella successione controversa di Monsignore Carlo Bartali, vescovo di Siena " is cited in the *Archivio di Stato di Siena, le Sale della Mostra* (Rome, 1956), vol. XXIII, n. 83. In 1459-1460, Mariano pronounced one of several favorable opinions, " De statu et approbatione religiosorum clericorum pauperum Christi Ihesuatorum vulgariter appelatorum, " Biblioteca Riccardiana, Firenze Cod. 1186, ff. 1 r.-21 v. His opinion, *c.* 1460-1462, in favor of the *Comune* of Siena in its litigation with Colle di Valdelsa over the boundaries of the two cities in the *Valle* di Strove and concerning possession of Montevasone is preserved in the Archivio di Stato, Siena: *Inventario dei Capitoli*, 183. In July, 1454 when a dispute broke out between the " foreign " readers and the Rector of the Sienese *Studio* over certain payments that should have been made in the latter's favor, the *Concistoro* decided to place the decision in the hands of Mariano. But after his impartiality in this case was assailed by two colleagues, Francesco Accolti and Giovanni d'Arezzo, representing the non-Sienese doctors, the case was removed from Sozzini's competence and delivered to the *Podestà* and to the *Capitano di Giustizia*. C. Corso, " Francesco Accolti d'Arezzo lettore di diritto nello studio di Siena, " *Bullettino della Società Senese di Storia Patria*, XV (1956), 28, 54-55.

Sozzini's famous " Tractatus de sortibus, " Biblioteca Vaticana, Cod. Reginense 1272, ff. 1 r.-37 r. was dedicated to Cardinal Bessarion. " Novissime opusculi de sortibus ad rev.mum Cardinalem Nicenum transmisi, " wrote Sozzini to Piccolomini on September 19, 1443, Biblioteca Vaticana, Cod. Urb. Lat. 402, f. 60 v.; and the latter replied from Gratz on December 8: " Tuas sortes si quando ad me miseris avide videbo. " *Ibid.*, f. 63 v. See also L. Zdekauer, " Dello scritto ' De Sortilegiis ' di Mariano Sozzini il vecchio, " *Archivio per lo studio delle tradizioni popolari*, XV (1896), 131-137 and " Sopra un'opera sconosciuta di Mariano Socino il vecchio, " *Studi Senesi*, II (1885), 341 f. Other Ms. versions of this treatise are preserved in the library of the Convent of San Domenico in Bologna. M. Laurent, *Fabio Vigili et les Bibliothèques de Bologne au début du XVIe siècle d'après le Ms. Barb. Lat. 3185* (Città del Vaticano, 1943), p. 60; in the Biblioteca Casanatense, Rome, Cod. F. III. 33 (619); Biblioteca Angelica, Rome: N. 90 A. 8. 2. N. 9; Biblioteca Nacional, Madrid, 2209. XXI. L. Hain, *Repertorium Bibliographicum*, n. 14894 attributes to Mariano a published work entitled, *Il libro delle sorti a instantia del Pigro Cerretano*. Florentiae, apud S. Iacobum de Ripoli (n. d.), but which he dates *c.* 1483-1484.

In view of his own descendant's condemnation by the Inquisition in the next century as a practicer of magic arts (see Cornelio, n. 46), it is interesting to note f. 36 v. of the *De Sortibus*: " Illud minime omittendum censeo quod hereticae pravitatis inquisitor ita demum de sortilegiis cognoscere possit si heresim sapiant manifestam; si autem heresim saperent sed non manifestam ad inquisitoris cognitionem non pertinerent. "

In the Biblioteca Classense, Ravenna (cf. Mazzatinti's, *Inventari*, IV, n. 373) is preserved the, " Repetitio domini Nicolai de Ubaldis de testamentis et ultimis voluntatibus Repetitiones Benedicti Caprae, Mariani de Sozinis, Antonii de Budino, Angeli (de Ubaldis), Iohannis de Imola, Pauli de Castro. " The Biblioteca del Convento di San Francesco at Assisi (cf. Mazzatinti, IV, n. 205) contains the " Repertorium iuris civilis. Significacio verborum, Explicit repertorium domini Mariani Cucini de Senis excellentissimi utriusque doctoris completum per manus Iacobi Colloniensis alias Iuliensis A.D. 1460, die X mensis octobris. " In the Library of the Metropolitni Kapitoly, Prague, Ms. 1133, ff. 289 r.-328 v., is preserved: " Mariani Socini de Senis contra sententiam sanguinis, " in which he declares that " Clericus nec dictare nec proferre sentenciam sanguinis debet. " In Madrid, Biblioteca Nacional, Ms. 2209-XIV, is preserved the " Marianus Socinus Senensis Tractatus ludi, per dominum.... Iste tractatus ludii examinatus est per peritissimum virum dominum Marianum Sozinum iuris utrisque profesorem in c. inter dilectos sub titulo de excesibus prelatorum....; " *Ibid.*, Ms. 2141-II, " Marianus Socinus Commentaria super de purgatione canonica rubricam. " In its *Prohemium* we read: " In nomine Ihesu Christi. Quoniam in superioribus titulis tractatum est de prelatorum et clericorum delictis. ". This contains chapters 1-6, and the 7th incomplete of the Commentary to the *rubrica* " De purgatione canonica " of the second part of the 5th Book of Decretals. (Cf. *Mariani Socini Nova et utilissima Commentaria super secunda parte libri quinti Decretalium, nunc primum in lucem edita...*, Parmae, ex typogr. S. Viothi, 1574). Also in the Biblioteca Nacional, Madrid, Ms. 735-VI is Mariano's " Commentaria super prima parte libri quinti Decretalium de homicidio voluntario, vel casuali.... " This treatise which was begun by him in June, 1437 and then abandoned was only completed in June, 1440 by a certain Gregory of Siscar " et aliorum scolarium " of Sozzini's at his urging. In Cortona, Biblioteca del Comune e dell'Accademia Etrusca (cf. Mazzatinti, XVIII, n. 187), are conserved the voluminous reminiscences of Mariano by one of his students: " Recollecte famosissimi atque preclarissimi utriusque iuris doctoris domini mei domini Mariani Sozzini de Senis legentis sub annis Domini MCCCCXLIIII die vero 26 ottobris. Ego Iohannes Cecchi de Cinughio minimus canonum scholaris collegi sub dicto domino in summa devotione. "

In 1465 Mariano was entrusted by the government of Siena with the defense of its claims over the Abbey of Sant'Anastasio. The Cardinal of Spoleto was attempting to sever Siena's ties with the Abbey and transfer it to Roman jurisdiction. N. Mengozzi, *Il Pontefice Paolo II ed i Senesi* (Siena, 1918), p. 277 f.

For the transfer in 1794 to the Biblioteca Laurenziana in Florence of legal manuscripts which had been handed down in the Sozzini family for generations, cf. N. Mengozzi, " Reliquie Sozziniane, " *Bullettino Senese di Storia Patria*, IV (1897), 155-181.

From what must have been a voluminous correspondence, a handful of letters only have been published: F. Marletta, " Una lettera volgare di Mariano Sozzini il vecchio, " *Bullettino Senese di Storia Patria*, XX (1942), 22-36. It is dated Modena, October 6, 1438 and is addressed to the *Signoria* of Siena. As a Doctor of Canon Law, Mariano had been attending the early sessions of the Council at Ferrara. After the first reports of its possible transfer, he had hoped to bring it to Siena and thus undercut Florence. In the present letter, he defends himself from the accusation that he had been motivated by a desire to subvert the ruling faction in Siena: " Hora o sentito che alcuni, e quali cercano di nuocermi con false calunnie, anno fabricato che io volevo fare venire el papa a Siena perchè lui dovunque va è mutatore di stati, conductore di perturbatione et operatore di scandoli. Queste quanto sieno calunniose infamie so certo ciascuno il cognosce.... " Another letter is published by F. Novati, " Una lettera ed un sonetto di Mariano Sozzini, " *Bullettino Senese di Storia Patria*, II (1895), 89-100. It is dated 12 kal. November, 1462 and addressed to Antonio Tridentone of Parma.

The epistolary exchange between Sozzini and Aeneas Sylvius Piccolomini has been preserved in the latter's already cited *Opera*. Cf. Epist. 39, 113, 160, 185 and 208. For references to Mariano in Piccolomini's correspondence, cf. Epist. 40, 112, 133, 146 and 149. A letter to Sozzini from another Piccolomini is in *Epistolae et Commentarii Iacobi Picolomini Cardinalis Papiensis* (Milan, 1506), f. 5 r. which closes with: " Saluta meis verbis Bartholomeum Iureconsultum filium tuum ac totam familiam. " Two letters of uncertain date (but probably c. 1457) to Mariano from Poggio Bracciolini are contained in T. De Tonellis, *Poggii Epistolae*, 3 vols. (Florence, 1832-

1861), I, 199 f. and III, 286 f. From the second letter and from others directed to Francesco Marescalco of Ferrara (Vol. III, 285 f. and 290 f.), it results that Poggio was intending to entrust the education of his adolescent son to Mariano Sozzini.

Three Ms. letters from Siena to Giovanni di Cosimo de' Medici, dated 27 December 1458, 24 September, 1459 and 5 May, 1461 are listed in the *Archivio Mediceo avanti il Principato*, 3 vols., (Rome, 1951-1957), I, 120, 164. Others are reported to be in the *Archivio Capitolare* of Siena. Cf. the special issue of the *Archivio Storico Italiano*, CXIV (1956), 625, devoted to "notizie degli Archivi Toscani"; it has been impossible to locate them.

In 1431 Mariano had married Niccola, daughter of Pietro Aldobrandini. J. F. von Schulte, *op. cit.*, II, 320. The celebrated Sienese artist, Lorenzo di Pietro detto il Vecchietta, executed a statue of Mariano which was intended to repose on his tomb. It is presently in the *Museo* del Bargello in Florence, although N. Mengozzi, *op. cit.*, p. 181 contends that there is not sufficient evidence to identify the subject of the statue with Mariano Sozzini. Mariano's funeral oration was pronounced by the Sienese humanist historian, Agostino Dati (d. 1478). It was printed as Bk. V, *Oratio* III in his *Opera* (Siena, 1503).

Legal *consilia* by Mariano Sozzini in the Biblioteca Nazionale, Firenze: Codici Panciatichiani are cited by P. Kristeller's *Iter Italicum* (London, Leiden, 1963), I, 146; another copy of Mariano's *Consilia* on the Jesuati is in Milan, Biblioteca Ambrosiana. *Ibid*, p. 297; other *consilia* are in Lucca, Biblioteca Capitolare. *Ibid.*, p. 253. A legal act dated September 25, 1467 executed "in domo domini Mariani Sozini et in studio domini Bartholomei, eius filii," is preserved in Siena, Archivio di Stato, *Carte di privati. Registro notarile*. Mariano died 5 days later. A great deal of manuscript material dealing with litigation that Siena and later the Grand Duchy of Tuscany conducted first with the Abbey of S. Anastasio and later with the Church over boundaries, census payments and jurisdictional questions in general, covering the period March 11, 1286-April 5, 1604, is in *A.S.S.*, Riformagioni Sant Anastasio. MSS. B. 16 and B. 18. Bishop Carlo Bartali who died on September 22, 1444 left the substance of his wealth to the *Spedale* and Cathedral of Siena. His testament was disputed and the ensuing controversy was not settled until 1446. Mariano and his colleague, a certain Ser Falasco, played key roles in settling the litigation. Cf. V. Lusini, *Il Duomo di Siena*, 2 vols., (Siena, 1911-1939), II, 45. According to Cantù (II, 507), at the suggestion of John of Capistrano, Mariano in 1449 founded a monastery for the "Padri osservanti d'Asinalunga" which was named Santa Maria di Monte Baldino. We have found no evidence supporting this, although Professor Myron Gilmore communicated in a recent letter from Rome that among Mariano's published *Consilia* was one on the necessity of taking communion once a week at Easter, written at the request of Capistrano.

According to the traditional account, Mariano received the title of Consistorial Advocate from Pius II. See instead the latter's *De viris illustribus* (Stuttgart, 1842), p. 27, the biographical sketch of Sozzini in which Piccolomini declares: "Hunc Eugenius Pontifex advocatum consistorialem creavit, libenterque in Romana curia habuisset, sed cives eum non permiserunt." A sonnet dedicated by Piccolomini "Ad Marianum" and which begins "Quicquid tu tangis, subito, Mariane fit aurum," is published in G. Cugnoni, "Aenae Silvii Piccolomini Senensis.... Opera inedita," *Atti della R. Accademia dei Lincei. Anno CCLXXX (1882-83). Ser. 3. Memorie della classe di scienze morali, storiche e filologiche*, vol. VIII, 676.

An undated letter from Poggio Bracciolini insinuates that Mariano had walked off with a precious coin from his archeological collection during a visit. But he accepts Sozzini's excuses and explanations. If he had held certain suspicions against him, he lays them aside for he esteems more Mariano's friendship than any coin, even of silver and gold. T. de Tonellis, *op. cit.*, I, 199 ff. dates the letter in 1426. See on this episode, E. Walser, *Poggius Florentinus leben und werke* (Leipzig, 1914), p. 149. The famous *insignia* of the Sozzini and other Sienese families related to them, supposedly painted by Mariano and cited by G. Panciroli, *op. cit.*, p. 359 still existed in the 18th century. See G. della Valle, *Lettere senesi sopra le belle arti*, 3 vols., (Venice-Rome, 1782-1786), III, 67: "Questa pergamena disegnata, e intagliata con pazienza indicibile dal celebre Mariano il vecchio si conserva tuttavia dal sudetto Signor Bartolomeo (Sozzini) insieme ad alcuni fiori vivissimamente da quegli dipinti in carta." The same distant descendant at that time also possessed the reclining statue of Mariano by Vecchietta now in the Bargello in Florence. P. Cellini, "La reintegrazione di un'opera sconosciuta di Lorenzo di Pietro detto il Vecchietta," *La Diana,* V (1930), 243. The long entry in the *Necrologio* of San Domenico marking the death of Sozzini is in L. Zdekauer, *Lo Studio,* p. 78.

22. (Giovanni).

b. 1432. Cantù, II, 508.

23. (Margherita).

Married Salimbene Capocci in 1459 with 1000 florins in dowry. Cantù, II, 508.

24. (Camillo).

b. 1434. Cantù, II, 508.

25. (Giovan Sozzino).

b. 1442. Cantù, II, 508.

26. (Bartolomeo).

1436-1507. Jurisconsult. Married Ludovica Orlandina. Progenitor of Branch A of the Sozzini family in Cantù's genealogy, II, 510-512. He surpassed even his celebrated father in fame and eccentricity. His legal studies were accomplished in Siena under Tommaso Dotti and Mariano, his father, and in Bologna under Alessandro da Imola and Andrea Barbazza. G. Tiraboschi, *Storia della Letteratura Italiana,* (Modena, 1790), VI, 569. His brilliant and turbulent career began in Siena where he read Canon Law in 1471. Tiraboschi, *ibid.,* cites Bartolomeo's commentary on the Falcidian Law composed "dum legeret ordinarie in Jure Canonico in almo Studio Senensi anno Domini MCCCCLXXI). He spent the following academic year, 1472-1473, teaching at Ferrara. At its completion, he broke his contract, a breach of faith that he would often repeat, to accept a lucrative appointment at the University of Pisa, under Florentine jurisdiction: 800 florins against the 350 that Ferrara could pay. A. Visconti, *La storia dell'università di Ferrara, 1391-1950* (Bologna, 1950), p. 25. A. Fabronio, *Historiae Academiae Pisanae,* 3 vols., (Pisa, 1791), I, 206 publishes the correspondence of 1473 between Filippo de' Medici, Archbishop of Pisa, and the Prefects of the University of Pisa, which describes their efforts to lure the celebrated jurist to their city. M. Gilmore, "The Lawyers and the Church in the Italian Renaissance," *Rice Institute Pamphlet,* XLVI (1960), 136-154 analyzes the high esteem enjoyed by the legal profession, the fierce rivalry among states to secure its most popular representatives for their universities, and the large salaries lavished upon them "altogether out of proportion to what was earned by anyone else in academic life," p. 141. According to L. Zdekauer, *Lo Studio,* p. 59, the Sienese authorities attempted in vain to impede Bartolomeo's departure by informing him on 12 May, 1473 that it had been deliberated on 12 February, 1338 "che nissuno dottore potesse andare a leggere in altra città, senza licenza speciale." This is somewhat puzzling since Bartolomeo was supposedly at the time already teaching in a "foreign" university, Ferrara.

Bartolomeo was often sought for his legal counsel: in 1478 by Lorenzo de' Medici on the Interdict of Sixtus IV. A. Fabronio, *op. cit.,* I, 217; in the controversy between Lucca and Jewish usurers (1493-1494), the opinions of Bartolomeo, Savonarola, and other leading jurists and theologians were sought. They are cited in the *Inventario del R. Archivio di Stato in Lucca* (Lucca, 1872), I, 362. On 29 August, 1501 Sozzini was paid 21 gold florins by the *comune* of Volterra "per il consiglio facto sopra le differenze delle gabelle del contado" and two days later, four more florins "per fare scrivere el consiglio nella causa delle Prunete," a contested section of land. M. Battistini, "Bartolomeo Sozzini consulente del Comune di Volterra," *Bullettino Senese di Storia Patria,* XXVII (1920), 110.

Like his father, before him, Bartolomeo was teacher to a future Pope. At Pisa, his most distinguished pupil (and subsequently his generous benefactor) was the young Giovanni de' Medici who, upon his elevation to the Cardinalate at the age of thirteen (1489), was despatched to Pisa to be educated. Bartolomeo, " il quale gli fe cinque argomenti, " was one of Giovanni's examiners at his *esame di laurea* in Canon Law. Cited from a contemporary letter in G. B. Picotti, *La giovinezza di Leone X* (Milan, 1928), p. 681.

In the summer of 1489, Bartolomeo returned to Siena, after he had duly warned the Florentine authorities, by a letter dated May 11, 1489, that he could no longer remain in Pisa. A. Fabronio, *op. cit.*, I, 209-210. The Florentines then sent Francesco Gaddi to Siena, to persuade Bartolomeo to return to Pisa. Gaddi even exerted pressure on the Sienese *Balìa* to use its influence on Sozzini, but in vain. When, in December, Bartolomeo attempted to flee to Padua where a magnificent offer of salary awaited him, he was seized at night on the road by the Florentines and thrown into prison. His release was eventually effected on March 9, 1490, only after relentless negotiation between Florence and Sienese Ambassadors, and the pledging of 15,000 florins as guarantee that Bartolomeo would respect the terms of his Pisan contract. Fabronio, I, 216 f. But his salary was set at the enormous figure of 1665 florins.

Sozzini's academic career ended in the famous *Studium* of Bologna. He had first taught there briefly in 1479 and in 1494 (reading Civil Law). On 26 October, 1496, the University offered him 605 gold ducats to persuade him to return to Bologna, and, as added inducement, the municipal government itself offered to pay for the transportation of his books and belongings. At the final examination of Bartolomeo Barbazza, on October 14, 1496, it was recorded that Sozzini was present, " gymnasii nostri unico splendore qui jura civilia stipendio publico florenorum sexcentorum auri largorum docet. " Two years later even the rent of his house was provided by the city. For Sozzini's Bolognese sojourn, see G. Zaccagnini, *Storia dello Studio di Bologna durante il Rinascimento* (Geneva, 1930), p. 103, f. He publishes a letter directed by one of Bartolomeo's students to the University Senate, lamenting the too frequent vacations, the inconvenient hours of the lectures, the ignorance and laziness of many of the readers, etc. It is dated, November 29, 1496. *Ibid.*, p. 52. According to G. Facciolati, *Fasti Gymnasii Patavini*, 3 vols. (Padua, 1757), I, 57, Bartolomeo also read at Padova for a triennium commencing in 1498. He had previously been invited to this *Studio* in 1479 and, again, a decade later. He was prevented from accepting the second invitation, as we have seen, by the forceful action of the Florentines.

Sozzini's political life followed the brilliant but uneven pattern of his academic career. In 1480 he was declared a rebel by Siena and his property confiscated after his faction, the *Dodici*, were excluded from the government. Cristoforo Cantoni, " Cronaca Senese, " L. A. Muratori, *op. cit.*, XV, Part 6², p. 887. (For a guide to the various rival parties and factions aspiring to power in Siena, cf. D. L. Hicks, " Sienese Society in the Renaissance, " *Comparative Studies in Society and History*, II [1959-1960], 412-420). However, on July 7, 1482, the Sienese populace revolted: " Ora circiter 15 levato lo popolo in arme con grandissimo impeto correndo al palazo, domandò che li forousciti (sic) dal Monte del Popolo et de' Nove, etiam ribelli di quelli due Monti, et Misser Bartolomeo Sozzini, rebelle del Monte de' Dodici, fussero chiamati et rimessi. " C. Cantoni, " Cronaca ", *op. cit.*, p. 894 f. " Misser Bartolomeo di Misser Mariano Sozzini, dottore, " appeared on the list of thirty six citizens who were given " plenaria auttorità et balìa " in this revolution. *Ibid.*, p. 897. In February, 1483, he was despatched to Florence to persuade the Medici not to support Nero Placidi, Lord of Piombino and Salvano Salvani of Lucca who had rebelled against Siena and were attacking her towns in the *contado*. *Ibid.*, p. 932 f. On the 24th of the same month, he was elected to the *Signoria* from the *Terzo* of San Martino. *Ibid.*, p. 935; and to the new *Balìa* in April and July, 1483. *Ibid.*, p. 938, 941.

Victim of the chronically unstable Sienese political situation, Bartolomeo found himself out of favor and in exile. In 1486, he was the representative of his party, the *Dodici*, in the peace made by the several groups of *fuorusciti* in Pisa. On July 22, 1487, with Pandolfo Petrucci who retained the reins of power for the next two decades, Bartolomeo reentered Siena at the head of a troop of horse, helped to overthrow the Popular *Balìa* and place in power one representing each of the five *Monti*. Tiraboschi, *op. cit.*, III, 52. He was sent off at once to Florence " a dar parte del presente ordinato Reggimento. " G. A. Pecci, *Memorie storico-critiche della città di Siena*, 2 vols., (Siena, 1755), I, 54. On 5 December, 1487, during his term as *Capitano del Popolo*, he delivered an important oration before the Senate convincing that body by a vote of 214-86 to support " che tutti gli Ordini di Siena a un Ordine, ò a un Monte si riducessero. " *Ibid.*, p. 64. Bartolomeo was elected *Capitano* and *Gonfaloniere* of Siena on four occasions: March 1-April 30, 1483; November 1-December 31, 1487; May 1-June 30, 1494; July 1-August 31, 1504. *Archivio del Concistoro del Comune di Siena, Inventario* (Rome, 1952), pp. 121, 126, 133, 143. During his term in June, 1494, he drew up extreme proposals to increase the powers of the *Balìe*, as a means of preserving peace in Siena. But the *Consiglio Generale*, jealous for its own prerogatives and suspicious of the centralization of authority in the hands of the *Balìe*, checked his efforts. Cf. G. Prunai & S. De Colli, " La Balìa dagli inizi del XII sec. fino alla invasione francese (1789), " *Bullettino Senese di Storia Patria*, LXV (1958), 70.

Due to his imprisonment by the Florentines (1489), it has been alleged that Bartolomeo's desire for revenge led him to plot the rebellion of Pisa against Florence in favor of Charles VIII. Ugurgieri, *op. cit.*, I, 430-432 and A. Fabronio, *op. cit.*, I, 219. The latter cites a *Libris Academiae*: " In anno 1494, mense novembris, cum defecisset Pisana civitas ob adventum Regis Francorum, ipse D. Bartholomaeus inimicus nostrae Reipublicae, ut pote Senensis, cum Pisanis faveret, beneficiorum immemor semper in omni actione Florentinis adversatus est. " In January, 1495, he sought to influence the *Balìa* to furnish the Pisans financial assistance against Florence, and on July 10, substantial quantities of grain were sent to the insurgent city. U. Mondolfo, *Pandolfo Petrucci, signore di Siena* (Siena, 1899), p. 28 f. Together with Pandolfo Petrucci, Bartolomeo was one of the seven members of that *Balìa* which on 16 June, 1495 signed a treaty with Charles VIII. A. Lisini, " Inventario dei Capitoli, " *Bullettino Senese di Storia Patria*, VI (1899), 223.

Bartolomeo was Ambassador to Alexander VI, the Borgia Pope, in 1492, conveying Siena's felicitations and obedience. A Lisini, *Relazioni tra Cesare Borgia e la Repubblica Senese* (Siena, 1900), p. 8 f. The magniloquent oration he delivered on this occasion was subsequently printed: *Senensium obedientia publica* (ad Alexandrum VI, auctore B. Socino). Rome (n. d) It is listed by Hain, *op. cit.*, n. 14675. Panciroli's slightly legendary account of this embassy (*op. cit.*, p. 225) would have Bartolomeo suffering a lapse of memory in the middle of his oration, which supposedly had been composed for him by Angelo Poliziano. When the Pope became aware of the orator's embarassment, he is said to have declared that the man's *virtù* had already been sufficiently demonstrated. Whereupon he bestowed upon Sozzini the title of Consistorial Advocate. Not satisfied with this, Panciroli adds that Bartolomeo was struck dumb on a second occasion, during the Venetian embassy in 1499.

In June, 1496 he was on a mission to Ludovico il Moro to negotiate an alliance with Milan against Florence. Cf. the letter of Bindaccio Ricasoli to the Florentine *Balìa*, dated 2 June, 1496: " Lo oratore Milanese che è in Siena et, per lettere, M. Bartolomeo Sozzini che è a Milano, ciascuno persuade et sollecita la legha.... " U. Mondolfo, *op. cit.*, p. 33. When Rinaldo Fungari returned to Siena from Milan, after the defeat of Ludovico, Siena simultaneously sent embassies to the Pope, the French sovereign and Venice. Bartolomeo and Giacomo Piccolomini were delegated to Venice. L. G. Pelissier, " Documents sur l'ambassade Siennoise envoyée a Milan en Octobre, 1499, " *Bullettino Senese di Storia Patria*, III (1896), 43-66 and G. Pecci, *op. cit.*, I, 155. A second embassy to the *Serenissima* followed several months later. Cf. the letter of *nuncio* Angelo Leonini to Alexander VI, dated Venice, 11 June, 1500: " His expectantur oratores senenses, d. nus Bartholomeus Sozinus et Fatius de Bencassai idem illi oblaturi huic ill.mo Dominio quod lucenses. " F. Gaeta, " Origine e sviluppo della rappresentanza stabile pontificia in Venezia (1485-1533), " *Annuario dell'Istituto Storico Italiano per l'età moderna e contemporanea*, IX-X (1957-1958), 139.

Bartolomeo was a prolific scholar. At least thirty editions of his writings appeared before the year 1500. The most important edition of his collected works was published by the Giunti in Venice in 1605 in three volumes. From his correspondence we can cite a letter to the Republic of Siena, dated Pisa, April 16, 1484, published in F. Donati, *Dieci lettere di Senesi illustri dei secoli XV e XVI* (Siena, 1878), p. 15 f. Several Ms. letters, all dated either Pisa or Prato, 1486 to Michelozzo Michelozzi, Puccio Pucci and the officers of the University of Pisa exist in Ms. B.I. 1, " Lettere dello Studio Pisano dal 1480 al 1486, " conserved in the Pisa University Library. This Codex has been studied by P. Arias, " Carte Quattrocentesche dello Studio Pisano, " *Rivista Storica degli Archivi Toscani*, II (1930), 1-28. A number of letters to Lorenzo de' Medici spanning the period from February 7, 1474-March 24, 1491 are recorded in the *Archivio Mediceo avanti il Principato*, II, 157, 200, 222, 250, 307, 351, 368 and 400. The two dated March and May, 1479 (p. 368) are addressed to Lorenzo in Naples. A number of letters to Piero de' Medici for the period from April 21, 1482 to May 16, 1494 are listed, *Ibid.*, I, 271, 318; II, 115; III, 40, 198, 487. Letters to the authorities of the University of Pisa, usually complaints and grievances of various kinds, are published by A. Fabronio, *op. cit.*, I, 90 ff. Twenty-seven letters from Lorenzo de' Medici to Bartolomeo for the period from July 25, 1477-August 26, 1491 are recorded by M. Del Piazzo, *Protocolli del Carteggio di Lorenzo il Magnifico per gli anni 1473-74, 1477-79* (Florence, 1956), p. 609. A single letter from another noted jurisconsult, Francesco Curtio, to Bartolomeo, dated Pavia, August 29, 1492, is recorded in the *Archivio Mediceo*, III, 425; and for a dateless document entitled, " Informazioni attinenti ad una domanda fatta da Bartolomeo Sozini per ottenere una pensione a mezzo di qualche beneficio del dominio fiorentino, " see *ibid.*, p. 338.

Bartolomeo was envied for his fame, his salaries and his following by jurisconsults obliged to read in his shadow, and Angelo Poliziano compared him to one of the immortal figures of the legal profession: " Quem equidem et Papinianum alterum videor audacter posse appellare seculo nostro. " *Angeli Politiani Opera, quae quidem extitere, hactenus omnia....* Basileae, apud Nicolaum Episcopium Iuniorem, 1552, p. 72. (From an undated letter to Jacopo Modesto of Prato). However, he died mute and penniless in his native Siena, brought there from Bologna by his young nephew, Mariano Sozzini. It is difficult to say how much truth underlies the low estimate of Bartolomeo's character which has been accepted since it was first pronounced by an early student of the Sozzini family, G. Panciroli, *op. cit.*, pp. 221-225. See most recently, L. Zdekauer, Lo *Studio*, p. 116; " Fraudulent in discussion, neglectful as an instructor, hypocritical in politics, venal as a writer, and, what is worse, as a teacher, he died in Siena, assisted by his relatives, after having dissipated his fortune at the gaming table to such a point that he did not leave sufficient funds to cover the expenses of burial. "

A.S.S. *Biccherna* (1132), f. 605 v. " Anno 1436. Bartolomeo Maria di miss. Mariano di Sozzino dottore si battezo adi XXVI di Marzo fu chonmare margarita dele povere daghobbio di Campansi et Madona Jacoma di Checco di Miss. Tilio da Pisa. " It was rather unusual to have two *conmari* rather than a *compare*. The first was a nun of the order of the Povere di Gubbio (Umbria) and belonged to the Convent of Campansi in Siena.

Additional *consilia* by Bartolomeo are indicated by Kristeller (p. 27) in Bologna, Collegio di Spagna; Lucca, Biblioteca Capitolare (p. 253); Biblioteca Nazionale, Firenze: Fondo Magliabecchiano (p. 122) and Strozziana (p. 127); in the Archivio di Stato, Firenze: Carte Strozziane (p. 68). Kristeller also indicates letters of Bartolomeo in Forlì, Biblioteca Comunale (p. 234); Mantova, Archivio di Stato (p. 265); Milano, Archivio di Stato (p. 277). Two letters from Innocent VIII to Lorenzo de' Medici, both dated Rome, January 4, 1490, interceding for " dilectus filius Bartholomeus Sozinus " who had been imprisoned by the Florentines for breach of contract are in A. Fabronio, *Laurentii Medicis magnifici vita*, 2 vols., (Pisa, 1784), II, 79 f. For a letter from the *Priori* of Pisa to Lorenzo dated August 11, 1475 complaining of Bartolomeo's insolence towards one of their body, *Ibid*, II, 78. For the opinions of the lawyers (including Bartolomeo and Bulgarino Bulgarini) consulted by Florence on the Interdict of Sixtus IV (1478), see A. Fabronio, *Ibid.*, II, 81 and *Fatti attenenti all'Inquisizione e sua istoria generale e particolare di Toscana* (Florence, 1782), p. 126.

A copy of Bartolomeo's oration, *Senensium obedientia Alexandro VI* (Romae, Stephanus Plannck, c. 1492) is in the Biblioteca Nacional, Madrid.

On his projected critical edition of the Pandects, Angelo Poliziano (1454-94) had intended to work in collaboration with Bartolomeo whom he esteemed highly. Cf. F. Calasso, *Medio Evo del Diritto* (Milan, 1954), p. 600. This tends to modify the view of the Sozzini as champions of the anti-humanistic and anti-philological approach to law.

27. (Alessandro).

1443-1503. Occupied several positions of authority in the Sienese government: *Priore* in 1493 and 1498; *Gonfaloniere* for the *Terzo* of San Martino in 1503. In 1477 he married Laura Arringhieri who died in 1500. Cantù, II, 508. A letter from him to Lorenzo de' Medici, dated August 26, 1472 is listed in the *Archivio Mediceo avanti il Principato*, II, 85. According to C. Cantoni, " Cronaca Senese, " *op. cit.*, XV, Part 6^2, p. 907: " Alesandro di Misser Mariano Sozzini, " appears on the list " del Monte de' Dodici abilitati per lo Monte del Popolo, " after the uprising led by his brother, Bartolomeo. Alessandro's name appears on a list published August 1, 1482 of fifty citizens from the *Dodici* who " s'intendano andare per lo Monte de' Riformatori " who were added to the *Consiglio del Popolo*. *Ibid.*, p. 912.

A.S.S. *Biccherna* (1133), f. 18 r. " Anno 1443. Alessandro Pietro Maria di miss. Mariano di Sozzino dottore fu battezzato adi XXI di ferraio fu compare miss. Cholantonio veschovo di Rieti et miss. Bartolomeo Rovarella et per lui tenne Donanbruogio di Nofrio priore di Santo Martino in Siena. "

An interesting document in the Archivio di Stato, Siena (*Biccherna* D. Vol. 706, f. 4) dated July 14, 1474 is the petition of Alessandro " ut possit libere et impune conducere in domum suam sitam in Pantaneto aquam fluentem ex fonte Pantaneti. "

28. (Bernardino).

b. 1492. Cantù, II, 508.

29. (Camilla).

Married Alessandro Borghesi with 1810 florins in dowry. Cantù, II, 508.

30. (Francesco).

b. 1483. He was a *Priore* in 1508 and 1519. On September 20, 1555, after the fall of republican Siena to the combined forces of Charles V and Cosimo de' Medici, he was among those who swore allegiance to France and the Sienese government in exile at Montalcino. Cantù, II, 508. His sons, Tiberio and Ottavio, distinguished themselves during the long siege.

The *Arte della Seta* in Siena was granted new statutes in 1513. They were compiled by " tre savi cittadini, " Agostino di ser Antonio (Savini ?), Bernardino Francesconi and Francesco Sozzini. Sozzini was one of the first three *Consoli* or governors of the guild following its reorganization, an indication that he was a prominent silk manufacturer in the city. See L. Banchi, *L'Arte della seta in Siena nei secoli XV e XVI. Statuti e documenti*. (Siena, 1881), pp. xviii ff.

31. (Niccolò).

b. 1488. Cantù, II, 508.

32. (Gianbattista).

b. 1496. Cantù, II, 508.

33. (Girolamo).

1480-1530. He was a *Priore* in 1505-1512. Cantù, II, 508. He was the father of the famous diarist of the Sienese rebellion against Charles V, Alessandro, b. 1518. The latter's diary is one of the most precious sources for Sienese history in the sixteenth century. Sozzini's manuscript work bore the title, " Il successo delle rivoluzioni della città di Siena, d'imperiale franzese e di franzese imperiale, scritto da Alessandro di Girolamo Sozzini, gentiluomo sanese." It was edited by G. Milanesi in the *Archivio Storico Italiano*, II (1842). On this period one can consult A. D'Addario, *Il problema Senese nella storia Italiana della prima metà del Cinquecento* (*la guerra di Siena*) (Florence, 1958), and R. Cantagalli, *La guerra di Siena* (Siena, 1963).

34. (Mariano junior).

1482-1556. Renowned jurisconsult of European fame. In Cantù's genealogy, II, 508, he is confused with his grandfather, especially in regard to the relationship with Pius II; and Ugurgieri, I, 432, probably led astray by the tendency to create a direct line of succession for the great jurists of the family, calls Mariano the son of Bartolomeo.

After having studied in Siena, the humanities under Angelo Fundo, and Civil Law under Francesco Turco, Bernardino Benvoglienti, Giovanni Battista Santo, Simone Borghesi and Antonio Bonafro, he completed his studies in Bologna under Bartolomeo, his uncle. G. Panciroli, *op. cit.*, p. 269. He returned with him to Siena in 1507 where he began his academic career by reading civil and canon law in alternate years. According to Panciroli, *ibid.*, he read in concurrence with another Sienese, Lancellotto Politi (1487-1553). Politi, as the Dominican Ambrogio Catarino, became one of the most virulent of the Catholic controversialists, writing against the booklet, *Il Beneficio di Cristo*, Luther, the flight of Bernardino Ochino to the Protestant north, etc. Earlier he had written against Savonarola and he was, according to Benedetto Nicolini, *Il pensiero di Bernardino Ochino* (Naples, 1939), p. 98, one of the first Catholic writers to take a position against the writings of Machiavelli.

Two of Mariano's *condotte* to read Civil Law in Siena are published in L. Sbaragli, *Claudio Tolomei* (Siena, 1939), pp. 154, 155. They pertain to the academic years 1516-1517, 1517-1518. The second contract specifies a salary of 80 florins.

He served as *Capitano* and *Gonfaloniere* from March 1-April 30, 1508. He held this post again, many years later, from July 1-August 31, 1524. *Archivio del Concistoro*, p. 147. In 1517 he was entrusted with an embassy of a ceremonial nature to Rome, conveying the gratitude of his city to Leo X for the nomination of two Sienese Cardinals, Giovanni Piccolomini and Raffaelle Petrucci. Pecci, *op. cit.*, II, 67. In the same year commenced his appointment at Pisa. In 1520, at the request of Cardinal Giulio de' Medici, the prefects of the University raised his salary to 700 golden florins. Fabronio, I, 274. In 1523, he was again in Siena, reading now in concurrence with Rainaldo Petrucci, who later became Auditor of the Roman Rota. Panciroli, p. 270. It is probably *c.* 1525 that we should date his admission to the Academy of the *Intronati* where he adopted the name of *Lo Sgualcito*. Although he was one of the early members, the account numbering him among the founders has been refuted. L. P. Costantini, *op. cit.*, p. 17. In the same year he was among the fifteen citizens elected *Conservatori della Libertà* by the *Consiglio Generale* to oversee that each of the parties in Siena (*Monti*) received equal representation in the government. Pecci, II, 177. Still in 1525, he was selected ambassador to the Florentines to confirm the existing alliance between the two states, after it became known in Siena that Giovanni Martinozzi, one of her rebels, had received Papal and Florentine permission to recruit troops in their states. Sozzini's two letters to the *Balìa* of Siena, reporting the progress of his mission, dated May 27 and 31, 1525 are in M. Callegari, "Il fatto d'armi di Porta Camollia nel 1526," *Bullettino Senese di Storia Patria*, XV (1908), 358.

Mariano was called to the University of Padua in October, 1525 to occupy the chair of "Prima Juris Civilis Schola Ordinaria Matutina" to read the first and second part of the Code of Justinian, at the salary of 625 florins. G. Facciolati, *op. cit.*, III, 116. However, at the death of Vincenzo Salviolo, a few months later, he was promoted to the "Secunda Juris Civilis Schola Ordinaria Pomeridiana" and, after three years, his salary was raised to 800 florins. As lecturer Sozzini was not an unqualified success. See the letter from Zuichemus, studying in Padua, to George Hermann (1531): "Post meridiem profitetur Socinus quidam, hereditaria jurisprudentiae dote insignis, sed tamen mire in legendo fastidiosus." Letter cited by A. Hartmann, *Die Amerbach-Korrespondenz*, 5 vols. (Basel, 1942-1958), IV, 148;

and on his method of teaching, Zuichemus wrote to Boniface Amerbach on June 3, 1532: " Alter (after Francesco Curtio), Socinus quidam, nimia accumulatione rerum seipsum etiam obruit, interea pulchrum existimans posse nudam materiam ampla commentariorum dote locupletare. Huius autem similes plerique sunt nunc per Italiam, qui cum videant ea, que ad legis interpretationem pertinent satis copiose ab maioribus tractata, ipsi ne nihil addidisse videantur, undique conquirunt, quod infarciant. Hoc nimirum est artem confundere et ad pristinum chaos nos reducere, videlicet cum ea, que suis sub titulis bene sita erant, ipsi sub alienos tractatus inculcent. " *Ibid.*, IV, 147. Nevertheless, in October, 1533, he took occupancy of the first law chair in the University, the " Prima Juris Civilis Schola Ordinaria Pomeridiana, " with the salary of 1000 florins, raised in 1535 and again in 1540. Facciolati, *op. cit.*, III, 134.

In October, 1529, John Stokesby, Bishop of London, and Dr. Richard Crook were sent to Italy by Henry VIII of England to ascertain the opinions of Italian jurists and theologians on his " divorce case. " Among the Italian Universities which were said to decide in favor of the King were Pavia, Ferrara, Bologna and Padua. P. Hughes, *The Reformation in England* (London, 1954), I, 216. They had come to this position, through the conviction that the Pope did not have the authority to grant the dispensation permitting a man to marry his brother's widow. J. S. Brewer, ed., *Letters and Papers, Foreign and Domestic of the reign of Henry VIII. 1529-1530* (London, 1876), IV, Part III, n. 6491. It is uncertain that the Law Faculty of Padua, despite its inclination to support the King, actually formally published its opinion. Permission to do this was withheld by the *Signoria* of Venice. The fear of offending so powerful a sovereign as Charles V (nephew of Catherine of Aragon) or of encroaching upon the jurisdiction of the Roman *Rota* helped to shape its resolve to compel the jurists in Padua to maintain a discreet silence. Cf. the letter sent to Charles V by his Ambassador at Venice, Rodrigo Niño, on 17 May, 1530. He informs that " the *Doge* and Council have, according to promise, dispatched a secret messenger to Padua with executorial letters to the doctors and professors of that university, forbidding them entirely to counsel or give opinion in the affair between the King and Queen of England.... The Doge and Signory could not possibly tolerate that doctors and professors in the pay of their treasury should give opinion in an affair of the kind, especially knowing, for it was public and notorious, that they had received grants and money, which excluded all idea of impartiality and justice on their part. " Out of the six Paduan jurists who were known to favor the King, five declared themselves ready to accede to the *Signoria*'s request. But, " the remaining one, whose name is Mariano di Sena, still persists in his resolution not to abide by the decision of his colleagues. He alleges that, although a professor at the University of Padua, he cannot be prevented from giving counsel to whomsoever pays him for it. He gave his opinion in writing more than six months ago and could not retrocede. " P. Gayangos, ed., *Calendar of Letters, Despatches, and State Papers, relating to the negotiations between England and Spain. Henry VIII, 1529-30* (London, 1879), IV, Part I, p. 547. (Mariano's views on the issue were discussed by Boniface Amerbach in a letter to Erasmus, dated February 2, 1530. A. Hartmann, *op. cit.*, III, 486: " quid quod et Marianus Socinus Pontificem tanquam fori penitentialis praesidem nuptias, quas se iuvenem non contrahendi animo sed amoris impotentia celebrasse praetexebat, post diutinam etiam cohabitationem dirimere posse pronunciavit ? Possem eius generis complura adferre.... ").

On the same day as Niño's report to the Emperor, May 17, 1530, the Council of Ten wrote to their agent in Padua, Marco Dandolo, directing him to make certain that Mariano express no further opinion on the subject of the divorce: " li faciate a bocha intender la preditta intention et desiderio nostro che il nome suo in tal causa de divortio non si intervegni si per luna come per l'altra parte, " N. Pocock, *Records of the Reformation: the Divorce case, 1527-1533*, 2 vols. (Oxford, 1870), I, 542-543. The instructions to Dandolo in English translation can be read in R. Brown, *Calendar of State Papers and Manuscripts existing in the Archives and collections of Venice, 1527-1533* (London, 1871), IV, pp. 242-243.

More than a year later, the scene of intrigue between Spanish and English had shifted to Rome. On December 17, 1531, Edward Carne, English Ambassador to the Pope wrote home that a disputation on the divorce case was being planned for the

Rota. The Imperialists were pressing to hold it at once, or else have the *Rota* deliver its opinion without benefit of a disputation. The first audience after Christmas had been assigned to the disputation. But Carne had informed the Pope that this date did not allow the English time to prepare themselves, " for no man here (in Rome) dared dispute (in defense of the King) and we should have to send for the most famous learned men in Italy.... It will be a great expense. The Bishop of Worcester has sent to Sienna for Decius and others, and to Perusio (sic) for Frisio, and was ready to pledge his office to pay them. Master Gregory has sent to Bologna for Parisio, to Padua for Corte and Sozino, and to Placentia for Burla, and intends to sell land for their expenses." J. Gairdner, *Letters and Papers, Foreign and Domestic of the reign of Henry VIII, 1531-1532* (London, 1880), V, n. 586. On January 20, Carne informed Henry VIII that his efforts to bring learned jurists to Rome to defend his cause were continuing. Most of the doctors, he wrote, would have already come if the decision had been theirs alone. The Paduan jurists had been refused permission by Venice, under pressure of the Imperialists: " .... Marianus Sozino had been forbidden by the King's adversaries. " *Ibid.*, n. 731. Thus the matter languished until May 23, 1533 when Thomas Cranmer declared Henry's marriage to Catherine of Aragon invalid. On the 28th, Henry was pronounced lawfully married to Anne Boleyn. Pope Clement, from Rome, fulminated the excommunication of the English sovereign and declared his divorce and new marriage null (July 11, 1533).

When the greatest Italian jurist of the first half of the sixteenth century, Andrea Alciato, was compelled by Imperial pressure to relinquish his chair at Bologna for his former position at the *Studium* of Pavia (under Milanese jurisdiction), in 1541, it was Mariano who was invited to replace him. In 1542 the vacancy was temporarily filled by Restauro Castaldi and Ansovino de' Medici. Mariano only began teaching in Bologna during the academic year, 1543-1544. G. Zaccagnini, *op. cit.*, p. 208. It is interesting that Cardinal Gasparo Contarini, then Legate in Bologna, interested himself in finding a suitable replacement for Mariano in Padua. In a letter of unspecified destination (but undoubtedly intended for the Rectors of the University of Padua) he recommends Ancuino da Camerino: " .... mi par poter securamente affermare che fra poco tempo egli non sarà punto inferiore ne al Sozzino ne al Salviato.... " A. Casadei, " Lettere del Cardinale Gasparo Contarini durante la sua legazione di Bologna (1542), " *Archivio Storico Italiano*, CXVIII (1960), 264. Alciato, under whom even Calvin had studied at Bourges, was the representative of a new method, a historical approach to the study of law which, beyond the glosses and traditional commentaries, sought to place the ancient statutes in their historical context. Opposed to this was the traditional method, the *mos italicus*. With Sozzini, the famous *Studium* of Bologna returned to this older form of instruction. On the Sozzini as upholders of the traditional approach to legal studies and their influence on Sienese legal scholarship, see P. Rossi, " La prima cattedra di Pandette nello Studio Senese, " *Studi Senesi*, XXVI (1903), 41-62. The crisis between the old and the new systems had been brought on by the mass of notes, comments and explanations which over the years had been added to the legal texts. Alciato's position represented the desire to view the *Corpus Juris Civilis* free from glosses and to reconstruct the text on the basis of critical methods. G. Barni makes the observation that the " mos italicus docendi " was viewed with a certain favor by the Catholic Church, locked in struggle with Protestantism. Rome was fully aware of the dangers existing in the critical, direct and personal examination of the sources. " Notizie del giurista e umanista Andrea Alciato, " *Bibliothèque d'Humanisme et Renaissance*, XX (1958), 25-35. One might also be tempted to underline the distance which separated Mariano from his sons (and nephew, Fausto) on this issue. It is ironic that Lelio was introducing in his approach to the study of the Scriptures and theology, a set of criteria which his father was rejecting for the Law. On Alciato, se the excellent article by R. Abbondanza in the *Dizionario Biografico degli Italiani* (Rome, 1960), II, 69-77.

Mariano's legal opinions were highly esteemed (as we have already seen in the divorce case of Henry VIII). In 1547, after Duke Ulrich of Württemberg had participated in the Schmalkaldic war, Ferdinand of Hapsburg started a suit against him for breach of the feudal oath. Although Ulrich had assumed Boniface Amerbach and the Basel Faculty of Jurisprudence for his defense, Ulrich's councillor, Dr. Nikolaus Meyer was dispatched to Italy to ascertain the opinions of Alciato and Sozzini. F. Church, *The Italian Reformers, 1534-1564* (New York, 1932), p. 191. For reading the records of the proceedings, Mariano received 35 crowns. C. F. Sattler, *Geschichte des Herzogtums Würtemberg* (Tübingen, 1771), Part III, p. 272. It was Nikolaus Meyer who wrote the famous letter of recommendation to the Swiss scholars and divines for the young Lelio about to start out on his northward journey.

In Goettingen, Universitätsbibliothek, Ms. Histor. 657, Band XVIII, f. 276 is conserved the " Originalgutachten (expert opinion) an die Königin Marie: von Marianus Sozinus Senensis, Bononie jura civilia legens. " The *Catalogue* of printed books in the British Museum lists several items connected with opinions delivered by Mariano on the bigamy and imprisonment of Philip of Hesse. (See under article *Socinus*, Mariano).

At Bologna, Sozzini's reputation and prestige reached its zenith. When the Paduan Franciscan, Lucio Anguissola, was arrested and confined to his monastery on suspicion of heresy on April 8, 1548, powerful voices were raised in his defense: the Bishop of Bitonto, Cornelio Musso, Cardinal del Monte and Mariano Sozzini. Cf. the letter from Massarelli, secretary to the Council of Trent, to Cardinal Cervino, dated August 18, 1548: " hoggi il Sozzino è stato da Mons. Rmo. de Monte et fattoli grande instantia, perchè concedesse gratia a.... Lutio di poter andar per Bologna dando una securità. " Cited from G. Buschbell, *Reformation und Inquisition in Italien um die mitte des XVI Jahrhunderts* (Paderborn, 1910), p. 190. A recent study cautions that Mariano's part in this affair is no more than a demonstration " di una solidarietà di amici dello Studio, Mariano Sozzini in testa. " A. Rotondò, " Per la storia dell'eresia a Bologna nel secolo XVI, " *Rinascimento*, XIII (1962), 149.

In 1551 Mariano was elected Consistorial Advocate by Julius III, and when Mariano temporarily abandoned Bologna in the same year, according to Zaccagnini, *op. cit.*, p. 208, he was recalled from Siena at the salary with which he had been lured away-1300 scudi, the highest ever paid in the Bolognese *Studium* up to that time. To dissuade him from future departures, priviledges and exemptions of various kinds were granted to him, his children and grand-children, which were to be valid even after his death. It was in this way, out of regard for Mariano, that his son Celso was granted a reading " de sero " in Canon Law. When Mariano was old and stricken by family misfortunes, Bologna caused relatives, servants and even vestments to be brought for him from Siena (G. Zaccagnini, p. 209). According to Panciroli, p. 271, a position was found even for a son-in-law entailing, " locus inter V. vir. litibus judicandis Bononiae Laelio ejus genero est donatus. " The *genero* who was thus favored must be that Lelio Pecci who married Porzia Sozzini in 1539. (See below, n. 40). In return for such attention, Mariano refused attractive invitations from Cosimo I for the University of Pisa, from Venice for Padua, from the King of Portugal, etc.

In 1508 Mariano had married Camilla, the daughter of Paolo Salvetti of Florence, who is said to have helped Pandolfo Petrucci regain Siena and who settled there himself. F. Bock, *Historia Antitrinitariorum* (Regiomonti & Lipsiae, 1784), II, 571. Cf. " Albero della famiglia Salvetti di Siena, " Cod. AZ, 23 in the Biblioteca Comunale, Siena. For the family tree of the Florentine branch of the family, see in the *Fondo* Magliabecchiano, Biblioteca Nazionale, Florence, Cod. 396, Cl. 25, p. 165. Camilla died in 1554. (See, however, the confused letter of Antonio Tiepolo, Venetian Ambassador in Rome, to the Council of Ten in 1578: " messer Marian Socino, gran dottor di leggi,... partendo di Padova andò a vivere a Bologna, dove si maritò et hebbe figliuoli, ma fu sfortunato perchè questi hanno grandemente degenerato dalla bontà di lui, essendone massime scoperto uno heretico, il quale si chiama Cornelio. " A. Stella, " Ricerche sul Socinianesimo: Il processo di Cornelio Sozzini e Claudio Textor (Bannière), " *Bollettino dell'Istituto di Storia della Società e dello Stato Veneziano*, III (1961), p. 10 of the extract. (On Cornelio, see n. 46 below). An Ottavio, who " militò in Germania " is also listed by Cantù, II, 508 as a son of Mariano's. This notice was undoubtedly taken from Ugurgieri, II, 152: " Ottavio Sozzini, nobil Sanese, havendo servito la Repubblica in carica di Sergente Maggiore andò a militare in Alemagna dove con la sua virtù fece molto celebre il nome Sanese. " He died from a leg wound received during the famous siege of Siena, on April 17, 1553. Ottavio was actually the son of Francesco Sozzini (and grand-son of Bartolomeo).

A. Sozzini, " Il successo delle rivoluzioni, " p. 211. The news of his mother's death was carried to Lelio Sozzini in Switzerland by " Caspar ille nobilis Pomeranus, qui nuper ex Italia redibat et cui tu scriptum Serveti ostendere te posse dicebas, nuntium mihi tristissimum attulit, matrem charissimam excessisse a vivis. " Letter from Lelio Sozzini to Bullinger dated Basel, February 5, 1554, in F. Trechsel, *Die Protestantischen Antitrinitarier vor Faustus Socin*, 2 vols. (Heidelberg, 1844), II, 436-437.

Mariano's relationship to Lelio remains ambiguous. F. Church (*op. cit.*, p. 164), suggests that Lelio was actually disinherited by Mariano to demonstrate his disapproval at his son's straying in religion. This certainly is the clear sense of Calvin's letter to Prince Radziwill, dated May 23, 1558 (*Calvini Opera*, XVII, col. 181). The Polish nobleman is asked by Calvin to favor Lelio because the latter had been disinherited, " quia tamen palam defecerat a Papatu seque ad nos contulerat, eum exheredavit. " But the idea of disinheritance does not seem to find support in a letter from Melanchthon to N. Pfauser, dated December 1, 1557: " Impediunt Laelius Inquisitores, ne patrimonio frui possit. Cogitat igitur proficisci ad urbem venetorum, ut ubi de patrimonio cum quibusdam paternis amicis agat. " C. Illgen, *Symbolarum ad vitam et doctrinam Laelii Socini* (Leipzig, 1826), p. 26. Cantimori states that, as long as he lived, Mariano had been able to keep the Inquisition at a distance, but, after his death, Celso, who succeeded to his Chair in Bologna, lacked his prestige and soon fell under suspicion of heresy himself. *Eretici Italiani del Cinquecento* (Florence, 1939), p. 232.

The shadow of moral improbity darkened Mariano's name, as it had that of his uncle, Bartolomeo. According to A. Fabronio, I, 274 f., " Vivens quoque uxorem amisit, qua extincta, homo voluptatis illecebris delinitus, temperantiae nuncium remisisse visus est.... Morbigenus, quo extinctus est, recens ex America ad Italos transvectum fuerat, et cogit sane multos, ut Marianum, incontinentiae poenitere. " (If his wife died in 1554, Mariano was already 72 years old)! From his Paduan period we do have the record, despite his high salary, of his substantial financial indebtedness to Gianbattista Campeggi, Bishop of Maiorca. A. Medin and G. Tolomei, " Per la storia aneddotica dell'università di Padova nel secolo XVI, " *Atti e Memorie della R. Accademia di scienze, lettere ed arti in Padova*, n. s. XXVII (1911), 91. Panciroli (*ibid.*, p. 272), who declares himself to have been a student of Mariano's, adds this description: " Marianus mediocris staturae fuit. Materna lingua, & musica delectatus, quandoque etiam in aleae (dice) ludo se detinuit. Vir fuit acutissimus, & acris judicii. " But he had a poor memory, so that usually he was compelled to lecture from written notes, and rarely did he dare to reply on a point of law extemporaneously. In view of Panciroli's remark that Mariano delighted in the study of the " materna lingua, " it is interesting to note that Bernardino Tomitano numbers Mariano among that group, including Benedetto Varchi, who in Padua in 1542 had gathered themselves about Sperone Speroni in the Academy of the *Infiammati*. *Ragionamenti della Lingua Toscana* (Venice, 1545), p. 12.

The *Catalogue of the British Museum*, under his name, lists several of Mariano's published works, including his opinion on the bigamy and imprisonment of Philip of Hesse. Sozzini's son Celso (see below n. 43) edited the major collection of his writings: *Commentaria cum profundissima, tum fructuosissima in quatuor lecturas vespertinas, quas ordinarias vocant, communi interpretum more in celebrioribus Italiae gymnasiis praelecta* (Venice, 1566). Subsequent editions appeared in 1571, 1575 and 1603 (the fifth edition). It has not been possible to verify the date of publication of the fourth. Mariano's famous *Consilia duo in materia duelli* (1545), published also in Italian translation in the same year, is studied by F. R. Bryson, *The sixteenth-century Italian duel. A study in Renaissance social history* (Chicago, 1938), p. 150 f.

In addition to the already cited published correspondence of Mariano, see also: F. Novati, *Dieci lettere di Senesi illustri dei secoli XV e XVI* (Siena, 1878), p. 24 f. for a letter dated February 23, 1551, from Bologna, to the *Signoria* of Siena, regarding the possibility of the purchase of grain by the latter; and G. Campori, *Lettere di scrittori Italiani del secolo XVI* (Bologna, 1877), pp. 371-373, for a letter dated Padova, October 19, 1540 addressed to Alessandro Donesmondo regarding a position for one of his sons (left unnamed, but perhaps Alessandro, already a jurist of some renown) in the forthcoming Council. Ms. letters of Mariano are to Francesco del Nero on March 28, May 6, and August 20, 1520 (complaints of tardy salary payments).

They are preserved in the Archivio di Stato, Florence: *Carte Strozziane, Signoria, Dieci di Balìa, Otto di Pratica*, Filza 72, f. 73, 64, and 8 respectively; to Niccolò Capponi, dated Pisa, October 19, 1523. *Ibid., Lettere concernenti lo Studio di Firenze e di Pisa. Serie Prima*, Filza CXXXIX, f. 22; to the German jurist, Hieronymus Schurf of St. Gall, dated September 22, 1542 from Padua. National Library, Berlin, Ms. Lat. Oct. 48, ff. 83-87.

According to E. Mattone-Vezzi, " Aonio Paleario e la riforma religiosa in Italia, " *Miscellanea Storica della Valdelsa*, LIV (1948), 53, Paleario corresponded with Mariano, while the latter was in Bologna. While this is indeed highly probable, Mattone-Vezzi unfortunately does not provide the source for his statement. In writing to Bullinger from Vicosoprano on July 10, 1552, Pietro Paolo Vergerio remarked that Mariano had written to him several times in the course of the year, expressing concern for Lelio who was at the time in Italy. In the words of Vergerio: " Lelium brevi expecto; pater scripsit illi non defuturum et hortatur ut extra Italian vivat. Quae literae si venissent in tempore, Lelius a me non discessisset.... " T. Schiess, *Bullingers Korrespondenz mit den Graubundnen*, 3 vols., (Basel, 1904-1906), I, 256. For a letter from Mariano, with a quite different destination, a letter of recommendation to Pope Paul IV for one of his former students, Gabriele Paleotti, see Appendix II, below. F. C. Church, *op. cit.*, p. 285 cites a letter from Boniface Amerbach to Mariano, dated July 31, 1555, which undoubtedly will be published by Hartmann in the appropriate volume of the *Amerbachkorrespondenz*. Two letters to Mariano from a distant relation, Claudio Tolomei (whose mother, Cornelia, was daughter of Bartolomeo Sozzini), are published in *Delle lettere di M. Claudio Tolomei Libri VII. Con nuova aggiunta ristampati* (Venice, 1578), f. 125 v. (135) and 251 v. The first from Bologna, undated (but before 1541), closes with the salutation, " greet.... my lady Camilla and your M. Alessandro whom I hear is making a fine jurisconsult of himself in the tradition of the Sozzini family. " The second letter is dated, Rome, October 25, 1546. For Tolomei, besides Sbaragli's already cited biography, see also P. Rossi, " Claudio Tolomei e il latino dei giuristi, " *Studi Senesi*, XXIX (1912), 365 where these letters are cited. On April 25, 1555, Mariano was named by Cosimo I and the representative of Charles V in Siena to serve on the first Balia of Siena after its capitulation to the Imperial forces and Florence. Mariano declined this invitation, citing the pressure of his academic duties, in a letter dated Bologna, May 18, 1555, which is published by C. Paoli, *Una lettera di Mariano Sozzini il giovane alla Balìa di Siena (1555)* (Florence, 1898).

Mariano died on August 20, 1556. The news of his passing was reported to Boniface Amerbach by his son Basil, who had studied with Mariano in Bologna from the winter of 1555 until a few days before the end. The letter, dated September 12, 1556 from Padua is cited by F. Trechsel, *op. cit.*, II, 192: " D. Socinus, quem discedens admodum infirmum reliqui, intra duos dies postea obiit. Habeo duos fasciculos ad D. Laelium filium ejus, quos mecum ipse adferam. " Mariano was buried under a magnificent tomb in the church of S. Domenico in Bologna. One of the several epitaphs composed at his death is printed in N. Mengozzi, " Reliquie, " p. 178. It reads: " Marianus.... LXXIV aetatis anno decessit. Germanorum studiosorum humeris in D. Dominici templum est elatus. Ex XIII filiis, quos suscepit tantum Celsus et Philippus superstites fuere.... Ei hoc monumentum filii posuerunt. " In small letters, the last line of the inscription on the tomb reads: " Filii moestiss. Patri opt. P. "

An engraving of a bust of Mariano's is reported to exist in Ms. 2774 (4086) f. 305 v.: " Gerardus Corselius: Ad Instituta Iustiniani auctarium. " It is cited in J. Van Den Gheyn, *Catalogue des Manuscripts de la Bibliothèque Royale de Belgique* (Brussels, 1904), p. 187.

A letter to the Balìa of Siena during his Florentine mission (1525) and not published by M. Callegari, *op. cit.*, is preserved in the Archivio di Stato, Siena: *Lettere al Reggimento*. It is dated June 5, 1525. Another letter, c. 1533 is in the Archivio di Stato, Mantova. Cf. Kristeller, p. 267. A later hand-written addition to the manuscript " Raccolta di notizie riguardanti le famiglie nobili di Siena, " compiled in the 19th century by A. Aurieri reads: " Mariano il Giovane fu creato Conte Palatino dal Card. Campeggi dal titolo di S. Maria in Trastevere nel 1532, perg. Borghesi, p. 278. Viene confermato il titolo comitale a Mariano ed Alessandro suo figlio dal Patriarca d'Alessandria, Cesare Riario, 1537, Marzo 5, p. 288". Biblioteca Comunale, Siena A. 15 f. 164 v.

When the death of Mariano became known in Siena, the Balìa wrote expressing its condolences to the comune of Bologna and to the surviving Sozzini in that city. The record of its deliberation reads: "1556, Sabato ali XXIX d'Agosto. Alli nobili figli di M. Mariano Sozzini deliberorno scrivarsi lettere amorevoli con dolersi della morte di lor padre, collega di lor Signoria. E ancora si scrivino lettere a chi fa di bisogno in raccomandatione di detti figli, secondo che domandarà M. Lelio Pecci loro già cognato." In the reply of the Bolognese ruling body, the *Quaranta*, on October 3 we have an interesting reference to the number and good reputation of Mariano's offspring: "Fa minore il nostro dispiacere il vedere che ha (Mariano) lasciato una molto bella et virtuosa creanza de figliuoli, li quali se per la memoria del padre, et per le degne qualità loro eravarno per haverli raccomandati come nostri cittadini...." The Bolognese letter is printed in the *Miscellanea Storica Senese*, I (1893), 136. In a note at the foot of the page, the record of his birth (1483) has been copied from the baptismal records: "Mariano Pietro Maria, figliuolo di Alessandro di Messer Mariano Sozzini si battezo a di XXVII di marzo, fu compare ser Domenico di Mariano prete e sagrestano di duomo."

35. (Camilla).

Married a Marco Tondi bringing a dowry of 1400 florins. Cantù, II, 508.

36. (Giulio).

1512-1525. Cantù, II, 508.

37. (Bartolomeo).

b. 1511. Cantù, II, 508.

38. (Marcantonio).

b. 1514. Cantù, II, 508.

39. (Ascanio).

1526-d. Padua, 1538. His epitaph was reprinted by Ugurgieri, I, 432.

40. (Porzia).

Married Lelio Pecci in 1539 with a dowry of 3000 florins. Cantù, II, 508. Their son, Scevola, was listed together with Fausto Sozzini and the two sons of Mariano (Carlo ? e Camillo) among the *Nobili* of Siena suspected of heresy. See the letter of Nofri Camajano to Cosimo I, dated September 5, 1558 published in Cantù, II, 448-449.

41. (Filippo).

He is known to Panciroli, *op. cit.*, p. 270 and included in Cantù's genealogy, II, 508. See above, n. 34, Mariano's epitaph).

42. (Alessandro).

1508-April 28, 1541. Jurisconsult. Despite his early death, he had already earned the title of "princeps subtilitatum." In Siena, he received his doctorate under the celebrated Filippo Decio and also began his own teaching career. In 1531 he was a *Priore* (Cantù, II, 509) and, soon after, he was reading Civil Law at Padua where his father, in October, 1533, took occupancy of the first Law Chair. Alessandro's appointment is described by Facciolati, III, 97: "1533 XVIII kal. dec. Alexander Socinus Senensis, Mariani filius, conductus est flor. LXXX anno superiore ad Institutionum scholam accitus fuerat, sed tempore adesse non potuit. Anno sequenti ad tertium Juris Civilis locum descendit, servato tamen stipendio." G. Facciolati, III, 97, and Ms. Passerini, *cit.*, 227, n. 36. In October, 1534, Alexander who, at the time, "locum secundum Juris Canonici pomeridianum tenebat," was promoted to the " Schola Tertia Juris Civilis Matutina. " This Chair, in Facciolati's words, had been created in 1525 " ad Juventutis ingenia exercenda, " (*op. cit.*, III, 126). Subsequently, Alessandro was invited to read Civil Law in the recently founded University at Macerata, where he also served as Rector. A youthful and glorious episode of his academic career, that occurred in 1531, is recorded by Panciroli (*op. cit.*, p. 271), a disputation during which Alessandro sustained 300 propositions for five days in Padua and later for two days in Siena.

Although no writings of Sozzini are listed in the collections of the British Museum, Bibliothèque Nationale, Paris or the Harvard College Library, he is reputed to have published certain *Repetitiones* and *Consilia*. Cf. under heading Alexander Sozinus in Conrad Gesner's, *Bibliotheca Instituta et Collecta....* (Tiguri [Zurich], 1583). No specific titles or editions are named.

It has been thought, traditionally, that Alessandro's wife, Agnese, was the daughter of Borghese Petrucci. (See, for example, Cantù's genealogy, II, 508 and Alexander Gordon, under the heading *Socinus* in the Encyclopedia Brittanica, 1956 ed.). However, in a strangely neglected passage, Pecci (*op. cit.*, II, 40) declares that Borghese had four daughters, two of whom died in childhood; and, of the surviving, Giulia married an Enea Borghesi in 1531 and Aurelia a Giacomo Petrucci in 1524. According to Pecci (*ibid.*, p. 127), Agnese was the daughter of Fabio Petrucci, Borghese's younger brother. Fabio's children were a Fabio, who died in infancy, Pandolfina who married Anton Maria Petrucci, an Agnese who died in childhood, a Sulpizia, and our Agnese who had three husbands: the first was Giovanni Sozzini, whom she married in 1531, and by whom, according to Cantù, II, 513, she had five children; the second was Alessandro whom (Cantù, II, 508) she married in 1538 and by whom she had Fausto and Fillide. Agnese's third husband was a certain Ghino Ghini Bandinelli.

At any rate, Agnese's grand-father, and thus Fausto's great grand-father, was Pandolfo Petrucci who, by his craft, wealth and generous display of force, reigned as the almost absolute lord of Siena from 1487-1512. (On the Petrucci, cf. U. Mondolfo's cited study). Agnese's uncle, Cardinal Alfonso Petrucci, was executed on July 16, 1517 in Rome for his part in the plot to assassinate Pope Leo X. F. Winspeare, *La congiura dei cardinali contro Leone X* (Florence, 1957).

43. (Celso).

1517-1570. Jurisconsult. Read first in Siena and later, in Bologna, Canon Law from 1551-1555 and Civil Law from 1556-1562. According to F. Bock, *op. cit.*, II, 596 f. and Illgen, *Symbolarum*, p. 80 f., a certain Hubert Lanquet, in a letter to Ulrich Mordesius, dated Wittenberg, December 7, 1559, reported that Celso had then assumed an engagement with the University of Jena: " Celsus Socinus, filius Mariani, condixit suam operam scholae Ienensi, cuius rei absque dubio sunt authores Vergerius et Illyricus.... Sed si ei veniat, ipsum procul dubio brevi poenitebit. " G. Strobel, *Beyträge zur Litteratur, besonders des sechszehnten Jahrhunderts*, 2 vols. (Nürenberg and Altdorf, 1784-1787), I, 122 suggests that in the place of Celso one could more plausibly read the name of Lelio. According to S. Mazzetti, *Repertorio di tutti i professori.... della famosa Università.... di Bologna* (Bologna, 1847), p. 293, Celso taught without interruption at Bologna from 1551-1563.

Celso periodically returned to Siena to occupy important political positions. He was *Capitano* and *Gonfaloniere* from September 1-October 31, 1565. *Archivio del Concistoro*, p. 202; *Priore* in 1543, 1549 and *Gonfaloniere* for the *Terzo* of S. Martino in 1568. Cantù, II, 509. In November, 1548, he was one of the Sienese citizens elected " to reform, expand and correct the municipal statutes of the city. " Pecci, *op. cit.*, III, 206.

As a young man in Padua, Celso formed an intimate friendship with Alessandro Piccolomini. (For the criticism of the latter's literary work by Fausto, more than two decades later, see the preceding article by Josephine von Henneberg). Celso's name appears frequently in Piccolomini's correspondence during the year 1541. F. Cerreta, " An account of the early life of the Accademia degli Infiammati in the letters of Alessandro Piccolomini to Benedetto Varchi, " *The Romanic Review*, XLVIII (1957), 249-264.

Besides membership in the *Intronati*, where he is listed as *Lo Scolorato* among those admitted after 1525 (L. Sbaragli, " ' I Tabelloni ' degli Intronati, " *Bullettino Senese di Storia Patria*, XLIX [1942], 192), Celso is reputed the founder (in 1554) of a Bolognese Academy known as the *Sizienti* or *Assetati* which had as its motto: " Non diu sitient sitientes. " L. P. Costantini, *op. cit.*, p. 61; M. Maylender, *Storia delle Accademie d'Italia*, 5 vols., (Bologna, 1926-1930), V, 193. Since an academy of this name flourished in Siena later in the century, it has been suggested that it was transferred there from Bologna either by Celso himself or by his returning Sienese students. C. Mazzi, *La Congrega dei Rozzi di Siena* (Florence, 1882), II, 416. However, Cantimori, following Fabiani in *Nuova Raccolta d'Opuscoli scientifici* (Venice, 1745), III, 8 reverses the process by indicating that the Academy, originally Sienese, was transferred to Bologna by Celso in 1554 (*Eretici*, p. 346).

Celso seems to have been implicated in the heresy of his brothers (see below), but the evidence is sparse, confused and second-hand. Our main sources are two 18th. century letters, namely the request for information about the Sozzini which was addressed by Anton Francesco Marmi of Florence to the Sienese Uberto Bentivoglio (published, with the latter's reply, by Cantù, II, 504-505). From Marmi's letter it appears that Celso and Cornelio were accused, *c.* 1560, by a Bolognese prisoner of the Sienese Inquisition, Paolo de' Cataldi, of living " da Luterani e eretici. " But after Cataldo had regained his freedom, he admitted that he had fabricated the charges at the instigation of the Inquisitor. Bentivoglio's reply provides the totally misleading information that Celso's writings were collected in the *Bibliotheca auctorum Polonorum* [sic] but that later in life he was thought to have recanted and returned to the Catholic faith. Cantimori, *op. cit.*, p. 236, assumes that he was arrested, together with the younger Camillo, by the ecclesiastical authorities late in 1559. (On the reaction of the Swiss reformers to the persecutions endured by the brothers of Lelio in Italy, see below under Camillo).

In 1549 Celso married Albina Bulgarini and, after she died, Lucrezia Sabbatini. The title of Count Palatine was conferred upon him by the Emperor. Cantù, II, 514. His principal literary remains are the edition of his father's *Consilia*. (See above, under Mariano, Jr.). A letter to Celso from Claudio Tolomei, dated Rome, May 30, 1543 was included in the latter's already-cited correspondence, *Delle lettere....* f. 144 r. and v. More important than his position as jurisconsult, academician and statesman is his traditionally-claimed zole as the closest parental authority and guide to Fausto Sozzini, during the latter's early years. Cantimori, *op. cit.*, p. 346.

On January 10, 1611 the Balìa of Siena appointed a committee of four individuals to draw up revised statutes for the guild of *Mercanzia*. One of them was "Alessandro del Dottor Celso Sozzini." Cf. *Statuti dell' Università de' Mercanti, e della corte de gl'offiziali della mercanzia della città di Siena. Riformati per comandamento del Sereniss. Don Cosimo II Gran Duca Quarto di Toscana.* (Siena, 1619), f. (2) v. Another son, " G. B. Sozzinus D. Celsi de Soczinis " is one of the councillors of the *Capitano del Popolo* in Siena during the term September-October, 1603. G. Bellissima, *Scipione Chigi* (Siena, 1922), p. 101. Cantù's genealogy (II, 509) lists eleven children for Celso, the first, Mariano, born on July 20, 1594, twenty-four years after his father's death. Cantù does not know of an Alessandro and as for Giovanni Battista he was born on June 27, 1604 and " morto l'anno appresso. "

44. (Camillo).

Twin brother of Lelio according to Bock, *op. cit.*, II, 576. In the annals of the *Accademia degli Intronati*, he is listed as *Il Ritirato* among those who were admitted during or after the year 1557. L. Sbaragli, *op. cit.*, p. 193. On the supposition of the arrest of Celso, Dario and the youngest, Camillo, in 1559 by the Inquisitor, see D. Cantimori, *op. cit.*, p. 232. In 1561 they were still apparently in prison, and the celebrated Conrad Gessner addressed a long consolatory letter to them from Zurich, January 6, 1561: " Ad Laelii Socini fratres et cognatos in Italia captos propter verbum Domini et de morte periclitantes. " It is published in J. Hanhart, *Conrad Gesner. Ein Beyträg zur geschichte des wissenschaftlichen Strebens u. der Glaubensverbesserung im 16ten Jahrhundert* (Winterthur, 1824), p. 34 f. Although he was publicly condemned in *contumacia* for heresy by the Inquisition in Bologna and Siena, Cosimo I nevertheless had prohibited the ecclesiastical authorities from confiscating his property. So we read in a letter from his nephew, Fausto, dated Cracow, December 14, 1588 to Ferdinand I de' Medici in which he appeals to Camillo's case as precedent. He pleads with the Florentine ruler to intervene with the Sienese Inquisitor who had ordered Sozzini's financial agent, Cornelio Marsili, to halt revenue payments to him. The letter is in A. Fabronio, *op. cit.*, II, 118-120. In the following decade, in the company of his brothers, Dario and perhaps Cornelio, he became a *persona non grata* to the Swiss reformers for his heretical, anti-trinitarian activity. See generally for his movements in the 60's and for Bullinger's undisguised hostility, " Quia tu Dei Filium blasphemas, ego te horreo et abhorreo, " D. Cantimori, *op. cit.*, p. 311 f. The Zurich reformer watched his movements closely. Cf. his letter to Johannes Fabricius, of December 24, 1563 (Schiess, *op. cit.*, II, 476), " Darius et Camillus Laelius, Ariani, hinc discessere, dicuntur in Rhetiam profecti. Proinde vigilate. " Fabricius replied on January 3 from Coira (*Ibid.*, p. 480), that he had already written fully to Zanchi, the minister at Chiavenna, concerning these two heretics. A few days later, Bullinger reported newer information to Fabricius (*Ibid.*) " Sunt hic, qui dicant Camillum et Darium profectos Constantiam ibi latitare. " From an original document, dated 1558, describing sojourners in Zurich for that year, we derive this precious, although mistifying notice: " By Hern Doctor Petro Martyr [Vermigli] gannd Zwey Italiener **zu** tisch. Ist der ein Lelii Soccini Bruder, der annder desselben bruders son. Hannd bi Felixen Sprungli ein kammer, unnd hannd kein andere begangenschafft dann das sy studierend. " The entire manuscript is published in F. Meyer, *Die evangelische Gemeinde in Locarno*, 2 vols., (Zurich, 1836), II, 388.

Finally Camillo was condemned, together with several other Italian radicals, at the Synod of Coira in 1571. P. D. R. De Porta, *Historia reformationis Ecclesiarum Raeticarum*, 3 vols. in 2 (Curiae Raetorum, 1772-1777), vol. I, Bk. II, Chapt. 20. Cf. also the long and important letter from Tobias Egli to Bullinger from Coira, dated June 20, 1571. T. Schiess, *op. cit.*, III, 251, 255. His treatment at the hands of this evangelical body was decried as an unjust act by another Sienese patrician, Mino Celso, who was a former *Intronato* and friend of the Sozzini family, himself a religious exile, and one of the champions of religious toleration in that century. His unpublished letter, probably directed to Niccolò Balbani, the Italian minister in Geneva, is preserved in Bern in Ms. A. 93. 11 and is carefully studied by D. Cantimori, *op. cit.*, p. 298 f.

Three documents concerned with Camillo's heretical activity in the Grisons are registered in H. Hagen, ed., *Catalogus codicum Bernensium* (Bern, 1875), Cod. Miscell. A. 93: 4 — " Disputatio inter Camillo Socino et Augustino de battesmo et cena sancta. " ff. 8; 7 — " Commentarii conventus synodalis convocati mense Jun. 1572 in oppido Chiavenna, de excommunicatione Hieronymi Turriani, ecclesiae Pluriensis ministri, et Camilli Sozzini. ff. 57; 11 — " Fragmentum libri contra haereticos Hieronymi Turrianum et Camillum Sozzinum. " ff. 2. References to Camillo may be contained in two letters: the first, from Bishop Delfino to [Carlo] Borromeo, dated Vienna, September 27, 1561, reporting that in Vergerio's organization for the diffusion of evangelical literature to Italy, " un figliuolo del Socino scrive a Senesi. " S. Steinherz, ed., *Nuntiaturberichte aus Deutschland 1560-1572* (Vienna, 1897), I, 311; the second, the famous letter from Bernardino Ochino to Friedrich von Salis of June 4, 1558 (in K. Benrath, *Bernardino Ochino von Siena*, 2nd. edition. (Braunschweig, 1892, p. 306, lamenting that Michelangiolo Florio had written to Vermigli and reported that in Chiavenna the brothers of Lelio Sozzini were saying that, he, Ochino, had preached "che Cristo habbia meritato o soddisfatto è una bestemmia."

A final reference to Camillo is probably contained in the denunciation of his brother, Cornelio, to the Venetian Inquisition by a certain Fra Girolamo on November 17, 1574. From the charges it appears that one of his brothers was then in Geneva, whither Cornelio himself might attempt to flee. A. Stella, *op. cit.*, p. 3.

45. (Dario).

As with Lelio's other brothers, the notices about him which have survived are fragmentary and often ambiguous. In fact, because of the very nature of the references, it is possible that we are actually dealing with more than a single Dario. One, is a Sozzini, the second, that Dario Scala or Dario Senese, whom we know carried on heretical activity in the Grisons. Cf. Cantimori, *op. cit.*, p. 288, and Da Porta's summary of a letter from Nicolao Camulio to Girolamo Turriani in Rhaetia: " exspectantur etiam Bettus quidam ac Darius haeretici. " (*op. cit.*, T. I, Bk. II, p. 544). F. Bock, *op. cit.*, II, 577 suggests that our Dario was a relative but not a brother of Lelio. Cantù's genealogy does not list him at all. Nevertheless, the references already cited in Bullinger's correspondence, despite the peculiar orthography (see above, n. 44 under Camillo), to " Darius et Camillus Laelius, Ariani, " seem sufficient to establish the fraternal relationship of a Dario to Lelio.

According to C. Sands, *Bibliotheca Antitrinitariorum* (Freistadii [Amsterdam], 1684), p. 18, the early historians of the Socinian tradition counted Dario Sozzini as a member of the Vicentine *Collegia* (*c.* 1546). He is listed also as one of the more celebrated participants in the Academy of the *Accesi* founded by Belisario Bulgarini " in his own home towards the fall of the Republic of Siena, " (1555). C. Mazzi, *op. cit.*, II, 345. A letter from Dario to Bulgarini dated " in fretta " from Bologna, October 14, 1561 and signed " come minor fratello " is preserved in the *Biblioteca Comunale*, Siena, Cod. D. VI. 7 f. 24. Dario is named in a letter addressed by his brother, Cornelio, to David Spilimberg, secretary to the Duke of Parma, dated March 12, 1571, in which he begged his friend to present his brother, " messer Dario, dottor, per servitore di casa sua.... " to Cardinal Farnese. A. Stella, *op. cit.*, p. 6. Remnants of Dario Sozzini's correspondence with the great Bolognese natural historian, Ulisse Aldrovandi, himself a former prisoner of the Inquisition, are cited in L. Frati, *Catalogo dei Manoscritti di U. Aldrovandi* (Bologna, 1907). Ms. 38^2 is a letter from Dario, dated Rome, 5 November, 1572. Ms. 136 entitled, " Ulyssis Aldrovandi Observationes variae, " at Tome XXVI, f. 204 r. contains notices " Ex literis Darii Sozzini, Senis datis, die 4 Maii 1597. "

According to G. Williams, *The Radical Reformation* (Philadelphia, 1962), p. 662, prior to or early in 1562, Dario Sozzini drew up with Nicholas Paruta in Moravia, twenty propositions on the doctrine of the Trinity which later were of some influence among the religious radicals in Poland. Illgen, *op. cit.*, p. 71 adds that Dario had been in Rhetia before going to Moravia. Even if Dario Sozzini was not included in the Inquisitorial persecution and imprisonment which befell certain of the brothers of Lelio *c.* the year 1560, the fact that he wrote to Bulgarini from Bologna in October, 1561 makes it difficult, although not impossible, to identify the " Moravian " Dario with Dario Sozzini. A Ms. writing (to be dated in the early 1560's) entitled " Scritto di Dario Senese presentato ai Ministri Seniori e Diaconi della Chiesa di Chiavenna dove si trovo presenti tre altri ministri cioè di Piur, di Morbegno, e di Tei, cavato puntualmente dal suo originale e da la sua propria mano che resto nelle mani di M. Augustino, " is ascribed to Sozzini by Cantimori, *op. cit.*, p. 287. It is preserved in Zurich, Universitâtsbibliothek, Simmlersammlung, Bd. 73, n. 37.

46. (Cornelio).

For Cornelio, we have now Aldo Stella's fine study, already cited above on several occasions, based upon the denunciations of Cornelio and a French companion, Claude Bannière, before the Inquisition in Rome and Venice in the late 1570's. We shall refer the reader to this article and content ourselves merely to glean from its abundance. Cornelio was denounced for heresy in Venice, where he had been residing, by a Fra Girolamo on November 17, 1574. Stella, *op. cit.*, p. 3. At the time, he was already in prison as a debtor. Only two years earlier he had been tried in Florence by the Inquisition as a " grand'heretico, " and his release on that occasion may have been due to the influence of his nephew Fausto, who was at the Medici court. *Ibid.*, p. 4. More than a decade earlier, he had shared in the persecutions which struck his family. It is likely that in the list of Sienese, suspected of heresy, which Nofri Camajani, Cosimo I's governor in Siena, sent to his master, " li duoi figliuoli di M. Maria [sic] Sozini, cioè Carlo e Camillo, " we should read Cornelio for Carlo. The former name never reappears in the history of the Sozzini, while Cornelio's extradition to Rome to stand trial for heresy is sought in a letter addressed to Cosimo by the Nuncio to Florence, cited by Cantù, II, 449. Cosimo replied on October 10: " I have seen the letter of Sozino, sent to me by your Excellency, which to me appears almost like a trial and clearly demonstrates his error.... ' Stella, *op. cit.*, p. 4.

In 1574, despite the seriousness of Fra Girolamo's charges, Cornelio was released. Following more serious accusations, he was rearrested in October, 1578. Because of Gregory XIII's strong solicitations, the Venetians released him from their custody and transferred him to Rome for trial. The records of these proceedings have not been located by Stella among the papers of the Roman Inquisition in Trinity College, Dublin, and, of course, the Archives of the Inquisition in Rome are still inaccessible. However, Cornelio's release, which was probably obtained by another recantation, is attested by his letter to Giovanbattista Pico, secretary to the Duke of Parma, dated Rome, April 22, 1581. Stella, p. 13.

In Venice, Cornelio had been engaged in alchemistic experiments. On his ambitious project, which he proposed to the *Signoria* of Venice, to remove filth from the streets and canals, see Stella, p. 6 f. It came to nothing, not only because of the expenditure it would require, but also because new charges of heresy were being lodged against him in 1578 (see above). At his own trial, Claude Bannière made interesting revelations about Cornelio's epistolary relationship with his nephew, Fausto, who was in Basel (Stella, pp. 26-27), important also, perhaps, for Cornelio's own religious sentiments in the late 1570's: " when the subject of his nephew Fausto, who is in Germany, came up, Socino showed impatience to the Jew [who had been the bearer of the letters from Fausto], saying that it had been a long time since he had taken any interest in his affairs, and showing that it displeased him to talk about these things. " Testimony of May 2, 1579 (Stella, p. 27).

Conserved in the Biblioteca Nazionale, Firenze and registered as Ms. Magl. Cl. XXVI. 131 is a selection made by a certain Del Migliore of the *Libri della Gabella dei Contratti*. Page 5 of this document has the following notice: " 95. M. Cornelio di M. Mariano Sozzini Citt. Sanese e Bolognese emit. " In the upper margin of the page in written " D 212 1564, " which is obviously the registration and the year of the book of the *Gabella*. After Cornelio's death, his nephew Fausto from Poland contested the claims of his (Cornelio's) daughter, Porzia, and her husband to his inheritance. See below (no. 49) Fausto's important letter to Cornelio Marsili (1587).

" 1553 Novembre 18. Cornelio Sozzini cav. e conte Palatino. " A. Aurieri, f. 164 v.

47. (Lelio).

b. Siena 1525, d. Zurich, 1562. The writings attributed to Lelio by the Socinian tradition are listed by D. Cantimori, " Serveto e Lelio Sozzini, " *Religio*, XII (1936), 437. Recent studies, however, have notably reduced their number. Thus, the famous *Apologia* of Alphonsus Lyncurius (see David Pingree's study and translation earlier in this volume) has been shown by S. Kot to belong to Curione; and an obscure anti-trinitarian writing attributed to Lelio by Bock, II, 651 has been fully shown to have issued from the pen of a German radical, once a Jesuit, Christian Francken. This little-known work is entitled: *Praecipuarum enumeratio causarum, cur Christiani, cum in multis religionis doctrinis mobiles sint et varii, in Trinitatis tamen retinendo dogmate sint constantissimi* (n. p., n. d.). Its actual authorship is fully demonstrated by L. Firpo, " Il vero autore di un celebre scritto antitrinitario: Christian Francken non Lelio Socino, " *Bollettino della Società di Studi Valdesi*, LXXVI (1958), 51-68; LXXVIII (1960), 27-35.

The great toleration plea, *In haereticis coercendis quatenus progredi liceat, Mini Celsi disputatio*. Christlingae [Basel], 1577 is still listed in the *Catalogue* of the Bibliothèque Nationale, Paris as a pseudonymous composition of Lelio Sozzini. Already in the 18th Century, Bock (III, 641) had rejected such an attribution on the basis of a reference in the *Disputatio* to Giacomo Aconcio's *Stratagemata Satanae* which was only published, in Basel, by Perna in 1564, two years after the death of Lelio.

Below follows a list of Lelio's letters and writings. The few surviving letters are given in chronological sequence. Of those which have been lost, it is possible to reconstruct the content of only a very few from their extant replies. See above the study of David Willis, who, through an analysis of Calvin's response to Lelio, sheds light on the latter's concept of the merits of Christ.

I. Letters of Lelio Sozzini:

To *Calvin*, Zurich, May 14, 1549 (*Calvini Opera*, XIII, coll. 272-274; cf. English translation above by Mr. Lazzaro).
To *Bullinger*, Basel, July 8, 1549 (*Calvini Opera*, XIII, coll. 322-323; Trechsel, II, 431-433).
To *Bullinger*, [Basel], July 8, 1549 (*Calvini Opera*, XIII, coll. 323-324; Trechsel, II, p. 431; Illgen, Particula III, p. 17).
To *Bullinger*, Basel, July 19, 1549 (Illgen, Particula III, p. 18; Trechsel, II, 433-434).
To *Calvin*, Basel, July 25, 1549 (*Calvini Opera*, XIII, coll. 336-340. See English translation above).
To *Bullinger*, Basel, end of July, 1549 (*Calvini Opera*, XIII, col. 340; Trechsel, II, pp. 434-436; Illgen, Particula III, 19-20).
To *Bullinger*, Basel, August 3, 1549 (Trechsel, II, p. 436; Illgen, Particula III, p. 21).
To *Calvin*, Zurich, February 1, 1550 (*Calvini Opera*, XIII, coll. 517-518; Illgen, Particula III, p. 22).
To *Calvin*, Zurich, April 20, 1550 (*Calvini Opera*, XIII, col. 554; Illgen, Particula III, p. 23).
To *Bullinger*, Nuremberg, July 6, 1550 (Simmler *Sammlung:* C. Illgen, Particula II, pp. 17-18).
To *Bullinger*, Wittenberg, August 20, 1550 (Simmler *Sammlung*: Illgen, Particula II, pp. 19-20).
To *Bullinger*, Wittenberg, August 28, 1550 (Simmler *Sammlung*: Illgen, Particula II, p. 21).
To *J. Crato*, Zurich, March 27, 1552 (E. Burnat, *Lelio Socin* [Vevay, 1894], p. 89 f.).
To *Ambrose Moibanus*, Zurich, April 29, 1552, *Ibid.*, pp. 90-91.
To *Rudolph Gualther* (Trechsel, II, pp. 452-454; Gualther's answer *Ibid.*, II, pp. 454-458. It is dated, Zurich, May 13, 1552).
To *Bullinger*, Siena, September 25, 1552 (Museum Helveticum, V, Particula XIX, pp. 489-490; Illgen, Particula III, pp. 25-26).
To *Bullinger*, Basel, February 5, 1554 (Trechsel, II, pp. 436-437; Illgen, Particula III, p. 26).
To *Bullinger*, Geneva, April 19, 1554 (Trechsel, II, p. 437; Illgen, Particula III, p. 27).
A tutta la santa e molto veneranda congregatione de fedeli amici di Jesu Christo. In Loccarno. Zurich, January 13, 1555 (Trechsel, II, p. 459. The letter is signed: "Lelio Sozzini vostro in Cristo frate, se ben ultimo e piccolissimo").
To *Martinus Cellarius* (Borrhaus), Zurich, October 14, 1557 (D. Cantimori, "Serveto e Lelio Sozzini," pp. 431-432.
To *Bullinger*, Tübingen, December 8, 1557 (Simmler *Sammlung*: Illgen, Particula II, pp. 27-28).
To *Bullinger*, Tübingen, July 17, 1558 (Illgen, Particula III, p. 32).
To *Bullinger*, Tübingen, July 18, 1558 (Illgen, Particula III, p. 31).
To *Bullinger*, Tübingen, July 25, 1558 (Illgen, Particula III, pp. 32-33).
To *Bullinger*, Augsburg, July 30, 1558 (Illgen, Particula III, p. 33).
To *Bullinger*, Cracow, January 23, 1559 (Illgen, Particula III, pp. 35-36).
To *Bullinger*, Vienna, May 10, 1559 (Trechsel, II, p. 438).
To *Bullinger*, Vienna, May 24, 1559 (Illgen, Particula III, p. 36).
To *Calvin*, Zurich, August 22, 1559 (*Calvini Opera*, XVII, coll. 604-605; Illgen, Particula III, pp. 36-37).
To *Calvin*, Zurich, October 2, 1559 (*Calvini Opera*, XVII, coll. 650-652; Illgen, Particula III, pp. 37-39).

To *John Wolff*, [s. d.] (The original is in the Hottingerische *Sammlung* in the Zentralbibliothek, Zurich, tom. VII, p. 198).

To *John Wolff*, [s. d.] (Hottingerische *Sammlung*, tom. V, p. 332, Zentralbibliothek, Zurich).

To *Lucas Pomisius* (with questions for Schwenckfeld); the latter's reply to Pomisius, to be relayed to Lelio, dated 27 february, 1560 is published in the *Corpus Schwenckfeldianorum*, XVII, 154-160.

Only a few of Lelio's writings have come down to us, and these works were printed after his death. It is doubtful that he published anything in his lifetime, yet F. Gardy remarks that among the books given to Vermigli by their authors was one by Lelio Socino (see F. Gardy, " Les livres de Pierre Martyr Vermigli conservés à la Bibliothèque de Genéve, " *Anzeiger für Schweizerische Geschichte*, n. s. XVII [1919], 1-6). We do know that in March, 1552 Lelio was occupied in translating a booklet of Bullinger's on the errors of the mass into Italian (see the letter above to Crato). If this work was carried through to completion and actually published, it could solve the mystery of Gardy's remark, but such a work has never been found.

II. Works of Lelio Sozzini:

A. *Confessio de Deo*, dated Zurich, July 15, 1555. (For the history of its printing, see Appendix I).

B. *Theses de Filio Dei et Trinitate a Socino aut Sociniano confectae.*

Exist in Ms. in a codex of the Universitatsbibliothek of Basel entitled, " Varia theologica et ecclesiastica Basiliensia. " It was located by Cantimori in Basel; the hand and the doctrinal content lead him to ascribe it to Laelius. The marginal notes are ascribed to Curione. Printed in D. Cantimori and E. Feist, *Per la Storia degli eretici Italiani....* (Rome, 1937), pp. 57-61.

C. *Brevis Explicatio in Primum Joannis Caput.*

Published by Giorgio Biandrata, founder of the Unitarian Church in Transylvania, as Chapter XI of his, *De falsa et vera unius Dei Patris Filii, et Spiritus Sancti cognitione....* " (Alba Julia [Gyulafehervar-Karlsberg], 1567), and also by F. De Jong (Junius) in his *Defensio Catholicae Doctrinae de S. Trinitate personarum in unitate essentiae Dei* (Leyden, 1650), col. 182. Copies of Biandrata's work are in the British Museum; the Nationalbibliothek, Dresden; and the Unitarian College, Cluj. The *Explicatio* has been reprinted by D. Cantimori, *op. cit.*, pp. 61-78.

D. *Fausti, & Laelii* / SOCINI / ITEM / ERNESTI SONNERI / Tractatus aliquot *Theologici*, / numquam antehac in lucem / editi. / . Quorum Catalogum se / quens pagina indicabit. /

ELEUTHEROPOLI. / Typis *Godfridi Philadelphi*, / ANNO 1654.

Since this work is little-known, a full description of it follows; one vol. in 12º of pp. [4], 100. It contains: p. [1], frontispiece; p. [2], blank; p. [3], list of the works in the volume; p. [4], blank; pp. 1-10, " BREVIS DISCURSUS, / DE CAUSA, / Ob quam creditur aut non / creditur Evangelio Jesu / Christi, & de eo, quod, / qui credit, proemio, qui / non credit, poena a Deo / afficiatur, " [of Fausto Socino]; pp.11-15, " Summa Religionis / CHRISTIANAE, / A *FAUSTO SOCINO* / Conscripta. "; pp. 16-29, " Coelii [sic] Socini / DE SACRAMENTIS / Dissertatio, ad Tigurinos & / Genevenses. " At the end, the date: " Anno 1560. " pp. 30-34, " Descriptum ex *D*. Curcel- / laei excerptis, quae & ipso Lae- / lii Socini autographo haec / descripserat. / De Resurrectione: ejusdem Auct- / oris, "; pp. 34-35, " Faustus Socinus, de Laelio So- / cino patruo ita alicubino- / tatum reliquit. " One reads this brief note: Laelius Socinus ingenii magnitudine, sacrarum literarum ex ipsis Hebraeis et Graecis fontibus cognitione, ipsarumque rerum divinarum scientia eximius atque singularis, qui non multorum annorum spatio (37 enim tantum annos vixit) errores fere innumerabiles [sic], maximaque ex parte gravissimos, ab aliis non animadversos in Christianam religionem invectos detexit, ac veram viam eam in integrum restituendi aperuit."

Pp. 36-69, " Ernesti Sonneri Demonstratio / THEOLOGICA / & / PHILOSOPHICA. / Quod aeterna impiorum sup- / plicia non arguant Dei justi- / tiam, sed injustitiam, "; p. 70, blank; pp. 71-100, with a separate frontispiece: " AN / *Doctrina Trinitatis* / SIT MYSTERIUM / a Seculis absconditum, / quod divini verbi pa- / tefactione hominibus / innotescere debuit. / E TRACTATU, / Qui de Origine Trinitatis / inscribitur, exscriptum. / ANNO MDCV. " On p. 73, the dedication: " MARTINO PISECIO / A MARTOWIC / Philos. & MEDIC. Doctori, / Nobili SILESIO, / Fratri suo, S. "

The two writings of Lelio Sozzini, in this collection, were reprinted by Trechsel with his emendations, *op. cit.*, II, 438-446. Most recently, the *De Resurrectione* has been critically edited by Lech Szczucki, " Z Eschatologii Braci Polskich, Dwa Pisma Leliusza I Fausta Socynow, " *Archiwum Historii Filozofii*, Nr. 1, 1957, pp. 5-13.

Copies of the *Tractatus* are in: British Museum 3900. a, 42. Bibliothèque Nationale, Paris. Res. D[2] 4962. Archiginnasio, Bologna 3 RR. III. 20 OP. 2; Biblioteca Nazionale, Firenze (Guicciardini 23-3-8).

An appraisal of Lelio's contribution to modern religious thought has been made by B. Matteucci, " Lelio e Fausto Sozzini ò l'anagrafe del liberalismo religioso, " *Studium*, LVI (1960), 258-263. An important contribution shedding light on the largely unknown youth of Lelio Sozzini is made by A. Rotondò's already cited study. The pertinent section of this article entitled, " Un episodio bolognese della giovinezza di Lelio Sozzini, " (p. 136 f.) is based primarily on the testimony issuing at an Inquistional trial of 1549 that meetings took place (1546) in the Bolognese home of Lelio Sozzini, during which heretical writings, including Camillo Renato's Ms. *Trattato* (del Battesimo e della Santa Cena ?), were read and discussed. In connection with the problem of reconstructing Lelio's correspondence, one should note a declaration by the accused (probably Ulisse Aldrovandi) that Sozzini had written to him on several occasions from Venice and " Germania, " exhorting him to " seguire la via già cominciata de l'evangelio " (p. 145).

A letter from the Florentine, Antonio Francesco Doni, dated Florence, April 1, 1547 and addressed to Lelio Sozzini in Bologna (neglected by all his biographers) is cited in: C. Marsili-Libelli, *Anton Francesco Doni, scrittore e stampatore* (Florence, Sansoni Antiquariato, 1960), letter n. 215 of the Index. It was published in several editions of Doni's letters, beginning with the: *Lettere del Doni, libro secondo* (Florence, 1547), n. 11 in Marsili-Libelli's bibliography. In the letter, Doni informs Sozzini that the pressure of affairs has prevented him from procuring the books that the Bolognese bookseller, Francesco Linguardo, had ordered for him. On Linguardo, who was imprisoned in 1548 for dealing in heretical books, see L. Carcereri, " Cristoforo Dossena, Francesco Linguardo e un Giordano libraio processati per eresia a Bologna (1548), " *L'Archiginnasio*, V (1910), 177-192.

48. (Fillide).

b. 1540. She married Cornelio Marsili with 4000 florins in dowry. Cantù, II, 509. After Fausto Sozzini's departure from Italy, Marsili served him as financial agent, administering his patrimony and regularly forwarding to him the rents from his holdings. (See at n. 44, the already cited letter written in 1588 by Sozzini to

Ferdinand de' Medici in which Marsili is named in this connection. At Fillide's death, Fausto composed the sonnet which is published below (Biblioteca Angelica, Rome. Cod. 1882, f. 28 r. Cantimori [*Eretici*, p. 356] thinks that the first line contains a reference to the death of Lelio, five years previously, and conjectures that Fillide died in 1568 [1567]).

In remembranza di mad.ª Fillide sua sorella già morta.

Volge il quinto anno, et lasso parmi un giorno
Ch'altri gli occhi chiudendo a me gli aperse
Ahi che megli richiuse et mi sommerse
Donde risurto ancora ho tema et scorno!

Donna gentile in questo uil soggiorno
Sol perche star piu tempo non sofferse
A me che pria giunto era, hoggi scoperse
Quel uer che puo far l'huom di stelle adorno.

Et ben sperar come un sol padre al mondo
Ambo dati'n' hauea ch' alaltra vita
Un sol padre celeste ambo accogliesse.

Et lo spero anco, poiche del profondo
Tratto de mali a la uia gia smarrita
Ritorno, in ch'ella alte uestigia impresse.

For a recently published letter from Fausto to Fillide's husband, Cornelio Marsili, see below (addenda for n. 49). An earlier letter (1584) from Fausto Sozzini to Ferdinand I de' Medici from Cracow pleads for his rents which the Inquisition had prohibited Marsili from forwarding to Poland. S. Ciampi, *Bibliografia critica delle antiche reciproche corrispondenze.... dell'Italia colla Russia, colla Polonia ed altre parti settentrionali,* 3 vols., (Florence, 1834-1842), I, 72. In another letter to the Medici ruler (Cracow, May 31, 1588) Sozzini mentions that he had been visited recently in Poland by his nephew, Rutilio Marsili, who was returning to Italy " informatissimo della devozione mia non men grande, che dovuta al glorioso nome di V.A. " *Ibid.*, p. 74.

49. (Fausto).

b. Siena, 1539, d. Luslowice, 1604. His birth is recorded in the Archivio di Stato of Siena. *Archivio della Biccherna. Serie Battezzati. Arm. 1521-1540.*

" Fausto Pavolo, fº di Mess. Alex.º Soziny si battezo alle 5 di Dicembre e nacque il di compare Messer Lodovico delle Armi gentilhomo bolognese. " (I was unable to find the record of Lelio's birth in this register). It is possible that Fausto's godfather is identical with that Ludovico dall'Armi who was beheaded by order of the Venetian Council of X on May 12, 1547. *Calendar of State Papers and Manuscripts.... Venice, 1534-1554,* (London, 1873), V, p. 217. The activities of this adventurer in the service of Henry VIII of England are noted by A. Stella, " Guido da Fano eretico del secolo XVI, al servizio dei re d'Inghilterra, " *Rivista di Storia della Chiesa in Italia*, XIII (1959), p. 211, n. 57.

Of all the Sozzini, Fausto was perhaps the most actively involved in the life of the Sienese Academies. In the Intronati, he was *Il Frastagliato*, and his *impresa*, a sea buffeted by winds with the motto, " Turbant sed extollunt. " It is reproduced by L. Costantini, *op. cit.*, p. 77. According to the *Tabelloni* of the Intronati published by L. Sbaragli, *op. cit.*, p. 193, Fausto's name appears for the first time (together with that of his uncle Camillo) among those admitted during or after 1557. But here, strangely, his name as an Intronato is given as *Il Ritagliato*. The names of two other " Frastagliati " have been recorded. The first was elected a member of the *Accademia de' Rozzi* in 1603 " per tutti lupini bianchi. " C. Mazzi, *op. cit.*, II, 454; the second, Girolamo Vieri, is listed among those admitted to the Intronati under the date, 1690. L. Sbaragli, *op. cit.*, p. 213.

In the *Dialogo de' giuochi che nelle vegghie Sanesi si usano di fare del Materiale Intronato* [Girolamo Bargagli], (Siena, 1572), dedicated to Fausto's patroness Isabella de' Medici, one of the principal interlocutors is *Il Frastagliato.* Bargagli's work, an account of Sienese games and feasts, begins with the return to Siena of *Il Sodo Intronato,* Marcantonio Piccolomini, after an extended sojourn in Venice. At this time when " finite le guerre, e mutato governo, sotto la speranza d'un sicuro et lungo riposo si era di nuova aperta l'Academia de gl'Intronati, la quale dalle discordie civili, et dalle torbolenze de tempi era stata tenuta molti anni serrata," p. 17. (This and the following quotations are from the second edition, Venice, 1581). Not long after the news of Piccolomini's return, his house overflowed with young men who came to pay their respects, " et fra gli altri non furono degli ultimi quell'Intronati, che si trovavano allora nella citta, et particolarmente.... quei giovani, che nella rinovatione dell'Academia erano stati novellamente adornati del nome Intronatico. Ma fra gli altri andandovi il Frastagliato e l'Attonito (*Ibid.*, p. 17). In fact, it is the *Frastagliato* who sets the stage for the book when he asks *Il Sodo*, an experienced *Intronato,* to describe the grand heritage of an *Intronato* for the benefit of his youthful audience: " Si che non vi sia grave il dare, come esperto nocchiero, qualche giovenal ricordo a quelli che nuovamente entrano in mare. " (*Ibid.*, p. 21). Throughout the book (cf. pp. 30, 48, 52, 91, 93, 124, 176) it is *Il Frastagliato* who interrupts Piccolomini to elicit further information or to register objections. See, especially, p. 30 ff. " Dico, ch'io dubito che non paia, che troppo in questa parte, [i. e. in Il Sodo's account], e a Senesi, e agl'Intronati s'attribuisca. Percioche si vede l'invention de' giuochi esser ancora ad altri commune, mostrando il Castiglione nel suo Cortigiano, che nella corte d'Urbino de giuochi s'usassero.... ".

Fausto was also a member of the *Corte de' Ferraiuoli* (or Accademia Ferraiuola) which " era fatta per un brio che si faceva nel giorno della befana.... " C. Mazzi, *op. cit.*, II, 357 ff. According to Scipione Bargagli, in the preface to his " Riverci di Medaglie della ventura Befana de' Cortigiani Ferraioli, " Cod. Y, II, 26 in the Biblioteca Comunale of Siena, " Fra l'altre maniere di piacevoli e ingegnosi et honorati trattenimenti che si costumava di dare in Siena a belle et valorose gentildonne, antica molto si trova esservi l'usanza che per la festa l'anno dell'Epifania si facciano et alla presenza di quelle si traggano, Sorti o Venture, le quali, dalla voce alquanto alterata di tal festa, venture della Befana or Befania sono nominate. " The *Corte Ferraiola* was not included in the closing of the other Academies of Siena decreed by Cosimo I. It was still active in 1574 but by 1603 it had ceased to exist. C. Mazzi, *op. cit.*, p. 359. Fausto composed several sonnets for these *Sorte* or *Venture*. Some have been published by A. Ferentilli, *Primo volume della scielta di stanze di diversi autori Toscani* (Venice, 1584), p. 49 ff. Several others remain in Ms. in the already cited Cod. 1882, f. 23 r. and following, Biblioteca Angelica, Rome. Single sonnets are preserved in several libraries: Bologna, Archiginnasio, Ms. A 2175-2181, " Raccolta di varie poesie di diversi stimatissimi autori, " vol. V, II, f. 101; Pistoia, Biblioteca Forteguerriana, Cod. For. B. 175, f. 7 v.; Biblioteca Nazionale, Firenze, Cod. Palatino, 225, VI, f. 16 r. The sonnet which Fausto composed at the death of his sister Fillide has been published above, n. 48. Another in the Angelica group, " In morte di L° C°, " was probably occasioned by the death of Lodovico Castelvetro. See the letter written by Fausto from Rome on April 27, 1571 to Scipione Bargagli in Siena: " La morte del Castelvetro mi ha dato tanto dolore che non potrei mai dirvelo a pieno, e mi ha fatto fare un sonetto il quale per essere indegno di pervenire alle vostre mani non credo che ardirò di mandarvelo. Ma se pure vel mando, pigliatelo per segno dell'amorevolezza et della confidenza mia in voi et non mostratela a persona. " Archivio di Stato di Siena, *Particolari*, *Bargagli.*

A further small ray is shed upon Fausto's literary activity (with perhaps even an interesting allusion to the limits of his ability in this direction) by an undated letter from Alessandro Piccolomini to the Grand Duke of Tuscany, written from Siena, probably in the early 1570's. Piccolomini had been requested to compose some comic pieces. He replies apologizing that he lacks both the physical strength and the heart for such a task. But he names two individuals who might serve in his stead. " Questi medesimi impedimenti furon causa che l'anno passato ricercandomi l'Ill.mo et R.mo Card. de' Medici d'una commedia, fui forzato a pregare S. S. Ill.ma che, perdonando, a l'impossibilità mia, si contentasse ch'io ponesse questo carico sopra di M. Girolamo Bargagli; et così si contentò ella et così fu fatto, perchè egli trovò il caso, egli distese le scene, le quali M. Fausto Sozzini rivedeva d'intorno a le parole in che egli vale et altro a me non toccò di fare se non di esser loro a le volte appresso et accomodar qualche cosetta. La qual cosa essendo il Bargagli in Firenze non si potrebbe di nuovo fare; ne altra persona conosco io oggi in Siena ch'a gran pezza fusse abile a fare il medesimo ch'egli faceva: perochè il Sozzino non è atto se non a quanto ho detto. " E. Casanova, " Lettere di Alessandro Piccolomini, *Bullettino Senese di Storia Patria,* XIII (1906), 218.

Later in his life, Fausto lamented the energy he had poured into literary pursuits. Writing to Valentinus Schmalz, he warns him not to imitate his own youthful error: " .... when I (who) had already tasted.... divine truth, was.... snatched away by certain other empty studies.... " (Letter dated Cracow, November 15, 1593). *Bibliotheca Fratrum Polonorum* (Irenopoli [Amsterdam]. Post annum Domini, 1656), I, 459.

An interesting account, touching upon several aspects of Fausto's life in Poland is contained in a letter from Alberto Bolognetti, Papal Nuncio in Poland, to Cardinal Jacopo Savelli, Prefect of the Inquisition in Rome, dated Cracow, April 23, 1583.

> Fausto Socino poi è in maggior concetto presso agl'heretici non solamente di letteratura, ma ancora d'una certa bontà dispregiatrice delle cose del mondo al qual concetto oltre che corrisponde quella sua natural palidezza del volto; pare anco ch'egli cerchi conformarsi et con l'habito (vestendo molto sprezzatamente benche forse per bisogno), et con le parole le quali quanto al suono sono tutte humili et tutte dolci; onde vien chiamato angelo mandato da Dio. Et per questo puo nuocere molto più d'ogni altro senza comparatione, quando voglia andare spargendo il suo veneno, come è opinione che faccia; che se bene egli dice di starsene ritirato, nondimeno credono molti che vada chetamente a questa casa et a quell'altra per discorrere delle cose della religione et persuadere la sua dottrina, et che se bene esso è ariano come si stima, faccia però congregatione in casa sua d'heretici di varie sette, anzi insino d'hebrei, di che s'ebbe a mesi passati assai certo ragguaglio....
>
> Scrissi già com'egli [Fausto] mi dava speranza di tornare alla fede cattolica, quand'io gl'avessi risolvere alcuni dubii, et che mentre si stava in questo, egli per una paura fattagli dal G. cancelliere [Possevino], più presto di quello c'havrei voluto, sene fuggì. Hor egli sta nascosto non so in che luogo, et perc'ha sospetto (per quant mi vien referto) ch'io non lo voglia far pigliare per mandarlo a Roma, come per ordine di N. S. feci in Venetia di Cornelio suo fratello, mi ha fatto dar intentione per un Meser Giovan Battista Fucci et anco per Prospero Provana che, s'io l'assicuro, tornerà et si seguirà il negotio incominciato della sua induttione. Tuttavia, considerando io questa possa essere una delusione, et ch'egli desideri più tosto di tornar in Cracovia a suoi soliti maneggi, non ho voluto dargli questa assicuratione senza scriverne prima a V. S. Illma., aspettando quel che da lei mi sarà commandato. (*Monumenta Poloniae Vaticana,* Cracow, 1938, VI, 257 f.).

Fausto's published works were collected and republished in the first two volumes of the famous *Bibliotheca Fratrum Polonorum.* The most complete listing of the separate editions of his writings is still Karol Estreicher's, *Bibliografia Polska* (Cracow, 1930), XXVIII, 379-402, which includes two Polish translations published in the sixteenth century. The largest collections of Socinian publications are in the British Museum and in the Guicciardini collection in the Biblioteca Nazionale, Firenze.

Many of Fausto's letters were published, after his death, in a small book entitled *Fausti Socini Senensis ad Amicos Epistolae* (Racow, 1618). Recently his correspondence appeared in Polish translation: *Listy,* edited by Ludwik Chmaj, 2 vols., (Warsaw, 1959). This edition contains thirteen " new " letters from Rumanian, Italian and other sources. A small, important, but curiously neglected printed collection of Fausto's letters is in S. Ciampi, *Bibliografia critica delle antiche reciproche corrispondenze.... dell'Italia colla Russia, colla Polonia...*, 3 vols., (Florence, 1834-1842), III, 70-75. Two letters are dated Lyon, July and September, 1561 and are addressed to Belisario Bulgarini in Siena. The remaining six, for the period 1583-1588, are written from Cracow to the Florentine Grand Duke (Ferdinand de' Medici).

Several Ms. letters from Fausto to Girolamo Bargagli and Bulgarini, with their replies, spanning the period 1561-1577 are conserved in the Biblioteca Comunale, Siena: Cod. D. VI. 7, ff. 17-25. A late copy of another letter to Bulgarini, dated Lyon, July 28, 1561 is registered as P. 3. 39. f. 422.

Of two Ms. letters in the Archivio di Stato, Siena, the first has already been noted in connection with the composition of the sonnet at the death of Lodovico Castelvetro. The second, a long letter to C. Marsili, dated Cracow January 30, 1587 is a document of extreme importance that has apparently remained unknown to students of the Sozzini family. It discloses that after the death of Cornelio Sozzini, his daughter Porzia, at the instigation of her husband, the " cancelliere, " had attempted to claim his inheritance. Fausto contests their right to succeed to Cornelio's property for two principal reasons. Firstly, because " Messer Mariano dispose che le femmine siano dotate quando non ci è maschi del medesimo padre, nel qual caso gli altri prossimi parenti maschi et discesi di maschi erano già da lui stati dichiarati eredi. " Secondly, Cornelio had been debtor for large sums of money to his brother, Camillo, and Fausto was the latter's heir: " Et lasciando da parte i figli di M. Celso, li quali non penso che per virtù del fidecomisso succedano altrimenti a Cornelio, dico che Camillo, di cui, s'egli è morto, che non ne so nulla, io pretendo d'essere erede, è o era creditore di Cornelio di molte centinaia di scudi. " On one occasion Cornelio had received 400 *scudi d'oro* from Camillo, through Turco Balbani of Lucca. This sum represented Camillo's share from the sale of the Sozzini property of Monte Giulio near Bologna. This money " Cornelio gettò insieme con tanti altri in quella sua benedetta impresa di Maremma. " After advancing as many arguments in his cause as he could considering that he wrote as a man who " già venti anni sono lasciò lo studio delle leggi, et quì non ha libri niuni di legge, " Fausto closes with the admonition that Marsili should forward his income punctually twice yearly. Moreover, " desidero che mi mandiate sempre scritto chiaro alla fine dell'anno in che modo mi avete finito di pagare. " Siena, Archivio di Stato, *Carte* Orlandi.

The earliest biography of Fausto Sozzini, on which all subsequent writers depended, is the famous *Vita Fausti Socini Senensis* (Rakow ?, 1636) by Fausto's own descendant Samuel Przypkowski. Excellent studies of the life and thought of Sozzini are S. Kot, *Socinianism in Poland* (Boston, 1957); Cantimori, *Eretici*, p. 340 f.; E. M. Wilbur, *A History of Unitarianism*, 2 vols. (Cambridge, Mass., 1947-1952), especially vol. I, 387 ff.; G. Williams, *op. cit.*, p. 749 ff. Giovanni Pioli's massive *Fausto Socino, vita, opere, fortuna* (Modena, 1952) suffers from hagiographic tendencies. Presently, the most exciting developments in the field of Socinian studies are coming out of Poland, especially from the group of able scholars connected with the *Studia Nad Arianizme*. The latest full-length biography is by Ludwik Chmaj, *Faust Socyn* (*1539-1604*) (Warsaw: Ksiazka Wiedza, 1963).

An Inquisitorial document concerning Fausto in the Società Napoletana di Storia Patria has been indicated by Kristeller (p. 438); additional sonnets are in the Biblioteca Governativa, Lucca. (Kristeller, p. 257). According to Aurieri, *loc. cit.*, Fausto rather than Celso was the founder of the Accademia dei Sizienti in Siena. A sonnet, " Ad Anum Suos Amores Odiose Servantem " (To an old woman who guards my loved one in a hateful way), copying Catullus, is published by W. M. Brady in *The Athenaeum*, n. 2598, August 11, 1877. On the lid of a snuff box preserved in the Library of Manchester College, Oxford is a painted portrait claimed to be of a youthful Fausto Sozzini from an original in Siena. It is reproduced in *The Hibbert Journal*, January, 1963, p. 75. I have published the previously cited letter written by Fausto to C. Marsili from Cracow on January 30, 1587 in the *Bibliothèque d'Humanisme et Renaissance*, XXVI (1964), 154-161. Sozzini's letter to Bargagli from Rome (1571), lamenting the death of Castelvetro, cited as in MS. was published by W. M. Bradi in *The Athenaeum*. (See above).

50. (Agnes).

The daughter of Fausto by his Polish wife, Elizabeta, daughter of the nobleman, Christophorus Morsztyn de Raciborsk. She married Stanislaus Wiszowaty.

51. (Andreas).

b. 1608-d. Amsterdam, 1678. From his marriage to Alexandra Rupnovia two children were born, Benedict and Andreas, both of whom became pastors. Wiszowaty was one of the greatest Socinian polemicists in the 17th century. His most famous work, *Religio rationalis seu de rationis iudicio in controversiis etiam theologicis ac religiosis adhibendo tractatus* has recently been republished in a critical edition by L. Chmaj and others (Warsaw, 1960).

52. (Theodor).

He had two sons and two daughters, one of whom married Przypkowski, the biographer of Fausto Sozzini.

Appendix I

A NOTE ON THE *CONFESSION OF FAITH* OF LELIO SOZZINI

We possess only a few writings that can claim to be unquestionably from the pen of Lelio Sozzini. Of these, perhaps the most celebrated is the so-called *Confession of Faith*, a Latin defence of his Trinitarian orthodoxy which Sozzini presented to his patron and friend Heinrich Bullinger in July, 1555.

The original autograph is contained in codex E II 367, ff. 54-57 of the Staatsarchiv of Zurich. It was first published in his encyclopedic nine volume history by Johann Hottinger.[1] More than a century later it was reprinted with many inaccuracies by Friedrich Bock on the basis of the Hottinger text.[2] An English translation by Edward M. Hulme appeared in 1931.[3]

Below are noted in parallel columns the instances where the Hottinger edition of the *Confession* unfaithfully renders the original text.

Zurich manuscript		*Hottinger edition*
Sozinus	p. 421, l. 25	Socinus
SpS sactus	p. 422, l. 26	S. Sp.
Jeovas	p. 422, l. 26	Jehovas
etiam	p. 423, l. 3	&
est Dei nostri beneficium	p. 423, l. 28	Dei beneficium

[1] Historiae Ecclesiasticae Novi Testamenti. Tomus IX. Seculi XVI. Tiguri, Typis Schaufelbergerianis, Anno MDCLXVII, pp. 421-427.

[2] *Historia Antitrinitariorum maxime Socinianismi et Socinianorum.... Tomus Secundus.* Regiomonti et Lipsiae, Impensis Gottl. Lebr. Hartungii, MDCCLXXXIV, pp. 599-602.

[3] " Lelio Sozzini's Confession of Faith, " *Persecution and Liberty. Essays in honor of George Lincoln Burr.* (New York, 1931), pp. 211-225. The text of the Confession itself is contained in pp. 216-218. Hulme's translation is not based on the original. See, for example, p. 218 where we read " my dear friend, " following Hottinger's, " mi Domine N. N. " rather than the original " Mi Domine Bullingere. " Moreover, see his remark that, " Lelio used the phrase ' with every wind, ' and the present writer has added the words ' of doctrine ' because the reference is unmistakable. " We have noted above that the original manuscript actually did contain the word *doctrinae* which had dropped out of Hottinger.

se non consolantur	p. 424, l. 6	non consolantur
suspitio ut minima	p. 424, l. 12	suspicio vel nimia
de re quae sit naturae	p. 424, l. 14	de re sit, quae sit naturae
(located in the margin)	p. 424, l. 21-22	Ita tamen ut nihil non respondeat vaticinio Ezech. 34.
quo circa	p. 424, l. 22	Quocirca
quia sibi	p. 424, l. 26	qua sibi
communico vobiscum Tigurini	p. 424, l. 28	communico vobiscum N. N.
sacri	p. 425, l. 1	Sacri
persuasum	p. 425, l. 2	suasum
christiano et apostolico	p. 425, l. 18	Christiano & Apostolico
Mi Domine Bullingere	p. 425, l. 22	mi Domine N. N.
si quis	p. 425, l. 27	siquis
cognitionen	p. 426, l. 7	agnitionem
satisfaciunt	p. 426, l. 10	satisfaciant
qui omni doctrinae vento fluctuet	p. 426, l. 17	qui omni vento fluctuet
proficiat	p. 426, l. 19	perficiat
IRH Tiguri 15 Julii 1555	p. 426, l. 28	Dabam 15 Julii 1555

Appendix II

AN UNPUBLISHED LETTER OF MARIANO SOZZINI JUNIOR

Everywhere during his travels in the early years of his exile, Lelio Sozzini was shown favor and hospitality by the great men of the age, from Bullinger, Calvin, and Melanchthon to Maximilian II, King of the Romans, and Sigismund Augustus of Poland.

The name Sozzini, rendered famous by several generations of eminent jurisconsults was an undeniable asset to the young sojourner in foreign lands. From the letters of Melanchthon, where Lelio is frequently described as " Socini filio, "[1] we obtain a glimpse of the immense respect which was reserved especially for Mariano Sozzini (d. 1556), the father of Lelio, professor of Law at the University of Bologna.

The letter which we publish below was addressed by Mariano to Pope Paul IV in the Autumn of 1555, the year of Lelio's defense of his orthodoxy before Bullinger.[2] It is a warm and rather ornate recommendation to a position as an Auditor in the Sacra Rota for a former Bolognese student, the future Cardinal, Gabriele Paleoti.

The autograph of Sozzini's letter is registered as AA. Arm. I. XVIII. 3106 in the Archivio Segreto Vaticano. It is known to Paleoti's recent biographer[3] who reprints the small section of it inaccurately quoted by A. Ledesma.[4]

Sanctissime Pater

Cum Sanctitas tua maximis assiduisque negocijs distineatur, non imprudenter opinor me facturum, si frequentius cum ea de ijs rebus agam, quae fortasse illi a publicis curis detrahuntur. Cum nuper intelligerem, exquiri a Beatitudine tua virum aliquem, nobilitate, literis, moribusque insignem, quem Auditorem Rotae Rom. eligeret, non potui statim tibi non commendare Gabrielem Palaeotum Bononiensem quippe qui omnibus his

---

[1] Christian F. Illgen, *Symbolarum ad Vitam et Doctrinam Laelii Socini Illustrandam, Particula II.* Lipsiae, Typis Vogelii, 1826, p. 18.

[2] See Appendix I.

[3] Paolo Prodi, *Il Cardinale Gabriele Paleotti* (*1522-1597*) (Rome, 1959), p. 94.

[4] A. Ledesma, *De vita et rebus gestis Gabrielis Palaeoti S. R. E. cardinalis primique bononiensis archiepiscopi et principis.* Bononiae, 1647, p. 18.

ornamentis abunde praestaret, et hoc Sanctitatis tuae iudicio dignissimus videretur. Scripsisque id, non adductus mea erga illum benevolentia, sed quod ita vere de eo sentirem: hocque a me officium, tum merita illius, tum meum erga hanc civitatem studium suo iure postularent. Nunc cum rem longius differri audiam, volui repetitis literis, meum hoc de eo testimonium Beatitudini tuae constare, ut ipsa sibi omnino persuadeat, si quicqunque est meum de ullo homine iudicium, existimare me, Sanctitatem tuam, hunc gradum apud Palaeotum optime collocaturam. Deus Sanctitati tuae vota omnia, rectaque consilia fortunet.

Datum Bononiae VI idus Octobris M.D.LV.

Filius et Servitor Humillimus
Marianus Sozinus

INDICES

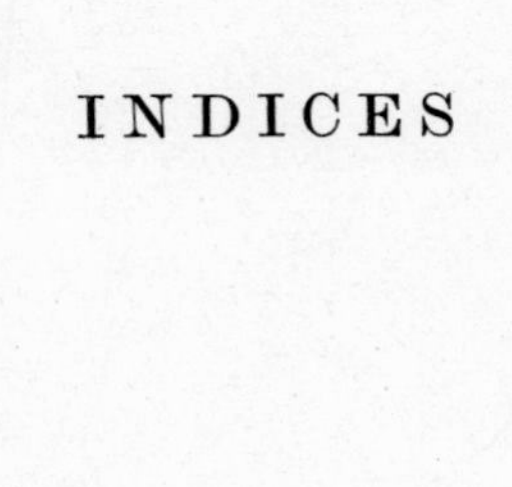

INDEX OF MODERN AUTHORS

GENERAL INDEX

CONTENTS

STAMPATO A FIRENZE
NEGLI STABILIMENTI TIPOGRAFICI
« E. ARIANI » E « L'ARTE DELLA STAMPA »
MAGGIO 1965

Bound by
DESS & TALAN
New York, N. Y.